True and False Allegations of Child Sexual Abuse

Assessment and Case Management

True and False Allegations of Child Sexual Abuse

Assessment and Case Management

Edited by

Tara Ney, Ph.D.

BRUNNER/MAZEL *Publishers* • New York

Library of Congress Cataloging-in-Publication Data

True and false allegations of child sexual abuse : assessment and case
    management / edited by Tara Ney.
        p.   cm.
    Includes bibliographical references and index.
    ISBN 0-87630-758-6
    1. Child sexual abuse–Investigation.   I. Ney, Tara.
HV6570.T78 1995
363.2' 59536–dc20   94-47941
                                                                        CIP

Published by
BRUNNER/MAZEL, Inc.
19 Union Square West
New York, New York 10003

Manufactured in the United States of America

10 9 8 7 6 5 4 3 2

Contents

Contributors

Brian R. Abbott, Ph.D., is the Executive Director of Giarretto Institute, San Jose, California, the first Child Sexual Abuse Treatment Program established worldwide.

Joyce A. Adams, M.D., is the former Director of the Child Sexual Abuse Evaluation Program at Valley Medical Center in Fresno, California. She has written numerous papers in the area of sexual abuse. She is currently with the Division of Adolescent Medicine, University of California, San Diego.

Lynne E. Baker-Ward, Ph.D., is an Associate Professor of Psychology at North Carolina State University, Chapel Hill, where she specializes in developmental psychology. She is coinvestigator with the Children's Memory Project, a research program that is concerned with children's abilities to remember and report personally experienced events.

Howard E. Barbaree, Ph.D., is a Professor of Psychology at Queen's Univeristy. He is also Head of the Impulse Control Disorders Program and Associate Head of the Forensic Division at the Clarke Institute of Psychiatry.

Debra A. Bekerian, Ph.D., is a research scientist at the Medical Research Council's Applied Psychology Unit, Cambridge, England. She is the principal author of many academic articles and chapters on memory, particularly on eyewitness memory and autobiographical memory. She is regarded as an expert on applied memory issues and serves as an advisor on training programs for the interviewing of sexually abused children.

Lorne D. Bertrand, Ph.D., is a Social Research Associate in the Canadian Research Institute for Law and the Family at the University of Calgary in Calgary, Alberta, Canada.

Floyd H. Bolitho, Ph.D., is Senior Lecturer, Faculty of Social Work and Social Policy, at the University of South Australia, Adelaide, South Australia.

Grant Charles, M.S.W., is the director of the Phoenix Centre, a treatment program for adolescent sex offenders, at Woods Homes in Calgary, Alberta, Canada.

Jon R. Conte, Ph.D., is Associate Professor at the School of Social Work, University of Washington, Seattle, Washington. He maintains a part-time private practice specializing in the treatment of trauma and a forensic practice dealing with various aspects of child abuse.

John L. Dennett is a Higher Scientific Officer at the Medical Research Council's Applied Psychology Unit, Cambridge, England. He is the coauthor of many academic articles and chapters on memory, particularly on psycho-legal issues. He serves as an advisor on training programs for the interviewing of sexually abused children.

Marion F. Ehrenberg, Ph.D., is an Assistant Professor of Psychology and Director of the Families in Transition Research and Information Centre at the University of Victoria, British Columbia, Canada. Her clinical practice includes child custody/access assessments and divorce-related interventions.

Michael F. Elterman, Ph.D., is a clinical psychologist who acts as a consultant to the Attorney General of British Columbia, the Ministry of Health, and the National Parole Board of Canada.

William N. Friedrich, Ph.D., is a Professor and Consultant at Mayo Medical School and Mayo Clinic in Rochester, Minnesota. He has authored or co-authored four books, including, *Bulimia: A Systems Approach to Treatment, Psychotherapy of Sexually Abused Children and Their Families*, and *Sexually Abused Boys: An Integrated Approach.*

Colleen Friend, M.S.W., is a licensed clinical social worker and field faculty at the University of California at Los Angeles School of Social Welfare. From

1990 to 1993, Ms. Friend was the Director of Stuart House, an innovative public/private partnership for the investigation and treatment of alleged child sexual abuse.

Betty N. Gordon, Ph.D., is an Associate Professor of Psychology at the University of North Carolina at Chapel Hill, where her specialty is clinical child psychology. She is coinvestigator with the Children's Memory Project, a research program that is concerned with children's abilities to remember and report personally experienced events.

Luise Greuel, Ph.D., is in forensic practice in Bonn, Germany. She has taught legal psychology at the Universities of Bonn and Hannover and is now active as a psychological expert for credibility assessment of child and adolescent victims.

Sandra K. Hewitt, Ph.D., is a child psychologist in private practice in Edina, Minnesota, and an adjunct faculty member at the Minnesota School of Professional Psychology. She is the cofounder and former codirector of the Midwest Children's Resource Center of the Children's Hospital of St. Paul, Minnesota.

Joseph P. Hornick, Ph.D., is the Executive Director of the Canadian Research Institute for Law and the Family at the University of Calgary in Calgary, Alberta, Canada.

Connie Burrows Horton, Ph.D., is a licensed clinical psychologist and an Assistant Professor of Psychology at Illinois State University, Normal, Illinois. She is involved in both research and clinical work in the area of child sexual abuse.

Toni Cavanagh Johnson, Ph.D., is a licensed clinical psychologist in private practice in South Pasadena, California. She is the coauthor, with Dr. Eliana Gil, of *Sexualized Children: The Assessment and Treatment of Sexualized Children and Children Who Molest.*

Kimberly A. Kochurka, B.A., a recent graduate of Illinois State University, collaborated with Connie Burrows Horton on this chapter as part of an undergraduate honors project. Ms. Kochurka began her graduate career in psychology in 1993.

Adelheid Kuehne, Ph.D., is a Professor of Clinical and Legal Psychology at the University of Hannover, Germany, Faculty of Education. She has also served as an expert for the credibility assessment of child and adult victims.

Susan P. Limber, Ph.D., M.L.S., is Clinical Assistant Professor of Neuropsychiatry at the University of South Carolina, and Director of the Division of School-Based Family Services at the Institute for Families in Society.

Elizabeth F. Loftus, Ph.D., is a Professor of Psychology and an Adjunct Professor of Law at the University of Washington in Seattle. She received her Ph.D. in Psychology from Stanford University. Since then she has published 18 books and over 200 scientific articles on the human memory and related topics. Her latest book, with Katherine Ketcham as coauthor, is *The Myth of Repressed Memory.*

David Marxsen, B.A., is a graduate student in the Department of Psychology, University of British Columbia, Vancouver, Canada.

Tara Ney, Ph.D., is a Registered Psychologist in private practice in Victoria, British Columbia. Her practice consists of assessing and treating children and adults who have experienced trauma. She is coeditor of *Smoking and Human Behaviour.*

Peter A. Ornstein, Ph.D., is a Professor of Psychology and the Director of the Developmental Psychology program at the University of North Carolina at Chapel Hill. He is coinvestigator with the Children's Memory Project, a research program that is concerned with children's abilities to remember and report personally experienced events.

Edward J. Peacock, Ph.D., is the Program Coordinator at the Warkworth Sexual Behavior Clinic, a federally sponsored treatment program for sex offenders at Warkworth Penitentiary.

Nancy Walker Perry, Ph.D., is an Associate Professor of Psychology at Creighton University in Omaha, Nebraska, where she has been a faculty member for 12 years. In addition, she was a practicing psychologist for five years. Her publications include *The Child Witness: Legal Issues and Dilemmas.*

Carolyn S. Schroeder, Ph.D., is a pediatric psychologist affiliated with Chapel Hill Pediatrics, P.A., and a Research Professor of Psychology at the University of North Carolina at Chapel Hill. She has been associated with the Children's Memory Project, a research program that is concerned with children's abilities to remember and report personally experienced events.

Monica Tymofievich, B.A., is a former research assistant, Department of Psychology, University of British Columbia, Vancouver, Canada.

Anne Graffam Walker, Ph.D., is a forensic linguist in private practice. A former court reporter, she has written several chapters on language and law, is the author of *Handbook on Questioning Children: A Linguistic Perspective,* and is coeditor with Judith Levi of *Language in the Judicial Process.*

Amye R. Warren, Ph.D., is a Professor of Psychology at the University of Tennessee in Chattanooga. She has written extensively on the topics of children's suggestibility, memory development, and language development.

Michael D. Yapko, Ph.D., is a clinical psychologist and marriage/family therapist in private practice in Solana Beach, California. He is the author of *When Living Hurts, Trancework,* and *Suggestions of Abuse.*

John C. Yuille, Ph.D., is a Professor of Psychology, University of British Columbia, Vancouver, Canada.

Foreword

Rediscovering Child Sexual Abuse

Around the turn of the century, Freud "discovered" sexual abuse while practicing psychoanalysis on middle-class Viennese women who presented with hysteria. He proposed that their hysterical symptoms were the result of experiences of sexual victimization—especially incest—during childhood. His theory met with widespread criticism. Because of this and Freud's own second thoughts, he soon repudiated his theory. Instead, he proposed that these claims of abuse derived from fantasies rather than reality. That is, these women, as children, wished sex with fathers and father figures and thereafter confused their thoughts with experiences. Based upon this redefinition, actual incest came to be considered quite rare: child sexual fantasies were easier to accept than child sexual abuse. The problem of sexual abuse was then buried for another 75 years (Masson, 1984).

Child sexual abuse was "rediscovered" in the late 1970s and early 1980s. In North America, reemergence of concern about sexual victimization can be traced to two phenomena: research on the prevalence of the problem and reports of child maltreatment to social service agencies mandated to investigate it. Studies in the United States first called professional and public attention to the problem of child sexual abuse. Similarly, although social welfare development in the United States has generally lagged behind that in Canada and Western Europe, in child abuse and neglect, the United States has been a leader.

The pioneering research in sexual abuse was a "college sophomore" study conducted by David Finkelhor (1979), who is a world leader in this field. He found that 19.2% of 530 women and 8.9% of 266 men from six New England colleges and universities had been sexually abused during childhood. These findings were particularly striking because college students are regarded as a low risk population. That is, assuming that sexual abuse has a negative impact on functioning, including academic achievement, one would expect a lower percentage of victims in a college population than in the general population.

Subsequent studies in the United States of low risk, high risk, and community samples have added support to Finkelhor's pioneering research. Although findings vary by gender and research methodology, they indicate that sexual abuse is a childhood experience for a considerable proportion of the population: about one in three or four women and between one in six to 10 men (Zellman & Faller, 1995).

The key social welfare development in the United States was the passage of the Child Abuse Prevention and Treatment Act in 1974. This act required states wanting federal discretionary funds to include certain provisions in their state child protection systems. Among these were mandatory reporting of child maltreatment, legal protections for reporters, and penalties for failure to report.

One consequence of the reporting provisions was a flood of referrals, including cases of possible sexual abuse. Moreover, each year, sexual abuse represents a larger proportion of reports. In 1976, the first year there were national data, 6,000 sexual abuse cases were reported, constituting less than 3% of all reports (American Association for Protecting Children, 1978). By 1993, about 300,000 sexual abuse cases were reported, representing 11% of reports (McCurdy & Daro, 1994), a 55-fold increase.

Comparable developments took place in Canada (Badgley, Allard, & McCormick et al., 1984). Although research into the problem of sexual abuse began a little later than in the United States, the Badgley Report (as it came to be known) was a ground-breaking study that was national in scope and representative of the Canadian population. Thirty-four percent of 1,833 respondents reported having been sexually abused as children (Badgley et al., 1984; Peters, Wyatt, & Finkelhor, 1986). Reanalysis of the data from this survey and subsequent studies demonstrate rates of sexual abuse comparable to those found in the United States (Bagley & King, 1990). As described in Bertrand, Hornick, and Bolitho's chapter in this volume, the Badgley Report, which included the national study findings, was instrumental in influencing far-reaching changes in the Canadian child welfare and criminal justice systems.

What to Do?

The flood of cases of children who may have been sexually abused caught child welfare professionals unprepared. They had virtually no skills or methodology for evaluating these allegations.

Child protection workers were, and are, often persons with no specific human services training. Law enforcement personnel were more accustomed to, and comfortable with, interrogating suspects than interviewing child victims about sexual matters. Mental health professionals may have considerable training in interviewing people about sensitive matters, but, as reflected in Limber's chapter in this book, they are not taught how to decide whether or not an event occurred. In addition, they have no special expertise in discerning whether a client is telling the truth.

Perhaps the legal system was the least prepared for the increased reporting of child sexual abuse and the consequent influx of criminal cases involving child witnesses. Long suspicious of children's motives and credibility (Myers, 1993), courts presented many obstacles to children's testimony, as described by Bertrand, Hornick, and Bolitho in their chapter.

Moreover, sexual abuse differs from physical abuse, whose hallmark is suspicious physical injury, and physical neglect, which is usually evident in the child's physical environmental conditions. Sexual abuse generally leaves no physical findings, as noted by Adams in this volume. It is a private undertaking—only involving the child and the adult. Therefore, in most cases, it comes down to the word of a child against the word of an adult.

In the late 1970s and early 1980s, practice was driven by necessity rather than knowledge. Pressured by the need to deal with sexual abuse allegations, professionals developed their techniques for investigation, assessment, and decision making by trial and error. There was a lack of uniformity in how cases were managed and an absence of empirical basis for much of the intervention. Indeed, many front-line workers lacked existing knowledge about child development, interview techniques, and the dynamics of sexual victimization.

The Backlash Against Child Protection

Although all child welfare mistakes are costly, perhaps those involving sexual abuse are even more costly than most. Among other tragedies, a false negative may doom the victim to a childhood of sexual abuse and teach the child that no adults can be relied upon. On the other hand, because child sexual abuse is treated foremost as a crime, a false positive can have equally devastating effects, such as unwarranted loss of liberty and unwarranted loss of custody to a beloved child.

Therefore, it is not surprising, that the process of investigation of child sexual abuse and its conclusions came to be challenged. This backlash against child protection began about 1983 and continues. It is interesting that the cases that galvanized the opposition to child protective practice were multivictim, multioffender cases that included descriptions of ritual abuse. These were the Jordan, Minnesota case, the McMartin Preschool case, and somewhat later a case in Hamilton, Ontario. Grant Charles's chapter in this book, and comments by Yuille, Tymofievich, and Marxsen, and Loftus and Yapko, in their respective chapters, attest to the continued divisiveness of these cases. It may be that the underlying reason for the instrumental role of ritual abuse in the backlash is the heinous crimes against children described are just impossible to believe. Nevertheless, these cases rightly highlighted flaws in child sexual abuse assessment and investigation.

Many well-meaning professionals working in child protection have been stunned and distressed by challenges to their assumptions, skills, and motivation. Nevertheless, the backlash has had a positive effect. It has caused professionals to respond to criticisms of their practices. To date, these responses include application of existing knowledge to practice, new research efforts relevant to sexual abuse evaluation and treatment, better training for child welfare professionals, and efforts to develop a consensus about what constitutes good practice.

Protecting the Future

It is important for society that the backlash not result in the reburial of the problem of child sexual abuse. Existing evidence indicates that child sexual abuse is a significant problem with considerable effects (e.g., Briere, 1989; Kendall-Tackett, Williams, & Finkelhor, 1993; Peters, Wyatt, & Finkelhor, 1986).

However, child sexual abuse professionals must also continue to respond to their critics. *True and False Allegations of Child Sexual Abuse* represents an important contribution to that effort. This book is about conducting evaluations of allegations of child sexual abuse that take into account research knowledge and practice wisdom.

True and False Allegations of Child Sexual Abuse is not a cookbook about how to do evaluations. Rather, it provides a great deal of food for thought. It is not for neophytes who are just learning about the problem of child sexual abuse. Rather, it is aimed at child abuse professionals who can critically read and test the material against their experiences in the field. The book does not present a party line. Rather, it includes a wide spectrum of information, approaches, and opinions about child sexual abuse evaluation. Since there are currently many perspectives and an expanding knowledge base, the chapters represent the state of knowledge and art about this problem. As such, *True and False Allegations of Child Sexual Abuse* ought to have a significant impact on the future quality of child sexual abuse evaluations.

Kathleen Coulborn Faller, Ph.D.
Professor, School of Social Work
Director, Family Assessment Clinic
Co-director, Interdisciplinary Project on Child Abuse & Neglect
University of Michigan

REFERENCES

American Association for Protecting Children. (1978). *Highlights of child neglect and abuse reporting: 1976.* Englewood, Col.: American Humane Association.

Badgley, R., Allard, H., McCormick, N., Proudfoot, P., Fortin, D., Ogilvie, D., Rae-Grant, Q., Gelinas, P., Pepin, L., & Sutherland, S. (1984). *Sexual offenses against children.* Ottawa: Canadian Government Publishing Centre.

Bagley, C., & King, K. (1990). *Child sexual abuse.* London: Routledge.

Briere, J. (1989). *Therapy for adults molested as children.* New York: Springer Publishing Company.

Finkelhor, D. (1979). *Sexually victimized children.* New York: The Free Press.

Kendall-Tackett, K., Williams, L., & Finkelhor, D. (1993). Impact of sexual abuse of children: A review and synthesis of recent empirical studies. *Psychological Bulletin, 113*(1).

Masson, J. M. (1984). *Assault on the truth.* New York: Farrar, Straus, & Giroux.

McCurdy, K., & Daro, D. (1994). *Current trends in child abuse reporting and fatalities.* Chicago: National Committee for the Prevention of Child Abuse.

Myers, J. (1993). *Legal issues in child abuse and neglect.* Newbury Park, Calif.: Sage.

Peters, S., Wyatt, G., & Finkelhor, D. (1986). Prevalence. In D. Finkelhor & associates, *Sourcebook on child sexual abuse.* Newbury Park, Calif.: Sage.

Zellman, G., & Faller, K. C. (1995). Reporting child abuse and neglect. In J. Briere, L. Berliner, & C. Jenny, (Eds.), *APSAC handbook on child maltreatment.* Newbury Park, Calif.: Sage.

Preface

The seeds for this volume were planted while I was being supervised as a psychologist intern. The case involved a four-year-old girl who, a year before, at age three, had used some sexually inappropriate language in the presence of her father. When the father (who was divorced from the child's mother) returned the child to the mother from a weekend visit, he told the child's mother what she had said. The mother, in turn, reported what had happened to the child-protection authorities. Within three weeks, all weekend visits with the father were stopped, and the child entered therapy.

An investigation ensued, although no criminal evidence could be found to charge the father with what he was first suspected of—perpetrating child sexual abuse. Nevertheless, the mother still would not allow the child to visit her father, since she firmly believed (as did the child's therapist) that the child had been molested by her father.

A year after the initial disclosure, I became involved in the case, along with my supervisor. The task was to determine the best case-management plans for this child. To this day, I recall the incredible anxiety I experienced in trying to do what was best for the child. Was the father a child molester? What if we recommended recommencement of visits and he began (or continued) to molest the child? On the other hand, what if he had never molested the child, and the child grew up believing her father had committed an offense against her that had never happened? I recall going through the research literature, looking for some material that could assist in our decision making. There was a remarkable dearth of applicable information that could help us to understand what had taken place.

I had many questions that I simply was not able to answer directly. What is normal child sexual development? What is truth telling for a young child? How suggestible are young children? Are there age differences in the suggestibility of young children? What is the memory capability of young children? What are the language and comprehension capabilities of young children? What are appropriate interviewing strategies and what influence can an interviewer have on what a young child reports? What are the risk characteristics of an incest offender? What are the dynamics of incest families and of families where there is intense anger between estranged parents? And above all, what are the implications of such questions for assessing and case managing an allegation of child sexual abuse?

Since first pondering these questions, a flood of research has appeared on all of these topics as they apply to assessing children who have been sexually abused. Many of the questions continue to be debated and much of the work is still in its infancy, but it is time for this research to be translated into practice. Hence this volume.

The chapters written for this book aim to increase the practitioner's knowledge base in order to improve skill level, competent assessment, and case management. Although they cover a great deal of complex theory and research, they are written in a style that is designed to be accessible to the layperson, regardless of background or training. Using everyday and legally relevant examples, complex principles are translated into comprehensible and feasible recommendations for practice.

Contributors have addressed the practical implications of the current research to related assessment and case management. They acknowledge the limits of our knowledge, drawing our attention to information that we appear to clearly understand and that which still remains problematic. Many of the chapters have coauthors: academics have teamed up with practitioners, pooling their knowledge, skills, and experiences. Such teamwork, I believe, is what was needed to make this volume applicable. The authors have also described useful strategies for proceeding in assessment and case management that are sensitive to information uncertainties.

Who will find this volume useful? The chapters were written by specialists in particular areas, and are suitable for both undergraduates and graduates training to be helping professionals, such as social workers, child and youth-care workers, probation officers, counselors, psychologists, nurses, medical practitioners, and teachers. Anybody training or working in the legal profession who is specializing in sexual abuse litigation will also find the volume useful. In addition, I know that more seasoned helping professionals working in the area of child sexual assessment or case management will benefit from the up-to-date research and practical strategies provided.

I would like to thank Dr. Francis Ricks for introducing me to case management in a "real world context." Thanks, of course, to all of the contributors for their willingness to write and rewrite these chapters. I am grateful, too, to Natalie Gilman of Brunner/Mazel for her patience and encouragement. I would also like to thank Kim Blank for his encouragement in pulling this volume together, his constant interest, and his assistance in many of the practical matters. And then to my own children, Acia and Jenner: thanks for your constant reminders about the day-to-day management of parental behavior!

−TARA NEY

PART I

Introduction

Assessing Allegations in Child Sexual Abuse: An Overview

Tara Ney

"First of all do no harm." Hippocrates

OVERVIEW

The Purpose of This Volume

CASE 1. A four-year-old girl, whose parents have been separated for six months, visits her father and his new girlfriend every other weekend. One weekend, she returns from a visit with her father and reports to her mother, "Daddy touched me in my private parts." She is unable to give further details, but when questioned in an interview with a police officer, she repeats what she has told her mother. The mother is guilt ridden, and feels she should have known that her daughter was being abused, as she had noticed her masturbating frequently. A medical examination finds no genital trauma. When confronted, her father first appears shocked, then becomes extremely angry. He reports that he has never touched his daughter's private parts, except when he applied a cream to her genitals to treat a yeast infection. He agrees to both a phallometric and lie detector test; in both instances, the findings are negative. The mother, who is now very anxious and upset, and is convinced that her daughter has been sexually molested by her husband, refuses to allow further visits with the girl's father. One afternoon, about two months after the allegation, the father by chance meets his daughter and her mother in a shopping mall. The daughter spontaneously jumps into her father's arms and says she misses him. The mother reports that shortly after this encounter, her daughter began to have nightmares and to wet her bed. The mother continues to refuse visits, and the young girl, after seven months of therapy, says to her counselor, "I don't want to see my daddy until I'm a teenager." The counselor also reports that the child has now disclosed memories of ritual abuse. The case goes to court.

Case 2. A 15-year-old girl claims that her paternal grandfather sexually molested her when she was eight and nine years old: she claims he would put her hands down his pants and have her rub his penis; he would also fondle her genitals. Charges are made. A few days before the court case, the adolescent recants her allegations, claiming that she made up the story because she was angry at her mother. A year later, she reports to her mother that sexual molestation really did occur, and that at the time she feared what her grandfather would do if she told her story.

Case 3. A 31-year-old woman approaches a therapist for counseling. She reports that two years earlier she had taken a hypnosis course, and shortly after this training, began to have memories of her father's sexually molesting her when she was a child. Her memories are vivid. She reports fondling, and recalls that later, in her teenage years, her father would take her on his business trips, wine and dine her, and then have sexual intercourse with her in the hotel room. About six months earlier, she had confronted her father in writing about what she claimed he had done. He responded in writing, denying everything, claiming that her previous therapeutic experiences had created "false memories." She is now filing a legal action for damages against her father.

What would you do if these allegations were presented to you? What would be the questions you would ask yourself and the individuals involved in such cases? Whom would you want to talk to? Are these allegations true or false?

Such are the day-to-day scenarios that are presented to front-line workers involved with children who allegedly have been sexually abused. The answers or the strategies are not always so clear cut. If we were to discuss these cases with a group of social workers, counselors, child-protection workers, police officers, general practitioners, and lawyers (prosecution *and* defense), a very heated discussion would likely develop about how to handle the allegations and what to do. Can you think of any colleagues, or coworkers in different professions, who might disagree with your perception of these events as presented here? And if your answer is "Yes," why might this be so, and what are the implications?

Increasingly, mental health professionals are participating in the adjudicatory stage of child sexual abuse proceedings: Did the abuse actually occur? If so, who did it, what happened, and what are the short- and long-term effects? The vicious debates among professionals involved in child sexual abuse cases often revolve around issues such as: Did it or did it not happen? Who could have done this? Is this child telling the truth? Do children lie? How was the original interview carried out? Could a child remember all of this? How suggestible is this child? What are the language capabilities of this child? What is in the child's best interest? The answers to such questions may differ among professionals, depending upon personal attitudes, skills, or the knowledge base to which one is referring. For example, the interpretation by professionals and laypersons of the research literature on whether children lie appears to have changed over the past decade, or at least is highly discrepant: children do lie; children never lie; under certain circumstances, children might lie (Ceci & Bruck, 1993). In fact, the circumstances under which children may lie, or are suggestible, continues to be the subject of ongoing debate. The task of the front-line worker—to be informed of the most recent research, and to integrate such knowledge into practice—is not an easy one.

More recently it has come to our attention that counselors, psychologists, psychiatrists, and other mental health professionals acting in the capacity of therapists must, like all front-line workers, also be aware of how young children may report a disclosure of sexual abuse, and the part they as therapists play in the assessment interview, disclosure, and therapeutic process of young children. In a recent court case in California, a therapist and psychiatrist were found guilty of negligent practice: they were held to have unnecessarily influenced their patient's memories of alleged, repeated rape by her father during her childhood.

This ruling suggests that while therapists and front-line workers play quite a different role from investigators of child sexual abuse, it is imperative that they too be knowledgeable and skilled in working with young children who have allegedly been sexually abused.

The inability of professionals to agree on the veracity of a statement made by a young child was demonstrated most recently in a study by Steve Ceci and colleagues (Ceci, Leichtman, & White, in press). Videos of more than 1,000 children recounting "memories" were shown to a panel of lawyers, doctors, and social workers. Some of the memories were fabricated by the children and some were not. The experts were correct about whether the child's account was accurate about one third of the time! This finding is astonishing, as the ability of a professional to determine the veracity of a child's statement is no better (and perhaps worse) than chance. But if professionals who work with young children are unable to agree, or to accurately identify when a child is or is not telling the truth based on what is said to them, then what else do we need to know in order to assess accurately what is being said by a young child?

Clearly, we do not have the critical tools for reliably distinguishing true from false accounts of sexual abuse. There is room, however, for improving our assessment skills and expanding our knowledge when working with young children who have been sexually abused. Professionals must build their knowledge and skill base to evaluate better the statements made about alleged child sexual abuse. The ability of the child-protection and legal systems to protect sexually abused children depends in part on the ability and willingness of professionals to assess children better and facilitate accurate testimony in court. I believe that these are the most difficult and complex cases that the front-line worker must deal with: it behooves us, therefore, as professionals, to ensure that we operate competently and responsibly, to be able to determine, as best as we can, what really happened and what meaning it may have had for a child. The aim of this volume is to translate, for the practitioner, the research issues into practice issues, and then to suggest useful strategies and techniques in the assessment and case management of child sexual abuse cases.

The Problem

Sexual abuse is prevalent and has a remarkably injurious impact on human development (Kendall-Tackett, Meyer Williams, & Finkelhor, 1993); however, there are a growing number of cases where allegations of child sexual abuse are misunderstood and mishandled by both professionals and non-professionals (Quinn, 1991). Inaccurately assessed allegations may result in determining that abuse didn't occur when it did, or that abuse did occur when it did not. For example, in a recent study, more than half of the adult survivors of child abuse surveyed for a university study said they weren't believed as children when they told someone about the abuse (Brown, Palmer, & Rae-Grant, 1994). On the other hand, several writers have written about the problem of false allegations (i.e., falsely identifying an individual as an abuser) (see Robin, 1991). Estimates indicate that the rate of false positives (i.e., cases where abuse is not occurring but is claimed to be) varies between 2% and 8%, and is somewhat higher in custody disputes (Green, 1991). Each of these mistaken assessments has horrific consequences for those involved: if the allegations are true but not believed, a child may continue to be subjected to abuse and suffer psychological aftereffects (in the Brown et al. study, 80% of those who told of the abuse said it continued or worsened after disclosure); if the allegations are false but believed, then unjustified consequences result for the alleged perpetrator and family. Until we understand better the circumstances under which both false positives and false negatives occur, then we will not learn of improved methods of assessing such cases.

In recent years, there have been trends in research that reflect efforts to understand better the validity of assessment techniques (e.g., Anson, Golding, & Gully, 1993; Horowitz, Lamb, Esplin, Boychuk, Krispin, & Reiter-Lavery, 1992; Landry & Brigham, 1992; Steller, 1989). Further, a recent increase in the number of edited volumes in the area of child development and child witness testimony is indicative of an acknowledgment of both the need to understand better the world of the young child who is required to provide a statement, and the need to bring together expertise from various disciplines (Ceci, Leichtman & Putnick, 1992; Ceci, Toglia, & Ross, 1987; Cicchetti & Toth, 1993; Dent & Flynn, 1992; Doris, 1991; Fivush & Hudson, 1990; Goodman & Bottoms, 1993; Peters, in press; Robin, 1991; Ross, Read, & Toglia, 1994; Snyder & Saywitz, in press; Zaragoza, in press). Together, the development of these research areas is evidence of the collaboration of researchers and clinicians in pooling their expertise and experiences, attempting to expand the limits of our knowledge and to improve our knowledge base about the circumstances under which we are able more accurately to assess the statements made by children about harm that may have been inflicted upon them.

OBJECTIVITY AND TRUTH

The task of assessing an alleged case of sexual abuse is formidable. The front-line worker is often encountering individuals at one of their darkest times, when feelings of fear, anger, and helplessness pervade. Individuals–caretakers, alleged victims, and abusers–may feel confused, violent, and/or despairingly suicidal. The transference and countertransference issues for the assessor can, at times, be overwhelming.

Moreover, at the time of assessment, families and individuals are typically in crisis. Everything comes into play: the assessment involves professionals of all sorts, and often the media. The practitioner is in a very vulnerable position: lives may change unalterably once an allegation is made–true or untrue. Often the assessor is in a no-win situation: there is almost always somebody who does not like what the assessor has formulated. Nethertheless, the evaluator is supposed to identify the problem, understand the nature of the allegation, provide formulations about the allegation of abuse, and make predictions about how various parts of the system will unravel and reshape themselves over time. In short, professionals are expected to provide these clients with the most competent, objective service available, in terms of assessment and case management.

The issue of objectivity is an interesting one, and requires extensive attention from practitioners and researchers. Throughout this volume, and in many others on the assessment of sexual abuse, the importance of objectivity in assessment is stressed. But what does this mean? The *Oxford English Dictionary* defines objectivity as "free from or independent of personal feelings, opinions, prejudice, etc." Yet, as noted here, emotional involvement is the subject of concern for both the professional and the client.

How, specifically, do our biases influence the assessment process? Personal biases may affect our decision making unknowingly. Remarkably, even with trained professionals, such factors as race, socioeconomic status, and the alleged victim's lack of affect may influence clinical judgments of sexual abuse, even though current knowledge would not support any of these criteria (Jackson & Nuttall, 1993)! It has also been demonstrated that clinicians who have a history of sexual abuse judge a case differently from those who do not have such a history (Jackson & Nuttall, 1993). Indeed, our interpretation of research is often reflected by our current positioning and experiences. It is impossible to present with a blank slate; we all have experiences and histories that affect our judgments. Jackson and Nuttall's findings suggest that the influence of personal biases is subtle but powerful in assessments of child sexual abuse.

Pettit, Fegan, and Howie (1990) also demonstrate how personal biases may have an impact on the assessment process. They found that interviewers who were misled about children's experiences prior to an interview elicited more inaccurate information from the children than did those who did not receive false information. This finding suggests that interviewer bias can unknowingly influence children's reports of what happened. In other words, an interviewer or therapist who has strong beliefs about what has happened to a child can influence a child to report events that did not occur. Such a finding has been demonstrated in other recent studies, with children of various ages, and with individuals other than interviewers (for an updated summary of these studies, see Ceci and Bruck, 1993). Moreover, this finding is not surprising, and has been described in the social psychological research as the Rosenthal Effect—the ability to influence another's behavior based on one's expectations (Rosenthal & Jacobson, 1966). In addition, social psychologists have long known that people tend to (1) form judgments extremely quickly, (2) attend and interpret information to confirm personal beliefs and preexisting theories, and (3) ignore or discount information that is ambiguous or contradictory (Rosenthal, 1985). It is only more recently that practitioners and researchers have begun to understand these phenomena in the context of child sexual abuse allegations. In short, this research suggests that practitioners' perceptions may be influenced by preexisting beliefs, and, perhaps more remarkable, that these *beliefs* may actually influence the behavior (statements) of the children being interviewed!

Thus objectivity and truth are clearly problematic in assessments of sexual abuse. Social constructivists argue that perceptions, opinions, beliefs, and the like are relative and socially constructed. This is an extraordinarily important point, for it suggests that although we strive for objectivity, in fact none of us is able to attain absolute objectivity. Perhaps the best we can do is to be aware that our realities are all relative and, at least according to social constructivists, socially constructed. Consider, for example, the following socially constructed realities: What might happen if the practitioner does not pay attention to his/her own gender when assessing a case? What problems might be incurred? Or, for example, where did the language used come from? Or what are your values and beliefs concerning children, women, abusers, etc.? If you are an incest survivor or if somebody you know is, or if you have been sexually molested in some way, how does this affect your approach to assessing such cases? At what school were you trained, and from what school of thought do you operate? What ideology is built into your approach, and what are the advantages and disadvantages for the individuals you are assessing and case managing? How does this affect your ability to assess and case manage? For whom are you working–child protective services, the defendant, the plaintiff? Such questions suggest differences among people, for which they are not at fault, but for which they must be accountable.

But if objectivity is so precarious, then what is the solution? It has been suggested that front-line workers be better trained in child development, assessment and case management, and interviewing (Yuille, Hunter, Joffe, & Zaparniuk, 1993). But training alone may give a false sense of "objective" security. For instance, in one study, one third of the interviewers who were trained to conduct a neutral interview and to avoid leading, suggestive questions later asked leading questions during interviews (Pettit et al., 1990). Why does this happen? As discussed above, the influence of our subjectivity is powerful; it is extremely difficult not to impose our own expectations on those with whom we work. Rather than insisting upon objectivity, perhaps we need to accept that we all operate from our subjectivity, and that perhaps the best we can do is to become aware of our biases, prejudices, and expectations. Thus, in addition to training, or better yet, included in the training, workers must reflect on their own beliefs and values. What am I bringing to this situation? When assessing sexual abuse, the following are questions the assessor could explore about himself or herself:

- What kind of people sexually abuse children?
- What kind of people are sexually abused?
- What does sexuality mean to me? How was it dealt with in my family? How was it expressed by my mother/father?
- What do I feel/think of men and/or women?
- Am I able to talk openly about sex? If yes, with whom? If no, with whom? Did I talk about sex openly with my family or with my friends?
- How did I view sex as a child? How does this affect me at present?
- Was I or were any of my friends sexually abused? If so, how does this experience affect me personally? Professionally? Does this affect my professional judgments? How?
- What are the *normal* ways in which families express sexuality in the home?
- Are children sexual?
- What is normal child sex play?
- What is normal sexuality?
- What is wrong with adult–child sex?
- Do I react differently to the topic of child sexual abuse professionally than I do personally?
- What are my attitudes about women? Men? Children? Sex roles? Rape? Wife battering? Sexual offenders? Homosexuality? Families? Punishment? Forgiveness?
- Do I come from a family of divorce? What does this mean to me?
- What are my attitudes toward my profession? Other professions? Government? Agencies?
- What are the ethical considerations?

The point is that our reality is constructed through our experiences: our perception is only what we need to promote. We are constantly experimenting with arbitrary rules, constructs, and theories. The issues of "truth" and "objectivity" are critical in the assessment of child sexual abuse. Always, truth and objectivity become what we need them to be—particularly in cases where there are many apparent truths: the child's, the child's parents', and the alleged offender's. Whose truth is truth? Achieving clinical objectivity in sexual abuse cases is difficult. Jackson and Nutall conclude that "attitudes and beliefs about sexuality, and the emotionally laden character of child and adolescent sexual abuse, make all clinicians vulnerable to defensive strategies that may cloud judgments and lead to inaccurate and, sometimes, unfortunate decisions" (Jackson & Nutall, 1993, p. 140). We must constantly be questioning and openly discussing our beliefs and values when conducting such assessments of children who have allegedly been sexually abused.

ASSESSMENT IS A PROCESS

All assessment is a process in time. From the beginning to the end of the assessment period, relevant and irrelevant information is gathered and synthesized. Judgments and formulations subsequently evolve. Information is integrated according to sets of criteria influenced by a *knowledge* base (e.g., theoretical orientation, training) and *personal position* (e.g., expectations, biases, etc.). The assessment process is not necessarily linear or sequential. The fluid nature of seeking, sorting, and integrating information means that assessments do not always go smoothly or in a straight line (Ricks, 1991). For example, the point at which an allegation of sexual abuse is made is only the starting point: information about the conditions prior to and following the allegation, as well as those prevalent at the time of the child's original report, must be examined. Specifically, such information would include the nature of the allegation, the people involved (alleged victim, alleged offender, family, friends, etc.) and their personal characteristics, and the context in which involved individuals live and the allegation was made. More specifically, based on recent research, the following information should be gathered, analyzed, sifted, and integrated before formulations are made.

Identify and Clarify the Problem

- Who originally made the report of alleged abuse?
- How was this dealt with?
- What is the allegation(s)?
- Who is involved?
- How are the various individuals involved?
- What meaning does the allegation have for various individuals?
- How did the allegation come about?
- When did the allegation first occur?
- What has been the consistency of the child's report over time?
- Has the allegation as reported by others remained consistent over time?
- What are the behaviors of all parties who are associated with this allegation?
- When do these behaviors occur?
- How frequent are these behaviors?
- What is the duration of these behaviors?
- What are the unmet needs of those involved?
- What are the various individuals' emotional reactions to the problem?
- How have the various parties attempted to cope with the allegation of abuse?

- What skills do various parties require to deal with this problem?
- What are the skills/strengths of individuals related to the problem?

Individuals Involved and Their Personal Characteristics

- Emotional, including affect, mood, content of thinking, energy level
- Physical health
- Cognitive, including memory, attention, thinking
- Judgment, including insight, perception, coherence
- Values and beliefs
- Self-concept

Characteristics of the Context

- What were the prevalent conditions at the time of the child's *original* report?
- What were the circumstances under which the initial report of concern was made?
- How many times has the child been questioned?
- Who has questioned the child?
- What are the hypotheses of those who have interviewed the child?
- What kinds of specific questions were asked of the child?
- Was the child's disclosure made in a nonthreatening, nonsuggestible atmosphere?
- Was the disclosure made after repeated interviews?
- Were any of the adults who have had access to the child before assessment motivated to distort the child's recollections (through suggestions or coaching)?
- What is the functioning capability of the child and key individuals, including their use of several key interpersonal subsystems?
- What is the motivation of the child/parents to work on specified target problems?
- Are there cultural problems embodied in the problem system, such as cultural norms and language?
- What are the interpersonal and communication dynamics involved in the spousal and family systems?
- Are there environmental factors that may affect various individuals?

These are examples of information to be collected.

Of course, the possibility of errors in assessment are increased when the assessor becomes single-minded. We must ask ourselves what we are bringing to the assessment situation. We must continually consider other causes, or even multiple causes, for the problem. The ability to keep our minds open to many possibilities while exploring one hypothesis is a difficult one. We need to be constantly thinking "process" on many levels throughout the assessment period.

Causality

Causality is an interesting notion. Frequently, if two events occur simultaneously, or one after the other, we will explain that one event caused the other: I haven't slept for 18 hours. I am tired. Therefore, I am tired because I haven't slept for 18 hours. Deductive reasoning is useful in solving problems of many kinds. In medicine, it is used all the time: for example, people who eat too many saturated fats are prone to heart disease; people who don't exercise are prone to heart disease; people who have a stressful lifestyle are prone to heart disease; people who have heart disease in their biological families are prone to heart disease. Of course, several of these explanations for heart disease were not possible until adequate research was completed to include them as contributing factors. For example, it was only in the past decade that the contribution of lifestyle *and* diet to heart disease became known empirically. Thus, while establishing causal mechanisms can be useful, it can be unhelpful, if not futile and confusing, if there are causal explanations that either are ignored or are as yet unknown. In the example of heart disease, we now know that all of these causes are valid. Heart disease may be caused in various ways. If a physician were not open to alternative explanations, he or she might mistakenly suggest that improper diet, for instance, caused the heart disease. Of course, a competent physician explores all of these possibilities. Likewise, when an allegation of sexual abuse is made, there are sometimes alternative explanations that must be explored.

Thinking unilinearly creates problems in assessment. For example, the child recanted, therefore she has been abused; the child recanted, therefore she hasn't been abused; the child has been masturbating, therefore she has been sexually abused; the father became angry and denied, therefore he is guilty; the mother has also been sexually abused, therefore she has suggested abuse to her child; the child lied about her marks at school, therefore she lied about the sexual abuse; preschool children are suggestible, therefore her story is not true; there is a custody dispute, therefore the allegations are false, etc. Our need to make quick decisions based on some form of deductive logic is tempting; however, the real world context is complex and formulations based on simple causations must be resisted. Cause and effect, especially when it comes to human behavior, is never a straightforward matter. The assessor must ask, "Are there other explanations that are consistent with these symptoms, yet inconsistent with allegations of child sexual abuse?" Assessment is a process that must incorporate many pieces of information.

Sometimes even with our best skills, and having access to the most up-to-date knowledge, it is impossible to determine whether abuse occurred (due to insufficient information). We must be prepared to recognize such cases, and then assess the risk and appropriately case manage them.

Chapter 2 provides some insight into the nature of allegations, true and false. A description of incidence and patterns of sexual abuse allegations helps us to understand what needs to happen to assess allegations more thoroughly and accurately. As Yuille et al. state, "Understanding the nature of false allegations can help investigators increase their level of confidence in dealing with all allegations."

Child Development

In assessments, knowledge refers to the assessor's frameworks that provide an understanding, description, explanation, and/or justification of the assessment judgment. One would assume that when assessing an alleged case of sexual abuse the assessor has, at minimum, knowledge in child growth and development (this would be among other areas of training in principles, processes, and models of adult development, assessment, research, family dynamics, communication theory, intervention, and ethics and legal systems).

Part II on child development demonstrates that the knowledge we are currently gaining from research is new and will continue to evolve over the years. While much of the research in this area is in its infancy (so to speak), it is expected that the management of these very difficult sexual abuse cases will reflect new discoveries in child development: clinicians will need to keep in touch with the empirically based research, and researchers will need to continue to keep in touch with the front-line workers' struggles.

At the very minimum, practitioners who work with young children must be trained in child development (Farr & Yuille, 1988). Frequently, however, this is not the case (Goodman & Helgeson, 1985). If practitioners have had child development training, typically, child development courses may cover cognitive, social, biological, and sometimes moral development, but are seriously deficient either in content or applicability to understanding children's reports of sexual abuse. In this section, writers cover the implications of children's sexual development, children's comprehension of truths and lies, suggestibility and memory development of young children and implications for the accuracy of reporting, developmental characteristics of very young (preschool) children, and the implications of developmental tasks of adolescents in allegations of child sexual abuse.

Interviews

The argument made at the beginning of this chapter suggests that we cannot be neutral when in conversation with someone, and typically, we have a way of seeing what we need to see in the world (social construction of reality). The task of interviewing, therefore, is not an easy one: interviewers of children who have allegedly been sexually abused must take into account a variety of factors that have been shown to influence children's statements. Generally speaking, the younger the child, the more vulnerable he or she is to a poorly conducted interview. Specifically, the interviewer must take into account the child's cognitive, language, and emotional levels. As well, interviewers who may have biases or expectations about what may have happened to the child, or who ask suggestive or misleading questions, will elicit incomplete and inaccurate information from the child. In Part III on interviews, contributors describe how an interview, or therapy session, can create misleading information about whether sexual abuse has occurred. To this end, the chapters deal with the use of language in interviews, psychotherapy and the recovery of repressed memories, and interview techniques which reportedly determine truthfulness of children's statements. Numerous useful suggestions are made to minimize making errors during interviews.

Special Issues

Difficulties in assessing allegations of child sexual abuse most frequently occur in the context of custody and access disputes. Often the assessor must establish: Which adult has distorted the truth? Why might a parent make such an allegation if it were not true? And, if this is the case, is it possible to obtain the truth from the child? What are the circumstances under which children may easily be guided by adults, friends, or therapists?

In Part IV, special topic areas are reviewed. These include allegations in custody/access disputes, medical assessments, offender assessments, family dynamic issues, assessing children with developmental disabilities, problems of indeterminacy in the "real world," and assessment of ritual abuse.

Legal Issues

Frequently, the point is made that the therapeutic role must be distinguished from the investigative role. However, there are many instances where investigation and therapeutic progress overlap. This is true, for instance, when the legal system discourages or does not provide opportunities for an accurate assessment. The legal system is not always sensitive to the subtle, interpersonal issues that arise when a child allegedly has been sexually abused. Sometimes the legal process breaks the family tapestry into more fragments, alienating and confusing children, and impeding an accurate account of what may have happened. Such discomfort with the system evokes a feeling that all is not well in our work, no matter how extraordinarily well we perform it. The two chapters in this section deal with some of the legal and ethical issues with which front-line workers must contend when working with young children who have allegedly been sexually abused.

Recommendations

To conclude, in an effort to obtain more accurate assessments of allegations of sexual abuse, a summary of a number of key recommendations made by the contributors to this volume is presented. It is recommended:

1. **THAT** interviewers and investigators be thoroughly trained in interviewing techniques before questioning the child about the abuse, and that training be competent and ongoing (Chapter 2).
2. **THAT** caution be exercised when ascribing meaning to children's sexual behaviors, as research data are in the early stages and most data are from clinical experience. Research so far indicates that few children, abused or not, draw genitals on human figures, and both abused and nonabused children engage in sexually suggestive behaviors with dolls (Chapter 3).
3. **THAT** clinicians conduct assessments of children's understanding of truths, lies, and false beliefs on a case-by-case basis (Chapter 4).
4. **THAT** an evaluation include the number and type of prior interviews done with the child. Any subsequent interviews should be video- or audiotaped so that each critical response can be evaluated in light of the stimulus that was required to elicit it (was the response spontaneous or heavily cued?), and then assessed in the context of any subsequent risk factors (Chapter 5).
5. **THAT** assessment of very young children utilize a protocol sensitive to the child's developmental level; this includes integrating the child's behavioral repertoire over time and across situations, and, in many instances, emphasizing protection rather than prosecution (Chapter 6).
6. **THAT** when conducting evaluations of sexual abuse of an adolescent, the evaluator be knowledgeable about relevant adolescent developmental tasks, such as gender self-concept and self-identity, and how these tasks may interfere with giving clear and accurate reports of sexual abuse (Chapter 7).
7. **THAT** a sample of the child's language be obtained by first discussing a neutral subject before approaching the subject at hand and the interviewer subsequently adapt his or her language

to the child. The interviewer must be knowledgeable and alert to simple words and phrases that may have unusual meaning for a child. The interviewer should conduct periodic checks to see if the child is understanding the conversation (Chapter 8).

8. **THAT** when using specific truth assessment techniques such as statement analysis, formal training first be obtained, and caution exercised in only using the technique with certain events and certain children who have specific developmental capabilities (Chapter 9).

9. **THAT** clinicians who are attempting to make a "diagnosis" of whether an individual had been sexually abused as a child understand that certain adults are suggestible in certain circumstances and so must not use leading questions or assume that repression is in force if the person cannot remember much from his or her childhood (Chapter 10).

10. **THAT** specific techniques for "facilitating" memory recall, such as the cognitive interview, be used at appropriate points in the investigation and with children who have reached a certain level of verbal competence (Chapter 11).

11. **THAT** when evaluating any allegation of child sexual abuse, assessors screen for divorce-related issues, and understand these dynamics in relation to the sexual abuse allegation (Chapter 12).

12. **THAT** since unusual genital or anal findings may or may not be due to abuse, a complete history be obtained from the child and caretaker in addition to the medical examination. More research is needed to establish the psychological effects of medical examinations on children and to understand better the healing of acute genital and anal injuries in children (Chapter 13).

13. **THAT** while the phallometric test is the best method for detecting pedophilia in men and is used increasingly to evaluate alleged offenders, its ability validly to identify an incest offender is unacceptably low. Negative results should not mean that a man is innocent or that he is safe with children, and, in fact, in most cases of allegations of child sexual abuse, the test should not be used (Chapter 14).

14. **THAT** while the disturbed family relationships found in incest cases cannot, in isolation, diagnose or predict the presence of child sexual abuse, it be recognized that increased understanding of the family dynamics is critical in the development of effective case-management plans where it is reported that a child allegedly has been sexually abused (Chapter 15).

15. **THAT** evaluators be aware of the pervasive myths that exist about children with developmental disabilities who allegedly

have been sexually abused, and that interfere with accurate, sensitive investigation (Chapter 16).

16. **THAT** there are a significant number of cases that are "difficult" and will not be substantiated. It is important, however, that these families also receive the required social and mental health services (Chapter 17).

17. **THAT** therapists and child-protection/criminal-justice investigators who are involved in ritual abuse cases continually keep their roles clear and separate, and that all professionals involved in such cases clearly delineate for themselves their personal and religious views about such abuses (Chapter 18).

18. **THAT** it be recognized that, typically, the more severe the abuse, the greater will be the anxiety experienced by a young child in anticipation of, during, and after the process of testifying in court. Since stress has been shown generally to interfere with a child's ability to communicate information accurately, then procedures now acceptable in courts of law should be utilized (Chapter 19).

19. **THAT** mental health professionals recognize their ethical and legal duty to report suspected cases of child sexual abuse, and that professionals who testify in court refrain from providing scientifically unfounded opinions about whether sexual abuse has occurred (Chapter 20).

The arguments and research basis for these recommendations can be found in the chapters to follow. Policy makers and front-line workers of all professions, it is hoped, will see the rationale of heeding these recommendations and adapt their existing skills and ways of working to the implications of the most recent research.

REFERENCES

Anson, D.A., Golding, S.L., & Gully, K.J. (1993). Child sexual abuse allegations: Reliability of criteria-based content analysis. *Law and Human Behavior, 17*(3), 331–341.

Brown, R., Palmer, S., & Rae-Grant, N. (1994). Preliminary findings of the long-term effects of childhood abuse: A study of survivors. Unpublished manuscript, School of Social Work, McMaster University.

Ceci, S.J., & Bruck, M. (1993). Suggestibility of the child witness: A historical review and synthesis. *Psychological Bulletin, 113*(3), 403–439.

Ceci, S.J., Leichtman, M., & Putnick, M. (Eds.). (1992). *Cognitive and social factors in early deception.* Hillsdale, N.J.: Erlbaum.

Ceci, S. J., Leichtman, M.D., & White, T. (in press). Interviewing preschoolers. In D. Peters (Ed.), *The child witness in cognitive, social, and legal context.* Dordrecht, Netherlands: Kluwer.

Ceci, S. J., Toglia, M.P., & Ross, D.F. (Eds.). (1987). *Children's eyewitness testimony.* New York: Springer-Verlag.

Cicchetti, D., & Toth, S. (Eds.). (1993). *Child abuse, child development, and social policy.* Norwood, N.J.: Ablex.

Dent, H., & Flynn, R. (Eds.). (1992). *Children as witnesses.* New York: Wiley.

Doris, J. (Ed.). (1991). *The suggestibility of children's recollections: Implications for eyewitness testimony.* Washington, D.C.: American Psychological Association.

Farr, V., & Yuille, J. (1988). Assessing credibility. *Preventing Sexual Abuse, 1*(1), 8–13.

Finkelhor, D. (1979). *Sexually victimized children.* New York: Free Press.

Fivush, R., & Hudson, J.A. (Eds.). (1990). *Knowing and remembering in young children.* New York: Sage.

Goodman, G., & Helgeson, V. (1985). Child sexual assault: Children's memory and the law. *University of Miami Law Review, 40,* 181–208.

Goodman, G.S., & Bottoms, B.L. (Eds.). (1993). *Child victims, child witnesses: Understanding and improving testimony.* New York: Guilford Press.

Green, A. (1991). Factors contributing to false allegations of child sexual abuse in custody disputes. In M. Robin (Ed.), *Assessing child maltreatment reports: The problem of false allegations* (pp. 177–189). New York: Haworth Press.

Horowitz, S.W., Lamb, M.E., Esplin, P.W., Boychuk, T., Krispin, O., & Reiter-Lavery, L. (1992, June). *Reliability of criteria-based content analysis of child witness statements.* Paper presented to the American Psychological Society, San Diego, Calif.

Jackson, H., & Nuttall, R. (1993). Clinician responses to sexual abuse allegations. *Child Abuse and Neglect, 17,* 127–143.

Kendall-Tackett, K.A., Meyer Williams, L., & Finkelhor, D. (1993). Impact of sexual abuse on children: A review and synthesis of recent empirical studies. *Psychological Bulletin, 113*(1), 164–180.

Landry, K., & Brigham, J.C. (1992). The effect of training in criteria-based content analysis on the ability to detect deception in adults. *Law and Human Behavior, 16,* 663–676.

Peters, D. (Ed.). (in press). *The child witness in cognitive, social, and legal context.* Dordrecht, Netherlands: Kluwer.

Pettit, R., Fegan, M., & Howie, P. (1990, September). *Interviewer effects of children's testimony.* Paper presented at the International Congress on Child Abuse and Neglect, Hamburg, Germany.

Quinn, K.M. (1991). False and unsubstantiated sexual abuse allegations: Clinical issues. In M. Robin (Ed.), *Assessing child maltreatment reports: The problem of false allegations* (pp. 145–157). New York: Haworth Press.

Ricks, F. (1991). *Accountability case management.* Victoria, B.C., Canada: Fotoprint.

Robin, M. (Ed.). (1991). *Assessing child maltreatment reports: The problem of false allegations.* New York: Haworth Press.

Rosenthal, R. (1985). From unconscious experimenter bias to teacher expectancy effects. In J.B. Dusek & V.C. Hall (Eds.), *Teacher expectancies* (pp. 37–65). Hillsdale, N.J.: Erlbaum.

Rosenthal, R., & Jacobson, L. (1966). *Experimenter effects in the classroom: Teacher expectations and pupil intellectual development.* New York: Holt, Rinehart & Winston.

Ross, D.F., Read, J.D., & Toglia, M.P. (Eds.). (1994). *Adult eyewitness testimony: Current trends and developments.* New York: Cambridge University Press.

Snyder, L.S., & Saywitz, K.J. (Eds.). Child abuse and communication disordered children. *Topics in Language Disorders, 14.*

Steller, M. (1989). Recent developments in statement analysis. In J.C. Yuille (Ed.), *Credibility assessment* (pp. 135–154). Dordrecht, Netherlands: Kluwer.

Yuille, J.C., Hunter, R., & Harvey, W. (1990). A coordinated approach to interviewing in child sexual abuse investigations. *Canada's Mental Health, 38* (2/3), 14–17.

Yuille, J.C., Hunter, R., Joffe, R., & Zaparniuk, J. (1993). Interviewing children in sexual abuse cases. In G. Goodman & B. Bottoms (Eds.). *Understanding and improving children's testimony: Clinical, developmental and legal implications.* New York: Guilford Press.

Zaragoza, M.S. (Ed.). (in press). *Memory, suggestibility and eyewitness testimony in children and adults.* New York: Sage.

2

The Nature of Allegations of Child Sexual Abuse

John C. Yuille,
Monica Tymofievich,
and David Marxsen

This chapter provides an overview of patterns and incidence rates of allegations of child sexual abuse. The authors draw on both professional experience and the literature to define allegations, determine their incidence rates, and ascertain their origins. It was found that although valid allegations are far more common, false allegations do occur. Investigations of sexual abuse allegations must be based upon knowledge and principles that maximize the likelihood of detecting both valid and false allegations. The issues of investigating sexual abuse cases, as well as the "false memory syndrome," are discussed. A need for more research in the area of allegations of child sexual abuse is necessary, as are investigators who are properly informed and trained.

NATURE OF THE PROBLEM

Legal professionals and social workers struggle with the difficult balance of protecting children while maintaining the rights of those suspected of abus-

21

ing children. Nowhere is this balance more difficult to maintain than in the area of child sexual abuse. The majority of cases have no physical or medical evidence and no other witnesses. These cases typically involve the allegations of the child juxtaposed with the denials of the suspect. Social workers, the police, prosecutors, defense attorneys, and judges must depend on such evidence to evaluate allegations of abuse. However, many of these professionals have been making such determinations with little or no specialized training (Yuille, Hunter, & Harvey, 1990). This chapter has grown out of the experience of the authors in providing training to professionals who must deal with allegations of sexual abuse.

Historically, family violence was viewed as a mental health problem. Before 1980, intervention in physical abuse and neglect, if attempted at all, occurred through the family court, a system designed to maintain family unity and reduce the role of the state. Such matters were considered to be private. It was not until the increased reporting of the sexual exploitation of children that the justice system became more involved. The increased involvement of children as witnesses in criminal proceedings has resulted in changed rules of evidence (e.g., Bala, 1991; Rogers, 1990; Spencer & Flynn, 1990; Whitcomb, 1992). Today, children as young as three years old testify in criminal courts. Testimony by a child is more common now than at any time in history (Goodman, 1984). One consequence of these changes is a renewed debate about the credibility of children's testimony (see Dent & Flin, 1992; Doris, 1991), which has centered on children's ability to separate fact from fantasy, on their understanding of the importance of telling the truth, and on their level of suggestibility (Ceci & Bruck, 1993a). This debate has been fueled by a proliferation of research on the development aspects of children's memory and cognitive abilities; for reviews see Ceci, Ross, & Toglia, 1987; Doris, 1991; Goodman & Bottoms, 1993; Steward, Bussey, Goodman, & Saywitz, 1993; Toglia, Ceci, & Ross, 1989.

Perhaps most central to the debate over children's eyewitness abilities concerns the issue of allegations of sexual abuse. This chapter explores the nature, frequencies, and causes of allegations.

A DEFINITION OF FALSE ALLEGATIONS

Many cases of alleged sexual abuse are labeled by investigative agencies as "unfounded" or "unsubstantiated." Our experience in working with the police and child-protection organizations is that as many as 50% of cases are labeled in this fashion (see Jones & McGraw, 1987). We caution that reports of sexual abuse classified as "unfounded" or "unsubstantiated" differ from allegations considered to be false. It is unfortunate that many investigations do not produce sufficient information to permit a determination of fact. For example, very young children may lack verbal or other communication skills and be unable to provide sufficient detail to determine whether abuse has occurred. Alternatively, children with communication problems (e.g., deaf and autistic children) may be unable to provide an account of their abuse (although see Chapter 16, this volume; Perlman, Ericson, Esses, & Isaacs, 1994; Porter, Yuille, & Bent, in press). Also, poor investigative techniques may prevent a child from telling what happened. For these and other reasons, many cases labeled as unfounded or unsubstantiated may be valid allegations of abuse. A false allegation, on the other hand, would be one of the following.

1. An allegation that is wholly untrue; that is, one in which none of the alleged events occurred.
2. An allegation in which an innocent person has been accused but the allegation is otherwise valid. This is a case of "perpetrator substitution" in which an abused child discloses his her abuse but accuses someone other than the actual perpetrator.
3. An allegation that contains a mixture of true and false features; that is, the child describes some events that actually occurred and adds others that did not.

Studies of false allegations of child sexual abuse show that such allegations are relatively rare (Benedek & Schetky, 1985; Corwin, Berliner, Goodman, Goodwin, & White, 1987; Everson & Boat, 1989; Jones & McGraw, 1987). Jones and McGraw found that 8% of the allegations in their first sample were fictitious. Of these, 6% originated with adults and only 2% came from children. Everson and Boat found that the estimated rate of false allegations fell between 4.7% and 7.6% of all child and adolescent reports of sexual abuse in their sample. Other studies have cited false allegation prevalence rates ranging from 2% to 50% (for a review, see Everson & Boat, 1989). The wide discrepancies in estimated rates reflect the consequences of studies' relying on small sample sizes that "may not be representative of the general population of sexual abuse cases or of a naturally occurring subpopulation of abuse reports" (Everson & Boat, 1989, p. 230). Also, many studies have employed biased samples, for example, cases referred to clinicians. Corwin et al. (1987) noted that "only the most perplexing and ambiguous cases are referred to forensic or specialist child psychiatrists, thus creating a potentially biased sample" (p. 94).

In summary, two methodologically sound studies (Everson & Boat, 1989; Jones & McGraw, 1987) suggest that the rate of false allegations is low (below 10% of all allegations), and that a false allegation arising solely from a child is even less common. Further, some forms of false allegation (e.g., perpetrator substitution, adding false elements to an otherwise true allegation) have not been researched at all. The rates of these forms of false allegations are unknown. However, the fact that false allegations occur at all emphasizes the need for investigators to detect them when they do occur. The causes of such false allegations are discussed later in this chapter.

DETERMINING THE VERACITY OF AN ALLEGATION

Attempting to determine whether an allegation of sexual abuse is true or false is fraught with difficulties. As noted earlier, these cases typically have only the allegations of the child as the key evidence. Thus a variety of techniques have been used to validate allegations or to determine when they are false. In the following section, we discuss some of the principal techniques: behavioral checklists, recantations, and credibility assessment.

Behavioral Checklists

In response to the need to identify children who have been sexually abused, many clinicians and researchers have used behavioral signs that are ostensibly indicative of sexually abused children. As a result, there has been a spate of behavioral indicator lists in the professional literature (Burgess & Holmstrom, 1980; Green, 1986; Jones & McGraw, 1987; MacFarlane, 1978; Sgroi, Porter, & Blick, 1982). Symptoms that have been cited as indicia of sexual abuse in children include sleep disturbances (nightmares), anxiety, regressive behaviors (e.g., clinging), enuresis, depression, and sexually inappropriate behaviors. While these behaviors may well be associated with a child who has been sexually abused, they are more accurately defined as behaviors that are symptoms of general stress or trauma rather than of sexual abuse per se. Of course, sexual abuse is one possible source of stress for children (Bala & Anweiler, 1987; Caffaro-Rouget, Lang, & Van Santen, 1989; Finkelhor & Dziuba-Leatherman, 1994; Terr, 1986). Also, some of these "indicators," such as nightmares, are normal for most children, both within and outside of clinical populations (Melton & Limber, 1989). Equally important, as Browne and Finkelhor (1987) have noted, not all sexually abused children will necessarily show behavioral symptoms in reaction to their sexual abuse. In short, some children may show these signs for reasons other than sexual abuse, and some abused children will show no signs (see Kendall-Tackett, Williams, & Finkelhor, 1993). Clearly, the job of assessment requires more than the knowledge that such symptoms do or do not exist.

The one behavioral sign that may be of some discriminative value in child abuse cases is sexualized behavior. It is a specific indicator that sexually abused children have been shown to exhibit (Brown & Finkelhor, 1986; Friedrich, 1993; Friedrich et al., 1992; Kolko, Moser, & Weldy, 1988; Yates, 1982), although it is noted that there are many kinds of sexual behavior that are normal or that may be explained by factors other than abuse (see chapter 3, this volume).

In summary, sexualized behavior by a child is a clear indication of something sexual in the child's history. That history may include sexual abuse by an adult; but, alternatively, it could reflect a hypersexual environment, peer sexual activity, boundary problems within the family, or the results of reinforcement (i.e., attention). Sexualized behavior by a child should always be given careful attention, but it may not, in itself, demonstrate abuse. Investigators must understand the difference between normal sexual play and sexualized behavior.

Some experts have taken indicator lists at face value and have used them as a partial or complete basis for their opinions in court cases (for example, see Cohen, 1985; Rabinowitz, 1990). Cohen comments that "the list of symptoms described by some experts as typical of sexual abuse victims is long and broad enough to encompass the experience of nearly all children who may be troubled by the turbulence of growing up, whether or not that turbulence entails sexual abuse" (p. 442).

The temptation to consult behavior indicator lists may be strong. Parents may be enticed because their perceptions of their children's behavior are already distorted due to suspected abuse (Benedek & Schetky, 1985). Experts, psychologists, psychiatrists, and social workers may also be attracted to them because they are under pressure to identify abused children.

Regardless of the presence or absence of abuse, if a child displays any number of concurrent behaviors that are on indicator lists, there is a legitimate cause for concern that something is wrong. A proper investigation must be made either to confirm or to rule out sexual abuse. If the investigation suggests abuse, the signs may then be attributed to abuse. If the investigation does not suggest abuse, then other sources of stress or trauma that may be causing these signs should be examined. In other words, behavioral indicators of stress should be used as one part of the fact gathering of a case and considered along with remaining facts to formulate a conclusion.

Recantations

It is not unusual for a child to retract an initial disclosure of sexual abuse (De Young, 1986; Faller, 1984; Robin, 1991). It has been suggested that because allegations of sexual abuse have the power to disrupt and destroy family structure, a child may recant because of immense family pressure to preserve family continuity (Cohen, 1985). After disclosing abuse, the child may feel responsible for the destruction of the family (Faller, 1984), and will recant to "restore a lie for the sake of the family" (Summit, 1983, p. 188). For example:

> Cathy, age 12, accused her father of raping her. One month
> later she insisted that she had lied about the rape in order to get
> back at her father for imposing strict curfews. In reality, Cathy
> had been raped by her father, but retracted her story under
> extreme pressure, humiliation, and rejection by her sister and
> mother. For fear of destroying the family structure, Cathy
> recanted her allegation.

In *U.S. v. Provost* (1992) the issue of recantation was central in the district judge's decision to refuse a retrial in a sex abuse case. In this case, a then 10½-year-old girl's half brother was convicted of sexually assaulting her. Four years later, she recanted her statement, claiming it was her stepbrother who abused her. The judge claimed "skepticism about recantations" (p. 621), adding that "[r]ecantation is particularly common where family members are involved and the child has feelings of guilt or the family members seek to influence the child to change her story" (p. 621).

Summit (1983) has defined recantation as one of the five symptoms of the "child sexual abuse accommodation syndrome." He claims that "unless there is special support for the child and immediate intervention to force responsibility on the father, the girl will follow the 'normal' course and retract her complaint" (p. 188). Despite the emphasis some authors have put upon Summit's syndrome, it has been criticized. Melton and Limber (1989) suggest that such syndromes lack the support of scientific data and are based on clinical intuition, which connotes a certainty that goes well beyond current knowledge and misleads the fact finder in a legal proceeding. Similarly, Robin (1991) noted that Summit's syndrome assumes that the child has been abused and "gives no account for the possibility of a legitimate retraction" (p. 103).

The literature contains opposing interpretations of whether or not recantation is a sign of true sexual abuse. For example, Jones and McGraw (1987) and McGraw and Smith (1992) found that recantations made up 9% and 12.5%, respectively, of the total number of founded cases of sexual abuse. They defined recantation as true allegations of child sexual abuse that were subsequently retracted by the child; the retraction was made under duress (McGraw & Smith, 1992). Other authors have supported the view that a child's recantation equates to sexual abuse (Goodwin, Sahd, & Rada, 1982). In contrast, Everson and Boat (1989) regarded recantation as a sign that the alleged sexual abuse may not have taken place. They found that 55% of the cases in their study were determined as false because of the child's subsequent retraction of allegations of sexual abuse.

In any event, it is clear that recantations are not a typical element of a child abuse investigation. For example, Sorensen and Snow (1991) researched 116 confirmed cases of child sexual abuse disclosures. They state that "in approximately 22% of the cases, children recanted their allegation," and "of those who recanted, 92% reaffirmed their abuse allegations over time" (p. 11). Another example is the London Child Witness Project conducted by the London Family Court Clinic (see Sas, 1990). This project received 221 referrals between 1988 and 1990. Of the 147 referrals that were evaluated, only four (less than 2%) recanted their original disclosure. The occurrence of recantations, no matter how small, is still cause for exploration and concern.

On the basis of the current literature, it is apparent that a retraction of a sexual abuse allegation does not mean either that the allegation was true or that it was false. Nonetheless, it is a sign that something is wrong in the child's life, be it sexual abuse, dysfunction within the child's family, or something amiss in the child's life outside the home. A complete investigation must be conducted to determine the nature of and motive for the recantation.

Assessing the Credibility of an Allegation

Clearly, there is a need for a method of assessing the credibility of children's statements. Wehrspann, Steinhauer, and Klajner-Diamond (1987) have summarized a set of criteria for determining the validity of an allegation of abuse. They state that "several authors have defined semiobjective criteria for determining the credibility of children's allegations given a sufficient data base to apply" (p. 618). Wehrspann et al. have attempted to integrate these criteria to provide an approach to assessment. They suggest that the child's allegation, obtained through a competent interview, should be assessed using 11 criteria. Some of the criteria, such as consistency in the face of challenge and embedded responses, have no foundation in current research knowledge. Thus this list is a mixture of criteria, some with and some without empirical foundation. There is no research that has tested the efficacy of the list or of most of its component criteria. Nor has there been any field testing of this approach.

A related approach, statement analysis, has a firmer foundation in both application and research. Statement analysis is based on a European technique known as statement reality analysis (Undeutsch, 1989; Wegener, 1989), which was developed in the early 1950s to assist German courts with cases in which children's evidence was central but uncorroborated. It is routinely used in such cases in Germany, and the statements of thousands of children, as well as of many adults, have been assessed over the past 40 years using statement reality analysis. More recently, variations in this approach have been given other titles (e.g., statement validity analysis; Raskin & Yuille, 1989; Steller & Koehnken, 1989; Yuille, 1989). For the sake of simplicity, the term statement analysis (SA) is employed here.

In order for SA to be used effectively, the child should describe the alleged abuse in a systematic interview. For example, the step-wise interview, a widely employed systematic investigative interview procedure for children (for a detailed description of the interview, see Yuille, Hunter, Joffe, & Zaparniuk, 1993b), can be used to obtain a statement from the child. After the child is interviewed, SA is then used to assess the credibility of the child's account of the abuse. The technique has two components: a criteria-based content analysis and a validity checklist. According to Yuille (1988), the analysis of the child's statement involves the following stages: "the application of a set of nineteen content criteria to the child's statement(s); the evaluation of a set of a dozen statement-related factors; the examination of a number of investigative issues; and the final overall evaluation of the child's statement(s)" (p. 257).

The results of the criteria-based content analysis and the validity checklist are combined to yield a final decision: the allegation is credible, it is not credible, it is indeterminate. Recently, there has been a flurry of research activity on the reliability and validity of the technique (for a review see Anson, Golding, & Gully, 1993; Boychuk, 1991; Horowitz, 1991; Horowitz, Lamb, Esplin, Boychuk, Krispin, & Reiter-Lavery, 1992; Joffe, 1993; Lamers-Winkelman, Buffing, van der Zanden, 1992; Landry & Brigham, 1992; Porter & Yuille, 1994; Raskin & Esplin, 1991; Steller, 1989; Steller & Koehnken, 1989; Yuille, Marxsen, & Ménard, 1993; Zaparniuk, Yuille, & Taylor, in press). The research indicates that there are two key features of SA:

1. It requires considerable training and practice before individuals become adept in its application.
2. Although SA is a useful and valid tool in assessing the credibility of children's allegations, particularly children of school age and older, caution should be exercised when using it with younger children, particularly those below the age of five years. It has been criticized for not being developmentally sensitive in assessing statements made by younger children (e.g., see Joffe, 1993). In order to improve SA for application with younger children, it must be modified to include criteria that are age appropriate and reflect the cognitive and linguistic abilities of preschool-age children. Evaluations should be based on children's use of interview aids (e.g., drawings of body part, a dollhouse to describe the layout of a room).

Summary of Determining Allegations

The only approach to determining the credibility of allegations that has both extensive practical application and a research foundation is SA. However, more research is needed on when the technique is useful and when it is not. There needs to be a clear understanding of the training and knowledge required to apply the techniques properly.

CLARIFICATION OF INCIDENCE RATES

Understanding the nature of false allegations can help investigators increase their level of confidence in dealing with all allegations. We suggest that professionals avoid conducting interviews with a preconceived notion that "children don't lie" or that "children can't be trusted." Personal objectivity is critical to the assessment process and requires an approach that is nonjudgmental (Mandel, Lehman, & Yuille, in press). Objectivity does not preclude being supportive of the child in the course of the investigation. It means only that the investigator will be as objective as possible in making a decision in the case. After all, children involved in false allegations of sexual abuse are in need of assistance, as they are often victims of another kind (e.g., pawns in a struggle between former spouses). An objective response will help investigators feel increasingly confident about the entire process of disclosure and investigation.

ORIGINS OF FALSE ALLEGATIONS

There are several reasons why false allegations might be made. Most allegations originate with adults, some are instigated by the child, and others are a result of poor investigations. Those instigated by an adult are often a result of custody/access disputes (see Chapter 12, this volume). Pathology, such as delusions found in folie à deux, may also play a role in an adult's making a false allegation of abuse concerning his or her child. Allegations solely instigated by a child are less common and less researched. The abuse may be either exaggerated or minimized by the child, depending on his or her situation. An older child may also allege abuse to seek revenge on an adult for some actual or perceived infringement. Alternatively, the child may be attempting to gain some control in a situation in which he or she feels powerless. Poor investigations can be a source of false allegations, where the interviewer is not equipped with the proper interviewing skills necessary for an objective, fact-finding investigation. Each of these motives for false allegations is explored in the following sections, which describe the patterns of false allegations.

Custody and Access Disputes

While studies demonstrate that the majority of false allegations occur in custody/divorce cases, these studies show an array of results that cannot be compared without a disclaimer about different methodologies or sample sizes. In order to determine the actual rate of false allegations in custody or divorce disputes and tighten up the estimates of false allegations, the investigative process must be standardized in two ways.

First, future studies must regulate and subsequently use consistent referral patterns, operational definitions, and data collection. Standardization would control for inconsistencies and changes in county, state, and countrywide abuse-counting systems (for an example of a standardized nationwide study, see the Study of National Incidence and Prevalence of Child Abuse and Neglect, 1988).

Second, these new, accepted standards of consistency should be applied to studies of consecutive divorce cases in various socioeconomic and geographic areas. A combination of these two improvements would give a more accurate estimate of false allegations in custody or divorce disputes.

A cautionary note should be sounded, particularly concerning the context of the original disclosure. A disclosure made by a child without any prompting or encouragement from outside sources such as parents or investigators is far different than one that is the product of an interview or parental prodding. A spontaneous "My daddy sticks his pee-pee in my bottom" to a playmate at school is easier to support in the court system than is an often frantic, or perhaps thought-out, phone call by a parent to a lawyer. The Ontario Court of Appeal *R. v. Khan* (1986) case, dealt with in the Supreme Court of Ontario, illustrates the greater weight put on spontaneous disclosures. Justice Robins admitted a then three-and-a-half-year-old child's spontaneous disclosure of sexual abuse into a court of law, claiming that "young children...are generally not adept as reasoned reflection or at fabricating tales of sexual perversion. They...are unlikely to use their reflective powers to concoct a deliberate untruth, and particularly on about a sexual act" (p. 19).

Despite the nature of spontaneous versus rehearsed disclosures, the same proper investigatory process must determine the credibility of the statement. More weight, however, should be placed on the spontaneous disclosure, and should be a large factor in determining the credibility of the abuse.

In summary, false allegations occur most often in the context of custody/access disputes. In spite of the diverse methodologies used, "the consistency of false allegation rates across studies is remarkable" (Everson & Boat, 1989, p. 235) and it appears that perhaps a third of all allegations in this context may be false. Note that even in this context, this means that the majority of allegations are true. Consequently, the investigator must be aware of the particular circumstances in which a false allegation may occur, and not conduct a biased investigation based simply on statistical probabilities.

Folie à Deux

In a state of stress or impaired functioning, a parent may misinterpret his or her child's behavior or statements as suggestive of sexual abuse when none has occurred (Schuman, 1986). In extreme cases, a folie à deux relationship may develop between a parent and child. The term "folie à deux," which was coined by Lastage and Falret in 1877, refers to "contagious insanity or the psychosis of association" (Dewhurst & Todd, 1956, p.451). Folie à deux has been said to occur in adults, primarily among women (Gralnick, 1942). However, due to a lack of research, it is difficult to assess how often it develops in children (Simonds & Glenn, 1976). Dewhurst & Todd (1956) list the following criteria to identify folie à deux: the intimate association of two people; similar general delusional content of the partners' psychosis; and the acceptance, support, and sharing of a partner's delusional ideas.

A symbiotic relationship between a parent and child may develop when the parent is overprotective, is oversolicitous, and tends to treat the child as an extension of himself or herself. He or she tends to be dominant and wishes to keep the child passive and dependent (Anthony, 1970). Green (1991) describes an example involving a mother and child: "The 'projection prone' mother readily projects her own sexual fantasies onto the spouse and child, while exploiting ambiguous physical or behavioral symptoms in the child as 'evidence' for molestation" (p. 183).

The submissive partner (the child) is immature, dependent, suggestible, and passive. The stability of the weaker partner's psychosis depends, to some degree, on his or her suggestibility. A highly suggestible child, for example, may take longer to acquire delusional ideas, but will hold these ideas longer (Dewhurst & Todd, 1956). Parent and child band together against a common enemy, namely, the spouse accused of sexually abusing the child.

Parents who make false allegations of sexual abuse may control the child in a variety of ways. For example, the parent may monitor the child's responses through the use of facial expressions and eye contact. The child may respond by "checking" with the parent before proceeding (Green, 1991). For example:

> Five-year-old Patrick was being interviewed about alleged
> sexual abuse at the hands of his stepfather. Patrick refused to
> continue the interview unless his mother was with him. Upon
> his mother's prompting, the boy described the abuse that
> occurred, frequently stopping and focusing on his mother for an
> indication of when to stop and to start the narrative.

There is little research to ascertain the rates, or even existence, of folie à deux. Jones and Seig (1988) claim that "enmeshed, symbiotic relationships were found in two thirds of the fictitious cases involving a mother and a child together" (p. 30). However, they do not define these terms operationally. The best the reader can do is assume that these relationships were diagnosed on the basis of observations during lengthy and in-depth interviews with the child and the caretaker.

Jones and McGraw (1987) found that two adults who had made fictitious allegations of abuse appeared to do so "based upon their delusions" (p. 30). Again, terms in this case are poorly defined. There is no way to determine whether these two cases were bona fide examples of folie à deux.

Most of the other literature describing folie à deux focuses on case studies (Kaplan & Kaplan, 1981; Schuman, 1986; Simonds & Glenn, 1976; Tucker & Cornwall, 1977). Quinn (1991) asserts that "[r]arely, [will] a child and care-taker mutually share a bizarre implausible belief concerning the perpetrator consistent with folie à deux" (p. 151). Despite Quinn's conclusion, the occur-rence of folie à deux in the general population and in the realm of fictitious allegations of child sexual abuse is difficult, if not impossible, to determine on the basis of the current literature.

Exaggeration

When giving an account of sexual abuse, some children may exaggerate the extent of the abuse. There are reasons for this. For example, one of the most consistent findings in the field is that the majority of child sexual abuse consists of genital fondling (e.g., Sorenson & Snow, 1991; Yuille et al., 1993). If a child wishes to see the offender severely punished (either out of a desire for vengeance or out of fear of the suspect), it might be tempting to agree to a leading question that a more "severe" form of abuse such as intercourse took place. A medical exam might then seemingly discredit the child's entire alle-gation, even though the child had in fact been fondled.

Another possible motivation for exaggeration is that it might be a way for some children to express the seriousness of the effect the abuse has had on them.

Minimization

Given the known seductive strategies of some pedophiles (Lanning, 1986) and the tautologically close relationship between incestuous offenders and their victims, some children may have every reason to protect their abusers and to minimize their abuse. In addition, the ubiquity of homophobia in our culture makes a boy's minimization of sexual abuse at the hands of another male very understandable. In any case, this minimization could lead to a poverty of both affect and detail in a child's account, which, in turn, could lead to its being taken as fictitious. The foregoing are purely speculative, of course, but they do pose possibilities that investigators and researchers should consider.

Revenge

The first author has been involved in investigating several cases in which a child, usually an adolescent, has made a false allegation against an adult who is in a position of authority (often a teacher). Usually the allegation has been made to exact a price for something the teacher has done that is resented by the child. To our knowledge, no research has been conducted on this pattern of false allegation. We do not know the rate of such allegations or, indeed, the rate of valid allegations against persons in such positions of authority. There is a need to explore these incidence rates.

Control

Sometimes a child finds himself or herself in a powerless position and uses a false allegation to try to gain some control. The pattern we have seen most often is captured in the following example.

Shirley, a 13-year-old girl, was sexually abused by her father. Subsequent to an investigation, she was placed in foster care. She reacted negatively to the foster home, and to her foster brother in particular. She asked to be moved to another facility, but the system could not accommodate her request. She then made a false allegation of sexual abuse against her foster father. As she continued to be abused by her biological father, she took what she had learned from that abuse and made a credible sounding allegation against her foster father.

Again, this is a pattern that is unexplored in research. We have no idea how common or uncommon this type of false allegation is. Also, we do not know how often children are actually the victims of abuse in such contexts. Clearly, researchers conducting incidence studies need to understand this pattern better and to improve investigations in this context.

Poor Investigations

Investigations of poor quality are the most easily preventable source of false allegations. Poor quality refers primarily to poor-quality interviewing, although other aspects of an investigation of an allegation may also vary in quality. As noted earlier, the typical sexual abuse allegation has no medical or physical evidence and consists of the allegations of the child and, typically, the denial of the suspect. Consequently, the quality of the investigative interview becomes central to the quality of the whole investigation (Yuille et al., 1993b). There is no question but that leading questions or the use of rewards or coercion by interviewers can lead children into making false statements (Doris, 1991; Mantell, 1988). The debate concerns whether poor interviewing can lead to false allegations of sexual abuse. Most authors in this field have adopted the position that it can (e.g., Ceci & Bruck, 1993b; Raskin & Yuille, 1989). However, Rudy and Goodman (1991) have argued that, although children are suggestible, this is true only for nonsexual questions. Others have argued that children are only suggestible about peripheral rather than central aspects of events (Fivush, 1993). While the debate about the precise nature of children's susceptibility to suggestion no doubt will occupy researchers for some years, there are enough instances of false allegations in actual cases of poor investigations to demonstrate that the problem exists.

INTERVIEWING. The McMartin case in Manhattan Beach, California, provides an example. The case lasted for seven years and cost the state over $15 million. Initially, seven defendants were charged with over 300 counts of abusing more than 100 children. In the end, not one of the accused was found guilty of a single count. Some of the jurors subsequently stated that the manner in which the children had been interviewed by social workers and the police made it impossible to determine what had happened. Although it is not clear that the allegations were false, it is evident that the poor quality of the interviews permanently damaged the case. The McMartin case is not unique. There have been a number of instances in which allegations were later dismissed or determined to be false, and the responsibility was placed on the poor quality of the interviews (e.g., for reviews of the Jordan County, Minnesota, and Bakersfield, California, cases, see Baker, 1992; Eberle & Eberle, 1986; Rabinowitz, 1990).

How prevalent is poor interviewing? There is no answer to this question at the present time. We do know that until recently police officers and social workers received little or no training in interviewing children (Yuille, 1991). Many investigators have expressed dissatisfaction with both the quality and the amount of training they have received (Yuille, 1986). Some of the training that has been available has encouraged the use of suggestion rather than reducing it. For instance, one text suggests that if, in the interview, a child denies being touched in a sexual manner, the interviewer should say to the child that the child's mother (or whoever else brought the concern to the interviewer's agency) told the interviewer "that someone had been touching them" (Halliday, 1986). This state of affairs raises the possibility that poor-quality interviews may not be rare.

There is one study that has compared trained and untrained interviewers. Yuille et al. (1993a) examined 202 statements from interviews of children suspected of being sexually abused. The interviews were conducted by child-protection workers and/or police officers. Forty-eight interviews (23.8%) were considered by the authors to contain sufficient inappropriate interviewing to render meaningless any assessment of the veracity of the child's account based on the interview alone. Of the 111 statements elicited by social workers and police officers trained in a standardized interviewing technique (the step-wise interview, Yuille et al., 1993b), only 16 (14.41%) were classified as "poor quality," compared with 32 of 91 statements (35.16%) elicited by untrained interviewers. There are two features of these results that bear on our current concern. First, the level of poor-quality interviews was over one third among the untrained workers, and this may be indicative of the extent to which problematic interviews are being conducted (although there is no indication as to how many, if any, of these interviews may have led to false allegations of abuse). Second, it is clear that even a small amount of training (four days in this instance)can substantially reduce the problem of poor interviews.

BIASED PROBLEM SOLVING. As noted at the beginning of this section, poor interview quality is only one aspect of poor investigations. Another issue concerns the extent to which biased problem solving or decision making occurs with front-line workers investigating abuse. That is, even if the interviewing is adequate, it is possible that a police officer or social worker may make an incorrect decision that abuse has occurred when it has not, or has not occurred when it has. This decision may be based on presumptions, base-rate assumptions, or some bias the worker holds. This issue has received some recent attention (Mandel, Lehman, & Yuille, in press), but the extent of bias in decision making is unknown. However, more experience in interviewing in these cases has been associated with a greater accuracy in assessing these reports (see Goodman, Batterman-Faunce, & Kenney, 1993).

It must be emphasized that poor interviewing not only may produce false allegations of abuse, but also can lead to abuses being ignored when it has actually occurred. That is, a child may attempt to provide a genuine account of abuse, only to have it significantly altered by inappropriate elements of the interview. Similarly, decision-making biases could lead front-line workers to decide that abuse did not take place when it actually did. Writers claiming that North America is undergoing "sex abuse hysteria" (Gardner, 1990) or a "child abuse witch hunt" (Eberle & Eberle, 1986, p. 285) may contribute to this problem.

Biases that assume that children never lie or that many allegations are false are problematic. Good interviewing must be coupled with nonbiased investigative decision making if children are going to be adequately protected and false allegations detected when they do occur. We do know what constitutes good interviewing (Yuille et al., 1993b). It would seem that further efforts toward ascertaining the prevalence of poor interviewing and research into how best to train investigators in interviewing and decision-making skills are warranted.

Latticed Allegations

A special type of allegation sometimes develops as a result of poor investigative techniques. We propose the label of "latticed allegations" to describe such cases, which include the following features.

1. There are several, sometimes many, alleged victims.
2. There are several, sometimes many, perpetrators.
3. The allegations are not "one to one" (although they may start out that way), but are multiple and overlapping, that is, child A alleges abuse at the hands of suspects W, X, and Y, while child B alleges abuse by suspects U, V, W, and X and child C alleges abuse by suspect Z.
4. The children and the suspects share a common context or are otherwise interconnected, for example, the suspects are the staff of a day-care center and their families while the alleged victims are children being cared for at the day-care center and their friends.
5. Most of the children are interviewed many times. The interviews are often of poor quality.
6. The allegations tend to increase in seriousness as the case progresses, sometimes becoming quite fantastic (monsters, incidents of mass murder with no accompanying evidence, cannibalism, etc.) by the end of the investigation.
7. There is often considerable media attention paid to the case during the investigation.
8. There is no clear resolution to the investigation.

It should be noted that, unlike such terms as "child sex ring," the term "latticed allegations" does not connote either guilt or innocence on the part of the suspects. The investigations of alleged abuse in Manhattan Beach, California; in Jordon, Minnesota (for reviews of these two cases, see Baker, 1992, and Eberle & Eberle, 1986); and in Hamilton, Ontario (see Marron, 1988) (while there were only two alleged victims in the Hamilton case, both sisters stated that many other, unknown children were victimized), fit the description of latticed allegations. As well, many of the so-called ritual abuse or satanic abuse cases, where the alleged victims are still children at the time of the allegations, match this pattern.

What might cause the confused pattern of allegations and the complete lack of resolution in many of these cases? Often the original allegation (whether genuine or not) seems to get lost during the investigation, buried under a series of increasingly bizarre allegations involving more and more suspects. There are several possibilities that could account for this, none of which is mutually exclusive.

A very distinctive feature of latticed allegation cases is the number of interviews each of the children undergoes and the often lamentable quality of many of those interviews. This in itself could account for some of the developing confusion in such investigations. If a child is subjected to a series of poorly done interviews, a dynamic might be established between the interviewer and the child whereby the interviewer, with the best intentions, subtly shapes the allegation of the child. The child may not disclose at all in the first interviews, but might eventually—through the interviewer's use of leading questions, rewards for disclosure, and other inappropriate actions such as making unrealistic promises—agree to a mild form of abuse. It could be that, during a subsequent interview, that level of disclosure does not get the same sort of reinforcement. The interviewer is trying to find out if anything else has happened to the child, and eventually gets the child to agree to a more serious allegation. As there are other alleged victims in the case, every time one of the children makes a new allegation, a new round of interviews is conducted to verify whether the newly "discovered" form of abuse occurred with any of the other children. This could result in the charges' increasing in seriousness until they verge on the fantastic. It becomes impossible to tell whether or not the children were in fact abused. This dynamic is, of course, purely conjectural, but it does offer one explanation for the progression of allegations in such cases.

Cross-contamination between the children and/or their families could also, in part, explain the latticed allegation problem. If most of the alleged victims know one another, then it is possible that the children will talk among themselves about their allegations, resulting in contamination. This would be especially problematic if the dynamic discussed above were in place. Knowledge of each other's allegations could be disastrous if an interviewer were to attempt to ascertain whether the children could confirm each other's story, and doubly so if the interviewer were to use inappropriate techniques. In addition, the parents will often either know one another or will be brought together because of the investigation. If the parents share with one another the allegations of each of their children, this, too, could lead to contamination. For example, the Smiths and the Wongs both have children who are suspected of having been sexually abused by their minister. The Smiths find out that the Wongs' daughter has alleged being forced to perform fellatio on the minister. It is only natural that the Smiths would fear that the same act might have been perpetrated on their child. This could be the case even if the Smith girl has already been interviewed and only made allegations concerning genital fondling. While the Smiths are both intelligent people, they are not well versed in the arcane subject of child interviewing, and they are very concerned about their daughter. Therefore, they do the obvious but incorrect thing: they ask her, "Did the reverend make you suck his penis?" Unfortunately, the Smith child tends to respond in the affirmative to direct inquiries from authority figures, and assents to this question even though she was not abused in that fashion.

Some authors have held that the reason for such seemingly fantastic allegations and the lack of resolution in such cases is the sophistication of the conspiracy behind the abuse. For instance, Hudson (1991) states that the phenomenon of the allegation's progressing to the fantastic is the result of disinformation planted by the perpetrators to discredit their victims. She describes "the incremental and progressive disclosure" of ritualized abuse as "peeling an onion layer after layer until your reach the center, only to find a light bulb." She writes that the abusers create illusions or simply lie to the children to make the entire allegation sound like a fantasy on the part of the victim. However, no evidence has ever been brought forward to support such claims. Indeed, the very existence of many of the techniques that the abusers are said to use, such as posthypnotic suggestion, is open to question.

There is some clinical lore that suggests that children may supplement their accounts of traumatic experiences with fantasy elements (Terr, 1988). This could account for some of the more bizarre and unsubstantiated accusations that arise in latticed allegations. But this alone cannot explain why the children's fantastic allegations in a particular case frequently share common elements. If some of the children's statements have similar impossible content then that impossible content must have arisen from some sort of contamination from the abusers, the interviewers, the parents, and/or the children.

Another important point to consider is the psychological profit gained by nonabused children during the course of an investigation. Not only do they receive the attention of their families, journalists, teachers, police officers, child-protection workers, and the community at large, but they also can potentially enjoy a sense of camaraderie with their fellow "victims." Lest this seem an overly harsh commentary on children, the extraordinary atmosphere of an investigation of latticed allegations should be considered. It is almost as if the incessant growth of the numbers of suspected victims and abusers, coupled with the steady increase in the seriousness of the suspected abuse, gives a form of "momentum" to the allegations. The children are often bombarded with suggestive questioning by their families, peers, and investigators, and they have much to gain from agreeing that they, too, were abused.

What would happen if the potential difficulties inherent in such an investigation were noted by the investigators early on? Of course, the complexity of the case may not become apparent until the investigation is under way, but several tactics may be of use when the investigators decide that they possibly are dealing with latticed allegations. To limit contamination among the children and their families, agencies could distribute booklets to the parents of the suspected victims. Such a booklet could give the parents guidelines about talking to their children and other families about the investigation and caution them against asking their children about their alleged abuse. If abuse is suspected, parents should notify the authorities. In addition, it could advise them to forbid their children to talk to other children, both other alleged victims and those not involved in the case. Indeed, it might be advisable to "spread the net widely" and distribute the booklets to all the families that realistically could be involved (e.g., all of the families with children in a particular day-care center). Obviously, the booklet must stress that the fact that a family receives the booklet does not mean that a child in the family is suspected of having been abused.

Even with this precaution, it is apparent that latticed allegation pose grave investigative difficulties. Those conducting the investigation should be extremely competent interviewers. Some child-protection agencies have very high worker turnover rates and may have no experienced interviewers on staff, or a small rural police force may not have an officer skilled in interviewing children. If the agency in question cannot commit an interviewer of the highest caliber to the investigation, then bringing in a practiced interviewer from outside should be considered.

"False Memory Syndrome" Versus Repression

There is another special type of poor investigation that can lead to false allegations of sexual abuse: misguided therapists in the role of investigators (see Chapter 10, this volume; Lindsay & Read, 1993). In the past few years, a great deal of controversy has been raised over the issue of adults who claim to have recovered repressed memories of childhood abuse in the course of therapy. Opinions have ranged from the claim that "an epidemic of false accusations is occurring" that "could be the worst crisis to hit the American family" (Goldstein & Farmer, 1992), to the oft-quoted assertions that "if you are unable to remember any specific instances...but still have a feeling that something abusive happened to you, it probably did" (p. 21) and "if you think you were abused and your life shows the symptoms, then you were" (Bass & Davis, 1988, p. 22).

Both of the extremes in this debate hold that this is a widespread phenomenon, with one side asserting that the recovered memories are genuine, while the other holds that they are not. Neither of these two tenets is supported by hard evidence. We simply do not know how prevalent the recovery of repressed memories is. Nor do we know what proportion, if any, are genuine. We do not even know whether such repression exists at all. Regardless of the rate of false allegations that arise out of therapy, we must acknowledge the fact that clients can be convinced that they have a memory of something that never happened to them (Loftus, 1993). Clinicians must discuss this issue and develop procedures to minimize the likelihood of creating a false memory in a client.

CONCLUSION

The intention of this chapter has been to provide an overview of the patterns of false allegations of sexual abuse. It is apparent that such allegations do arise, although they are relatively uncommon as compared with valid allegations. Nonetheless, it is essential that both the rate and nature of false allegations are understood in order to improve the investigation of and response to all allegations of sexual abuse. The consequences of investigations that err, deciding that abuse did not occur when it did, or that it did occur when it did not, are enormous, for both the child victim and the suspect. If the allegations are true but not believed, a child could continue to be victimized, and may be more reluctant to report subsequent abuse. If the allegations are false, the potential for false imprisonment, unnecessary family disruption, unjustified loss of a job or career, etc., exists.

Halliday (1986) suggests that "one of the biggest factors in false allegations, has generally been the lack of expertise and training of those professionals assigned to conduct the investigation and interview" (pp. 27–28). Yuille et al. (1990) have similarly stressed that investigators must be properly trained if the systemic response to child abuse is to be effective. Part of that training must involve an examination of false allegations, and when and how they occur. This chapter has demonstrated that although some knowledge exists that can be useful to investigators, there is a need for research to understand better the incidence rates and nature of false-allegation patterns. Perhaps this volume can both encourage that research and serve as a resource for investigating allegations of child sexual abuse.

Recommendations

1. **THAT** investigators and interviewers be thoroughly trained in interviewing techniques before questioning a child about abuse. A properly conducted interview is the only way to obtain good statements.

2. **THAT** the training given to interviewers and investigators be competency based. Standards of interviewing should be met before the interviews are conducted, and not gradually reached during the course of several investigations.
3. **THAT** the training of interviewers be done on a continuous basis. It is imperative that information, courses, and training sessions be available to update, as well as to refresh, the interviewers.
4. **THAT** objectivity in the investigation of child abuse be promoted. All possible alternative explanations should be examined and fleshed out before a conclusion is reached.
5. **THAT** the interviewing process be investigative, rather than therapeutic. In order to maintain investigative integrity, the interview must obtain the facts from the child in a way that still meets the systematic goals of the legal system.

REFERENCES

Anson, D. A., Golding, S. L., & Gully, K. J. (1993). Child sexual abuse allegations: Reliability of criteria-based content analysis. *Law and Human Behavior, 17*(3), 331–341.

Anthony, E. J. (1970). The influence of maternal psychosis on children—folie à deux. In E. J. Anthony & T. Benedek (Eds.), *Parenthood: Its psychology and psychopathology* (pp. 571–595). Boston: Little, Brown.

Baker, R. A. (1992). *Hidden memoirs: Voices and visions from within.* Buffalo, N.Y.: Prometheus Books.

Bala, N. (1991). *Prosecuting child sexual abuse cases in Canada: A measure of progress.* Kingston, Ont.: Queen's University.

Bala, N., & Anweiler, J. (1987). Allegations of sexual abuse in a parental custody dispute: Smokescreen or fire? *Canadian Family Law Quarterly, 2,* 343–415.

Bass, R., & Davis, L. (1988). *The courage to heal.* New York: Harper & Row.

Benedek, E. P., & Schetky, D. H. (1985). Allegations of sexual abuse in child custody and visitation disputes. In D. H. Scotch & E. P. Benedek (Eds.), *Emerging issues in child psychiatry and the law* (pp. 145–156). New York: Brunner/ Mazel.

Boychuk, T. D. (1991). *Criteria-based content analysis of children's statements about sexual abuse: A field-based validation study.* Unpublished doctoral dissertation, Arizona State University.

Browne, A., & Finkelhor, D. (1987). Impact of child sexual abuse: A review of the research. *Psychological Bulletin, 99,* 66–77.

Burgess, A. W., & Holmstrom, L. L. (1980). Sexual trauma of children and adolescents: Pressure, sex, and secrecy. In L. Schultz (Ed.), *Sexual victimology of youth,* (pp. 67–82). Springfield, Ill.: Thomas.

Caffaro-Rouget, A., Lang, R. A., & van Santen, V. (1989). The impact of child sexual abuse on victims' adjustment. *Annals of Sex Research, 2,* 29–47.

Ceci, S. J., & Bruck, M. (1993a). Child witnesses: Translating research into policy. *Social Policy Report, 20*(10), 34–38.

Ceci, S. J., & Bruck, M. (1993b). Suggestibility of the child witness: A historical review and synthesis. *Psychological Bulletin, 113*(3), 403–439.

Ceci, S. J., Ross, D. F., & Toglia, M. P. (1987). Suggestibility of children's memory: Psycholegal implications. *Journal of Experimental Psychology, 116*, 38–49.

Cohen, A. (1985). The unreliability of expert testimony on the typical characteristics of sexual abuse victims. *Georgetown Law Journal, 74*(429), 429–456.

Corwin, D. L., Berliner, L., Goodman, G., Goodwin, J., & White, S. (1987). Child sexual abuse and custody disputes: No easy answers. *Journal of Interpersonal Violence, 2*(1), 91–105.

Dent, H., & Flin, R. (Eds.). (1992). *Children as witnesses.* Chichester, England: John Wiley & Sons.

Dewhurst, K., & Todd, J. (1956). The psychosis of association—folie à deux. *Journal of Nervous and Mental Diseases, 124*, 451–459.

De Young, M. (1986). A conceptual model for judging the truthfulness of a young child's allegation of sexual abuse. *American Journal of Orthopsychiatry, 56*(4), 550–559.

Doris, J. (Ed.). (1991). *The suggestibility of children's recollections.* Washington, D.C.: American Psychological Association.

Eberle, P., & Eberle, S. (1986). *The politics of child abuse.* Secaucus, N.J.: Lyle Stuart.

Everson, M. D., & Boat, B. W. (1989). False allegations of sexual abuse by children and adolescents. *Journal of the American Academy of Child and Adolescent Psychiatry, 28*(2), 230–235.

Faller, K. C. (1984). Is the child victim of sexual abuse telling the truth? *Child Abuse and Neglect, 8*, 473–481.

Finkelhor, D., & Dziuba-Leatherman, J. (1994). Victimization of children. *American Psychologist, 49*(3), 173–183.

Friedrich, W. N. (1993). Sexual victimization and sexual behavior in children: A review of recent literature. *Child Abuse and Neglect, 17*, 59–66.

Friedrich, W. N., Grambisch, P., Damon, L., Hewitt, S., Koverola, C., Lang, R., Wolfe, V., & Broughton, D. (1992). The child sexual behavior inventory: Normative and clinical findings. *Psychological Assessment, 4*, 303–311.

Gardner, R. (1990). *Sex abuse hysteria.* Cresskill, N. J.: Creative Therapeutics.

Goldstein, E., & Farmer, K. (1992). *Confabulations: Creating false memories, destroying families.* Boca Raton, Fla.: SIRS Books.

Goodman G. (1984). Children's testimony in historical perspective. *Journal of Social Issues, 40*(2), 9–32.

Goodman, G. S., & Bottoms, B. L. (Eds.). (1993). *Child victims, child witnesses: Understanding and improving testimony.* New York: Guilford Press.

Goodman, G. S., Batterman-Faunce, J. M., & Kenney, R. (1993). Optimizing children's testimony: Research and social policy issues concerning allegations of child sexual abuse. In D. Cicchetti and S. L. Toth (Eds.), *Child abuse, child development and social policy: Advances in applied developmental psychology. Volume 8.* (pp. 139–166). Norwood, N. J.: Ablex.

Goodwin, J., Sahd, D., & Rada, R. T. (1982). False accusations and false denials of incest: Clinical myths and clinical realities. In J. Goodwin (Ed.), *Sexual abuse: Incest victims and their families* (pp. 17–26). London: John Wright.

Gralnick, A. (1942). Folie à deux–the psychosis of association. *Psychiatry Quarterly, 16,* 230–263.

Green, A. H. (1986). True and false allegations of sexual abuse in child custody disputes. *Journal of the American Academy of Child Psychiatry, 25*(4), 449–456.

Green, A. H. (1991). Factors contributing to false allegations of child sexual abuse in custody disputes. In M. Robin (Ed.), *Assessing child maltreatment reports: The problem of false allegations* (pp. 177–189). New York: Haworth Press.

Halliday, L. (1986). *Sexual abuse interviewing techniques for police and other professionals.* Campbell River, B. C., Canada: Ptarmigan Press.

Horowitz, S. W. (1991). Empirical support for statement validity assessment. *Behavioral Assessment, 13,* 293–313.

Horowitz, S. W., Lamb, M. E., Esplin, P. W., Boychuk, T., Krispin, O., & Reiter-Lavery, L. (1992, June). *Reliability of criteria-based content analysis of child witness statements.* Paper presented to the American Psychological Society, San Diego, Calif.

Hudson, P. S. (1991) *Ritual child abuse.* Saratoga, Calif.: R&E Publishers.

Joffe, R. (1993). *Criteria-based content analysis: An experimental investigation with children.* Unpublished doctoral dissertation, University of British Columbia, Vancouver, Canada.

Jones, D. P. H., & McGraw, J. M. (1987). Reliable and fictitious accounts of sexual abuse to children. *Journal of Interpersonal Violence, 2*(1), 27–45.

Jones, D. P. H., & Seig, A. N. (1988). Child sexual abuse allegations in custody or visitation cases: A report of 20 cases. In E. G. Nicholson & & J. Bulkley (Eds.), *Sexual abuse allegations in custody and visitation cases: A resource book for judges and court personnel* (pp. 22–36). Washington, D.C.: American Bar Association.

Kaplan, S. L., & Kaplan, S. J. (1981). The child's accusation of sexual abuse during a divorce and custody struggle. *Hillside Journal of Clinical Psychiatry, 3*(1), 127–134.

Kendall-Tackett, K. A., Williams, L. M., & Finkelhor, D. (1993). Impact of sexual abuse on children: A review and synthesis of recent empirical studies. *Psychological Bulletin, 113*(1), 164–180.

Kolko, D. J., Moser, J. T., & Weldy, S. R. (1988). Behavioral/emotional indicators of sexual abuse in child psychiatric inpatients: Controlled comparison with physical abuse. *Child Abuse and Neglect, 12,* 529–541.

Lamers-Winkelman, F., Buffing, F., & van der Zanden, A. P. (1992, May). *What children can or will tell about sexual abuse: Preliminary results.* Poster presented at the conference of the Child Witness in Context: Cognitive, Social, and Legal Perspectives, Lucca, Italy.

Landry, K., & Brigham, J. C. (1992). The effect of training in criteria-based content analysis on the ability to detect deception in adults. *Law and Human Behavior, 16,* 663–676.

Lanning, D. V. (1986). *Child molesters: A behavioral analysis for law enforcement.* Quantico, Va.: FBI Academy.

Lindsay, S., & Read, D. (1993). *Psychotherapy and memories of childhood sexual abuse: A cognitive perspective.* Unpublished manuscript, University of Lethbridge, Alberta, Canada.

Loftus, E. (1993). The reality of repressed memoirs. *American Psychologist, 48*(5), 518–537.

MacFarlane, K. (1978). Sexual abuse of children. In J. Chapman & M. Gates (Eds.), *The victimization of women* (pp. 81–109). Beverly Hills, Calif.: Sage Publications.

Mandel, D. R., Lehman, D. R., & Yuille, J. C. (in press). Should this child be removed from home? Hypothesis generation and information seeking as predictors of case decisions. *Child Abuse and Neglect.*

Mantell, D. (1988). Clarifying erroneous child sexual abuse allegations. *American Journal of Orthopsychiatry, 58*(4), 618–621.

Marron, K. (1988). *Ritual abuse.* Toronto: McClelland-Bantam.

McGraw, J. M., & Smith, H. A. (1992). Child sexual abuse allegations amidst divorce and custody proceedings: Refining the validation process. *Journal of Child Sexual Abuse, 1*(1), 49–62.

Melton, G. B., & Limber, S. (1989). Psychologist's involvement in cases of child maltreatment: Limits of role and expertise. *American Psychologist, 44*(9), 1225–1233.

Perlman, N. B., Ericson, K. I., Esses, V. M., & Isaacs, B. J. (1994). The developmentally handicapped witness: Competency as a function of question format. *Law and Human Behavior, 19*(2), 171–187.

Porter, S., Yuille, J. C., & Bent (in press). Credibility assessment of criminal suspects through statement analysis. *Child Abuse and Neglect.*

Quinn, K. M. (1991). False and unsubstantiated sexual abuse allegations: Clinical issues. In M. Robin (Ed.), *Assessing child maltreatment reports: The problem of false allegations* (pp. 145–157). New York: Haworth Press.

R. v. Khan (1986). Ontario Court of Appeal.

Rabinowitz, D. (1990, May). From the mouths of babes to a jail cell: Child abuse and the abuse of justice. *Harper's Magazine,* pp. 52–63.

Raskin, D. C., & Esplin, P. W. (1991). Statement validity assessment: Interview procedures and content analysis of children's statement of sexual abuse. *Behavioral Assessment, 13,* 265–291.

Raskin, D. C., & Yuille, J. C. (1989). Problems in evaluating interviews of children in child sexual abuse cases. In J. J. Ceci, M. P. Toglia, & D. F. Ross (Eds.), *Perspectives on children's testimony* (pp. 184–207). New York: Springer-Verlag.

Robin, M. (1991). Beyond validation interviews: An assessment approach to evaluating sexual abuse allegations. In M. Robin (Ed.), *Assessing child maltreatment reports: The problem of false allegation* (pp. 93–114). New York: Haworth Press.

Rogers, R. (1990). *Report of the special advisor to the administer of Health and Welfare Canada on child sexual abuse in Canada: Reaching for solutions.* Ottawa: National Clearinghouse on Family Violence.

Rudy, L., & Goodman, G. S. (1991). Effects of participation on children's reports: Implications for children's testimony. *Developmental Psychology, 27*(4), 527–538.

Sas, L. (1990). *London child witness project.* Ottawa: Health and Welfare Canada.

Schuman, D. C. (1986). False accusations of physical and sexual abuse. *Bulletin of the American Academy of Psychiatry Law, 14*(1), 5–21.

Sgroi, S. M., Porter, F. S., & Blick, L. C. (1982). Validation of child sexual abuse. In S. M. Sgroi (Ed.), *Clinical intervention in child sexual abuse* (pp. 39–79). Lexington, Mass.: Lexington Books.

Simonds, J. F., & Glenn, T. (1976). Folie à deux in a child. *Journal of Autism and Childhood Schizophrenia, 6*(1), 61–73.

Sorensen, T., & Snow, B. (1991). How children tell: The process of disclosure in child sexual abuse. *Child Welfare, 70*(1), 3–15.

Spencer, J. R., & Flynn, R. H. (Eds.). (1990). *The evidence of children: The law and the psychology.* London: Blackstone.

Steller, M. (1989). Recent developments in statement analysis. In J. C. Yuille (Ed.), *Credibility assessment* (pp. 135–154). Dordrecht, Netherlands: Kluwer.

Steller, M., & Koehnken, G. (1989). Criteria-based statement analysis. In D. C. Raskin (Ed.), *Psychological methods in clinical investigation and evidence* (pp. 217–245). New York: Springer.

Steward, M. S., Bussey, K., Goodman, G. S., & Saywitz, K. J. (1993). Implications of developmental research for interviewing children. *Child Abuse and Neglect, 17,* 25–37.

Study of national incidence and prevalence of child abuse and neglect. (1988). Washington, D.C.: National Center on Child Abuse and Neglect.

Summit, R. (1983). The child sexual abuse accommodation syndrome. *Child Abuse and Neglect, 7,* 177–193.

Terr, L. C. (1986). The child psychiatrist and the child witness: Travelling companions by necessity, if not by design. *Journal of the American Academy of Child Psychiatry, 25*(4), 462–472.

Terr, L. C. (1988). What happens to the memories of early childhood trauma? *Journal of American Academy of Child and Adolescent Psychiatry, 27,* 96–104.

Toglia, M. P., Ceci, S. J., & Ross, D. F. (1989, April). *Prestige vs. source monitoring in children's suggestibility.* Paper presented to the Society for Research in Child Development, Kansas City, Mo.

Tucker, L. S., & Cornwall, T. P. (1977). Mother–son folie à deux: A case of attempted patricide. *American Journal of Psychiatry, 134*(10), 1146–1147.

Undeutsch, U. (1989). The development of statement reality analysis. In J. C. Yuille (Ed.), *Credibility assessment* (pp. 101–119). Dordrecht, Netherlands: Kluwer.

U.S. v. Provost, 969 F.2d 617 (8th Cir. 1992).

Wegener, H. (1989). The present state of statement analysis. In J. C. Yuille (Ed.), *Credibility assessment* (pp. 121–133). Dordrecht, Netherlands: Kluwer.

Wehrspann, W. H., Steinhauer, P. D., & Klajner-Diamond, H. (1987). Criteria and methodology for assessing credibility of sexual abuse allegations. *Canadian Journal of Psychiatry, 32*(7), 615–623.

Whitcomb, D. (1992). Legal reforms on behalf of child witnesses: Recent developments in the American courts. In H. Dent and R. Flin (Eds.), *Children as witnesses* (pp. 151–165). Chichester, England: John Wiley & Sons.

Yates, A. (1982). Children eroticized by incest. *American Journal of Psychiatry, 39,* 482–485.

Yuille, J. C. (1986). Meaningful research in the police context. In J. C. Yuille (Ed.), *Police selection and training: The role of psychology* (pp. 225–243). Dordrecht, Netherlands: Martinus Nijhoff.

Yuille, J: C. (1988).The systematic assessment of children's testimony. *Canadian Psychology, 29,* 247–262.

Yuille, J. C. (Ed.). (1989). *Credibility assessment.* Dordrecht, Netherlands: Kluwer.

Yuille, J. C. (1991). Training programs and procedures for interviewing and assessing sexually abused children. In C. Bagley & R. Thomlinson (Eds.), *Child sexual abuse: Critical perspectives on prevention, intervention and treatment* (pp. 121–134). Toronto: Wall & Emerson.

Yuille, J. C., Hunter, R., & Harvey, W. (1990). A coordinated approach to interviewing in child sexual abuse investigations. *Canada's Mental Health, 38*(2/3), 14–17.

Yuille, J. C., Marxsen, D., and Ménard, K. (1993). *Interviewing and assessing children in child sexual abuse investigations: A field study.* Unpublished manuscript, Ministry of Social Services, British Columbia, Canada.

Yuille, J. C., Hunter, R., Joffe, R., & Zaparniuk, J. (1993b). Interviewing children in sexual abuse cases. In G. Goodman & B. Bottoms (Eds.), *Understanding and improving children's testimony: Clinical, developmental and legal implications* (pp. 95–115). New York: Guilford Press.

Zaparniuk, J., Yuille, J. C., & Taylor, S. (in press). Assessing the credibility of true and false statements. *International Journal of Law and Psychiatry.*

PART II

Child Development Issues

3

Assessing Young Children's Sexual Behaviors in the Context of Child Sexual Abuse Evaluations

Toni Cavanagh Johnson
and Colleen Friend

Assessing children's sexual behavior for the purpose of examining whether they are within the natural and healthy range, or signify distress, is discussed. Fifteen guidelines are provided to help determine children's sexual behaviors that are of concern and require further evaluation. As problematic sexual behaviors in children can be an indication of sexual abuse or other disturbance in the family, methods of utilizing information regarding the child's sexual behaviors during evaluations are described.

When it is alleged that a child has been sexually abused, a thorough assessment of the child and family is often warranted. Evidence shows that

The authors thank Cathy McCarrel, MSW, Director of the Los Angeles County Child Sexual Abuse Crisis Center at Harbor/UCLA in Torrance, California; Kathy Singletarry, MFCC, Director of CAST in Orange County, California; Dominique Cattaneo, L.C.S.W., Clinical Services Supervisor, Center for Child Protection, Children's Hospital, San Diego, California; and Thomas McGuire, Director of Act Three in Vancouver, B.C., Canada.

children who have been sexually abused often show an increase in their sexual behaviors (Deblinger, McLeer, Atkins, Ralphe, & Foa, 1989; Finkelhor, 1979; Friedrich, 1991; Friedrich, 1993; Friedrich, Beilke, & Urquiza, 1988; Friedrich, Grambsch, Broughton, Kuiper, & Beilke, 1991; Friedrich, Grambsch, Damon, Hewitt, Koverola, Lang, Wolfe, & Broughton, 1992; Gale, Thompson, Moran, & Sack, 1988; Kolko, Moser, & Weldy, 1988; White, Halpin, Strom, & Santilli, 1988). This aspect of the child's behavior is often assessed in the evaluation, but with little understanding of normal sexual behavior. Johnson (Gil & Johnson, 1993) points out that children's sexual development proceeds along seven distinct developmental lines: biological, sensual/erotic, behavioral, gender-related, cognitive, relational, and sexual socialization.

When a child has been sexually misused, abused, or overly exposed to adult sexuality, disruptions in multiple areas of the child's sexual development may occur. For example, the child may be prematurely eroticized or overly concerned about his or her gender identity or gender object choice, or be too knowledgeable about sex or have confused ideas about sexual relationships. A child who has lived in an incestuous home or in a home with poor boundaries may not have been adequately socialized regarding sexuality. Disruptions in any of these developmental lines may result in increased or problematic sexual behaviors.

This chapter examines problematic sexual behaviors and compares them with more natural and healthier sexual behaviors in children. A discussion of the assessment of young children's sexual behaviors in the context of child sexual abuse evaluations is presented, and specific recommendations for assessing these behaviors are made.

The authors caution that there are very little empirical data available regarding children's sexual behaviors and their meaning. The data provided in this chapter, when not specifically noted as research data, are derived from clinical practice and thus have not been subjected to empirical validation. Caution should be exercised in their use.

There are many aspects to interviewing children. The authors assume that the reader is familiar with the intricacies and legal issues related to evaluations of children when there are allegations of sexual abuse. This chapter builds on that knowledge, addressing only issues related to interviewing children with problematic sexual behaviors.

RESEARCH ON CHILD SEXUAL BEHAVIORS AND SEXUAL VICTIMIZATION

A fairly consistent finding in the literature is that there is a higher frequency of sexual behavior in sexually abused children than in nonabused samples (Deblinger et al., 1989; Finkelhor, 1979; Friedrich, 1991, 1993; Friedrich et al., 1988, 1991, 1992; Gale, Thompson, Moran, & Sack, 1988; Kolko et al., 1988; White et al., 1988). Yet some studies do not find this to be so (Cohen & Mannarino, 1988; Allen, Jones, & Nash, 1989; Mannarino, Cohen, & Gregor, 1989; Weinstein, Trickett, & Putman, 1989). For instance, comparisons between sexually abused children and children with psychiatric diagnoses but with no sexual abuse history show no significant differences in sexual behavior (Cohen & Mannarino, 1988). Another study, which compared precocious pubescent children, physically abused children, sexually abused children, and a control group of nonabused girls, found no significant differences among the groups (Weinstein et al., 1989).

While sexualized behaviors and PTSD are the only two symptoms that occur more frequently in sexually abused children than in clinical comparison groups of nonabused children, less than half of sexually abused children manifest sexual behaviors of concern. Across six studies of preschoolers (the age group most likely to manifest such symptoms) an average of 35% exhibited sexualized behaviors of concern. Friedrich (Friedrich et al., 1992), using the Child Sexual Behavior Inventory, found a slightly higher percentage (Kendall-Tackett et al., 1993).

An important variable relates to family disturbance. When looking at two small samples of emotionally disturbed preschoolers with similar levels of family disturbance, one group sexually abused and the other group not sexually abused, no significant differences were seen as related to sexual behaviors (Allen et al., 1989). Friedrich (Friedrich et al., 1992) found that the intensity of the children's life events was a *significant* predictor of sexual behaviors in children. Wolfe and Mosk (1983) observed that in families with high levels of chaos and disruption, there is an increased level of overall behavioral problems in the children, regardless of whether or not they were sexually or physically abused. In addition, Johnson and Aoki (1993) found that children who had been both physically and sexually abused engaged in a greater variety of sexual behaviors than did children who had experienced only sexual abuse. Together, these findings suggest caution when assessing the determinants of increased sexual behaviors.

Friedrich's (1991) research indicates that children with a more severe history of sexual abuse involving a greater number of perpetrators, and with whom force was used, engage in more sexual behaviors than do children whose abuse was not characterized by these features. He also found that there are no sexual behaviors that are exclusively engaged in by sexually abused children (Friedrich et al., 1992).

The studies cited here refer to a clinical population of sexually abused children. This limits the generalizability of findings: the observed sexual behaviors may only be characteristic of sexually abused children who have sought professional help. Clinical populations consist of children who are experiencing enough difficulties to seek professional help. Many sexually abused children do not receive or require psychological services, and thus would not be included in these studies. For a lengthy review of studies regarding the sexual behaviors of children as they relate to abuse, see Friedrich (1993).

CURRENT TECHNIQUES FOR ASSESSING CHILDREN'S SEXUAL BEHAVIORS

Many different approaches have been taken to assessing children's sexual behaviors, including looking for depictions of the genitals in children's drawings, observing the child's play with toys or dolls, and noting sexual behaviors by the child during the interview. Unfortunately, none of these assessment approaches are supported by empirical research.

Children's Drawings

While several studies indicate a significant difference between sexually abused and nonabused children regarding the drawing of genitalia, very few sexually abused children draw genitalia. Waterman and Lusk (1993) found that 7% of a sample of ritualistically abused children drew genitalia on their pictures while none of the control children did so. Hibbard and colleagues found that 10% of an alleged sexually abused group of children drew genitalia, while only 2% of the nonabused sample did (Hibbard, Roghmann, & Hockelman, 1987). Yet, in a more recent study, Hibbard (Hibbard & Hartman, 1990) found no significant difference in the drawings of a sample of abused children compared to those of nonabused children. Therefore, the relevance of genitalia on children's drawings is not clear.

Anatomically Detailed Dolls

Observing children's sexual play with dolls or the use of anatomically detailed dolls in interviews is another method that has been used to gain information related to abuse. Although there are guidelines on the use of the anatomically detailed dolls (APSAC, 1990), there are scant empirical data that offer clear evidence regarding the behavior of abused and nonabused children's sexual behavior with the dolls.

Studies in the 1980s indicated that nonabused children under eight years of age were unlikely to demonstrate sexual acts spontaneously with anatomically detailed dolls (Jampole & Weber, 1987; Sivan, Schor, Koeppl, & Noble,

1988; White, Strom, Santilli, & Halpin, 1986). However, recent work by Everson and Boat (1990) indicates that in a demographically diverse sample of 223 children, ages two to five, who were screened for the *absence* of sexual abuse, touching and exploration of the dolls' genitalia were common behaviors, occurring in over 50% of the children at each age level. Explicit sexual play in the form of apparent demonstrations of vaginal, oral, or anal intercourse (i.e., penile insertion, sexual placement with "humping" motions, or mouthing a doll's genitals) was seen in only 6% of the total sample. The frequency of this explicit sexual play was significantly related to the child's age and socioeconomic status; over 20% of the four- and five-year-old, low-socioeconomic-status, black males in this sample demonstrated clear sexual intercourse of some type during the sessions. The presence of an adult did not inhibit these children from engaging in the behavior.

Boat and Everson (1988) asked child-protective-service workers, mental health professionals, law enforcement officers, and physicians to rate the normality of a list of behaviors with anatomically detailed dolls for nonabused children. The behaviors were divided into two groups: (1) the less overtly sexual behaviors, such as undressing the dolls, looking at the dolls' genitals, touching the dolls' genitals, and placing dolls on top of each other; and (2) highly sexualized behaviors, such as showing vaginal or anal penetration or showing oral–genital contact. Most of the professionals agreed that the overtly sexual behaviors were abnormal for nonabused children ages two to 5.9 years of age. There was disagreement about some of the less overtly sexual behaviors, and there were no behaviors on which there was unanimous agreement.

Kendall-Tackett's (1992) study of men and women in law enforcement and mental health who work clinically or in an investigatory role with sexual abuse victims is instructive regarding the use of observations of children's play with anatomically detailed dolls. When Kendall-Tackett asked which sexual behaviors demonstrated by a child with the dolls were normal, questionable, or abnormal, she found differences based on profession, experience with child victims, length of experience, and gender. As in the Boat and Everson (1988) study, there was more agreement on the abnormality of the more highly sexual behaviors but less on those that were less overtly sexual.

There are no clear guidelines based on research and no consensus among professionals regarding what constitutes normal, questionable, and abnormal doll play among abused and nonabused children. Presently, the most reliable use of anatomically detailed dolls in evaluations is as a tool for children to demonstrate what happened to them after verbally disclosing some history of abuse. In this way, the professional is not extrapolating from a child's free play with the dolls, but getting a visual and verbal representation of what has occurred. Each piece of information an evaluator gathers during an interview is integrated into the professional's final assessment or decision regarding abuse status. Extreme caution must be exercised as to which pieces of information are used and how the information informs the opinion.

Observing Children's Sexual Behaviors

In a survey by Conte, Sorenson, Fogarty, and Roasa (1991), professionals who evaluate children when sexual abuse is alleged were asked to rank various criteria as to their importance in influencing their belief about whether a child was sexually abused. Six items that related to children's sexual behaviors were among the top 20 (of 41) items that the professionals said would influence them to believe that sexual abuse had taken place:

- (2) Age-inappropriate sexual knowledge
- (6) Sexualized play during the interview
- (8) Precocious or apparently seductive play
- (9) Child's behavioral and/or affective response to anatomically correct dolls
- (12) Excessive masturbation
- (13) Preoccupation with genitals

It is interesting to compare the Conte survey with Friedrich's research. The data in Table 1 represent the outcome of a survey of 880 mothers of nonabused children (normative sample) and 276 mothers of children with a confirmed history of sexual abuse (Friedrich et al., 1992). The mothers were asked to describe the sexual behaviors of their children by filling in an inventory.

While the data indicate that there is a significant difference between the number of different sexual behaviors engaged in by the nonabused sample and by the abused sample, it is important to look at the frequency of the behaviors observed in both populations. "Touching of sexual parts in pub-

TABLE 1
Normative Versus Clinical Sample of Children's Sexual Behaviors

Behavior	Normative Sample, %	Clinical Sample, %	P Level
Masturbates with hand	15.3	28.6	.0001*
Masturbates with object	0.8	11.2	.0001*
Talks flirtatiously	10.6	15.0	.04*
Touches sex parts in public	19.7	21.8	.0035*
Touches sex parts at home	45.8	42.2	.0022*
Imitates sexual behavior with dolls	3.2	17.5	.0003*

From Friedrich et al., 1992.
*Indicates significant differences between groups.

lic," while significantly different between the samples, occurs in a fairly similar number of children in both groups. "Touches sex parts at home" actually was observed significantly more in nonabused children than in abused children! "Talks flirtatiously" was witnessed more frequently in the sexually abused sample (15%) than in the nonsexually abused sample, but 10.6% of nonabused children have been observed to engage in this behavior. "Masturbating with hand" has been seen by approximately twice as many mothers of sexually abused children as of nonabused children. Children imitating sexual behavior with dolls was observed five time more frequently in the abused than in the nonabused sample. Unfortunately, the data do not describe what "type" of sexual behavior the children engaged in with the dolls.

While Friedrich's data indicate what sexual behaviors have been observed by mothers, it does not tell us the frequency of each of the behaviors. For instance, while more of the normative sample than of the abused sample "touch their sex parts at home," it may be that the sexually abused children engage in this behavior more frequently.

Friedrich's data provide some substantiation for the clinicians in the Conte survey. Yet many children who exhibit these behaviors have not been sexually abused. While Friedrich's Child Sexual Behavior Inventory is able to statistically separate a majority of children into an abused or nonabused group based on the sexual behaviors, it cannot determine whether or not a particular child was abused. Unfortunately, there is virtually no research-based information to help the evaluator determine when a child's specific sexual behaviors are indicative of sexual abuse and when they are not. Research indicates that there are no sexual behaviors that are observed only in sexually abused children.

There are no easy answers to these complex questions. The research is useful to the evaluator in amplifying experience, creating hypotheses, following up on information, and seeing the big picture. The caveat for evaluators remains: it is important to use multiple sources of information to come to a decision about whether sexual abuse has occurred; no sexual behaviors are pathognomonic of sexual abuse. It is more valuable to look for a pattern of distress in the child's sexual behaviors, the context in which the sexual behaviors take place, any verbalizations by the child, the precursors of the behavior, and with whom the child associates the behaviors.

NATURAL AND HEALTHY SEXUAL BEHAVIORS

It is expected that 40–75% of children will engage in at least some sexual behaviors before 13 years of age (Finkelhor, 1983; Friedrich et al., 1991; Goldman & Goldman, 1988; Johnson, 1994). The following definition will assist in understanding natural, expected sexual expression in children. This will be contrasted with characteristics of childhood sexual expression that becomes problematic.

Natural and expected sexual exploration during childhood is an information-gathering process wherein children explore each other's bodies visually and tactually (e.g., playing doctor), as well as explore gender roles and behaviors (e.g., playing house). Children involved in natural and expected sex play are of similar age, size, and developmental status and participate on a voluntary basis. While siblings engage in mutual sexual exploration, most sex play is between children who have an ongoing, mutually enjoyable play and/or school friendship. The sexual behaviors are limited in type and frequency and occur during several periods of the child's life. The child's interest in sex and sexuality is balanced by curiosity about other aspects of his or her life. Natural and expected sexual exploration may result in embarrassment, but does not usually leave children with deep feelings of anger, shame, fear, or anxiety. If the children are discovered in sexual exploration and instructed to stop, the behavior generally diminishes, at least in the view of adults. The affect of the children regarding the sexual behavior is generally lighthearted and spontaneous (Johnson, 1993a).

It is important to bear in mind that children's natural and expected sexual behaviors, as well as their level of comfort with sexuality, will be affected by the amount of exposure they have had to adult sexuality, nudity, and explicit television, videos, and pictures, as well as their level of sexual interest. Parental, cultural, societal, and religious attitudes and values will also influence children's sexual behavior.

CHILDREN'S SEXUAL BEHAVIORS THAT CAUSE CONCERN

When presented with a child who is engaging in sexual behaviors, parents, teachers, medical professionals, school and public health nurses, and others who come into contact with children sometimes find it difficult to decide whether a referral to the police or child protective services should be made. Is this sex play? Are the increased sexual behaviors of the child attributable to the print, video, and television media, or culture, which seems to be overly focused on sexuality? Is it possible that the child's sexual behaviors are indicative of sexual misuse?

The following will assist in determining whether a child's sexual behaviors fall outside of what is generally considered natural and healthy in children under 12 years of age (Johnson, 1994).

1. *Sexual behaviors that are engaged in by children of different ages or developmental levels or who do not have an ongoing, mutual play relationship.* In general, chil-

dren who engage in sexual exploration seek out as partners good friends who will keep a secret, as most children are aware of adults' prohibitions on overt sexual play. Children do not generally choose someone whom they distrust or with whom they have an antagonistic relationship, as the other child may tell on them. Childhood playmates are generally within the same age range and on the same developmental level, unless the child is isolated from same-age children. The wider the age difference, the greater the concern.

2. *Sexual behaviors that are out of balance with other aspects of the child's life and interests.* Children are interested in every aspect of their environment, from the sun's rising to how babies are made. While they may explore some aspects of their world more extensively at certain periods of their lives, their interests are generally broad and intermittent. Children's sexual behaviors follow the same pattern. At one period, they may be very interested in finding out about sexuality, and at another time in how the dishwasher works or what will make Mommy mad. Many fluctuations occur during a day, a week, or a month. When a child is preoccupied with sexuality, this raises concern. If a child would prefer to masturbate rather than play with friends, this also raises concern.

3. *Children who seem to have too much knowledge about sexuality and behave in ways more consistent with adult sexual expression.* As children develop, they acquire knowledge about sex and sexuality from television, movies, videos, magazines, their parents and other relatives, school, and peers. Knowledge gathered in these time-honored ways is generally assimilated, without disruption, into the child's developing understanding of sex and sexuality; this translates into additional natural and healthy sexual interest. When children have been overexposed to explicit adult sexuality, or have been sexually misused, they may engage in or talk about sexual behaviors that are beyond age-appropriate sexual knowledge and interest.

4. *Sexual behaviors that are significantly different from those of other same-age children.* The frequency and type of children's sexual behaviors depend, to a certain extent, on the environment (home, neighborhood, culture, religion) in which they have been raised, their parents' attitudes and actions related to sex and sexuality, and their peers' behaviors. If a child's sexual behavior stands out among his or her neighborhood peers, this raises concern.

5. *Sexual behaviors that continue in spite of consistent requests to stop.* Most adults are consistent in their admonitions against children openly engaging in sexual behaviors. While adults may be inconsistent regarding other behaviors, and children may persist in engaging in them, children generally learn very quickly that there is a strong taboo concerning overt sexual behavior.

When children continue sexual behaviors within the sight of adults, despite requests to stop or even punishment, this may be a conscious or unconscious way of signaling that they need help. When children "cry for help," they may persist in the behavior until adults pay heed, discover, and curtail the antecedents of the sexual behavior.

6. *Sexual behaviors that occur in public or in other places where the child has been told they are not acceptable.* When a child has been told not to engage in sexual behaviors or told to do so in private, the child generally responds so as not to be reprimanded. When a child does not conform to these requests, it may indicate the sexual behavior is driven by anxiety or other discomforting or overwhelming emotions. This type of sexual behavior is generally not within the full conscious control of the child. The child who feels anxious when in the presence of certain precipitating stimuli may respond directly by masturbating or engaging in other sexual behaviors. Hiding the sexual behaviors or finding friends with whom to engage in the behaviors in private may not be possible for these children. Anxiety-, guilt-, or fear-driven sexual behavior often does not react to normal limit setting.

7. *Children's sexual behaviors that are eliciting complaints from other children and/ or adversely affecting them.* Generally, children complain when something is annoying or discomforting to them. When a child complains about another child's sexual behaviors, it is an indication that the behavior is upsetting to the child and should be taken seriously. In natural and healthy sexual play, both children agree, overtly or indirectly, to engage in it willingly and in secret. It is quite unlikely that either would tell on the other; therefore, if one child is telling, this is cause for concern.

8. *Children's sexual behaviors that are directed at adults who feel uncomfortable receiving them.* Children often hug adults and give them kisses, as spontaneous expressions of caring to a well-known adult, or because they have been told by a caretaker to do so. When a child continues to touch an adult in a manner more akin to adult–adult sexual contact, offers himself or herself as a sexual object, or solicits sexual touch from adults, this raises concern. Children who have been groomed and seduced into ongoing sexual behaviors may engage others in similar sexual behaviors.

9. *Children (four years of age and older) who do not understand their rights or the rights of others in relation to sexual contact.* Children who do not understand who has the right to touch their bodies, or whose bodies they can touch, may have had their own personal boundaries violated. Some children may live with persons who do not respect their emotional, physical, or sexual privacy. These children may not have learned proper boundaries, and hence they may violate the boundaries of others. Sexual abuse may involve teaching children to touch adults or other children in a sexual way.

10. *Sexual behaviors that progress in frequency, intensity, or intrusiveness over time.* While sexual behavior in children is natural and expected, its frequency is not generally high, it is sporadic, and it occurs outside the sight and knowledge of others. When a pattern of sexualized behavior develops unabated,

and the behaviors encroach upon others' emotional and physical space, this raises concern.

11. *When fear, anxiety, deep shame, or intense guilt is associated with the sexual behaviors.* Children's affect regarding sexuality is generally lighthearted, spontaneous, giggly, or silly. In some cases, if a child has been caught engaging in sexual behaviors, the adult's response may have generated embarrassed or guilty feelings in the child. Yet these feelings are qualitatively different from the deep shame or intense guilt, fear, or anxiety of a child who has been fooled, coerced, or threatened into sexual behaviors or overexposed to adult sexuality.

12. *Sexual behaviors that cause physical or emotional pain or discomfort to self or others.* Any behaviors by children, including sexual behaviors, that induce pain or discomfort in themselves or others are a cause for concern.

13. *When anger precedes, follows, or accompanies the sexual behavior.* In healthy development, sexual expression and exploration are accompanied by positive emotions. Children who have been sexually abused may feel anger and suspicion about all sexual expression. When they associate negative and hostile emotions with sexual behavior, this may be their response to having been coerced, forced, bribed, fooled, manipulated, or threatened into sexual contact or of being aware of its happening to someone else.

14. *When verbal and/or physical aggression precedes, follows, or accompanies the sexual behavior.* Verbal or physical aggression that accompanies children's sexual behaviors is a learned response to sexuality. In general, children who exhibit this behavior have witnessed repeated instances in which verbally and/or physically aggressive behavior has occurred, often in the context of sex. They may have witnessed their parents or other adults hitting each other when fighting about sexual matters. Some children may have seen a parent being sexually misused. Some parents use highly sexual words when verbally assaulting their partners. When sex and aggression are paired with the child's sexual expression, this is a cause for great concern.

15. *When coercion, force, bribery, manipulation, or threats are associated with sexual behaviors.* Healthy sexual exploration may include teasing or daring. Unhealthy sexual expression involves the use of emotional or physical force or coercion to engage another child, perhaps one who is emotionally or physically vulnerable.

If any of the foregoing concerns are pertinent to the child who is being assessed, it is important to remember that there are many causes for problematic sexual behaviors. This is discussed in the section entitled "Causes of Children's Problematic Sexual Behaviors."

Tables 2 and 3 provide a tabulation of specific sexual behaviors exhibited by preschool and school-aged children. They can be used to distinguish among particular sexual behaviors that are *natural and expected*, those *of concern*, and

TABLE 2
Behaviors Related to Sex and Sexuality in Preschool Children

Natural and Expected	Of Concern	Seek Professional Help
Touches/rubs own genitals when diapers are being changed; when going to sleep; when tense, excited, or afraid.	Continues to touch/rub genitals in public after being told many times not to do this.	Touches/rubs self in public or in private to the exclusion of normal childhood activities.
Explores differences between male and females, boys and girls.	Continuous questions about genital differences after all questions have been answered.	Plays male or female roles in an angry, sad, or aggressive manner. Hates own/other sex.
Touches the genitals, breasts of familiar adults and children.	Touches the genitals, breasts of adults not in family. Asks to be touched himself/ herself.	Sneakily touches adults. Makes others allow touching, demands touching of self.
Takes advantage of opportunity to look at nude persons.	Stares at nude persons even after having seen many persons nude.	Asks people to take off their clothes. Tries forcibly to undress people.
Asks about the genitals, breasts, intercourse, babies.	Keeps asking people even after parent has answered questions at age-appropriate level.	Asks strangers after parent has answered. Sexual knowledge too great for age.
Erections	Continuous erections	Painful erections
Likes to be nude. May show others his/her genitals.	Wants to be nude in public after the parent says "No."	Refuses to put on clothes. Secretly shows self in public after many scoldings.
Interested in watching people doing bathroom functions.	Interest in watching bathroom functions does not wane in days/weeks.	Refuses to leave people alone in bathroom, forces way into bathroom.
Interested in having/birthing a baby.	Boy's interest does not wane after several days/weeks of play about babies.	Displays fear or anger about babies, birthing, or intercourse.
Uses "dirty" words for bathroom and sexual functions.	Continues to use "dirty" words at home after parent says "No."	Uses "dirty" words in public and at home after many scoldings.
Interested in own feces.	Smears feces on walls or floor more than one time.	Repeatedly plays or smears feces after scolding.
Plays doctor, inspecting others' bodies.	Frequently plays doctor after being told "No."	Forces child to play doctor, to take off clothes.
Puts something in the genitals or rectum of self or other *due to curiosity or exploration.*	Puts something in genitals or rectum of self or other child after being told "No."	Uses coercion or force in putting something in genitals or rectum of other child.
Plays house, acts out roles of Mommy and Daddy.	Humps other children with clothes on.	Simulated or real intercourse without clothes, oral sex.

© 1993b Toni Cavanagh Johnson.

TABLE 3
Behaviors Related to Sex and Sexuality in
Kindergarten Through Fourth-Grade Children

Natural and Expected	Of Concern	Seek Professional Help
Asks about the genitals, breasts, intercourse, babies.	Shows fear or anxiety about sexual topics.	Endless questions about sex. Sexual knowledge too great for age.
Interested in watching/ peeking at people doing bathroom functions.	Keeps getting caught watching/peeking at others doing bathroom functions.	Refuses to leave people alone in bathroom.
Uses "dirty" words for bathroom functions, genitals, and sex.	Continues to use "dirty" words with adults after parent says "No" and punishes him/her.	Continues use of "dirty" words even after exclusion from school and activities.
Plays doctor, inspecting others' bodies.	Frequently plays doctor and gets caught after being told "No."	Forces child to play doctor, to take off clothes.
Boys and girls show interest in having/birthing a baby.	Boy keeps making believe he is having a baby after months.	Displays fear or anger about babies or intercourse.
Shows others his/her genitals.	Wants to be nude in public after the parent says "No" and punishes child.	Refuses to put on clothes. Exposes self in public after many scoldings.
Interested in urination and defecation.	Plays with feces. Purposely urinates outside of toilet bowl.	Repeatedly plays with or smears feces. Purposely urinates on furniture.
Touches/rubs own genitals when going to sleep; when tense, excited, or afraid.	Continues to touch/rub genitals in public after being told "No." Masturbates on furniture or with objects.	Touches/rubs self in public or in private to the exclusion of normal childhood activities. Masturbates on people.
Plays house, may simulate all roles of Mommy and Daddy.	Humps other children with clothes on. Imitates sexual behavior with dolls/stuffed toy.	Humps naked. Intercourse with another child. Forcing sex on other child.
Thinks other-sex children are "gross" or have "cooties." Chases them.	Uses "dirty" language when other children *really* complain.	Uses bad language about other child's family. Hurts other-sex children.
Talks about sex with friends. Talks about having a girl/ boyfriend.	Sex talk gets child in trouble. Romanticizes all relationships.	Talks about sex and sexual acts a lot. Repeatedly in trouble with regard to sexual behavior.
Wants privacy when in bathroom or changing clothes.	Becomes very upset when observed changing clothes.	Aggressive or tearful in demand for privacy.

(*continued*)

Natural and Expected	Of Concern	Seek Professional Help
Likes to hear and tell "dirty" jokes.	Keeps getting caught telling "dirty" jokes. Makes sexual sounds, e.g., moans.	Still tells "dirty" jokes even after exclusion from school and activities.
Looks at nude pictures.	Continuous fascination with nude pictures.	Wants to masturbate to nude pictures or display them.
Plays games related to sex and sexuality with same-aged children.	Wants to play games related to sex and sexuality with much younger/older children.	Forces others to play sexual games. A group of children forces child/ren to play.
Draws genitals on human figures.	Draws genitals on one figure and not another. Genitals' size disproportionate to body.	Genitals stand out as most prominent feature. Drawings of intercourse, group sex.
Explores differences between males and females, boys and girls.	Confused about male/female differences after all questions have been answered.	Plays male or female roles in a sad, angry, or aggressive manner. Hates own/other sex.
Takes advantage of opportunity to look at nude child or adult.	Stares/sneaks to stare at nude persons even after having seen many persons nude.	Asks people to take off their clothes. Tries forcibly to undress people.
Pretends to be opposite sex.	Wants to be opposite sex.	Hates being own sex. Hates own genitals.
Wants to compare genitals with those of peer-aged friends.	Wants to compare genitals with those of much older or much younger children or of adults.	Demands to see the genitals, breasts, buttocks of children or adults.
Interested in touching genitals, breasts, buttocks of other same-age child or have child touch his/hers.	Continuously wants to touch genitals, breasts, buttocks of other child/ren. Tries to engage in oral, anal, vaginal sex.	Manipulates or forces other child to allow touching of genitals, breasts, buttocks. Forced or mutual oral, anal, or vaginal sex.
Kisses familiar adults and children. Allows kisses by familiar adults and children.	French kisses. Talks in sexualized manner with others. Fearful of hugs and kisses by adults. Gets upset with public displays of affection.	Overly familiar with strangers. Talks/acts in a sexualized manner with unknown adults. Physical contact with adult causes extreme agitation.
Looks at the genitals, buttocks, breasts of adults.	Touches/stares at the genitals, breasts, buttocks of adults. Asks adult to touch him/her on genitals.	Sneakily or forcibly touches genitals, breasts, buttocks of adults. Tries to manipulate adult into touching him/her.
Erections	Continuous erections	Painful erections

Puts something in own genitals/rectum *out of curiosity and exploration.*	Puts something in own genitals/rectum when it feels uncomfortable. Puts something in the genitals/rectum of other child.	Uses coercion or force in putting something in genitals/rectum of other child. Anal, vaginal intercourse. Causing harm to own/others' genitals/rectum.
Interest in breeding behavior of animals.	Touching genitals of animals.	Sexual behaviors with animals.

© 1993c Toni Cavanagh Johnson.

those for which a *professional consultation* should be sought immediately. The tables illustrate how the same sexual behavior can change from being natural and expected to being of concern by altering some of its characteristics. As when assessing any behavior, it is important to attend to the children's age and emotional and cognitive development when assessing their sexual behaviors.

In both Tables, behaviors listed in the first column are those that are in the expected range. This range is wide, and not all children will engage in all of the behaviors; some may engage in none, whereas others will be involved in many. If a child were to engage continuously in all or most of the behaviors, this might be a cause for concern.

The second column describes behaviors that are seen in some children who are overly concerned about sexuality, who lack adequate supervision, or who live in sexualized environments, and in others who have been, or are being, sexually and emotionally maltreated.

When a child exhibits several of these behaviors, or the behavior persists in spite of interventions, a full assessment, including the child and all family members, is indicated. As it is possible that the child is being sexually misused or abused, a full assessment should be completed by a professional who specializes in child sexual abuse (Gil & Johnson, 1993).

The third column describes behaviors that are often indicative of a child who is experiencing deep confusion in the area of sexuality. This child may or may not have been sexually and emotionally abused or physically maltreated. It may be that the level of sex and/or aggression in the child's environment has overwhelmed his or her ability to integrate it and the child is acting out the confusion. A full assessment to determine the precipitants and sustainers of the behavior and to delineate the goals of treatment will be necessary. Consultation with a professional who specializes in the treatment of sexual abuse or sexual offending should be sought. If it is determined that the child is engaging in coercive sexual behavior, treatment will need to be specific and focused on the sexually abusive behavior (Gil & Johnson, 1993).

ASSESSING THE SEXUAL BEHAVIORS

It is often very difficult for parents to discuss the sexual behaviors of their children. Some do not have the vocabulary or are fearful that they do not know the correct terms for sexual behaviors, the genitals, and other body parts. To have to describe from memory a child's sexual behaviors can be difficult. Parents who feel anxious about their own sexuality may be embarrassed or ashamed to speak about sexual matters. For this reason, it is useful to utilize a list of sexual behaviors to gather information. Johnson's Child Sexual Behavior Checklist (Gil & Johnson, 1993) or Friedrich's Child Sexual Behavior Inventory (Friedrich et al., 1991) can be helpful in this regard. It is important to note the range (variety), as well as the frequency, of the child's sexual behaviors. Unfortunately, neither instrument has been adequately normed. The Child Sexual Behavior Inventory has some data providing preliminary information regarding differences between sexually and nonsexually abused children (Friedrich et al., 1991, 1992).

Clarifying the Child's Sexual Behaviors

After the parent(s) or caretaker has described the type and frequency of the child's sexual behaviors, the evaluator will decide if any of the behaviors seem to be outside the realm of what can be expected naturally. The following questions, which parallel the 15 guidelines (described above), can be asked about specific behaviors that may be of concern.

- How and when did the parent/caretaker first find out about the sexual behavior?
- How long have the sexual behaviors persisted?
- Where do the sexual behaviors usually take place?
- With whom does the child engage in the sexual behaviors?
- If there are two or more children involved, what is the relationship between them? What is the age difference?
- Generally, what are the immediate precipitants of the sexual behaviors?
- What is the child's affect regarding sexuality in general?
- What is the affect of the child before, during, and after engaging in the sexual behaviors?
- What has the child said about the sexual behaviors?
- Do the child's sexual behaviors seem different from those of his or her peers?
- Is any force, coercion, bribery, or threat used in relation to the sexual behaviors?

- Does the child hurt himself or herself or anyone else in relation to the sexual behaviors?
- Does anyone complain about the child's sexual behaviors?
- What interventions have been made to assist the child to stop the sexual behaviors?
- What has been the child's response to the interventions?
- What kinds of things do you say to the child or have you done about the sexual behaviors?

Causes of Children's Problematic Sexual Behaviors

Children exposed to certain conditions engage in problematic sexual behaviors (Gil & Johnson, 1993). Such children include

- those who lack adequate supervision.
- those who live in sexualized environments in which the sexual boundaries are diffuse or unstable. Pornography, explicit videos or R-rated movies, or adults who expose children to their own sexual behaviors and feelings contribute to a sexualized atmosphere.
- those who have lived in environments in which sex routinely is paired with aggression.
- those who have lived in sexually explicit environments in which sex was used as an exchange commodity.
- those who have been physically and emotionally abused or neglected.
- those who have been sexually abused by being made to observe, for the titillation of adults, genitalia or sexual behaviors.
- those who have been sexually abused by being observed or photographed naked for the sexual stimulation of others (two children may have been forced to engage in sex acts).
- those who have been sexually abused by direct physical contact with their bodies or by being used to stimulate others' bodies, sexually.

Also, while unknown at this time, it may be that physiological or hormonal differences account for variations in young children's sexual behaviors (Gil & Johnson, 1993). When children's emotional and physical space is routinely violated, this may leave an unconscious residue of distress related to sex, which then becomes manifest in increased sexual behaviors. In some children, the level of adult sexuality has simply overwhelmed their ability to integrate it into their developing sexuality, and they engage in the sexual behaviors to try to diffuse their confusion, tension, and anxiety.

Assessing Children's Problematic Sexual Behaviors

When it is determined that the child is engaging in some problematic sexual behaviors, further questioning of the child's parents/caretakers may provide helpful information prior to interviewing the child. The following are pertinent to each problematic sexual behavior.

- When did these sexual behaviors begin to really concern you?
- What is the context in which the behaviors occur (while dressing, bathing, playing, changing diapers, watching someone change clothes, etc.)?
- What was going on in the child's life at the time of the change in the child's sexual behaviors?
- What was happening in the life of the family at the time?
- Were there new or different people in the child's life during that time?
- Does the child say anything before, during, or after these sexual behaviors?
- Does the child ask to carry out these sexual behaviors with others? With whom?
- Has the child used any names when engaging in the sexual behaviors?
- Does the child have a preferred gender or age of a person with whom to engage in the sexual behaviors?

The answers to these questions may help the evaluator frame questions to the child. The child may feel more comfortable knowing that the evaluator already has a great deal of information, thus alleviating the need to describe the sexual behaviors himself or herself.

When evaluating children, it is essential that interviewers be aware of their own issues regarding sexuality. They should bear in mind that the child's purpose for engaging in the sexual behaviors may be different from that ascribed by an adult. Countertransference reactions by the evaluator may inhibit a child's ability to describe his or her experience.

The evaluator's attitude and style will assist the child to feel less apprehensive. A straightforward, positive, forthright, matter-of-fact attitude that lets the child know the interviewer is not judgmental, and expects to hear what has happened in order to understand what is going on, will help the child. Children are generally afraid that they will get into trouble if they engage in sexual behaviors. Thus it may be helpful if the evaluator, after talking with the parents, can offer honest reassurances that they are not in trouble.

When an evaluation is carried out to determine whether the child has been sexually misused or abused, the attention of the interviewer is not on the actual behaviors themselves, but on their antecedents. When the child and interviewer are clear about this, the child is less likely to be shy or ashamed or to deny the behaviors.

Interviewers should be aware of their physical contact with children. Children who engage in problematic sexual behaviors generally should not be touched during the interview, as this can cause them anxiety about the intent of the interviewer. Exceptions may arise in some cultures, but the interviewer should be very aware of the meaning of touch to the child.

Some children engage in sexual behaviors or say things that may fluster the evaluator during the interview. Rather than stopping the child, the interviewer may want to use the incident to further the aim of the interview. For example, one child grabbed the breast of an evaluator. Her reaction was a desire to scream and to slap the child! Instead, she said with composure, "That is my breast and not for you to touch. Do you do that to other people? Does someone want you to do that to them?" Another child tried to put her hand up the interviewer's dress. Shocked, the interviewer started to recoil from the little girl. But then, instead of admonishing the child, she said, "It seems like you have a hard time knowing what is okay and not okay about touching in private areas. With whom else do you do this?" When the child looked stymied, the interviewer asked, "With whom do you do the touching?" The girl said, "My mom, but I really don't like it."

Some children get anxious in evaluations and become physically assaultive. If they try to hurt the interviewer, a helpful rejoinder is, "I don't want you to hit me, but I do want to talk to you. Does anyone hit you like this?

When children repeatedly touch their own genitals during an interview, the interviewer should decide whether the behavior should be addressed. If addressing the behavior will further the aims of the interview, questions such as this may help: "You touched yourself. Do you ever see people touching their privates?"

The following questions are useful for questioning the child regarding the sexual behaviors. All standard procedures for child sexual abuse evaluations should be followed. These would be used only after the rapport-building and developmental-assessment phases of the evaluation.

- "I know that you have been doing some 'touching stuff.' Your mom and dad (whoever told) told me about it. I was wondering where you got the idea."
- "Today we are just trying to find out where you got the idea."
- "Did someone else give you the idea, or was it your idea?"
- "Did you see someone do the same kind of 'touching stuff' you do?"
- "Is the 'touching stuff' you are doing copycatting something you have seen?"

- "Where did you see it?" (Pursue relevant details to determine if the child saw it in person, on a video, etc.)

When a child is engaging in sexual behaviors with other children, these additional questions can be useful.

- "I know that you have been doing some 'touching stuff' with other children. Your mom and dad (whoever told) told me about it. How did the touching start?"
- "Did you want to do the touching?"
- "Did anyone say you had to do the touching?"
- "Did anyone say that something bad would happen if you didn't do it?"
- "Did you ask the other person to do the touching?"
- "Is there anyone else you did this with?"
- "Are there any other people who like to do the touching with you?"
- "Do any bigger people like to do this touching with you?"

These questions focus on the question of abuse of the child. If there is a concern that the child has abused another person, a separate interview will be necessary (see Gil & Johnson, 1993).

If abuse or neglect is not revealed in the interview, yet there is concern for the child due to his or her sexual behaviors, diffuse physical, emotional, and sexual boundaries in the family can be assessed (Gil & Johnson, 1993).

The first author is currently developing a boundary questionnaire to be filled out by the adults in the home to aid in this assessment. It should be noted that when children have lived in environments with very poor boundaries, they may not know what to report to an evaluator. They do not inherently know what rights they can expect regarding emotional space and privacy. Having no doors on the bathrooms or bedrooms could be highly intrusive. There may also be exhibitionistic behavior by an adult that the child would not know to report to the evaluator. What children know when they are young is what they have become accustomed to. Sleeping or bathing with adults might be improperly sexualized by the adult and the child would not know that this could be sexual misuse.

Children find it more difficult to know when a female is being sexually inappropriate or abusive with them than they do with a male. This is an additional area for assessment. Mothers' or other female caretakers' overly diligent washing of a child's genitals, observation and measurement of a child's genitals and breast development, and sleeping nude with the child are examples that are frequently unreported by children. A mother who bathes with her child and asks the child to wash her breasts or buttocks may not be behaving in ways that seem inappropriate to a child. While they may not think to report such behavior, gentle questioning can allow children to describe behaviors by adult females with which they feel uncomfortable. Determining whether the behavior is sexually abusive may prove difficult, but if the child feels uncomfortable, the mother/female caretaker can be alerted to desist from the behavior. Follow-up will be necessary to assure that the behavior has stopped.

CONCLUSION

In some instances, suspicion arises regarding sexual abuse or misuse of a child based on an increase in sexual behaviors. Research on children who have been sexually abused indicates that many of these children engage in more sexual behaviors than do children who have not been sexually abused; however, importantly, many children who have not been sexually abused also engage in similar sexual behaviors.

This chapter provides the evaluator with some guidelines regarding natural and healthy sexual behaviors in young children. Further, 15 points are discussed that are indicators of when children's sexual behaviors become of concern. Tables 2 and 3 allow the evaluator to see whether a specific behavior is within the natural and healthy range, is of concern, or requires immediate evaluation by a professional trained in sexual abuse.

Standard methods of assessing children's sexual behaviors are discussed and relevant literature is reviewed.

The many different antecedents of problematic sexual behaviors in children are also discussed. Note is made that family disruption, without abuse, can be an antecedent of increased behavioral problems, including sexual behaviors.

Suggestions regarding questioning parents and children regarding problematic sexual behaviors are made.

Recommendations

1. **THAT** evaluators be familiar with the everyday behaviors of nonabused young children. Without this ongoing contact, interviewers can misperceive children's actions or behaviors. When professionals are only around children with problem behaviors, they may lose their ability to distinguish between what is natural and healthy and what is problematic.

2.   **THAT** evaluators for sexual abuse routinely ask about the sexual behaviors of children. If not questioned, the parent/caretakers may not bring this area up. Parents often rely on the professionals to ask the applicable questions. A written questionnaire format is suggested.

3.   **THAT** if a child is referred due to problematic sexual behavior but an evaluation does not reveal sexual abuse, the evaluator remember that there are many reasons for problematic sexual behaviors other than overt abuse. Physical and emotional abuse, neglect, overly sexualized environments, violence mixed with overt sexuality in the home, and homes with poor boundaries also produce children with increased sexual behavior. These cases may require diligent intervention, both protective and therapeutic.

4.   **THAT** a clinician assess whether to accept for treatment a child who is engaging in highly sexualized behaviors, or first to call in law enforcement or child protective services for a sexual abuse evaluation, and then proceed with an evaluation for treatment.

5.   **THAT** caution be exercised regarding the understanding of children's sexual behaviors, as research data are in the early stages and most are from clinical inference.

6.   **THAT** empirically based research on children's sexual behaviors be undertaken to fill a gap in our knowledge.

7.   **THAT** evaluators use caution when ascribing meaning to children's sexual behaviors. Research regarding children's drawings and children's play with dolls indicates that few children, abused or not, draw genitals on human figures, and that both abused and nonabused children engage in sexually suggestive behaviors with dolls.

REFERENCES

APSAC. (1990). *Guidelines for psychosocial evaluation of suspected sexual abuse in young children.* Task Force of the American Professional Society on the Abuse of Children, Chicago, Ill.

Allen, M. E., Jones, P. D., & Nash, M. R. (1989). Detection of sexual abuse among emotionally disturbed preschoolers: Unique effects of sexual abuse as observed on doll play and the standard assessment procedures. Paper presented at the Annual Convention of the American Psychological Association, New Orleans, La.

Boat, B. W., & Everson, M. D. (1988). Use of anatomical dolls among professionals in sexual abuse evaluations. *Child Abuse and Neglect, 12,* 171–180.

Cohen, J. A., & Mannarino, A. P. (1988). Psychological symptoms in sexually abused girls. *Child Abuse and Neglect, 12,* 571–577.

Conte, J., Sorenson, E., Fogarty, L., & Roasa, J. (1991). Evaluating children's reports of sexual abuse: A survey of professionals. *American Journal of Orthopsychiatry, 61,* 428–437.

Deblinger, E., McLeer, S. V., Atkins, M. S., Ralphe, D., & Foa, E. (1989). Post-traumatic stress in sexually abused, physically abused, and nonabused children. *Child Abuse and Neglect, 13,* 403–408.

Everson, M., & Boat, B. W. (1990). Sexualized doll play among children: Implications for the use of anatomical dolls in sexual abuse evaluations. *Journal of the American Academy of Child and Adolescent Psychiatry, 29,* 736–742.

Faller, K. (1993). *Child sexual abuse: Intervention and treatment issues.* Washington, D.C.: U.S. Department of Health and Human Services, National Center on Child Abuse & Neglect. (Contract number: HHS-105-89-1730)

Finkelhor, D. (1979). *Sexually victimized children.* New York: Free Press.

Finkelhor, D. (1983). *Childhood sexual experiences: A retrospective survey.* Unpublished manuscript, University of New Hampshire, Durham.

Friedrich, W. (1991). Sexual behavior in sexually abused children. In J. Briere (Ed.), *Treating victims of child sexual abuse* (pp. 15–27). San Francisco: Jossey-Bass.

Friedrich, W. (1993). Sexual victimization and sexual behavior in children: A review of recent literature. *Child Abuse and Neglect, 17,* 59–66.

Friedrich, W., Beilke, R., & Urquiza, A. (1988). Behavior problems in young sexually abused boys. *Journal of Interpersonal Violence, 3*(1), 21–27.

Friedrich, W., Grambsch, P., Broughton, D., Kuiper, J., & Beilke, R. (1991). Normative sexual behavior in children. *Pediatrics, 88*(3), 456–464.

Friedrich, W., Grambsch, P., Damon, L., Hewitt, S., Koverola, C., Lang, R., Wolfe, V., & Broughton, D. (1992). The Child Sexual Behavior Inventory: Normative and clinical comparisons. *Psychological Assessment, 4*(3), 303–311.

Gale, J., Thompson, R. J., Moran, T., & Sack, W. H. (1988). Sexual abuse in young children: Its clinical presentation and characteristic patterns. *Child Abuse and Neglect, 12,* 163–170.

Gil, E., & Johnson, T. C. (1993). *Sexualized children: Assessment and treatment of sexualized children and children who molest.* Rockville, Md.: Launch Press.

Goldman, R., & Goldman, J. (1988). *Show me yours: Understanding children's sexuality.* London: Penguin Books.

Hibbard, R. A., & Hartman, G. L. (1990). Emotional indicators in human figure drawings of sexually victimized and nonabused children. *Journal of Clinical Psychology, 46,* 211–219.

Hibbard, R. A., Roghmann, K., & Hockelman, R. A. (1987). Genitalia in children's drawings: An association with sexual abuse. *Pediatrics, 79,* 129–137.

Jampole, L., & Weber, M. K. (1987). An assessment of the behavior of sexually abused and nonsexually abused children with anatomically correct dolls. *Child Abuse and Neglect, 11,* 187–192.

Johnson, T. C. (1993a, July). Definition of sex play. Paper presented at the Indian Health Service Conference, Seattle, Wash.

Johnson, T. C. (1993b). Behaviors related to sex and sexuality in preschool children. Self-published.

Johnson, T. C. (1993c). Behaviors related to sex and sexuality in kindergarten through fourth-grade children. Self-published.

Johnson, T. C. (1994). Children's natural and healthy sexual behaviors and characteristics of children's problematic sexual behaviors. Self-published.

Johnson, T. C., & Aoki, W. (1993). Sexual behaviors of latency-aged children in residential care. *Residential Treatment for Children and Youth, 11*(1), 1–22.

Kendall-Tackett, K. A. (1992). Professionals' standards of "normal" behavior with anatomical dolls and factors that influence these standards. *Child Abuse and Neglect, 16,* 727–733.

Kendall-Tackett, K., Williams, L., & Finkelhor, D. (1993). Impact of sexual abuse on children: A review and synthesis of recent empirical studies. *Psychological Bulletin, 113*(1), 164–180.

Kolko, D. J., Moser, J. T., & Weldy, S. R. (1988). Behavioral/emotional indicators of child sexual abuse in child psychiatric inpatients: A controlled comparison with physical abuse. *Child Abuse and Neglect, 12,* 529.

Mannarino, A. P., Cohen, J. A., & Gregor, M. (1989). Emotional and behavioral difficulties in sexually abused girls. *Journal of Interpersonal Violence, 4,* 437–451.

Sivan, A. B., Schor, D. P., Koeppl, G. K., & Noble, L. D. (1988). Interaction of normal children with anatomical dolls. *Child Abuse and Neglect, 12,* 295–304.

Waterman, J., & Lusk, R. (1993). Psychological testing in evaluation of child sexual abuse. *Child Abuse and Neglect, 17,* 145–159.

Weinstein, R. J., Trickett, P. K., & Putnam, F. W. (1989). Sexual and aggressive behavior in girls experiencing child abuse and precocious puberty. Paper presented at the Annual Convention of the American Psychological Association, New Orleans, La.

White, S., Halpin, B. M., Strom, G. A., & Santilli, G. (1988). Behavioral comparison of young sexually abused, neglected, and nonreferred children. *Journal of Clinical Child Psychology, 17,* 53–61.

White, S., Strom, G. A., Santilli, G., & Halpin, B. M. (1986). Interviewing young sexual abuse victims with anatomically correct dolls. *Child Abuse and Neglect, 10,* 519–529.

Wolfe, D. A., & Mosk, M. D. (1983). Behavioral comparisons of children from abusive and distressed families. *Journal of Consulting and Clinical Psychology, 51,* 702–708.

4

Children's Comprehension of Truths, Lies, and False Beliefs

Nancy Walker Perry

Do children understand what it means to tell "the truth, the whole truth, and nothing but the truth" in cases of alleged sexual assault? Professional opinion on that question is divided. Because the consequences of sexual assault allegations are so serious, professionals must actively seek the truth in each case, eschewing preconceived notions of outcome and fanatic advocacy. Objectivity is essential. But truthseeking involves more than an attempt to be impartial; it also involves assessment of the belief systems of those children who provide testimony. In other words, it is important for professionals to understand how children comprehend such concepts as truths, lies, and false beliefs. Moreover, it is vital to understand how children's comprehension of those concepts may affect their testimonial accuracy. The purpose of this chapter is to describe children's understanding of different types of beliefs and their comprehension of the obligation to tell the truth. The chapter also discusses factors that may influence truthtelling, and outlines some strategies for maximizing truthtelling in cases involving allegations of child sexual assault.

Do children understand what it means to tell "the truth, the whole truth, and nothing but the truth" in cases of alleged sexual assault? Professional

---

Portions of this chapter appear in Perry, N.W., and Wrightsman, L. S. (1991). *The child witness.* Newbury Park, Calif.: Sage. Reprinted with permission from Sage Publications, Inc.

73

opinion on that question is divided. Mental health, legal, and scientific communities disagree over whether, or to what extent, children's reports of sexual assault are truthful. Some argue that children are especially prone to suggestion, fabrication, confabulation, serious memory distortions, and outright lying (e.g., Raskin, 1992; Varendonck, 1911, cited in Goodman, 1984). In fact, in some cases, young children have been excluded as witnesses at trial because of a judicial ruling that they could not distinguish the truth from a lie (e.g., *State of New Jersey v. DR*, 1988). Others argue emphatically that children have superb memories and are quite capable of accurately reporting what they know (e.g., Faller, 1984; Goodman, 1992). In support of this argument is the fact that even children of very tender years (ages two to three) have been ruled competent at trial, and their testimony has, in some cases, been perceived as highly credible (e.g., Jones & Krugman, 1986).

Which viewpoint is correct? Should children's accounts of sexual assault be trusted? Under what circumstances should children's allegations be believed? These questions are vital for everyone who is party to a sexual assault investigation—victims, defendants, and society.

Because the consequences of sexual assault allegations are so serious, professionals must actively seek the truth in each case, eschewing preconceived notions of outcome and fanatic advocacy. Objectivity is essential. But truthseeking involves more than an attempt to be impartial; it also involves assessment of the belief systems of those children who provide testimony. In other words, it is important for professionals to understand how children comprehend such concepts as truths, lies, and false beliefs. Moreover, it is vital to understand how children's comprehension of those concepts may affect their testimonial accuracy. In this regard, Haugaard (1992a) notes:

> How children define the truth influences their ability to distinguish it from a lie and to provide what adults consider truthful testimony. If children define certain types of statements or actions as the truth, while most adults define them as lies, then a child could speak the truth from his or her perspective and yet tell a lie from the perspective of most adults. This could result in the child unintentionally providing misleading information during an investigation or courtroom proceeding. (p. 1)

As Haugaard notes, "It is unclear, however, whether these differences could have a meaningful influence on a child's ability to provide truthful testimony" (p. 1).

The purpose of this chapter is to help practitioners avoid the problem described by Haugaard. Toward that end, it describes children's understanding of different types of beliefs and their comprehension of the obligation to tell the truth. The chapter also discusses factors that may influence truthtelling, and outlines some strategies for maximizing truthtelling in cases involving allegations of child sexual assault.

DEVELOPMENTAL CHANGES IN COMPREHENSION

A truthful statement is characterized by five elements: (1) the statement is true; (2) the speaker believes the statement to be true; (3) in uttering the statement, the speaker intends the statement to be truthful; (4) the speaker wants to convey truthfulness; and (5) the speaker expects the listener to believe the statement because, of course, it is truthful (see Table 1). The great majority of children, even at the tender age of three, have a grasp of the difference between truth and falsehood (Leekam, 1991), and of the duty to tell the truth in court (Johnson & Foley, 1984).

Although information on children's definitions of the truth is sparse, some evidence indicates that young children's definitions may differ from those of older children and adults. For instance, four-year-old children may label any verbal indiscretion (such as swearing) a lie (Haugaard, 1992b; Peterson, Peterson, & Seeto, 1983; Piaget 1932/1965). Although older children may not follow such "logic," even most six-year-olds do not consider the speaker's intention (i.e., "good" or "bad") when assessing whether an inaccurate statement is a mistake or a lie (Wimmer, Gruber, & Perner, 1984).

By age four, children distinguish lies from truth on the basis of the factuality of the statement (Strichartz, 1980; Strichartz & Burton, 1990). Although factuality remains a critically important element of children's definition of lies, its centrality decreases as age increases (Burton & Strichartz, 1991), so that sometime between the ages of six and 10, children begin to place more emphasis upon the belief system of the speaker than upon the factuality of the statement (Strichartz & Burton, 1990). In other words, with increasing age, they begin to focus more on whether the speaker *believes* the statement to be true than on the objective truth of the utterance.

Haugaard, Reppucci, Laird, and Nauful (1991) and Haugaard (1992a) examined one aspect of children's definitions of the truth: whether young children (ages 4 to 10) categorized an inaccurate statement, made at the instruction of a parent, to be the truth or a lie. They found that 95% of the children accurately reported that the false statement constituted a lie. The form of the instruction to lie, provided by the mother of a child depicted in a videotaped incident, did not influence their conclusions. Indeed, 71% of the children were able to articulate that it was the inaccuracy of the statement that made it a lie. The three children who said that the statement was the truth were in preschool or kindergarten. Haugaard (1992a) says:

It appears that two of the children believed that by making the
statement to a police officer the girl must have been telling the
truth. The responses of these few children raises [sic] some
concern that a small percent of young children may have a
definition of the truth that does not correspond with the definition held by most adults. The results suggest that this concern is
most relevant for 4- and 5-year-old children and not for older
children. (p. 5)

Thus a "mature" concept of truthtelling usually emerges by the time children
enter school. Of course, the ability to comprehend the concepts of "truth"
and "truthtelling" does not necessarily predict moral action (Burton, 1976).
For example, an elementary school child may be able to articulate convincingly that children should not cheat on tests, but when given the opportunity
to copy from another child's paper during an exam, the seemingly scrupu-
lous child may cheat with abandon. Similarly, in a case of assault, the child
victim may talk persuasively about the importance of truthtelling, yet may
knowingly make false statements.

Verbal Falsehoods

The category of "verbal falsehood" includes such disparate elements as
lies (i.e., intentional deceptions), false beliefs (i.e., mistakes), and innocent
deceptions (e.g., jokes, irony, and hyperbole). These elements can be distinguished from one another, and from truthfulness, on the basis of (1) the
veracity of the statement, (2) the speaker's belief in the statement, (3) the
speaker's intention in conveying the statement, and (4) the speaker's expectation regarding the listener's belief in the statement (see Table 1).

LIES. A lie is characterized by five elements: (1) the statement is false; (2)
the speaker believes the statement to be false; (3) in uttering the statement,
the speaker *intends to deceive* the listener; (4) the speaker *wants to convey truthfulness*; and (5) the speaker expects the listener to believe the statement
(Coleman & Kay, 1981; see Table 1). Definitions of lying are similar to definitions of deception; however, deception incorporates a wide range of behaviors, including gesture, silence, and mimicry, whereas lying typically is
defined as an intentionally deceptive, stated message (Leekam, 1992a).
Leekam (1992b) argues that "the ability to manipulate *beliefs* and not just
behavior is the hallmark of intentional deception" (p. 48, italics added). In
other words, lying involves convincing the listener that the speaker's statement is credible (whether or not the statement is, in fact, truthful).

TABLE 1
Distinctions Among Truths, Lies, False Beliefs, and Innocent Deceptions

	Category			
	Truth	*Lie*	*False Belief*	*Innocent Deception*
Statement:	True	False	False	False
Speaker believes statement is:	True	False	True	False
Speaker intends statement to be:	Truthful	Deceitful	Truthful	Deceitful
Speaker wants to convey:	Truthfulness	Truthfulness	Truthfulness	Deceitfulness
Speaker's motive is:	Good	Bad	Good	Good
Speaker expects listener to:	Believe statement	Believe statement	Believe statement	Not believe statement
False statement is:	(not applicable)	Intended	Unintended	Intended
Examples:	Accurate reports	Lies, hoaxes, "white" lies, hypocrisy	Misperceptions, inaccurate interpretations	Jokes, teasing, irony, sarcasm, hyperbole, understatement, banter

Leekam (1992b) notes that the ability to lie requires too much sophistication for most young children (that is, those under age seven):

> Young children's lies often fail. They seem to miss the point that the success of a lie depends on the listener believing what you say. This doesn't mean that young children do not attempt to lie. Nor that they have no notion of how to deceive. But to be successful at lying you need to be aware of what the listener will think–whether they will believe or disbelieve what you say. (p. 47)

Thus young children may try to lie, but most often they will be unsuccessful in their attempts to deceive others intentionally. For example, in cases of alleged sexual assault, they may tell simple but untrue stories suggesting that abuse did or did not occur, but when pressed for details, the stories are likely to fall apart (Raskin & Yuille, 1989).

FALSE BELIEFS. A false belief is a mistaken notion characterized by several elements: (1) the statement is false; (2) the speaker believes the statement to be *true*; (3) in uttering the statement, the speaker has *no* intention to deceive; (4) the speaker wants to convey truthfulness; and (5) the speaker expects the listener to believe the statement (see Table 1). False beliefs arise from misperceptions and inaccurate interpretations rather than from motives to deceive. Under certain circumstances, a child's false belief may become a central element in a case of alleged sexual assault. Suppose, for instance, that the child's parents are in a bitter custody battle. During a regularly scheduled visit, the noncustodial parent bathes the child, including washing genitalia and applying ointment to soothe a genital rash. Upon returning home, the child reports that the noncustodial parent "did something bad and touched me in my private parts." In this case, the child's statement is based on a false belief (that washing and treating the genitalia constituted "bad" actions). Because children younger than age nine or 10 have difficulty interpreting situations and making inferences (Perry & Wrightsman, 1991), their statements may be more likely to result from false beliefs.

INNOCENT DECEPTIONS. Innocent deceptions are characterized by several elements: (1) the statement is false; (2) the speaker knows that the statement is false; (3) the speaker *intends the statement to be deceitful, but in a playful sense*; (4) the speaker intends to convey deceitfulness; and (5) the speaker expects the listener to *not* believe the statement (see Table 1). In other words, innocent deceptions involve false statements that are intended to "hoodwink" the listener—for example, jokes, teasing, hyperbole, and sarcasm. It is very unlikely that innocent deceptions will be part of the investigation of a sexual assault allegation.

Developmental Norms

At what age are children capable of understanding the differences among truths, lies, and false beliefs? The results of empirical studies (e.g., Leekam, 1992; Wimmer & Perner, 1983; Wimmer et al., 1984) suggest some developmental norms for children's comprehension of these concepts (see Table 2).

According to Flavell, Mumme, Green, and Flavell (1992), "The majority view is that most 3-year-olds do not yet possess a representational conception of the mind [i.e., knowledge that the mind is a place to store symbolic representations of the real world] and consequently really do not know what beliefs are—either false beliefs or true ones" (p. 974). A variation of this perspective is offered by Wellman (1990), who suggests that three-year-olds do have some understanding of what true beliefs are (namely, internal, mental representations of reality), but they do not yet understand false beliefs. However, even children who are too young to define such concepts as "truth" and "lie" can deceive others by manipulating their *behaviors*, an "ability" that

TABLE 2
Truth, Lies, and False Beliefs: Some Developmental Norms

Age of Attainment	Ability
3–4	Can deceive by manipulating *behaviors* (rather than beliefs), but not very skillfully.
4	Can distinguish mistakes from lies, but still tend to characterize false statements as lies.
4–5	Can distinguish deceitful lies from joking lies (i.e., innocent deceptions). Can deceive by manipulating listener's belief of speaker's *statement* (rather than of speaker).
6	Can understand the concept of "lie."
5–7	Can distinguish white lies from irony when asked about speaker's intention about listener's *belief*.
7	Can deceive by manipulating listener's belief of speaker's *intention* (rather than statement alone). Can lie skillfully.
8	Can distinguish sarcasm from other forms of falsehood.

emerges at about the age of three. For example, through pleading or whining, a three-year-old may be capable of manipulating an adult into giving the child a piece of candy. In such a case, the manipulation is successful, although the child had formed no mental intent to *deceive* the adult.

Wimmer and Perner (1983) and Perner, Leekam, and Wimmer (1987) argue that children exhibit an understanding of false beliefs at four to five years of age. In this regard, Sodian, Taylor, Harris, and Perner (1991) note:

> For example, [four- to five-year-old children predict] that a
> person who has placed an object in a container and does not
> witness its unexpected transfer to another container will mistak-
> enly search for the object in the original container; similarly,
> they realize that a person who is shown a familiar candy box
> will expect it to have its standard contents [i.e., candy] if that
> person has not witnessed their surreptitious replacement. By
> contrast, most children younger than 3½ years do not under-
> stand such false beliefs: they predict that a person will search
> for a hidden object where it really is, or will know the actual
> rather than the apparent contents of a closed container. (p. 468)

Thus, at ages four to five, children become capable of deceiving others by manipulating the listener's *belief in an untrue statement.* For example, young children are notorious for convincing their peers that monsters and goblins really exist. If a child of this age actually believes in monsters, then telling others of their "existence" does not constitute lying, but rather the promulgation of a false belief.   On the other hand, if the child does not believe in monsters but still tries to convince others of their presence, then the child is engaging in verbal deceit (either lying or innocent deception).

At approximately age seven, children develop the capacity to deceive others by manipulating the *belief of the speaker's intention.* In other words, children become capable of making adults think that they are speaking truthfully when the children know that, in fact, they are not doing so.   At that point, children can lie skillfully (Quinn, 1988). For example, a child at this stage may intentionally deceive an adult by convincing the adult that the child is speaking truthfully in alleging that abuse occurred when the child knows that it did not.

Within another year (i.e., age eight), children can begin to make finer discriminations among various types of falsehoods (e.g., sarcasm, hyperbole, understatement, banter).   At that point, therefore, they may become more aware of subtle attempts at manipulation by adults with ulterior motives (e.g., "coaching" the child to falsely allege sexual abuse).

What is the practical implication of all this information about truths, lies, and false beliefs? The point is that, although a child under the age of seven may make a false statement in court or to an adult assessing an allegation of child sexual abuse, it is most likely that such a statement will be born of false beliefs rather than of an intention to deceive. After a child reaches the age of seven, the investigator should be more concerned with discerning intentional deceits from false beliefs.

THEORIES OF MORAL DEVELOPMENT

An understanding of the child's comprehension of truths, lies, and false beliefs is helpful but insufficient when assessing allegations of sexual assault. It also is important to consider the combination of child's age, stage of moral reasoning, and gender when assessing the youngster's comprehension of the duty to be truthful. Several individuals have provided useful theories of the development of morality (Gilligan, 1982; Kohlberg, 1963; Lickona, 1983).

A review of Lickona's theory of the stages of moral reasoning (based on the work of Kohlberg, 1963) suggests that when children are asked to speak truthfully about events, their responses may depend on their age and moral frame of reference (see Table 3). According to Lickona's theory, children in stage 1 of moral development (four and younger) tend to believe that it is right that they get their own way. They are motivated by rewards and punishments. Their concepts of good and bad are not yet well defined; therefore, they may be persuaded more easily to stray from the truth. At this level, truth can mean what is most advantageous for the child. For example, if the child wants to live with a particular parent—regardless of the objective qualifications of that adult to care for the child—then the child may testify that the chosen parent is the better caregiver. In order to avoid this problem, the assessor should encourage the child to tell about events as they really happened. Questions that ask for simple descriptions of specific actions—not conclusions or inferences—should help to avoid pitfalls lurking at this stage. For example, it is better to ask, "What does Mommy/Daddy do when you are put to bed?" than to ask, "Is Mommy/Daddy a good parent?"

At stage 2 of moral development (generally kindergarten age), being good (and, therefore, truthful) rests on obedience to authority. With children at this level, descriptions of the truth can change depending on the child's allegiances. This potential problem is of particular importance in cases involving incest or child custody. For instance, the investigator may need to know with which parent the child wants to live. However, if the child has some understanding that one parent may be sent to prison on the basis of the child's testimony, the youngster may be reluctant to speak the truth. If this problem arises, it may be helpful to impress upon the child that the judge—not one of the parents—is the authority who must be obeyed, and that the judge wants to know how things really happened.

From ages six through eight or nine, children operating at stage 3 tend to believe in a "you scratch my back and I'll scratch yours" philosophy of reciprocal benefit. At this stage, children need to understand what they have to gain by testifying truthfully. Because they are not at the level of conscience-

TABLE 3

Lickona's Stages of Moral Reasoning: Implications for the Courtroom

Level	Stage	Age Attained	Motivation for Good Behavior	Techniques for Maximizing Truthful Responses
1	Reward and punishment	Before age 4	To obtain rewards and avoid punishments.	Ask for simple descriptions of specific actions; do *not* ask for conclusions or inferences.
2	Obedience to authority	5–6	To be perceived as obedient.	Impress upon the child that the judge must be obeyed.
3	Reciprocal benefit	7–8	To help others, so long as self also benefits.	Explain in simple terms how testifying truthfully will serve justice, and benefit the child as well.
4	"Good girl"/ "good boy"	9–12	To be perceived as "nice."	Impress upon the child that telling the truth is "good."
5	Social contracts	Adolescence	To maintain social order.	Explain how our system of justice is meant to function.
6	Principled action	Some adults	To uphold universal ethical principles.	No explanations or reminders are necessary.

guided behavior, they may be frightened out of testifying truthfully if they believe that they may be more harmed than helped by telling what actually happened. (Indeed, this problem may arise for adults when they have been threatened or intimidated.) With youngsters at stage 3, it is important to explain in simple terms how testifying truthfully will serve justice, and benefit the child as well. It may be helpful to refer to other incidents from the child's personal experience that show how justice was served when the child spoke truthfully.

Lickona suggests that children at stage 4 are eager to please others and to be seen as "nice." This stage typically encompasses the middle to upper elementary grades (ages nine through 12). Children at this level usually want to say whatever pleases important adults. As their ability to make inferences improves, they become adept at reading the intentions and desires of adults. Thus testifying truthfully can be compromised when the child says what he or she thinks an important adult wants to hear. Those in authority should impress upon the child that what the judge wants to hear is what actually happened, no matter how unpleasant the events may have been, and no matter how much distaste others' expressions may show.

Adolescents at stage 5 usually want to keep social systems operating smoothly. They understand the need to meet personal obligations, including the need to testify truthfully. At this stage, explanations of our system of justice may be helpful.

Stage 6 focuses on adherence to universal ethical principles. It is rare even for adults to attain this level of moral reasoning.

Some children (and adults) never progress beyond the rudimentary levels of moral reasoning (Kohlberg, 1963). Moreover, if a person has been traumatized or threatened, regression to an earlier level of functioning may occur (see Pynoos & Eth, 1984). In such a case, use of instructions and techniques associated with earlier levels of functioning (described above) may prove beneficial.

Gender also may be an important variable to consider. Kohlberg's (1963) six-stage theory of moral reasoning was based on his study of developing boys. His approach has a "rules" orientation, with emphasis on abstract concepts, including the notion of justice. In order to progress in moral reasoning, according to Kohlberg, an individual must move toward increasingly abstract notions of conscience based upon "universal ethical principles"— that is, principles that transcend gender and culture. However, research by Gilligan (1982) suggests that, unlike most men, most women possess a "responsibility" orientation, rather than a "rules" orientation. In other words, women and girls tend to emphasize sensitivity to others and to the concepts of compassion and care, rather than adherence to abstract principles of justice. Applying Gilligan's theory, one might expect female victims to be more concerned with the welfare of everyone concerned in the case than with punishing the offender. Research on that prediction, however, is lacking. The point is that when children are called to testify in court, their moral frame of reference—and, therefore, their understanding of what it means to speak "truthfully"—may be influenced by both stage of moral reasoning and gender. Therefore, clinicians should attempt to discern the level of each child's moral reasoning ability, and how closely the child's behavior conforms to his or her reasoning.

CHILDREN'S COMPREHENSION OF THE OBLIGATION TO TELL THE TRUTH

Many courts administer an oath as a means to ensure the witness's understanding of the obligation to testify truthfully. The purpose of the testimonial oath is twofold: "to alert the witness to the moral duty to testify truthfully and to deter false testimony by establishing a legal basis for perjury prosecution" (*People v. Parks*, 1976, p. 366).

Use of the oath requirement harks back to the common-law practice of barring from the stand individuals who either did not understand the religious implications of an oath or would not or could not take an oath (Myers, 1987). Today, the oath continues to play a role in legal proceedings, although some jurisdictions now allow witnesses to substitute a secular affirmation for a religious oath (see Cleary, 1984). For example, Rule 603 of the U.S. Federal Rules of Evidence states, "[B]efore testifying, every witness shall be required to declare that he will testify truthfully, by oath or affirmation administered in a form calculated to awaken his conscience and impress his mind with his duty to do so" (Fed. R. Evid.). The United States statute from the state of Georgia is representative, stating in part, "Children who do not understand the nature of an oath shall be incompetent witnesses" (Georgia Code Ann., 1982).

Under this approach, the child need not be able to define the term "oath," or even to give an example of an oath, in order to be judged competent. Consider the case of *State v. Eiler* (Mont. 1988), heard by the supreme court of the state of Montana. In that case, an eight-year-old sexual abuse victim was judged competent to testify to incidents that had occurred four years earlier, although she could not remember where she had lived at the time of the alleged abuse or what clothes she and the defendant had been wearing when the acts took place. The child's testimony undoubtedly influenced the jurors' verdict of guilt. The defendant appealed the decision, partly on the

grounds that the child did not appreciate "the duty to tell the truth," a corol-
lary of the oath requirement. In order to show that the girl did not know the
difference between the truth and a lie, counsel for the defendant quoted a
portion of the child witness's deposition (762 P.2d 210 [Mont, 1982], p. 214):

Q: Is there a reason for telling the truth?
A: Yes.
Q: What's the reason for telling the truth?
A: (No response)
Q: Do you believe in God?
A: Yes.
Q: Okay. And does God have anything to do with you telling the truth?
A: Yes.
Q: What does God have to do with that?
A: I don't know.

In citing this testimony, counsel for the defendant argued that the child did
not know what it meant to tell the truth. An alternative explanation, of course,
is that the child found the questions abstract, and therefore confusing; she
could not answer the questions if she did not understand them (Perry,
McAuliff, Tam, Claycomb, Dostal, and Flanagan, in press). Moreover, the
appeals court ruled that defense counsel had neglected to call attention to the
statements made immediately prior to and immediately following the foregoing testimony:

Q: Okay. Now do you know what it means to tell the truth?
A: Yes.
Q: What does it mean to tell the truth?
A: To tell what really happened.
...
Q: Okay. Does God care if you tell the truth?
A: Yes.
Q: And do you wish to please God?
A: Yes.
Q: Okay. What do you think happens if you don't tell the truth?
A: You won't be resurrected.
...
Q: Okay. Do you get in trouble for not telling the truth, not telling the
     truth at school?
A: Yes.
Q: What happens if you don't tell the truth at school?
A: You have to go to detention.
Q: What is detention?

A: You have to stay in at recess.

Q: And do you ever—would you get in trouble at home for not telling the truth?

A: Yes.

Q: What happens if you don't tell the truth?

A: You have to go to bed.

The appellate court ruled that the child in this case did understand the difference between the truth and a lie, and, having agreed to tell the truth with the understanding that telling a falsehood results in punishment, the child had complied with the spirit of the oath requirement. Similarly, the state of Texas oath statute was considered fulfilled in *Gonzales v. State* (1988) when questions asked by the judge and the prosecutor were sufficient to "impress" witnesses who were minors with their duty to be truthful.

Even a witness who has been "duly impressed" may not be disqualified if he or she has shown some tendency to prevaricate outside the courtroom. The fact that a child has lied previously does not render him or her incompetent. Indeed, Myers (1987) notes that there are few, if any, witnesses who have not "stretched the truth" (p. 99). Past moral lapses do not relate to competence; rather, such weaknesses speak to the credibility of the witness, an attribute that must be assessed by the judge or jury during the course of the trial.

Professionals who work with children who are called to testify need to understand that, as witnesses, children must be judged both competent and credible. In order to be found competent as witnesses, children must possess (among other attributes) a sense of the obligation to tell the truth. If speaking truthfully is defined for them, and if the obligation to tell the truth is impressed upon them, absent other influences, most children—even very young ones—speak the truth as they understand it. However, certain factors can substantially influence truth telling.

FACTORS THAT MAY INFLUENCE TRUTHTELLING

Two sets of factors may have an impact on truthtelling: (1) intrapersonal variables and (2) external influences. Professionals who attempt to ascertain the veracity of a child's report of sexual assault should consider both of these sets of factors.

Intrapersonal Variables

Intrapersonal variables that may influence children's truthtelling include developmental sophistication, ability to record memories and to use memory strategies, and ability to communicate.

DEVELOPMENTAL SOPHISTICATION. Clinicians should assess children's developmental sophistication and attempt to determine how their intelligence and developmental level may influence interpersonal relationships and the reporting of events (see discussion of Lickona's stages of moral reasoning, above). For example, brighter children may be more articulate and complete in their descriptions. One caveat is in order, however. It stands to reason that gifted children also might be more adept at deceiving others. Similarly, children who are more mature socially are likely to be more aware of the details of sexual intimacy than are less mature children (Everson & Boat, 1990).

The point is that it is important to assess more than the *statement* provided by a child. The statement's validity must be judged in the context of both the situation and the personal characteristics of the particular child. For example, spontaneous statements (situation) provided by younger, more naive children (personal characteristics) are more likely to be credible than are statements provided by "savvy" teens (personal characteristics) who have something to gain from lying (situation) (see Perry & Wrightsman, 1991).

ABILITY TO RECORD MEMORIES AND TO USE MEMORY STRATEGIES. Before a child can provide an account of an event, the child must be able to perceive, attend to, and record the event in memory. No matter how well intentioned, a child cannot tell the truth about an incident if a memory for the event does not exist. Even if events are recorded in memory, children differ in their ability to retrieve the relevant information. For example, on free recall tasks, kindergartners and first graders typically recall only one or two facts about an incident, third and fourth graders about three, seventh and eighth graders about six, and adults between seven and eight (Marin, Holmes, Guth, & Kovac, 1979; Perry, Neilsen, Burns, Cunningham, & Jenkins, 1987). Children often know more than they can freely recall, but their ability to use memory strategies is limited. Memory strategies may include repeatedly rehearsing the material to be remembered, creating mnemonic rhymes, or putting small bits of information into larger chunks that can be remembered easily. Young children typically do not use memory strategies spontaneously. Without such strategies at their disposal, children under the age of six experience difficulty in freely recalling events, and it is only where such strategies are not needed that these children perform as well as do older children or adults (Brown, Bransford, Ferrara, & Campione, 1983). (See Perry, 1993, and Chapter 5, this volume, for discussion of these factors.)

ABILITY TO COMMUNICATE. After an event has been perceived and the details have been recorded in memory, the child must be able to communicate the particulars of the stored recollections. Some children generally are talkative (even about stressful events), whereas others are more reticent by nature. In addition, interviewer skill and other situational factors are likely to have a major impact on whether children of either communicative style discuss stressful events (see below; see also Chapter 8, this volume).

External Influences

A variety of external factors also may influence a child's recollection of events: salience of the events and details to be remembered, suggestions provided to the child (see Chapter 10, this volume), inducements given to the child to withhold information about the event in question, and the stress associated with the initial event and with the postevent interviews.

EVENT SALIENCE. In general, school-age children recall the details of familiar situations better than those associated with novel events (Johnson & Foley, 1984). This phenomenon was demonstrated in two studies of children who experienced group trauma. Elementary school children who had witnessed a sniper attack at their own building (a familiar setting) tended not to err in sequencing or estimating the duration of the event (Pynoos & Nader, 1989). In contrast, children kidnapped from Chowchilla, California, and buried in a school bus (an unfamiliar setting) produced significant memory errors in sequencing and estimating event duration (Terr, 1979).

On the other hand, when novel events are particularly salient, as often is true in cases of trauma, they are more likely to be remembered accurately. However, individuals' recollections of traumatic events may be influenced by their perceptions of life threat. For example, Pynoos and Nader (1989), researchers who interviewed the elementary school children who had witnessed a school-yard sniper attack, found that:

> [the children] altered their memory, or spatial representation of
> the incident, i.e., how far they were from the direct line of fire,
> in order to alter their degree of life threat. The exposed chil-
> dren apparently altered their spatial representations in order to
> minimize the renewal of traumatic anxiety or fear. In contrast,
> the nonexposed children, who exhibited no apparent fear of
> renewed anxiety, increased their proximity to the danger.
> (p. 240)

These findings suggest that while a salient event may be remembered, if it is perceived as life threatening, the details may be minimized (and, therefore, may be inaccurate). This conclusion has clear implications for the assessment of sexual assault. For example, if an assaulted child has been threatened with grave bodily harm, the details of the assault may be minimized because they are too traumatic to recall.

Children's memory of the "truth" also may be affected by their own imagined actions. A series of experiments conducted by Johnson and Foley (1984) demonstrated that school-age children (ages six to 12) have difficulty distinguishing plans they actually carry out from those they only think of doing. Thus, "inner plans of action may be more likely to become an inextricable part of memory in school-age children than in adults" (Pynoos & Nader, 1989, p. 240). Practically speaking, these findings suggest that clinicians must take care to determine whether a child's account is the product of actual experience or only of thoughts. In this regard, it may be helpful to ask for details of the account, as an imagined plan may be less likely to include rich detailing (Undeutsch, 1982; see also Chapter 9, this volume).

SUGGESTION. According to conventional wisdom, children are more suggestible than adults (see Goodman, Golding, & Haith, 1984). Certainly children, like adults, are subject to suggestion, but children are not as suggestible as many adults believe (see Duncan, Whitney, & Kunen, 1982). Indeed, several studies have shown that children are no more easily swayed into incorrect answers by the use of misleading questions than are adults (Duncan et al., 1982; Marin et al., 1979).

In contrast, other studies have found that, under certain circumstances, children may be more suggestible than adults (see Doris, 1991; Goodman & Reed, 1986). Because the effect of suggestion on material that has been encoded well tends not to be significantly different across age groups (Cohen & Harnick, 1980), it is likely that younger children's inferior performance on suggestive tasks results from inferior encoding strategies. In other words, younger children simply may not comprehend a situation initially. In this regard, Loftus and Davies (1984) conclude:

> If an event is understandable and interesting to both children and adults, and if their memory for it is still equally strong, age differences in suggestibility may not be found. But if the event is not encoded well to begin with, or if a delay weakens the child's memory relative to an adult's, then age differences may emerge. In this case the fragments of the event that remain in the child's memory may not be sufficient to serve as a barrier against suggestion, especially from authoritative others. Of course, if the child's grasp of the language is so weak as to make him or her oblivious to the subtle implications in the suggestive information, then the child may be immune to the manipulation regardless of the interest value or memorability of the stimuli, or the loss of an accurate memory record. (p. 63)

Even unintentional suggestions can profoundly influence truthtelling. For example, Dent (1982) asked experienced police officers to question eight- to 12-year-old child witnesses following a staged incident. She found that all of the police officers elicited very inaccurate, descriptive information from the children by succumbing to the temptation of using suggestive, leading questioning. Consider this example, in which an officer questioned a child concerning the appearance of a woman suspect (pp. 290–291).

OFFICER: Wearing a poncho and a cap—?

CHILD: I think it was a cap.

OFFICER: What sort of a cap was it? Was it like a beret, or was it a peaked cap, or—?

CHILD: No, it had sort of, it was flared with a little piece coming out (demonstrates with hands). It was flared with a sort of button thing in the middle.

OFFICER: What—sort of—like that—was it a peak like that, that sort of thing?

CHILD: Ye-es.

OFFICER: Like a sort of orange segment thing, like that, do you mean?

CHILD: Yes!

OFFICER: Is that right?

CHILD: Yes.

OFFICER: That's the sort of cap I'm thinking you're meaning, with a little peak out there.

CHILD: Yes, that's top view, yes.

OFFICER: That sort of thing, is it?

CHILD: Yes.

OFFICER: Smashing. Um—what color?

CHILD: Oh! Oh—I think this was um black or brown—

OFFICER: Think it was dark, shall we say?

CHILD: Yes—it was a dark color I think, and I didn't see her hair.

In fact, the woman was not wearing anything on her head, nor was she wearing a poncho!

As this example illustrates, even an experienced interviewer may unwittingly lead a child into compounding an initial error by requesting increasingly specific details and offering "helpful" suggestions. Deliberate coaching—that is, implanting suggestions to serve some ulterior motive—is even more pernicious, in part because it often is coupled with intimidation and/or inducements to keep secrets.

In summarizing the current research on suggestibility, Goodman and Clarke-Stewart (1991) conclude that "children are especially likely to accept an interviewer's suggestions when they are younger, when they are interrogated after a long delay, when they feel intimidated by the interviewer, when the interviewer's suggestions are strongly stated and frequently repeated, and when more than one interviewer makes the same strong suggestions" (p. 103). In addition, the risk of obtaining inaccurate information in response to suggestive questions increases when children are asked to interpret ambiguous events (Goodman & Clarke-Stewart, 1991). Therefore, clinicians should ask children to describe events, but not to make inferences. The important point is that those who assess allegations of sexual assault should interview children meticulously. (See Myers, 1991, and Walker, 1994, for excellent guidelines for conducting forensically sound interviews.)

INDUCEMENTS TO KEEP SECRETS. Another factor that may influence the accuracy and completeness of children's reports is the use of incentives to keep secrets. Particularly in cases of sexual abuse, children may be motivated to keep secrets by (1) physical threats to the child or to loved ones, (2) being told that a perpetrator will get into trouble if the child discloses the secret (which may lead to disruption of the family, the child's main source of support), or (3) promises of tangible rewards if the child keeps quiet (Bottoms, Goodman, Schwartz-Kenney, Sachsenmaier, & Thomas, 1990).

Even young children have some knowledge of secrets (Marvin, Greenberg, & Mossler, 1976) and may keep secrets when given only moderate motivation to do so (Bottoms et al., 1990). This proclivity was investigated by Bottoms and colleagues, who explored three- to six-year-old children's accuracy in reporting events their own mothers had told them to keep secret. The mothers, serving as confederates of the experimenters, "broke" and hid a toy they had been instructed not to touch, and then told their children to keep the secret. The researchers found that younger children (ages three and four) tended to disclose the secret, whereas five- and six-year-olds generally kept the secret, "omitting information about the most salient activities of the session [i.e., breaking and hiding the toy]" (p. 9). Even a completely leading interview did not result in the children's telling the secret. Bottoms and colleagues conclude: "We can speculate that if a child will keep a secret about an innocuous, nonthreatening act in our laboratory for the reward of a toy and so as not to get the parent in trouble, we should not automatically discount the testimony of a child who delays in disclosing a crime—that child may be responding quite understandably to pressure from a trusted person to keep the event a secret" (p. 10).

In other laboratory studies, Wilson and Pipe (1989) and Perry, Kern, Eitemiller, Mohn, Fischer, and Stessman (1991) found that children (ages three to six) who kept a confederate's secret were not less accurate in other respects than were children who mentioned the secret. Moreover, like Bottoms et al. (1990), Wilson and Pipe (1989) and Perry et al. (1991) found that errors made by the children tended to be ones of omission (i.e., omitting actions that actually had occurred), rather than of commission (i.e., actively falsifying information).

Thus an inducement to keep a secret may not alter the memory itself. However, such an incentive may have a significant effect on the manner in which the memory is reported to others. Specifically, the child may report "the truth" and "nothing but the truth," but not "the *whole* truth." Therefore, clinicians should take care to question children about ways in which they may have been encouraged or threatened into keeping the "secret" of abuse.

STRESS AND INTIMIDATION. Stress alone may not impair memory processes. Indeed, it can lead to arousal, heightened attention, and improved encoding (Deffenbacher, 1983). However, stress that results from intimidation may lead to either impairment in encoding or problems in recalling or reporting memories.

For example, Peters (1990) found that "confrontational" stress had a negative effect on school-age children's reports of their memories of a staged robbery. In postevent interviews, half of the children were questioned in the presence of the thief, while the remaining half were interrogated in the perpetrator's absence. Peters found that accuracy of the child eyewitnesses was compromised severely when the thief was present; that is, when they were confronted and intimidated. Bussey (1990) also found that when three- to five-year-old children expected negative sanctions for disclosing information, truthtelling was compromised. Similarly, Perry et al. (1991) found that three- to six-year-old children experienced distress (as measured by heart rate, skin temperature, and self-report) when they testified in front of an alleged perpetrator, and that the distress experienced was associated with less complete and less accurate reports.

Clinical anecdotes also suggest that confrontational stress may have a negative effect on children's reports of their memories of abuse. The following example is a case on point.

> Three young children (ages three, four, and six) provided their therapist with independent and consistent reports of repeated sexual assault by their stepfather. Charges were filed with the county attorney. Subsequently, the therapist was asked to provide details of the children's accounts for a bill of discovery, the legal document filed for the purpose of compelling a defendant to answer the charges against him or her. The therapist was reluctant to do so, fearing that the children might be harmed or threatened if their stepfather were informed of the details of their allegations. But without her report, no further legal steps could be taken. Reluctantly, she complied

with the request of the defense counsel. At the next therapeutic visit–which followed the youngsters' regular visitation with "Daddy Don"–the children, who had been "warm, open, and expressive" on previous occasions, acted "withdrawn and fearful," and adamantly refused to discuss topics relating to physical intimacy. The therapist speculated that, during the delay, the defendant had threatened or coerced the children, causing the changes in their behavior. (V. Bones, personal communication, 1990)

This anecdote, coupled with the research cited above, suggests that stress generally may not have a negative effect on the reports of young children unless it is coupled with intimidation. However, if a child has been intimidated by a perpetrator, then truthtelling may be severely compromised. Although the child may not actively lie, he or she may not tell "the whole truth."

MAXIMIZING THE LIKELIHOOD OF OBTAINING THE TRUTH: STRATEGIES AND TECHNIQUES

Clinicians may employ several strategies that should increase the likelihood of obtaining "the truth, the whole truth, and nothing but the truth" when questioning children.

Recommendations

1. **THAT** professionals maintain objectivity when assessing children's allegations of sexual assault. Brooks and Milchman (1990) offer a description of one useful approach, the clinician-as-researcher model. The authors suggest that, when conducting interviews or assessments, clinicians (and others) must collect data without having preconceived conclusions about whether the child was or was not abused (see Chapters 1 and 2). Instead, the child's observed and reported behaviors should be considered in light of the following guidelines.
    a. Empirical standards of normality for the behavior of children of the same age, developmental level, gender, and cultural group.
    b. Reported behaviors of the same child before the alleged incident occurred.
    c. Alternative explanations for the behaviors (observed or reported).

Such guidelines are simple and straightforward, but very power-ful, considering all of these factors improves the likelihood that the clinician-as-researcher will reach a valid conclusion.

2. **THAT** all persons working with cases involving child witnesses receive general education regarding child development and family dynamics, as well as specialized training in interviewing children (see Chapters 5, 9, 10, and 15; also Myers, 1991), as the guidelines articulated here presuppose a certain knowledge base. Such training should help clinicians to avoid techniques that unintentionally obstruct truthtelling.

3. **THAT** courtrooms and investigative settings and procedures should be made "child friendly" to the degree possible without infringing upon the rights of the defendant (see, for example, Parker, 1982; Perry, 1992; Perry & McAuliff, 1993; Perry & Wrightsman, 1991). For example, if a child is unduly trauma-tized by the prospect of testifying at trial, the court should consider hearing the child's statement via closed-circuit televi-sion, a provision allowed by statute in most U.S. states, as well as in Canada, Israel, Japan, and several European countries (Perry & McAuliff, 1993). This approach serves to reduce the intimida-tion of child witnesses, which, in turn, should lead to obtaining more complete and accurate reports (see Chapter 19).

4. **THAT** interviews of children be conducted only by trained personnel, and, in most cases, be videotaped (using a running time record) (see Perry & McAuliff, 1993). The number of interviews held, and the number of people conducting such sessions, should be limited to the bare minimum. Preferably, a multidisciplinary team involving the prosecutor, police, and social services resource personnel should investigate and pros-ecute cases in which a child is alleged to be the victim of or a witness to abuse (see ABA, 1985; Brooks & Milchman, 1990; Perry & Wrightsman, 1991). The interview must be conducted in a forensically sound manner (see Myers, 1991; also Chapter 20).

5. **THAT** clinicians conduct assessments of children's understand-ing of truths, lies, and false beliefs on a case-by-case basis. Specifically, the clinician should:

   - ascertain whether the child understands the difference be-tween the truth and a lie, keeping in mind that children under the age of five do not understand the word "difference" (Matthews & Saywitz, 1992). Therefore, instead of asking, "What's the difference between the truth and a lie?" it is better to ask such questions as, "If I said you were a boy/girl, would

that be the truth or a lie?" or "If I said your shirt was blue,
would that be the truth or a lie?" (See Chapter 9, this volume.)
* determine whether the child can define the "truth" as telling
  what actually happened.
* inform the child that, in legal proceedings, the judge is the
  authority figure to be obeyed.
* ascertain whether the child understands that knowingly telling
  a falsehood typically results in punishment, such as losing a
  privilege, being sent to bed, or falling into disfavor with a
  supreme being.
* impress upon the child that he or she has a duty to tell the
  truth, keeping in mind the stages of moral development
  outlined by Lickona (1983) (see above).

The information obtained using these approaches should be
helpful in determining how a particular child's comprehension of
the concepts of truths, lies, and false beliefs may affect testimonial
accuracy.

REFERENCES

American Bar Association. (1985). *ABA guidelines for the fair treatment of child
witnesses in cases where child abuse is alleged.* Washington, D.C.: Author.
Bottoms, B. L., Goodman, G. S., Schwartz-Kenney, B., Sachsenmaier, T., &
Thomas, S. (1990, March). *Keeping secrets: Implications for children's testimony.*
Paper presented at the biennial meeting of the American Psychology–Law
Society, Williamsburg, Va.
Brooks, C. M., & Milchman, M. S. (1990). Child sexual abuse allegations in the
context of child custody litigation: A multi-disciplinary project to resolve
conflicts between mental health professionals' testimony. In *Lawyers for children.*
Washington, D.C.: American Bar Association Center on Children and the
Law.
Brown, A. L., Bransford, J. D., Ferrara, R. A., & Campione, J. C. (1983). Learn-
ing, remembering, and understanding. In J. H. Flavell & E. M. Markman
(Eds.), *Handbook of child psychology* (4th ed.). Vol. 3: *Cognitive development* (pp.
77–166). New York: Wiley.
Burton, R. F. & Strichartz, A. F. (1991). *Developmental and Behavioral Pediatrics, 12,*
121–128.
Burton, R. V. (1976). Honesty and dishonesty. In T. Lickona (Ed.), *Moral develop-
ment and behavior* (pp. 173–197). New York: Holt, Rinehart and Winston.
Bussey, K. (1990, March). Adult influences on children's eyewitness testimony. In S.
Ceci (Chair), *Do children lie? Narrowing the uncertainties.* Paper presented at the
biennial meeting of the American Psychology–Law Society, Williamsburg, Va.

Cleary, E. W. (1984). *McCormick on evidence.* St. Paul, Minn.: West.

Cohen, R. L., & Harnick, M. A. (1980). The susceptibility of child witnesses to suggestion. *Law and Human Behavior, 4,* 201–210.

Coleman, L., & Kay, P. (1981). Prototype semantics: The English word "lie." *Language, 57,* 26–44.

Deffenbacher, K. A. (1983). The influence of arousal on reliability of testimony. In S. M. A. Lloyd-Bostock & B. R. Clifford (Eds.), *Evaluating witness evidence* (pp. 235–251). London: Wiley.

Dent, H. R. (1982). The effects of interviewing strategies on the results of interviews with child witnesses. In A. Trankell (Ed.), *Reconstructing the past: The role of psychologists in criminal trials* (pp. 279–297). Stockholm: Norstedt.

Doris, J. (Ed.). (1991). *The suggestibility of children's recollections: Implications for eyewitness testimony.* Washington, D.C.: American Psychological Association.

Duncan, E. M., Whitney, P., & Kunen, S. (1982). Integration of visual and verbal information in children's memories. *Child Development, 53,* 1215–1223.

Everson, M. D., & Boat, B. W. (1990). Sexualized doll play among young children: Implications for the use of anatomical dolls in sexual abuse evaluations. *Journal of the American Academy of Child and Adolescent Psychiatry, 29,* 736-742.

Faller, K. C. (1984). Is the child victim of sexual abuse telling the truth? *Child Abuse and Neglect, 8,* 473–481.

Fed. R. Evid. 603.

Flavell, J. H., Mumme, D. L., Green, F. L., & Flavell, E. R. (1992). Young children's understanding of different types of beliefs. *Child Development, 63,* 960–977.

Georgia Code Ann. § 24-9-5 (1982).

Gilligan, C. (1982). *In a different voice.* Cambridge, Mass.: Harvard University Press.

Gonzales v. State 748 S.W.2d 513 (Tex.app.–Beaumont 1988).

Goodman, G. S. (1984). Children's testimony in historical perspective. *Journal of Social Issues, 40,* 9–31.

Goodman, G. S. (1992, May). *The reliability of children's testimony.* Paper presented to the NATO Advanced Study Institute: The Child Witness in Context: Cognitive, Social, and Legal Perspectives, Il Ciocco, Lucca, Italy.

Goodman, G. S., & Clarke-Stewart, A. (1991). Suggestibility in children's testimony: Implications for sexual abuse investigations. In J. Doris (Ed.), *The suggestibility of children's recollections* (pp. 92–105). Washington, D.C.: American Psychological Association.

Goodman, G. S., Golding, J. M., & Haith, M. M. (1984). Jurors' reactions to child witnesses. *Journal of Social Issues, 40,* 139–156.

Goodman, G. S., & Reed, R. S. (1986). Age differences in eyewitness testimony. *Law and Human Behavior, 10,* 317–332.

Haugaard, J. J. (1992a, March). *Children's definitions of the truth: A replication and extension.* Paper presented at the biennial meeting of the American Psychology–Law Society, San Diego, Calif.

Haugaard, J. J. (1992b, March). *Young children's classification of the corroboration of a false statement as the truth or a lie.* Paper presented at the biennial meeting of the American Psychology–Law Society, San Diego, Calif.

Haugaard, J. J., Reppucci, N. D., Laird, J., & Nauful, T. (1991). Children's definitions of the truth and their competency as witnesses in legal proceedings. *Law and Human Behavior, 15*, 253–271.

Johnson, M. K., & Foley, M. A. (1984). Differentiating fact from fantasy: The reliability of children's memory. *Journal of Social Issues, 40*, 33–50.

Jones, D. P. H., & Krugman, R. D. (1986). Can a three-year-old child bear witness to her sexual assault and attempted murder? *Child Abuse and Neglect, 10*, 253–258.

Kohlberg, L. (1963). The development of children's orientations toward a moral order: I. Sequence in the development of moral thought. *Vita Humana, 6*, 11–33.

Leekam, S. (1991). Jokes and lies: Children's understanding of intentional falsehood. In A. Whiten (Ed.), *Natural theories of mind* (pp. 159–174). Cambridge, Mass.: Basil Blackwell.

Leekam, S. (1992a, May). *Understanding intention to deceive.* Paper presented to the NATO Advanced Study Institute: The Child Witness in Context: Cognitive, Social, and Legal Perspectives, Il Ciocco, Lucca, Italy.

Leekam, S. (1992b). Believing and deceiving: Steps to becoming a good liar. In S. J. Ceci, M. D. Leichtman, & M. Putnick (Eds.), *Cognitive and social factors in early deception* (pp. 47–62). Hillsdale, N.J.: Erlbaum.

Lickona, T. (1983). *Raising good children: Helping your child through stages of moral development.* New York: Bantam Books.

Loftus, E. F., & Davies, G. M. (1984). Distortions in the memory of children. *Journal of Social Issues, 40*, 51–67.

Marin, B. V., Holmes, D. L., Guth, M., & Kovac, P. (1979). The potential of children as eyewitnesses. *Law and Human Behavior, 3*, 295–306.

Marvin, R. S., Greenberg, M. T., & Mossler, D. G. (1976). The early development of conceptual perspective taking: Distinguishing among multiple perspectives. *Child Development, 47*, 511–514.

Matthews, E., & Saywitz, K. J. (1992). Child victim witness manual. *California Center for Judicial Education and Research Journal, 12*, 3–81.

Myers, J. E. B. (1987). *Child witness law and practice.* New York: Wiley.

Myers, J. E. B. (1991). *Legal issues in child abuse and neglect.* Newbury Park, Calif.: Sage.

Parker, J. (1982). The rights of child witnesses: Is the court a protector or perpetrator? *New England Law Review, 17*, 643–717.

People v. Parks, 41 N.Y.2d 36, 359 N.E.2d 358, 390 N.Y.SS.2d 848 (1976).

Perner, J., Leekam, S., & Wimmer, H. (1987). Three-year-old's difficulty with false belief: The case for a conceptual deficit. *British Journal of Developmental Psychology, 5*, 125–137.

Perry, N. W. (1992). When children take the stand: Permissible innovations in the U.S. courts. *Expert Evidence, 1*, 54–59.

Perry, N. W. (1993). Accuracy and suggestibility of children's memory for witnessed events. In L. VandeCreek, S. K. Knapp, and T. L. Jackson (Eds.), *Innovations in clinical practice,* Vol. 12., 35–47.

Perry, N. W., Kern, S., Eitemiller, J., Mohn, S., Fischer, M. P., & Stessman, L. J. (1991, April). *Factors affecting children's ability to provide accurate testimony.* Paper presented at the annual meeting of the Western Psychological Association, San Francisco, Calif.

Perry, N. W., & McAuliff, B. D. (1993). The use of videotaped child testimony: Public policy implications. *Journal of Law, Ethics, and Public Policy, 7,* 387–422.

Perry, N. W., McAuliff, B. D., Tam, P., Claycomb, L., Dostal, C., & Flanagan, C. (in press). When lawyers question children: Is justice served? *Law and Human Behavior.*

Perry, N. W., Nielsen, D., Burns, D., Cunningham, E., & Jenkins, S. (1987, April). *Young children's ability to provide accurate testimony following a witnessed event.* Paper presented at the spring meeting of the Nebraska Psychological Association, Lincoln, Neb.

Perry, N. W., & Wrightsman, L. S. (1991). *The child witness.* Newbury Park, Calif: Sage.

Peters, D. P. (1990, March). *Confrontational stress and children's testimony: Some experimental findings.* In S. Ceci (Chair), *Do children lie? Narrowing the uncertainties.* Paper presented at the biennial meeting of the American Psychology–Law Society, Williamsburg, Va.

Peterson, C. C., Peterson, J. L., & Seeto, D. (1983). Developmental changes in ideas about lying. *Child Development, 54,* 1529–1535.

Piaget, J. (1932/1965). *The moral judgment of the child.* New York: Free Press.

Pynoos, R. S., & Eth, S. (1984). The child as witness to homicide. *Journal of Social Issues, 40,* 87–108.

Pynoos, R. S., & Nader, K. (1989). Children's memory and proximity to violence. *Journal of the American Academy of Child and Adolescent Psychiatry, 28,* 236–241.

Quinn, K. M. (1988). The credibility of children's allegations of sexual abuse. *Behavioral Sciences and the Law, 6,* 181–199.

Raskin, D. C. (1992, May). *Issues in psychological techniques and testimony in child sex abuse cases.* Paper presented to the NATO Advanced Study Institute: The Child Witness in Context: Cognitive, Social, and Legal Perspectives, Il Ciocco, Lucca, Italy.

Raskin, D. C., & Yuille, J. C. (1989). Problems in evaluating interviews of children in sexual abuse cases. In S. J. Ceci, D. F. Ross, & M. P. Toglia (Eds.), *Perspectives on children's testimony* (pp. 184–207). New York: Springer-Verlag.

Sodian, B., Taylor, C., Harris, P. L., & Perner, J. (1991). Early deception and the child's theory of mind: False trails and genuine markers. *Child Development, 62,* 468–483.

State v. Eiler 762 P.2d 210 (Mont. 1988).

State of New Jersey v. DR 537 A.2d 667 (1988).

Strichartz, A. F. (1980). Truth or consequences: *The concept of lies and truth in children three through seven years old.* Unpublished undergraduate honors thesis, Cornell University, Ithaca, N.Y.

Strichartz, A. F., & Burton, R. V. (1990). Lies and truth: A study of the development of the concept. *Child Development, 61,* 211–220.

Terr, L. (1979). Children of Chowchilla: Study of psychic trauma. *Psychoanalytic Study of the Child, 34,* 547–623.

Undeutsch, U. (1982). Statement validity analysis. In A. Trankell (Ed.), *Reconstructing the past: The role of psychologists in criminal trials* (pp. 27–56). Stockholm: Norstedt & Soners.

Walker, A. G. (1994). *Handbook on Questioning Children.* American Bar Association Center on Children and the Law.

Wellman, H. M. (1990). *The child's theory of mind.* Cambridge, Mass.: MIT Press.

Wilson, J. C., & Pipe, M. E. (1989). The effects of cues on young children's recall of real events. *New Zealand Journal of Psychology, 18,* 65–70.

Wimmer, H., Gruber, S., & Perner, J. (1984). Young children's conception of lying: Lexical realism–moral subjectivism. *Journal of Experimental Child Psychology, 37,* 1–30.

Wimmer, H., & Perner, J. (1983). Beliefs about beliefs: Representations and constraining function of wrong beliefs in young children's understanding of deception. *Cognition, 13,* 103–128.

5

Clinical Implications of Research on Memory Development

Betty N. Gordon, Carolyn S. Schroeder, Peter A. Ornstein, and Lynne E. Baker-Ward

Research on memory processes among children is reviewed as it is relevant to children's testimony. An organizing framework is proposed that includes four broad themes: (1) not everything gets into memory, (2) what gets into memory may vary in strength, (3) the status of information in memory changes over time, and (4) retrieval is not perfect. Factors that can influence children's memory are discussed in the context of each of these themes. Finally, guidelines for clinicians that are based on the research reviewed are presented.

Preparation of this chapter was supported in part by grant MH 43904 from the National Institute of Mental Health.

Can a nine-year-old be believed when she suddenly discloses sexual abuse that allegedly occurred when she was three years old? How should the report of sexual abuse by a four-year-old be evaluated when he has been questioned by a day-care worker, pediatrician, social worker, and police officer before coming to you for further assessment? What effect does treatment have on a child's testimony about sexual abuse? Why would a child deny that he or she has been abused when there is clear physical evidence of sexual abuse?

Difficult questions such as these are commonly faced by clinicians who are charged with the management of children who may have been sexually abused. The answers require some familiarity with the research on the development of memory in children. Given that children cannot provide accurate reports about events that cannot be remembered, memory is clearly central to effective testimony (Ornstein, Larus, & Clubb, 1991). Yet memory is itself determined by a complex set of factors and must be understood in the context of children's cognitive, language, emotional, and social development, as well as of the broader environmental setting in which events take place and interviews are conducted. Together these factors can influence what is committed to memory, how memory changes over time, and, finally, what is reported by the child.

The clinician's role in cases of child abuse is complex and often can be confusing. Depending on the case, the clinician can be called upon to be either therapist or investigator or both. In practice, these two roles are often intertwined, but it is important to recognize that they have very different implications for case management, especially in cases where the child must eventually testify in court. As the child's therapist, the clinician is charged with helping the child understand and deal with the trauma that he or she has experienced. In these cases, the clinician may use whatever methods seem appropriate and effective regardless of the effect on the child's later testimony. As an investigator, however, the clinician's role is to help the child provide information from memory that is accurate and detailed, and to evaluate that information in the context of all of the factors that might influence the validity of the child's report. The focus of this chapter is on the implications of research in memory development for the clinician in the role of investigator. However, some of the implications of therapeutic methods are discussed briefly, as these methods can potentially influence what the child subsequently remembers about the abuse experience.

To understand the issues involved in obtaining accurate testimony from children, it is useful to have some knowledge of the flow of information within the memory system; that is, how information is encoded, stored, and retrieved. Ornstein and colleagues (Ornstein et al., 1991; Ornstein, Baker-Ward, Gordon, & Merritt, 1993) outline a framework that allows one to consider the wide range of factors that can influence children's memory at each of these stages. This framework includes four very general themes: (1) not everything gets into memory, (2) what gets into memory may vary in strength, (3) the status of information in memory changes over time, and (4) retrieval is not perfect. In this chapter, we use these themes to integrate the memory literature as it is relevant to children's testimony. A final section outlines the implications of the research for clinicians.

NOT EVERYTHING GETS INTO MEMORY

In the management of child sexual abuse cases, professionals who interview child witnesses are concerned with the retrieval of details related to the events the children have experienced. It is important, however, to keep in mind that some presumed problems in remembering may not reflect retrieval failures. Indeed, some things may not be remembered because they were not entered into memory in the first place. In cases of child sexual abuse, incidental rather than deliberate memory is involved at the encoding phase of the memory process (Ornstein, Gordon, & Baker-Ward, 1992a). That is, the child is not aware that he or she will be given a "memory test" at some later time. Thus the information entered into memory is acquired in an incidental fashion. Given the complexity of abusive experiences, what factors influence the information that enters the child's memory system?

Knowledge

One important determinant of encoding is what one knows about an event before it happens. Prior knowledge influences how an individual monitors the world, interprets events, and selectively attends to certain types of stimuli while excluding other types (Bjorklund, 1985; Chi & Ceci, 1987; Ornstein & Naus, 1985). A considerable body of evidence indicates that children's understanding of the events to which they are exposed will have a profound effect on what is encoded and stored in memory (Chi, Glasser, & Farr, 1988; Clubb & Ornstein, 1992; Schneider & Korkel, 1989; Spilich, Vesonder, Chiesi, & Voss, 1979). Moreover, given that knowledge in most, if not all, domains clearly increases with age, there should be comparable developmental differences in the types of specific details that are noticed, encoded and stored. Thus, for example, based on Gordon, Schroeder, and Abrams' (1990a) recent demonstration of developmental differences in knowledge of sexual anatomy and behavior, it would be expected that older children would understand and encode more organized information about their experiences of sexual abuse than would younger children.

One implication of the research literature for the relation between knowledge and memory is that in cases in which the abuse is less severe and less obviously sexual from the child's perspective, knowledge gained at a later date through sex education or other means may influence recall long after the event in question has occurred (Ornstein et al., 1991). In these cases, however, it must be recognized that what is remembered represents a reinterpretation of the information that was originally placed in memory, and, as such, the details recalled may be substantially altered. Moreover, the original events may not have been well encoded because of the child's lack of understanding of the events in question at the time they took place.

Interest Value of Stimuli

Another factor that can influence what is stored in memory is the salience or interest value of the stimuli to which the child is exposed (Renninger & Wozniak, 1985). Details about persons, actions, or objects in which a child is interested are more likely to be encoded than are less salient stimuli. It should not be surprising to find developmental differences in the types of stimuli that are of interest to children, in part because interest value covaries considerably with prior knowledge. The more a child knows about something, the more likely he or she is to be interested in it, and, therefore, more highly motivated to remember it.

Conversely, children are often intensely interested in some things about which they have little knowledge. Goodman, Rudy, Bottoms, and Aman (1990) suggest that events or actions that affect a child's sense of well-being, safety, and social acceptance are personally significant and thus may be more likely to be remembered. They argue that sexual behavior, particularly that which is also abusive, is likely to be particularly salient to children, regardless of what a child understands about the topic. However, to the extent that children are aware of societal taboos regarding sexuality, sexually abusive behavior may cause the child to be embarrassed. As a consequence, although the behavior may be well remembered, the child may not report it (Goodman et al., 1990).

What types of information are children most likely to remember? Several researchers have reported that children's memory for central actions is better than their memory for peripheral information (Fivush, Gray, & Fromhoff, 1987; Goodman, Hirschman, & Rudy, 1987; Goodman et al., 1990). More specifically, preschool and school-age children are more likely to remember information about activities and objects than details concerning people or locations (Fivush & Shukat, in press; Schwartz-Kenney & Goodman, 1991). Moreover, the type of information most likely to be recalled does not appear to change with age (Fivush & Shukat, in press). To our knowledge, there is no research concerning the extent to which children remember sexual information, although it seems reasonable to assume that sexual abuse likely would be remembered because it typically involves actions. Gordon, Schroeder, and Abrams (1990b), however, demonstrated that sexual experience does not necessarily lead to greater knowledge. They found that children who had been sexually abused did not know more about sexual anatomy and behavior than did nonabused children of the same age.

Stress

Given that child witnesses will undoubtedly be asked to remember experiences that are quite stressful, it is important to determine the effects of high levels of stress on the encoding and storage of information. Unfortunately, however, the literature examining the impact of stress on children's memory is characterized by inconsistency (Ceci & Bruck, 1993). Some researchers suggest that high levels of stress increase children's abilities to focus, and thus to encode information (e.g., Goodman, Aman, & Hirschman, 1987; Goodman et al., 1990). In contrast, others argue that stress experienced at the time of the to-be-remembered event typically impedes memory performance (Merritt, Spicker, & Ornstein, 1993; Peters, 1987, 1991).

These conflicting findings are probably a result of both methodological problems in some studies and procedural differences across investigations. For obvious ethical reasons, it is not possible to control the levels of stress experienced by participants in various studies. As a consequence, researchers have examined a variety of naturally occurring events that involve differing levels of stress (e.g., visits to the doctor or dentist for a routine checkup versus an invasive radiological procedure; see Baker-Ward, Gordon, Ornstein, Larus, & Clubb, 1993; Merritt et al., 1993), and have measured the effects of stress on different types of recall (e.g., picture lineups versus details of the event; see Goodman et al., 1987; Peters, 1987, 1991). Clearly, further research is required to clarify the effects of stress on the encoding of information, but there is an emerging consensus that high levels of stress at the time of encoding interfere with the acquisition of information (Ceci & Bruck, 1993; Peters, 1993).

Overview

Taken together, the results of a growing body of research suggest that children who have been sexually abused are likely to encode some central actions, even if they do not have a great deal of knowledge about sexual behavior and may not understand what has happened to them. They are less likely to encode details about the location or person(s) involved, despite the fact that these details are usually necessary for the successful prosecution of a case. Although research on the effects of stress on encoding has revealed some inconsistencies, it seems reasonable to assume that children who have experienced very traumatic events may not encode as much detail as will those whose experiences were more benign.

WHAT GETS INTO MEMORY MAY VARY IN STRENGTH

Given that information about an event is encoded and stored, many factors can potentially influence the strength of that information in memory, and consequently the ease with which it may be retrieved at a later time. Stronger representations may be readily retrieved, even in response to open-ended questions, such as, "What happened when you were with Bob?" In contrast, weaker representations may be more difficult to retrieve and may require more cues from the interviewer, perhaps in the form of more direct questions, such as, "What was Bob wearing?" or "Did Bob have his clothes on?" Differences in the strength of the representation may be reflected in the age differences that typically characterize children's recall. After comparable exposure to the same event, for example, older children may have stronger memory representations than do younger children. Thus differences in strength may explain why older children give more information in response to open-ended questions and provide more integrated and coherent accounts of their experiences than do younger children (Baker-Ward et al., 1993; Dent & Stephenson, 1979; Ornstein, Gordon, & Larus, 1992b).

Research on the development of memory suggests at least three factors that can potentially affect the strength of the representation in memory: (1) the amount of exposure to an event, (2) the status of the individual as a participant or observer, and (3) the age of the witness (Ornstein et al., 1991).

Amount of Exposure

Variations in the extent of exposure to an event (in terms of both its duration and frequency) are associated with differences in the strength of the resulting memory trace. Indeed, since the time of Aristotle, a fundamental principle of memory has been that repetition facilitates performance (Brainerd & Ornstein, 1991; Crowder, 1976)! Thus, in the case of a single occurrence of an event, the longer the exposure time to relevant features, the stronger will be the resulting representation in memory. Similarly, repeated exposures to a stimulus will yield stronger representations. It is important to note, however, that when children are exposed to multiple repetitions of the same event, they form generalized representations, or "scripts," of that event (Myles-Worsley, Cromer, & Dodd, 1986; Nelson, 1986). Thus recall in a case of repeated abuse may represent the child's memory of what "usually happens" rather than of the details of a specific episode.

Children's scripts for repeated events are important to understanding memory performance in another sense. As the strength of a memory trace for a specific experience deteriorates with time, children may increasingly "fill in the gaps" of their recall by relying quite unconsciously on generalized knowledge (Brainerd & Ornstein, 1991). Thus, with the passage of time, the details of a particular experience may be lost and the information in memory altered to be more consistent with what a child knows usually happens (Myles-Worsley et al., 1986).

This research on children's scripts highlights the important distinction between memory as a *reconstructive* versus a *reproductive* process. As events are repeated and as the representation of the event weakens over time, a child's memory performance increasingly reflects a reconstruction based on the child's generalized knowledge rather than on an exact reproduction of the events in question.

Participant Versus Observer

When a child is an active participant in an event, greater attention may be directed to the details of the event than when the child is simply an observer. Consequently, the resultant memory representations may be stronger than those stemming from observation. Recent research provides support for the view that recall is enhanced when the child actively participates in an experience rather than simply acts as an observer (Baker-Ward, Hess, & Flanagan, 1990; Goodman et al., 1990).

Age

With increasing age, there are corresponding changes in a variety of cognitive functions that influence the acquisition and storage of information in the memory system (Ornstein et al., 1991). As a result of the increased efficiency of information processing, more effective use of memory strategies, and greater knowledge, for example, comparable exposures to an event should result in stronger memory traces for older children than for younger children. Moreover, Brainerd and Ornstein (1991) indicate that memory traces fade over time, and that these "storage failures" decrease with age. It thus is likely that the age differences in forgetting that are commonly found in studies of children's autobiographical memory (Baker-Ward et al., 1993;

Ornstein et al., 1992b) reflect corresponding changes in the status of under-lying memory representations.

Overview

To summarize, research suggests that the memories of children who are abused repeatedly will be stronger than those of children who experience just one incident. However, repeated episodes of abuse are also likely to result in generalized representations of abuse, and the child may have difficulty in distinguishing the details of a particular episode. Because children are typically not passive observers when they are being abused, it is likely that the memory representations of the details encoded will be relatively strong. It is clear, however, that age will interact with these factors such that, other things being equal, the memory representations of younger children will be weaker than those of older children. Taken together, this research points out the importance of understanding children's memory performance as reflecting a reconstructive process. The weaker the memory representation, the greater is the possibility that the child's recall is a reconstruction of the actual events.

THE STATUS OF INFORMATION IN MEMORY CHANGES

Once information about an experience is in the memory system, its status can be altered during the interval between the occurrence of the event and the memory interview. Both passage of time and prior knowledge can exert a substantial influence on the underlying memory representation. Moreover, children may be exposed to a variety of experiences in the time between encoding and recall, some of which can act to strengthen memory, whereas others can interfere with performance. In cases of sexual abuse, experiences happening after an event that may alter the status of information in the memory system include (1) the length of the interval between the occurrence of the event and the subsequent report, (2) exposure to repeated interviews, (3) provision of information that is misleading or is inconsistent with the original event, and (4) participation in various therapeutic procedures.

The Delay Interval

As discussed in the section on the strength of the representation, memory traces deteriorate over time. Accordingly, the more closely the interview follows the event, the greater is the likelihood of obtaining accurate and complete accounts of the details of children's experiences. Unfortunately, it is typical for interviews in child sexual abuse cases to be conducted weeks, months, and even years after the events in question.

Although some research has shown that preschool children's recall of experienced events can be quite good even over relatively long periods of time (e.g., Fivush & Hammond, 1990; Fivush & Shukat, in press), others have consistently shown that the younger the child, the more vulnerable he or she is to forgetting over time (e.g., Baker-Ward et al., 1993; Brainerd, Kingman, & Howe, 1985; Goodman et al., 1990; Ornstein et al., 1992b; Poole & White, in press). As the interval between encoding and retrieval increases, moreover, the memory trace becomes weaker, and it is increasingly likely that the information in memory will be altered as a result of prior knowledge. Myles-Worsley et al. (1986), for example, demonstrated that over a five-year period, children's memories of events experienced in a preschool class increasingly came to be reconstructions involving a combination of actual remembered information and general knowledge about similar experiences. Thus there is evidence that as memory fades over time, children's delayed reports may represent more reconstruction and less reproduction than their initial reports (Ornstein et al., 1991).

Repeated Interviews

In the absence of suggestive questions or misleading information, multiple interviews can have both positive and negative effects on memory performance. On the positive side, repeated questioning can enable the individual to recall information not recalled earlier, and under some conditions may "inoculate" the individual against forgetting (for reviews, see Poole & White, in press; Warren & Hagood, in press). In some sense then, repeated questioning may serve to maintain information in memory, in a process that is analogous to Campbell and Jaynes' (1966) construct of "reinstatement." For Campbell and Jaynes, partial repetitions (e.g., repeated interviews) of an initial event during a delay can serve to reinstate information that ordinarily would be forgotten.

Recent research, however, suggests that more than just simple repetition is necessary to reinstate memory. Poole and White (in press), for example, state that the timing and number of repeated interviews may be important in determining their effects. Thus an interview carried out immediately after the event in question may be more effective in maintaining memory than one that takes place some time later. A child who is interviewed on several occasions, moreover, may remember more information than a child who is interviewed only once or twice (Gordon, Ornstein, Clubb, Nida, & Baker-Ward, 1991). But the effects of the number and timing of repeated interviews may be different for children of different ages. Rovee-Collier and Hayne

(1987), for instance, argue that for infants, a reinstating stimulus has the most beneficial effect when it comes very late in the delay interval, at a point when the original response has been forgotten. Gordon et al. (1991) present preliminary evidence that suggests that the same phenomenon may be true for older children. Thus, in timing interviews, the critical issue for researchers and clinicians may be to determine the point at which forgetting occurs for children of different ages.

In contrast to these positive effects, others have found negative effects or no effects of repeated interviews. Baker-Ward et al. (1993) reported that an interview conducted immediately after an event had no effect on recall at three weeks, and Gordon et al. (1991) found no effects of an immediate interview or one conducted six weeks after the event on memory performance at 12 weeks. Moreover, Warren and Hagood (in press) argue that with multiple interviews, errors are typically repeated, intrusion errors are more likely, and speculation tends to be confirmed.

Suggestibility

Despite the positive effects of repeated interviews, because of the potential for exposure to misleading or suggestive information as a result of the interview process, many have cautioned against repeatedly questioning children in cases of sexual abuse (e.g., Flin, 1991). Studies have shown that individuals exposed to misleading or inconsistent postevent information typically perform less well than do those who do not receive such information (e.g., Loftus, 1979; Loftus & Palmer, 1974). Moreover, preschool children have consistently been found to be more suggestible than older children and adults (Ceci, Leichtman, & White, in press; Ceci, Ross, & Toglia, 1987a, 1987b). Indeed, Ceci et al. (in press) have shown that preschool children will provide elaborate details about things that did not happen when they are subjected to pre- and postevent suggestive information, and that some children will hold to their misguided beliefs even in the face of mild challenges. It is important to note, however, that not all children are suggestible at all times. Even in the Ceci et al. (in press) study, under the most suggestive conditions, one quarter of the three- to four-year-olds and two thirds of the five- to six-year-olds resisted suggestion (see also Stein & Trabasso, 1991).

Clearly, the question of suggestibility is quite complex, and the important issue is not whether children are more suggestible than adults or whether younger children are more suggestible than older children. Rather, research must begin to address the question, "Under what circumstances are children more or less vulnerable to suggestion?" (Baxter, 1990). Factors that have been identified as influencing suggestibility include the timing of the inconsistent information, the perceived prestige of the person providing the information, the relative strength of the memory trace, and the degree of certainty about what is to be remembered. Warren and Hagood (in press), for example, have demonstrated that inconsistent information is more detrimental to memory when it is given just before the memory interview than when provided earlier in the delay interval. Moreover, others have found that children are more suggestible when the inconsistent information is provided by an adult, as opposed to by a child (Ceci et al., 1987b), and also when the adult furnishing the misleading information is perceived as being knowledgeable or credible (Toglia & Ross, 1991).

Children (and probably also adults) are more likely to be vulnerable to suggestion when the memory representation is weaker. Thus, as the interval between encoding and recall increases, the risk of altering the information stored in the memory system by providing misleading information also increases. The increased vulnerability to suggestion seen among younger children may be in part a function of the fact that their memories fade sooner than do those of older children. Moreover, given that memory representations for more salient stimuli are stronger than traces for less interesting details, certain types of information are apt to be more vulnerable to suggestion than other types. Schwartz-Kenny and Goodman (1991), for instance, demonstrated that the memory of six- and nine-year-olds for action items (which are also more likely to be encoded) was less vulnerable to misleading questions than was their memory for person and location information.

Treatment Procedures

Little is known about how children's memory for the details of sexual abuse experiences is influenced by treatment procedures. Based on their research demonstrating that stereotypes and suggestion can influence children to say that something happened when it did not, Ceci et al. (in press) warn that many therapeutic procedures have the potential to elicit false disclosures of abuse, particularly when the therapist has a strong bias about what happened. In addition, recent research with adults indicates that it is possible, by suggestion, to create memories (and hence false reports) of early traumatic experiences that never happened (Loftus, 1993). In contrast, Bussey, Lee, and Grimbeek (1993) argue that false disclosures, although possible, are less likely than denials of actual abuse. Moreover, Tate and Warren-Leubecker (1989) demonstrated that when coached to lie about an event, children's false statements were not particularly credible.

There is some concern that the use of sexually anatomically detailed dolls in the investigation and treatment of cases of suspected abuse will elicit false reports of sexual abuse from children. The empirical evidence regarding this concern is inconsistent. In a recent review of research on the use of such dolls, Boat and Everson (1993) concluded that sexually naive children who have not been abused do not typically engage in explicit sexual play with the dolls. Further, work by Goodman and her colleagues (Goodman & Aman, 1990; Goodman et al., 1990; Saywitz, Goodman, Nicholas, & Moon, 1991) indicated that the dolls do not elicit false reports of genital or other touching. However, others (Bruck, Ceci, Francoeur, & Renick, in press) have found that some preschool children falsely reported genital touching during a physical examination when interviewed with these dolls.

For children who have recently experienced abuse, certain therapeutic procedures may have the potential to alter their recollections of the details of their experience of sexual abuse. Reading the child a story about another child who was abused may introduce information that is inconsistent with the child's experience, and this information may, in turn, become incorporated into the child's memory. Thus, it is possible that what takes place during therapy, particularly when the therapist has a strong bias regarding what happened to the child, may influence the child's subsequent remembering of the experience, or may lead to a false allegation in a child who has not been abused.

The research indicates that the process of remembering is, to a large extent, one of reconstruction. Information in memory is almost certainly altered as time passes. Moreover, the more time goes by, the more likely it is that memory will be reconstructed on the basis of knowledge and intervening experiences, with the resultant recall representing less and less a reproduction of what actually happened. Repeated interviews increase the risk of exposing children to misleading or inconsistent information, which, in some cases, will affect the validity of the child's report. Furthermore, interviewers or therapists who have strong beliefs about a child's experience can influence the child to report events that did not happen. Nonetheless, *neutral* repetitions of the original experience, perhaps through repeated opportunities to discuss the events in question, can reinstate memory and prevent forgetting to some extent. However, repetitions also can make children more sure about something they were uncertain about originally, and can cause perseveration of errors.

RETRIEVAL IS NOT PERFECT

The final phase of the memory process involves retrieval of the stored information. Yet not everything can be retrieved at all times. Many factors, both social and cognitive, influence the child's ability to gain access to previously acquired information. The task of the interviewer is one of "cognitive diagnosis" (Flavell, 1985; Ornstein, 1991), a process involving a complex assessment of the characteristics of the child, the interviewer, and the interview context. Individual differences among children in such areas as language, temperament, memory, and intelligence can influence the reporting of information during an interview. Moreover, the clinician must evaluate the child's responses in the interview in the broad context of the child's pattern of strengths and weaknesses, the types of questions asked, and the physical and psychological environment in which the memory interview is conducted.

Language Development

A child's level of language competency can have an important impact on memory performance, particularly that of the preschool child (see Chapter 8). Saywitz, Nathanson, and Snyder (1993) outline a number of variables related to language comprehension and production that are important in understanding children's recall. They suggest that children will not be able to retrieve information in response to a particular question if they fail to understand the syntactic constructions or the particular words used by the interviewer. Children typically try to answer questions that they do not understand, and their performance may also be impaired if the meanings that they have assigned to words only partially overlap with those of adults (see, e.g., Donaldson & Wales, 1970; Saywitz & Snyder, 1993; Saywitz et al., 1993). As Saywitz and colleagues point out, children may think that they understand a term when, in fact, they do not (e.g., allegations = alligators). Language concepts involving measurement, time, number, and kinship relationships may also be beyond the skills of the child, especially if under the age of seven. Saywitz and Snyder (1993) demonstrated that school-age children can be trained to monitor their comprehension of complex questions and indicate when they do not understand. Training successfully enhanced the memory performance of these children as compared with untrained children.

Language development also plays a role in the amount and content of the information children retrieve from memory. Children's reports depend a great deal upon what they have attended to and encoded, as well as on the questions asked (Fivush & Shukat, in press; Saywitz et al., 1993), but they also reflect their facility with expressive language. Moreover, with increases in age, there are corresponding changes in the ability to use narrative structure to report what can be remembered (Mandler, 1990). Thus some of the age-related improvement in recall may stem from increased narrative skill. Consistent with this perspective, there is considerable evidence that young children give less information when asked open-ended questions than do older children (Baker-Ward et al., 1993; Ornstein et al., 1992b). The information that a preschool child gives in answer to nonsuggestive, open-ended questions may be quite accurate (although not at the level of older children), but it is nonetheless limited in elaborative details (Baker-Ward et al., 1993; Fivush & Hammond, 1990; Fivush & Shukat, in press; Gordon & Follmer, 1994; Ornstein et al., 1992b).

Because of the limited amount of information given in response to open-ended questions, interviewers typically must rely on more specific questions when working with younger children. Unfortunately, when preschool children are asked specific questions, their accuracy decreases, and when the questions are of the yes/no type, their accuracy may not be above the level of chance (Clubb & Follmer, 1993; Gordon & Follmer, 1994). As well, children may respond to only part of a yes/no question, but their responses may be interpreted as applying to the entire question.

Because preschool children's limited verbal skills are reflected in their difficulty in reporting all of the information they remember, efforts have been made to enhance their reports through the use of dolls or other props. The results of this research have been consistent in indicating that the use of dolls to enhance nonverbal communication and recall is not effective for three-year-olds, but may facilitate the recall of older children (DeLoache & Marzolf, 1993; Goodman & Aman, 1990; Gordon, Ornstein, Nida, Follmer, Crenshaw, & Albert, 1993; Saywitz et al., 1991). As DeLoache and Marzolf (1993) point out, very young children may not yet have the cognitive skills to use a doll to represent the self.

Metacognitive Factors

As children develop, they learn strategies for organizing material and retrieving it from memory. Their narrative accounts of *who, what, why, where,* and *when* become more detailed, organized, and coherent. In addition, as suggested above, as children learn how narratives are structured, they are better able to retrieve specific information about an event, such as its setting, participants, conversation, affective states, and consequences (Mandler, 1990; Saywitz et al., 1993; Stein & Glenn, 1978).

Just as children's responses depend on their comprehension of the questions asked, performance on cognitive tasks is influenced strongly by their understanding of what is required (Ornstein, 1991; Saywitz et al., 1993). For optimal performance, it is essential that the child and the interviewer share some common assumptions about the task (Ornstein et al., 1991). When these perceptions differ, the child may be responding to a task that is different from the one intended by the interviewer. Also, when the task in question involves remembering, the child's report may underestimate what is available in memory. Because very young children lack the ability to take another person's perspective, they may assume that the interviewer already knows the answers to the questions, and so may fail to provide sufficient information for the interviewer to make sense out of the response (Saywitz et al., in press). This may be particularly true in the case of repeated interviews (Best & Ornstein, 1986; Ornstein, 1991). Moreover, the child's report might be changed somewhat in response to repeated questioning, particularly when the questions are posed by the same interviewer within the same interview, because the child may believe that his or her first responses must not have been correct (Ornstein et al., 1991; Siegal, Waters, & Dinwiddy, 1988; Warren & Hagood, in press).

These metacognitive factors may also contribute to the lack of consistency that is often noted in the reports of young children. Several studies have shown that the consistency of information recalled by children increases with age (Fivush & Hammond, 1990; Gordon & Follmer, 1994). Thus preschool children are likely to remember different bits of information in response to different interviews. The information they recall may be inconsistent because they are less sophisticated regarding the use of strategies for remembering, their memories may be less organized, they may be responding to different questions asked during different interviews, or they may not understand what is important to report. Recent research has focused on incorporating these metacognitive factors into training programs designed to maximize the recall of children (Saywitz & Lamphear, 1989; Saywitz & Snyder, 1993). Preinterview training in providing the types of information and the level of detail required for a forensic interview, in resistance to misleading questions, and in comprehension monitoring has been shown to improve the performance of children of school age (Saywitz & Snyder, 1993). It may or may not be possible to develop similar techniques to enhance younger children's reports as well.

Emotional Factors

The temperamental and emotional status of the child can also influence recall performance. Gordon et al. (1993) found evidence that children who were more at ease in new situations than were their peers provided more information, both verbally and nonverbally, about a physical examination. Similar findings were reported by Merritt et al. (1993) in their study of young children's recall of the details of an invasive radiological procedure. In this study, the children's adaptability and tendency to approach others were found to correlate strongly with recall.

Saywitz et al. (1993) also note that children with different temperamental characteristics may react to the communicative demands of the courtroom in very different ways. Further, there is some evidence indicating that suggestibility may be viewed as a personality "trait" that is related to recall performance. Clarke-Stewart, Thompson, and Lepore (1989), for example, found that children's suggestibility in recalling an event sequence was related to their suggestibility in other contexts. Thus leading questions or postevent misleading information may affect some children's recall more than that of others (but see Baxter, 1990). Saywitz et al. (1993) also point out that there are individual differences in children's reactions to trauma, and that these reactions may differentially affect what children are able to recall or have the motivation to recall.

The prevailing social views concerning a topic can also influence children's recall, and this would be especially true for reports of sexual experiences. Goodman et al. (1990) suggest that when children are aware of societal taboos, they may associate nudity and sexuality with embarrassment and secrecy, if not punishment. The extent to which this association arises or how it affects memory is not known. However, Saywitz et al. (1991) found that five-year-olds more readily reported vaginal and anal touch in free recall, as compared with seven-year-olds. In contrast, the use of doll-aided direct questions increased the disclosure of genital and anal touch for the older children, suggesting that socialization experiences had affected the reports of these children.

The Interview Context

A general principle of the psychology of memory is that remembering is facilitated to the extent that the psychological and physical conditions prevailing at the time of recall resemble those in place when the information was acquired. Thus the interview conditions can determine to a considerable extent what is recalled (Ornstein, 1991; Saywitz et al., 1993). Even without returning physically to the scene of an event, a skilled interviewer can reinstate the context in which the alleged event took place through the use of props (e.g., a dollhouse or other play equipment), resulting in a greater likelihood of retrieval. The interviewer also can help the child to feel comfortable and at ease in the setting, and this, in turn, can exert a strong influence on the child's performance (Gabarino & Stott, 1989).

Another aspect of the interview context that is just beginning to be studied is that of stress during the interview process. Peters (1991) suggests that in addition to the stress experienced at the time of encoding, the combination of a stressful event and a stressful, potentially confrontational interview can result in impaired performance. Saywitz and Nathanson (1993) also demonstrated that children's perceived stress while being interviewed in a mock courtroom interfered with recall. Such stress can arise from many other sources, as well, including direct contact with the defendant, as well as the failure of interviewers to establish appropriate rapport with the child or to consider the child's limited understanding of the legal process (Ornstein et al., 1991).

As discussed in previous sections, the nature of the questions posed to the child during the interview (e.g., free recall, nonsuggestive direct questions, suggestive or leading questions) can also greatly influence recall, as can the interviewer's preexisting ideas about what happened. Pettit, Fegan, and Howie (1990; cited in Ceci et al., in press), for instance, found that interviewers who were misled about the children's experience prior to the interview elicited more inaccurate information than did those who did not receive false information. Thus it appears that interviewer bias can influence children's reports.

It would seem important for interviewers to be trained to conduct a neutral interview and to avoid leading, suggestive questions. Unfortunately, it has been shown that such training may not be effective. Pettit et al. (1990) trained interviewers to ask neutral questions, but found that about one third of the questions later asked in child interviews could be classified as leading.

To summarize, the research on retrieval indicates that professionals who interview children must take into account a variety of factors that have been shown to influence children's reports of what they remember. Preschool children, because of their relatively less developed cognitive and language skills, appear to be most vulnerable to poorly conducted interviews. Interviewers who are insensitive to the child's language, cognitive, and emotional needs; who are biased in their beliefs about what the child experienced; or who ask suggestive or misleading questions will receive incomplete and inaccurate information from children.

CONCLUSION

As more and more children become involved in the legal system as witnesses, research concerning their abilities to provide accurate testimony has become increasingly important. When sexual abuse is alleged to have occurred, the legal system relies heavily on the accounts of children in determining which cases to prosecute. Clinicians assume the primary responsibility for assessing the reports of these children, yet they often have little training and few guidelines for conducting effective interviews. As Saywitz (in press) points out, the task of the clinician who interviews children is to capitalize on their strengths, compensate for their weaknesses, and create an optimal environment for their remembering and fully communicating credible information about potentially traumatic experiences. Furthermore, the interviewer must gain accurate information that not only will protect children from harmful situations, but also will protect adults from false accusations.

As this review of research on memory development indicates, the reliability of the child's report ultimately depends on the characteristics of the child, the interviewer, the context of the interview, and the relations among these factors. There is no right way to interview all children, but current research offers important information for clinicians about memory processes and the factors that potentially influence remembering in clinical settings. This information has been organized below in the form of recommendations for professionals who work with child witnesses in sexual abuse cases. Although these guidelines have been derived from the memory literature, it must be recognized that they are just a beginning, and it is expected that they will continue to evolve as new research is conducted. Ultimately, the goal is to provide clinicians with empirically based resources that will enable them to manage these very difficult sexual abuse cases most effectively.

Recommendations

Setting the Stage

1. **THAT** relevant background information about the alleged abuse be gathered, including the number and type of prior interviews, the nature of the child's initial disclosure, behavioral changes evidenced by the child, and a brief family and developmental history. This allows the clinician to plan for the interview and to put the recalled information in context. One must, however, remember that interviewer bias can influence children's reports. Being neutral as to whether the event actually occurred is critical. One must always entertain the hypothesis that the "data" that have been obtained could be explained in a different way.

2. **THAT** the setting in which the interview is conducted be arranged to facilitate the child's recall. Although it is usually not possible to have a setting that is similar to the event setting, one can provide a child-friendly environment with age-appropriate toys and props, such as crayons and paper, a dollhouse, and dolls.

3. **THAT** video- or audiotaping be arranged. Although some argue against taping the interview, we think this record serves two important purposes. First, it can help to minimize the number of interviews to which the child is exposed. Second, after the interview is completed, the clinician can review the questions asked and the manner in which they were asked, and evaluate the child's responses to these questions.

4. **THAT** the interview be conducted as soon after the initial report of the alleged incident as possible. A speedy interview is particularly important for preschool children. We would recommend

that the interview take place within a few days, or at most a week, for these younger children.

Conducting the Interview

1. **THAT** rapport with the child be established by being friendly and showing interest in the child's activities. Children should be prepared for what will happen and what is expected in the interview (see Saywitz, Geiselman, & Bornstein, 1992, for preparation instructions). The purpose of the interview should be explained, as well as the importance for the child to tell only what really happened. Moreover, the interviewer should stress that he or she does not know what happened to the child, so it is important for the child to provide as much detail as possible.

2. **THAT** the developmental level of the child be assessed (formally or informally). Areas to be assessed include language comprehension and expression, intellectual level, memory skills, emotional status, and knowledge of sexuality (see Schroeder & Gordon, 1992, for suggested methods of assessment). This provides the framework for deciding how questions will be asked, what props will be used, and how the child's responses will be evaluated. Yuille, Hunter, Joffe, and Zaparniuk (1993) suggest that the child be asked to describe two specific past experiences. This allows the interviewer to model the form of the interview, and the child to practice giving complete descriptions.

3. **THAT** the language used in the interview be consistent with the language-comprehension level of the child. This is particularly important for preschool children who have trouble with vocabulary, multiple-syllable words, and syntax. Use the child's words for body parts and functions. Check out what the child understands, since children often think that they know the meaning of a word or a question when, in fact, they do not, or have only a partial understanding. To assess the child's understanding, request definitions or explanations, rather than accepting "Yes" responses to "Do you understand?" When changing the topic, make sure that the child is aware of the transition (see Geiselman, Saywitz, & Bornstein, 1993, for suggestions on conducting a "cognitive interview").

4. **THAT** questioning begin with open-ended questions (e.g., "Tell me about your stepfather. What do you like/dislike about him?"). This is important because the types of questions asked can affect the accuracy and completeness of the child's recall, as

well as the interviewer's (and others') impressions of the credibility of the child's report.   Preschool children will require more
specific questions, but their responses to these questions may be
difficult to interpret.   In particular, yes/no questions are problematic for preschoolers, and the validity of their responses must be
viewed cautiously.

Evaluating the Child's Responses

1.   **THAT** the clinician recognize that sometimes it is not possible to
     determine what has happened, and be willing to state this.   There
     are two types of cases that increase the probability of an improp-
     erly conducted interview.   First, some children who are referred
     for evaluation have not been abused.   Second, some children
     have been abused, but for various reasons will not admit that it
     has happened.   In these cases especially, but also in all cases,
     although the clinician is uncertain about the occurrence of abuse,
     he or she may nonetheless be concerned about the child's safety.
     In such cases, it is usually possible to negotiate a reasonable plan
     with child protective services for the protection of the child and
     family.   This plan should include provisions for sexuality educa-
     tion and abuse prevention for the child and information for the
     family on the potential effects of sexual abuse.

2.   **THAT** the clinician not expect the recall of young children to be
     very organized, consistent, or detailed.   This is so in spite of the
     fact that research on children's memory has consistently indi-
     cated that, when interviewed in a nonbiased, nonleading manner
     and in the absence of misleading or suggestive questions, even
     very young children can remember important events.

3.   **THAT** the clinician review the video- or audiotape and evaluate
     each critical response in light of the stimulus that was required to
     elicit it.   Was the response spontaneous or heavily cued (e.g.,
     "Tell me about Uncle Joe," versus "Did Daddy touch your private
     parts?")?

4.   **THAT** the child's responses be evaluated in light of the back-
     ground information that has been gathered.   Walker, Bonner,
     and Kaufman (1988) delineate the risk factors associated with
     child sexual abuse (e.g., alcoholism, stepfamilies, social isolation,
     unemployment or underemployment, parental psychopathol-
     ogy).   They also provide a framework that incorporates these risk
     factors, and is useful for organizing and interpreting the back-
     ground information obtained during the assessment, evaluating

the child's responses to the interview, and making case-management decisions and recommendations. In cases in which the clinician is uncertain about whether abuse has taken place but where the family has numerous risk factors, recommendations regarding treatment or monitoring by social services may be warranted.

REFERENCES

Baker-Ward, L. E., Gordon, B. N., Ornstein, P. A., Larus, D., & Clubb, P. A. (1993). Young children's long-term retention of a pediatric examination. *Child Development, 64,* 1519–1533.

Baker-Ward, L. E., Hess, T. M., & Flanagan, D. A. (1990). The effects of involvement on children's memory for events. *Cognitive Development, 5,* 55–70.

Baxter, J. S. (1990). The suggestibility of child witnesses: A review. *Applied Cognitive Psychology, 4,* 393–407.

Best, D. L., & Ornstein, P. A. (1986). Children's generation and communication of mnemonic organizational strategies. *Developmental Psychology, 33,* 845–853.

Bjorklund, D. F. (1985). The role of conceptual knowledge in the development of organization in children's memory. In C. J. Brainerd & M. Pressley (Eds.), *Basic processes in memory development* (pp. 103–142). New York: Springer-Verlag.

Boat, B. W., & Everson, M. D. (1993). The use of dolls in sexual abuse evaluations: Current research and practice. In G. S. Goodman & B. L. Bottoms (Eds.), *Child victims, child witnesses: Understanding and improving testimony* (pp. 47–70). New York: Guilford Press.

Brainerd, C. J., Kingman, J., & Howe, M. L. (1985). On the development of forgetting. *Child Development, 56,* 1103–1119.

Brainerd, C. J., & Ornstein, P. A. (1991). Children's memory for witnessed events: The developmental backdrop. In J. Doris (Ed.), *The suggestibility of children's recollections: Implications for eyewitness testimony* (pp. 10–20). Washington, D.C.: American Psychological Association.

Bruck, M., Ceci, S. J., Francoueur, E., & Renick, A. (in press). Anatomically detailed dolls do not facilitate preschooler's reports of a pediatric examination involving genital touching. *Journal of Experimental Psychology: Applied.*

Bussey, K., Lee, K., & Grimbeek, E. J. (1993). Lies and secrets: Implications for children's reporting of sexual abuse. In G. S. Goodman & B. L. Bottoms (Eds.), *Child victims, child witnesses: Understanding and improving testimony* (pp. 147–168). New York: Guilford Press.

Campbell, B. A., & Jaynes, J. (1966). Reinstatement. *Psychological Review, 73,* 478–480.

Ceci, S. J., & Bruck, M. (1993). Suggestibility of the child witness: A historical review and synthesis. *Psychological Bulletin, 113,* 403–439.

Ceci, S. J., Leichtman, M. D., & White, T. (in press). Interviewing preschoolers. In D. Peters (Ed.), *The child witness in cognitive, social, and legal context.* Amsterdam, Netherlands: Kluwer.

Ceci, S. J., Ross, D. F., & Toglia, M. P. (1987a). Suggestibility of children's memory: Psycholegal implications. *Journal of Experimental Psychology: General,* *116,* 38–49.

Ceci, S. J., Ross, D. F., & Toglia, M. P. (1987b). Age differences in suggestibility: Narrowing the uncertainties. In S. J. Ceci, M. P. Toglia, & D. F. Ross (Eds.), *Children's eyewitness testimony* (pp. 79–91). New York: Springer-Verlag.

Chi, M. T. H., & Ceci, S. J. (1987). Content knowledge: Its role, representation, and restructuring in memory development. In H. W. Reese (Ed.), *Advances in child development and behavior* (vol. 20, pp. 91–142). New York: Academic Press.

Chi, M. T. H., Glasser, R., & Farr, M. (Eds.). (1988). *The nature of experience.* Hillsdale, N.J.: Erlbaum.

Clarke-Stewart, A., Thompson, W. C., & Lepore, S. (1989, April). Manipulating children's interpretations through interrogation. In G. S. Goodman (Chair), *Can children provide accurate eyewitness reports?* Symposium conducted at the biennial meeting of the Society for Research in Child Development, Kansas City, Mo.

Clubb, P. A., & Follmer, A. (1993, March). *Children's memory for a physical examination: Patterns of retention over a 12 week interval.* Poster presented at the biennial meeting of the Society for Research in Child Development, New Orleans, La.

Clubb, P. A., & Ornstein, P. A. (1992, April). Visiting the doctor: Children's differential retention of individual components of the physical examination. In D. Bjorklund & P. A. Ornstein (Chairs), *Children's memory for real-world events: Implications for testimony.* A symposium presented at the Conference on Human Development, Atlanta, Ga.

Crowder, R. G. (1976). *Principles of learning and memory.* Hillsdale, N.J.: Erlbaum.

DeLoache, J. S., & Marzolf, D. P. (1993, March). *Young children's testimony may not be improved by using dolls to question them.* Poster presented at the biennial meeting of the Society for Research in Child Development, New Orleans, La.

Dent, H. R., & Stephenson, G. M. (1979). An experimental study of the effectiveness of different techniques of questioning child witnesses. *British Journal of Social and Clinical Psychology, 18,* 41–51.

Donaldson, M., & Wales, R. J. (1970). On the acquisition of some relational terms. In J. R. Hayes (Ed.), *Cognition and the development of language* (pp. 235–268). New York: Wiley.

Fivush, R., Gray, J., & Fromhoff, F. A. (1987). Two-year-olds talk about the past. *Cognitive Development, 2,* 393–409.

Fivush, R., & Hammond, N. R. (1990). Autobiographical memory across the preschool years: Toward reconceptualizing childhood amnesia. In R. Fivush & J. A. Hudson (Eds.), *Knowing and remembering in young children* (pp. 223–248). New York: Cambridge University Press.

Fivush, R., & Shukat, J. (in press). What young children recall: Issues of content, consistency and coherence. In M. S. Zaragoza, J. R. Graham, G. N. N. Hall, R. Hirschman, & Y. S. Ben-Porath (Eds.), *Memory and testimony in the child witness.* Thousand Oaks, Calif.: Sage.

Flavell, J. H. (1985). *Cognitive development* (2nd ed.). Englewood Cliffs, N.J.: Prentice-Hall.

Flin, R. (1991). Commentary: A grand memory of forgetting. In J. Doris (Ed.), *The suggestibility of children's recollections: Implications for eyewitness testimony* (pp. 21–23). Washington, D.C.: American Psychological Association.

Garbarino, J., & Stott, F. M. (1989). *What children can tell us.* San Francisco: Jossey-Bass.

Geiselman, R. E., Saywitz, K. J., & Bornstein, G. K. (1993). Effects of cognitive questioning techniques on children's recall performance. In G. S. Goodman & B. L. Bottoms (Eds.), *Child victims, child witnesses: Understanding and improving testimony* (pp. 71–94). New York: Guilford Press.

Goodman, G. S., & Aman, C. (1990). Children's use of anatomically detailed dolls to recount an event. *Child Development, 61*, 1859–1871.

Goodman, G. S., Aman, C., & Hirschman, J. (1987). Child sexual and physical abuse: Children's testimony. In S. J. Ceci, M. P. Toglia, & D. F. Ross (Eds.), *Children's eyewitness memory* (pp. 1–23). New York: Springer-Verlag.

Goodman, G. S., Hirschman, J., & Rudy, L. (1987, April). Children's testimony: Research and policy implications. In S. Ceci (Chair), *Children as witnesses: Research and social policy implications.* Symposium conducted at the meeting of the Society for Research in Child Development, Baltimore, Md.

Goodman, G. S., Rudy, L., Bottoms, B. L., & Aman, C. (1990). Children's concerns and memory: Issues of ecological validity in the study of children's eyewitness testimony. In R. Fivush & J. A. Hudson (Eds.), *Knowing and remembering in young children* (pp. 249–284). New York: Cambridge University Press.

Gordon, B. N., & Follmer, A. (1994). Developmental issues in judging the credibility of children's testimony. *Journal of Clinical Child Psychology, 23*, 283–294.

Gordon, B. N., Ornstein, P. A., Clubb, P. A., Nida, R. E., & Baker-Ward, L. E. (1991, October). *Visiting the pediatrician: Long-term retention and forgetting.* Paper presented at the annual meeting of the Psychonomic Society, San Francisco, Calif.

Gordon, B. N., Ornstein, P. A., Nida, R. E., Follmer, A., Crenshaw, M. C., & Albert, G. (1993). Does the use of dolls facilitate children's memory of visits to the doctor? *Applied Cognitive Psychology, 7*, 1–16.

Gordon, B. N., Schroeder, C. S., & Abrams, J. M. (1990a). Age and social class differences in children's knowledge of sexuality. *Journal of Clinical Child Psychology, 19*, 33–43.

Gordon, B. N., Schroeder, C. S., & Abrams, J. M. (1990b). Children's knowledge of sexuality: A comparison of sexually abused and nonabused children. *American Journal of Orthopsychiatry, 60*, 33–43.

Loftus, E. F. (1979). *Eyewitness testimony.* Cambridge, Mass.: Harvard University Press.

Loftus, E. F. (1993). The reality of repressed memories. *American Psychologist, 48*, 518–537,

Loftus, E. F., & Palmer, J. C. (1974). Reconstruction of automobile destruction: An example of the interaction between language and memory. *Journal of Verbal Learning and Verbal Behavior, 13*, 585–589.

Mandler, J. M. (1990). Recall and its verbal expression. In R. Fivush & J. A. Hudson (Eds.), *Knowing and remembering in young children* (pp. 317–330). New York: Cambridge University Press.

Merritt, K. A., Spicker, B., & Ornstein, P. A. (1993, March). *Distress and memory: Implications for autobiographical recall.* Paper presented at the biennial meeting of the Society for Research in Child Development, New Orleans, La.

Myles-Worsley, M., Cromer, C. C., & Dodd, D. H. (1986). Children's preschool script reconstruction: Reliance on general knowledge as memory fades. *Developmental Psychology, 22,* 22–30.

Nelson, K. (1986). *Event knowledge: Structure and function in development.* Hillsdale, N.J.: Erlbaum.

Ornstein, P. A. (1991). Commentary: Putting interviewing in context. In J. Doris (Ed.), *Suggestibility of children's recollections: Implications for eyewitness testimony* (pp. 147–152). Washington, D.C.: American Psychological Association.

Ornstein, P. A., Baker-Ward, L. E., Gordon, B. N., & Merritt, K. A. (1993, March). Children's memory for medical experiences. In N. L. Stein (Chair), *Children's memory for emotional events: Critical issues and implications for development.* Symposium at the biennial meeting of the Society for Research in Child Development, New Orleans, La.

Ornstein, P. A., Gordon, B. N., & Baker-Ward, L. E. (1992a). Children's memory for salient events: Implications for testimony. In M. L. Howe, C. J. Brainerd, & V. F. Reyna (Eds.), *Development of long-term retention* (pp. 135–158). New York: Springer-Verlag.

Ornstein, P. A., Gordon, B. N., & Larus, D. M. (1992b). Children's memory for a personally experienced event: Implications for testimony. *Applied Cognitive Psychology, 6,* 49–60.

Ornstein, P. A., Larus, D. M., & Clubb, P. A. (1991). Understanding children's testimony: Implications of research on the development of memory. In R. Vasta (Ed.), *Annals of child development* (vol. 8, pp. 145–176). London: Jessica Kingsley Publishers.

Ornstein, P. A., & Naus, M. J. (1985). Effects of the knowledge base on children's memory strategies. In H. W. Reese (Ed.), *Advances in child development and behavior* (vol. 19, pp. 113–148). Orlando, Fla.: Academic Press.

Peters, D. P. (1987). The impact of naturally occurring stress on children's memory. In S. J. Ceci, M. P. Toglia, & D. R. Ross (Eds.), *Children's eyewitness memory* (pp. 122–141). New York: Springer-Verlag.

Peters, D. P. (1991). The influence of stress and arousal on the child witness. In J. Doris (Ed.), *The suggestibility of children's recollections* (pp. 60–76). Washington, D.C.: American Psychological Association.

Peters, D. P. (1993, March). Stress, emotional arousal, and the child witness. In N. L. Stein (Chair), *Children's memory for emotional events: Critical issues and implications for development.* Symposium at the biennial meeting of the Society for Research in Child Development, New Orleans, La.

Pettit, R., Fegan, M., & Howie, P. (1990, September). *Interviewer effects of children's testimony.* Paper presented at the International Congress on Child Abuse and Neglect, Hamburg, Germany.

Poole, D. A., & White, L. T. (in press). Tell me again and again: Stability and change in the repeated testimonies of children and adults. In M. S. Zaragoza, J. R. Graham, G. N. N. Hall, R. Hirschman, & Y. S. Ben-Porath (Eds.), *Memory and testimony in the child witness.* Thousand Oaks, Calif.: Sage.

Renninger, K. A., & Wozniak, R. H. (1985). Effect of interest on attentional shift, recognition, and recall in young children. *Developmental Psychology, 21,* 624–632.

Rovee-Collier, C. K., & Hayne, H. (1987). Reactivation of infant memory: Implications for cognitive development. In H. W. Reese (Ed.), *Advances in child development and behavior* (vol. 20, pp. 185–283). New York: Academic Press.

Saywitz, K. J. (in press). Improving children's testimony: The question, the answer, and the environment. In M. S. Zaragoza, J. R. Graham, G. N. N. Hall, R. Hirschman, & Y. S. Ben-Porath (Eds.), *Memory and testimony in the child witness.* Thousand Oaks, Calif.: Sage.

Saywitz, K. J., Geiselman, R. E., & Bornstein, G. K. (1992). Effects of cognitive interviewing and practice on children's recall performance. *Journal of Applied Psychology, 77,* 744–756.

Saywitz, K. J., Goodman, G. S., Nicholas, E., & Moan, S. (1991). Children's memories of physical examinations involving genital touch: Implications for reports of child sexual abuse. *Journal of Consulting and Clinical Psychology, 59,* 682–691.

Saywitz, K. J., & Lamphear, V. S. (1989, August). *Preparing child witnesses for pretrial interviews and testimony.* Paper presented at the 97th Annual Convention of the American Psychological Association, New Orleans, La.

Saywitz, K. J., & Nathanson, R. (1993). Children's testimony and their perceptions of stress in and out of the courtroom. *Child Abuse and Neglect, 77,* 613–622.

Saywitz, K. J., Nathanson, R., & Snyder, L. (1993). Credibility of child witnesses: The role of communicative competence. *Topics in Language Disorders, 13,* 59–78.

Saywitz, K. J., & Snyder, L. (1993). Improving children's testimony with preparation. In G. Goodman & B. Bottoms (Eds.), *Child victims, child witnesses: Understanding and improving testimony* (pp. 117–146). New York: Guilford Press.

Schneider, W., & Korkel, J. (1989). The knowledge base and text recall: Evidence from a short-term longitudinal study. *Contemporary Educational Psychology, 14,* 382–393.

Schroeder, C. S., & Gordon, B. N. (1991). *Assessment and treatment of childhood problems: A clinician's guidebook.* New York: Guilford Press.

Schwartz-Kenney, B. M., & Goodman, G. S. (1991, April). *The effects of misleading information on children's memory for a real-life event.* Paper presented at the biennial meeting of the Society for Research on Child Development, Seattle, Wash.

Siegal, M., Waters, L. J., & Dinwiddy, L. S. (1988). Misleading children: Causal attributions for inconsistency under repeated questioning. *Journal of Experimental Child Psychology, 45,* 438–456.

Spilich, G. J., Vesonder, G. T., Chiesi, H. L., & Voss, J. F. (1979). Text processing of domain-related information for individuals with high and low domain knowledge. *Journal of Verbal Learning and Verbal Behavior, 18,* 275–290.

Stein, N. L., & Glenn, C. (1978). *The role of temporal organization in story comprehension* (Tech. Rep. no. 71). Urbana, Ill.: University of Illinois, Center for Study of Reading.

Stein, N. L., & Trabasso, T. (1991, April). Children's and parents' memory for emotional events: Conditions for convergence at polarization. In N. L. Stein & P. A. Ornstein (Chairs), *The development of autobiographical memory for stressful and emotional events.* Symposium at the biennial meeting of the Society for Research in Child Development, Seattle, Wash.

Tate, C. S., & Warren-Leubecker, A. (1989, April). *The effects of adult coaching on children's willingness to provide false reports.* Paper presented at the biennial meeting of the Society for Research in Child Development, Kansas City, Mo.

Toglia, M. P., & Ross, D. F. (1991, April). *Children's suggestibility: The role of biaser credibility.* Paper presented at the biennial meeting of the Society for Research in Child Development, Seattle, Wash.

Walker, C. E., Bonner, B. L., & Kaufman, K. L. (1988). *The physically and sexually abused child: Evaluation and treatment.* New York: Pergamon.

Warren, A. R., & Hagood, P. L. (in press). Effects of timing and type of questioning on eyewitness accuracy and suggestibility. In M. S. Zaragoza, J. R. Graham, G. N. N. Hall, R. Hirschman, & Y. S. Ben-Porath (Eds.), *Memory and testimony in the child witness.* Thousand Oaks, Calif.: Sage.

Yuille, J. C., Hunter, R., Joffe, R., & Zaparniuk, J. (1993). Interviewing children in sexual abuse cases. In G. S. Goodman & B. L. Bottoms (Eds.), *Child victims, child witnesses: Understanding and improving testimony* (pp. 95–116). New York: Guilford Press.

6

Assessment and Management of Abuse Allegations with Very Young Children

Sandra K. Hewitt and
William N. Friedrich

Assessing cases of child sexual abuse with very young children is difficult, because children 18 to 36 months of age cannot talk very well about what has happened to them. This chapter integrates information about basic child development and research on early memory, normal and abnormal sexual behavior, and the characteristics of young abused children into a format for assessment that is developmentally appropriate. Suggestions for changes in interview style to accommodate the status of young children are also offered. Finally, a procedure for court-ordered reunification is outlined for use when abuse has not been proved, but the child's age and status make him or her vulnerable to possible future abuse.

How do we assess or manage cases of alleged sexual abuse when the child alleged to have been abused is too young to talk about what has happened?

Portions of this chapter appear in Hewitt (1994), "Preverbal sexual abuse: What two children report in later years." *International Journal of Child Abuse and Neglect, 18*(10), 819–824. Reprinted by permission.

What can we do to protect children aged 18 months to three years who are the least able to report their abuse or to separate themselves from their abuser?

Rates for substantiation of abuse are low in this population. In a study of families in divorce courts, it was found that the perceived veracity of alleged sexual abuse reports for children ages one through three is lower than for all other ages (Thoennes, Pearson, & Tjaden, 1988). This age group thus had the largest percentage of indeterminate abuse. Ironically, the children who are among the most vulnerable to being abused, because of their dependency on caretakers and their need for regular diapering and help with bathing, appear to be some of the children for which it can be most difficult to determine abuse.

This chapter briefly reviews the research on very young children's memory; normal sexual behaviors; and the behaviors of young, sexually abused children, and incorporates this information into an outline for the assessment of sexual abuse. The chapter concludes with suggestions for handling cases that cannot be proved, but that have elements that appear to place a child at risk by being reunited with an alleged perpetrator.

MEMORY IN VERY YOUNG CHILDREN

The period from 12 to 36 months marks a transition from preverbal to verbal functioning. Often, because children cannot speak well in these years, people assume that they do not remember or retain information from this period. Hewitt (1994) documents two case studies in which young children had the capacity later to recall and report sexual abuse experiences that took place at the age of two years. Meyers, Clifton, and Clarkston (1987) have documented memory for a behavioral action sequence in children "almost three" years of age who were exposed to repeated experimental procedures administered when they were six to 40 weeks old. Fivush and Hammond (1990) found that children aged two and a half remembered the routine sequences of events, whereas children aged four recalled more of the unique and distinguishing events. Terr (1988) reported behavioral memories for trauma in children under a year old at the time of the event(s), and verbal memory for events happening when they were older than 28 to 36 months of age. Such evidence of early memory and its developmental change has implications for the sexual abuse evaluation of children 18 to 36 months old and for the manner in which such information can be elicited from young children.

SEXUAL BEHAVIOR IN YOUNG CHILDREN

The behaviors of sexually abused children two to 12 years of age were contrasted with the sexual behaviors in a sample of nonabused children

(Friedrich, Grambsch, Damon, Hewitt, Koverola, Lang, Wolfe, & Broughton, 1992). Using the Child Sexual Behavior Inventory (CSBI), a measure specifically designed to assess the nature and intensity of sexual behaviors, Friedrich and colleagues found that sexually abused children showed a greater frequency of sexual behaviors than did the normative sample. Behaviors such as "puts mouth on sex parts, asks to engage in sex acts, masturbates with object, inserts objects in vagina/anus, imitates intercourse, imitates sexual sounds, and French kisses" were among some of the more powerful discriminating items.

A survey of 564 day care providers by Phipps-Yonas, Yonas, Turner, and Kauper (1993) found some developmental differences in the sexual behavior displayed by preschool children. Their research echoed Friedrich and colleagues' findings, and included information on normative sexual behavior in children ages one to three.

> The younger group (aged one to three)...was judged to be more comfortable with their own nudity, both with peers and adults...(while) older children (aged four to six) were viewed as much more curious than the younger ones regarding the mechanics of sexual activity and reproduction. They were also much more likely to engage in exploratory "sexual" games, such as "I'll show you mine, if you show me yours" or doctor or house...touching of other children's genitals is relatively common; more than one-third of the providers describe the older group as doing this and just less than a third report it among the younger children...certain behaviors were reported as having a very low probability...especially for children under age four. These include: efforts to engage in pretend sexual intercourse; French-kissing; requests to have another suck, lick, or kiss their genitals; and attempts to insert objects into their own or another's buttocks or vaginas. (pp. 3–4)

BEHAVIORS OF YOUNG, SEXUALLY ABUSED CHILDREN

Hewitt and Friedrich (1991) found that levels of elevated sexualized behaviors on the CSBI and sleep disturbance significantly differentiated "probably abused" from "probably not abused" children ages one to three. Hewitt, Friedrich, & Allen (1994) found spontaneous sexualized play a significant discriminator between "probably abused" and "probably not abused" children in a sample of 21 two-year-old children. In addition, this research pointed toward the importance of careful behavioral chronicling, plus the need for immediate attention with these cases as initial behavioral responses dissipated over time and substantiation became more difficult.

Although not all children display sexualized behaviors following abuse (Kendall-Tackett, Williams, & Finkelhor, 1993), this beginning body of research with very young children points toward discernible differences in the behaviors of some sexually abused versus nonabused young children, and for the interviewer, it underlines the importance of careful assessment of the sexualized behaviors of young children, as these can be a factor in helping to differentiate abuse from nonabuse cases.

CURRENT EVALUATION PROCEDURES

Most cases of child abuse are proved or not proved on the basis of a child's statements about the events that have or have not happened. If adequate verbalization is the requirement for determining the veracity of cases involving very young children, then assessment will fail because these children cannot give adequate verbal disclosure. Because of their dependency on adults, their inability to escape abuse, and their repetitive needs for diapering, bathing, and toileting help, young children are extremely vulnerable: sexual abuse assessment of these children needs to look beyond words. What is necessary is a thorough, developmentally sound assessment of the child's overall status, plus an exploration of a young child's behaviors, over time and across situations.

Young children's sexual behaviors can be powerful "statements" about their experiences. For example, a two-year-old girl during her bath repeatedly stuck the end of the bowl brush she had grabbed into her vaginal introitus. When asked what she was doing, she responded, "Daddy do." Her actions and her few words are unusual bathing play and talk, and demand follow-up attention. Abuse was later determined in this case.

SHIFTING THE ASSESSMENT PARADIGM

Effective assessment procedures need to reflect the developmental stage of the child. The evaluation of cases of sexual abuse with very young children requires a paradigm shift: a change in philosophical view from verbal disclosure to an emphasis on the "behavioral repertoire" of the young child, over time and across situations. It also requires a new consideration of the significance, or risk level, of unusual sexual behavior as it relates to new research on the sexual behaviors of young children. To fail to explore the behaviors of young children systematically, and to build a case primarily on a child's verbalizations, ignores the preverbal developmental status of the child, and may result in a failure to identify sexual abuse and to protect a child in this vulnerable population.

In another study (Hewitt & Friedrich, 1991), children ages one to three were separated and more closely examined. The most clearly substantiated cases in this sample were found to have four elements: the child had unusual sexual behaviors; he/or she made some limited verbal statement relative to the behaviors; the behaviors/statements were calmly received by a caretaker who did not contaminate, lead, or suppress the expression; and the child was able to repeat the behavior and/or verbalization to someone qualified to assess child abuse. In addition to these findings, the review also noted that the unusual behaviors often did not occur just once, but were frequently part of a "behavioral repertoire" that took place over time and across situations. There would be, for example, unusual expressions of behavior in napping, diapering, or bathing situations that may have evoked some behavioral memory of the original abuse.

Although the 1991 research found significant levels of sexualized behavior, a survey of the literature across all ages of sexually abused children by Kendall-Tackett, Williams, and Finkelhor (1993) found approximately one third of the population of abused children to be asymptomatic. Obviously, if very young children cannot talk and their behaviors are not unusual, sexual abuse may not be suspected and such children are not referred. The approach proposed here, with its emphasis on behavioral repertoire, may underidentify some cases.

An initial outline for assessing abuse in very young children was developed from the case review of previously determined cases, from information on children's memory and play, and from research on the behaviors of abused and nonabused children. This initial outline was expanded for use in current research assessment (Friedrich & Hewitt, 1993).

Developmental History

Effective evaluation of very young children needs to combine both developmental history and current history. Because young children are not carriers of their own history, the primary caretaker needs to be carefully interviewed about the child's background.

Developmental changes need to be surveyed. Are there any unusual lags or problems, any difficulties that may affect the way the child functions, perceives or stores life events? For example, one mother stated that her child had anoxia at birth with resulting brain damage that could affect the child's ability to report. Information about premorbid status, and the overall integrity of the child, is essential in sorting out the effects of possible abuse from other developmental problems.

Medical problems or medical procedures need delineation. Some symptoms of abuse, such as repeated yeast infection exams or a diaper rash that does not respond to treatment, may mimic medical procedures and encourage attention on the genital area of the child, resulting in the child's having a more genitally directed focus and behavior than would a child without such history. For example, one child had been born with a congenital kidney condition, and had been subjected to repeated catheterizations that required her to be strapped down. The child's subsequent reactions to other forms of genital attention were clearly traumatic. Knowledge of the child's history can allow the examiner to understand better the child's reactions.

Attachment history and the documentation of any problems or prolonged separations need to be considered. Some negative reactions to a parent on visitation may reflect problems of separation and attachment, and not abuse reactions. For example, a child whose father had left the home when the child was about nine months old had no contact with him until he was legally restored to visitation when she was 16 months of age. When the father arrived to pick up the child for a visit, there was no time for transition or reacquaintance because of the parents' animosity toward each other. The mother's anxiety was heightened by contact with the father, and the child–being primarily attached to the mother–began to resist not only the separation from the mother, but also any contact with the father. The father was accused of sexual abuse given the child's fearful avoidance of him. A careful behavioral history of the child indicated no unusual sexualized behaviors over time, and the father's psychological evaluation, plus observation of the child and father, gave no evidence of sexual problems. Later, as visits were better arranged (i.e., no contact between the parents and supervised gradual reintegration of the child and her father), the relationship normalized.

Sometimes the normal attachment and separation issues that are salient during these early years may give rise to avoidant behaviors during visitation and abuse may be suspected. Careful evaluation is necessary to look at both the sexual abuse concerns and the attachment issues. It is important to remember that children with poor attachment histories may have more difficulty in making a transition, but even poor attachment histories by themselves do not create a pattern of unusual sexual behaviors.

Any illnesses, injuries, prolonged fevers, and the like, that could affect a child's overall ability and integrity must be noted, as they also could affect the child's capacity to remember or disclose past experiences. For example, although a child had once fallen and sustained injuries with subsequent neurological damage, that child would be expected to respond normally upon observation or in an interview unless the examiner was aware of the medical history. If such a history is not ascertained beforehand, the child's reactions might be misinterpreted. For each new case, the examiner must weigh a complex matrix of variables in reaching a conclusion.

A Review of Relevant Predisposing Factors

Associated risk factors (Friedrich & Hewitt, 1993) include a maternal history of abuse, the level of maternal social support (number of friends, social isolation), the relationship of the mother with her mother and family (the availability of support, as well as assistance, in child rearing), plus such issues as domestic violence (the child may exhibit more fearfulness and/or aggression), chemical dependency, and sexual boundaries in the home (Does the child see nudity, intercourse, X-rated videos, or pornography? What opportunities are there to sleep or bathe with the child?). Exposure to explicit sexual acts either in or outside the home is important to consider in understanding the child's behavior. For example:

A two-year-old girl abruptly began "humping" her dolls and toys. Her mother reported the change to child protection and the child was referred for evaluation. In the evaluator's office, the child mounted a female AC doll and "rode" her, jockey fashion. The mother denied any sexual activity in her home as she was now living with her parents. The husband was living with a new girlfriend, and he vigorously denied that his daughter had witnessed any of their sexual contacts. After he was issued a warning to keep sexual activity private, however, the "humping" behavior significantly decreased, and after about six weeks, it ceased altogether.

Behavioral Repertoire Detailed

Careful documentation of a child's unusual and/or sexualized behaviors over time and across situations is critical. Caregivers usually report one precipitating incident, but often have a list of behaviors of concern before and after that incident. Careful questioning of the caretaker about "the first time you were concerned," as well as about other, subsequent incidents, sometimes can reveal patterns of behavior prior to the reporting. For example:

When taking her nap, two-year-old Nicki would insist that her mother lie down with her, and she would then grab her mother's hand and place it on her vulva. Even when told "No," Nicki would persist; she was giggly and very active during this activity. At one point, while in her bath, Nicki tried to poke a toy, and then some soap, into her vaginal introitus. After she was dried off, she sat up, pulled apart her labia, and again tried to insert things into the introitus. All of this behavior had begun approximately two months before Nicki's referral to a pediatrician for sexual abuse evaluation. With an evaluation finally planned, she returned home from a visit with her father, who was estranged from her mother, and exhibited a reddened vaginal area. All cultures were negative. The father denied any abuse, but was evaluated for sexual abuse by an expert of his choosing. This expert later stated in court that Nicki's father had the characteristics of a sexual offender. Nicki's behavioral repertoire over time was much broader and richer than the precipitating incident of a reddened vulva, and the behavioral documentation helped to create a stronger argument for her protection.

When discussing the behavioral repertoire, the interviewer should ask what the child said and did, where the behavior/statement occurred, what might have triggered the behavior/statement, and how the caretaker responded.

Response to the Disclosure

It is imperative to ask about the method of inquiry used with the child. Parents may be poor observers of their own behavior, and leading and suggestive questioning can contaminate a child's information; however, careful listening and subsequent documentation can provide a powerful log of the child's reactions and responses. Angry, shaming statements by the caretaker or indications of distress can inhibit the child, or even shut the child down to further or later inquiry; a parent's receipt of information in a calm, factual manner is much less suppressing or censuring.

Children's verbal disclosures can sometimes be contaminated by poor interviewing, but the behavioral repertoire is less susceptible to interview contamination and is often one of the most spontaneous child-driven forms of disclosure.

Objective Behavioral Assessment

The use of standardized measures to assess developmental status, behavioral adjustment, and the quality of sexualized behaviors is important. Ask the caretaker to complete objective measures to assess the child's overall development (e.g., Child Development Inventory [CDI], Ireton, 1992), behavioral adjustment (e.g., Child Behavior Checklist [CBC], Achenbach, 1989), and sexualized behaviors (e.g., Child Sexual Behavior Inventory [CSBI], Friedrich et al., 1992). Comparing results from a target child with the standardized scores on the CDI or CBC can help to determine problem areas that might require follow-up and referral. Results on the CSBI can be compared with the scores obtained by abused versus nonabused children.

Even if abuse is not determined, referred children will often have some behavioral or developmental problem. If this is documented, then they can be referred for such services as early childhood intervention, special education, or Head Start. Other trained observers can continue to observe the child while helping him or her to develop additional relationships and communication skills.

Collateral Source Information

Data on the child's statements/behaviors should be gathered from other observers or situations, such as a day-care provider, the medical exam, or behavior noted during the initial police/CPS interview. Some children with abuse histories may vigorously refuse genital exams, while others may invite the physician or nurse to observe or touch their genitals. The children's reactions need to be integrated with their histories, and the reactions may give a clue as to the nature of the abuse—forceful and intrusive or pleasant and manipulative. Day-care providers can validly complete the CBC and CSBI and this provides a direct comparison to the parent report that can be useful in determining the validity of the parent report.

Interview with the Child

The child may be seen for an individual interview, but the task of interviewing a two-year-old is a formidable one. The following are some guidelines for conducting an interview with this age group.

1.   Take time to make friends with the child. Unlike older children who understand the role of the police or child-protection services in helping them, the very young child responds to the quality of the relationship, not the role of the interviewer. As you take time to develop a relationship, carefully assess the child's overall status. Watch how well the child understands speech, how well he or she attends, how much speech the child has, how intelligible the speech is, and how long the child can stay on track with your general questions.

2.   Watch how well the child plays with dolls or toys. There is a developmental progression in the capacity to represent (McCune-Nicolich, 1981). Development moves from play concerning everyday activities (e.g., a car that goes "vroom, vroom"), to more symbolic representations (e.g., dolls taking their clothes off and going "potty" or to bed), and, eventually, to an ability to pretend carrying out other people's activities and their own (e.g., "Mommy is fixing my hair bows"). Representing the self externally is a more complex cognitive task, and often does not appear until the child is about three and a half. This is a critical concept to understand when asking young children to demonstrate with dolls what has happened to them. Because very young children often cannot represent themselves, it is most helpful to let one doll stand for an alleged perpetrator and allow the young child to use his or her own body to show what happened. Do not ask children to use dolls to represent themselves until you are sure they have this capacity. In addition, very young children may not be able to move from abstractions to specifics; that is, to respond to: "Why don't you pick one of these dolls (from a group of dolls) to be a mommy?" For the very young, the interviewer may

need to choose a representative doll and label it for the child ("Let's have this doll be your mommy"), and then proceed with questioning (S. Sgroi, personal communication, February 1993).

3.   Be sure the language used is concrete and clear. The use of "tickle" or "hurt" is more concrete and often better understood than the global, abstract, and sometimes confusing word "touch." Asking a child "How did they do that?" requires the child to organize a body of experience, and that may be difficult for two-year-olds. Asking instead, "What did they do?" followed by, "What did they do next?" may be more helpful. Asking if "somebody" versus "anybody" hurt the child again appeals to a more specific vocabulary (A. Graffam-Walker, personal communication, October 1992). Use simplified and concrete words. For example, a two-year-old was asked if she had a baby sister. Although, in the waiting room, her mother was holding an infant wrapped in a pink blanket, the child replied, "No." But when asked if she had a baby at her house, she said, "Yes," and when asked if it was a girl or a boy, she replied that it was a girl. The fact that two-year-olds are quite young and inexperienced often means that they require more careful and knowledgeable interviewing skills than are needed for older children.

4.   Be sure the child has the necessary concepts to answer your questions. If you ask, "Who touches your pee pee?" you need to screen for the concepts of who, what, or where (Boat & Everson, 1986). Preschoolers do not have temporal or quantitative concepts and cannot meaningfully answer such questions as "When?" and "How many?" You need to know the names the child has for genitals, and you also need a knowledge of what kinds of "touch" words the child understands.

5.   Young children cannot generate extended answers to open-ended questions. They do not have the cognitive complexity and maturity to group information, scan for multiple bits of information, and integrate their experience into a narrative. They are concrete, egocentric thinkers. They need to rely on the interviewer's structure and direction to lead them toward important information. For example, young children cannot respond well to questions like, "Did anything happen at your babysitter's?" Instead ask, "Who tickles you? Show me where _____ tickles you." It is best to let the child generate unprompted responses; however, sometimes you may have to be more direct, for example, "Does Ms. Claire tickle you?" Always, with yes-or-no questions, ask the child to show you what happened. Recognize that with more interviewer-directed questioning a certain degree of freedom is lost; yet, with children at risk, more direct questioning sometimes is necessary to screen safety concerns.

6.   Young children do not relate their history well; in their egocentric thinking, they assume that you see the world in the same way that they do

and that you know about all of their experiences. Therefore, it is important to get the names of significant people in the child's life, as well as any idiosyncratic names for places, people, or genitals. The child may refer to someone or something, and unless you know his or her history, you will not understand the child and may miss some significant information.

Observing the Child with the Alleged Perpetrator

This activity is optional, and is not desirable if it may be traumatic for the child; for example, if the child has been shown to decompensate in the past when in contact with the alleged perpetrator, and if such decompensation would compromise the child's present status. If the alleged abuse is not considered threatening or potentially harmful, then observation of the two may be conducted.

It is important to note that much more research needs to be done to determine what kinds of behaviors are associated with sexual abuse of varying intensity and duration, and how the passage of time affects their presence or absence on observation. Sometimes graphic behavioral interactions may be seen in an abused child, but the lack of such behaviors does not rule out abuse. Very young children are resilient and can regroup quickly with abuse-related behaviors. If the abuse is not reinforced through repetition, the child's behaviors may fade over time.

APPLYING THE PROTOCOL

This assessment protocol is different from the usual sexual abuse protocol because it emphasizes the unique developmental context of the young child; it focuses on behaviors, and then integrates interview approaches to match the child's minimal language skills. It also focuses on behaviors over time and place, not just on the event that prompted the reporting. Attempts to understand the significance of the very young child's sexual behavior against the background of beginning research is also integrated into the assessment protocol.

The protocol is, however, only a working draft. More research remains to be done: more data from larger numbers of sexually abused two-year-olds are needed; data from offender populations (both male and female, adult and adolescent) documenting the type and frequency of abuse are lacking; more work is needed to identify initial behaviors present after abuse and their history of dissipation over time; and, finally, the relationship between the types and length of a child's sexualized behavioral presentation and the nature and extent of the abuse experience must be more fully explored.

A SECOND PARADIGM SHIFT

Even with the use of a developmentally appropriate method of gathering information on possible sexual abuse in children 18 to 36 months of age, few cases of abuse in this age range are substantiated. A second paradigm shift is required—a shift in focus from assessing the perpetrator for prosecution to assessing the child for protection. Although there may be a good behavioral repertoire and a short, clear statement by the child about the abuse, the child is still too young to testify in court and these cases are rarely criminally prosecuted. Careful data collection, with analysis of the behavior against research findings, can help to substantiate a risk level for the young child. If the findings point to a high level of risk, then care can be taken to protect the child, such as allowing only supervised visits until the child is capable of better reporting and better self-protection. Assessment at this age level may best be directed toward "buying time" and affording protection until the child matures and is less vulnerable.

WHEN HIGH-RISK CASES CANNOT BE PROVEN, AND CONTACT WITH AN ALLEGED PERPETRATOR IS ORDERED

One of the realities of child protection is that cases do not sort themselves into neat piles of abused versus not-abused children. There are many "gray" cases; cases in which abuse may be suspected, but information sufficient to substantiate it is lacking. In some of these cases, the children may be ordered to resume contact with the alleged abusers. For some children, the risks may be minimal; for others, they may be more formidable. For some, the reunion may be joyful; for others, it may be frightening or painful. One procedure for therapeutically managed reunification in cases of alleged but unsubstantiated sexual abuse involves a process of careful reunion that seeks to minimize the risk of additional abuse by explicit agreements about touch and ongoing monitoring of the child and the alleged perpetrator (Hewitt, 1991).

This process is best used when court ordered, after a hearing in which abuse is undetermined, and when both parties agree that the ordered reunification should be handled in a therapeutic manner. The initial process includes clarifying forms of touching the child likes and does not like by both the alleged perpetrator and the other parent. Efforts to strengthen the bond between the nonalleged parent and the child are enhanced, and the parent is directed to therapy to help manage his or her anxiety and concern over the prospect of reunification. This parent is also directed not to do any more questioning if abuse-related information surfaces; rather, the child's therapist, or a designated child-protection worker, is identified as the one to follow up with the child. When the child and alleged abuser are reintroduced, the reunion is carefully scripted and timed to promote the child's safety and comfort. Then the alleged abuser is asked to review and affirm the child's desired and not-desired touches, and, finally, to state clearly to the child the "rules" about genital touching and secrets. This explicit instruction about appropriate and inappropriate touching should help to impede the alleged abuser's use of a child's naivete or ambiguity to continue the perpetration. The cases are then followed over time and the behavior of the child carefully monitored.

Cases in need of the longest monitoring are those in which the child is very young and cannot voice opposition to the alleged perpetrator, or cannot fully comprehend the rules. Additionally the alleged perpetrator is seen as controlling, minimizing, marginally cooperative, lacking in role-taking and empathy skills, and unresponsive to boundary violations.

Young children need protection, particularly in view of their vulnerabilities and needs for constant care as compared with older children. Because they cannot speak well, they cannot describe their abuse, and some investigators may conclude that it is useless to try to assess for abuse. Some may feel that there is nothing to be done with this population, and besides, "they probably won't remember anything anyhow." This chapter challenges that assumption and outlines a procedure that can lend structure to a difficult area. Much research is still needed, but the format outlined here does present an alternative for assessment that is better than the other option—that of doing nothing. Even very young children have the right to protection.

Recommendations

1. **THAT** greater attention be paid to the probability of abuse with a population of very young children.
2. **THAT** a more developmentally appropriate protocol for assessment be used to evaluate these cases.
3. **THAT** the assessment emphasize an integration of behavioral repertoire over time and across situations, and that the assessor understand the behaviors in light of the research on the sexual behaviors of both abused and nonabused children.
4. **THAT** assessments shift from a prosecution focus to one of protection and an effort to "buy time" for children until they are more able to report problems.
5. **THAT** when abuse is unproved and children must be reunified, the reunification be handled in a way that honors a child's right to a careful and safe reintegration.

REFERENCES

Achenbach, T. (1988). *Child behavior checklist.* Burlington, Vt.: University Associates in Psychology.

Boat, B., & Everson, M. (1986). *Using anatomical dolls: Guidelines for interviewing young children in sexual abuse investigations.* Chapel Hill, N.C.: University of North Carolina, Department of Psychiatry.

Fivush, R., & Hammond, N. (1990). Autobiographical memory across the preschool years: Toward reconceptualizing childhood amnesia. In R. Fivush & J. Hudson (Eds.), *Knowing and remembering in young children.* New York: Cambridge University Press.

Friedrich, W. N., Grambsch, P., Damon, L., Hewitt, S., Koverola, C., Lang, R., Wolfe, V., & Broughton, D. (1992). Child sexual behavior inventory: Normative and clinical comparisons. *Psychological Assessment, 4*(3), 303–311.

Friedrich, W. N., & Hewitt, S. (1993). *Preschool structured interview.* Unpublished manuscript. Rochester, Minn.: Mayo Clinic.

Hewitt, S. (1991). Therapeutic management of preschool cases of alleged but unsubstantiated sexual abuse. *Child Welfare, 70*(1), 59–67.

Hewitt, S. (1994). Preverbal sexual abuse: What two children report in later years. *International Journal of Child Abuse and Neglect, 18*(10), 819–824.

Hewitt, S., & Friedrich, W. N. (1991). Effects of probable sexual abuse on preschool children. In M. Q. Patton (Ed.), *Family sexual abuse* (pp. 57–74). Newbury, Calif.: Sage.

Hewitt, S., & Friedrich, W. N. (1993). *Assessing sexual abuse in the preverbal child.* Unpublished manuscript.

Hewitt, S., Friedrich, W. N., & Allen, J. (1994, January). Factors in assessing sexual abuse allegations in a sample of two-year-old children. Research presentation at the conference on Child Maltreatment, San Diego, Calif.

Ireton, H.(1992). *Child development inventory.* Minneapolis: Behavior Science Systems.

Kendall-Tackett, K., Williams, L. M., & Finkelhor, D. (1993). Impact of sexual abuse on children: A review and synthesis of recent empirical studies. *Psychological Bulletin, 113*(1), 164–180.

McCune-Nicolich, L. (1981). Toward symbolic functioning: Structure of early pretend games and potential parallels with language. *Child Development, 52,* 785–797.

Meyers, N. A., Clifton, R. K., & Clarkston, M. (1987). When they were very young: Almost threes remember two years of age. *Infant Behavior and Development, 10,* 123–132.

Phipps-Yonas, S., Yonas, A., Turner, M., & Kauper, M. (1993). Sexuality in early childhood: The observations and opinions of family day care providers. *Cura Reporter,* University of Minnesota, Center for Urban and Regional Affairs, Minneapolis.

Terr, L. (1988). What happens to early memories of trauma: A study of twenty children under age five at the time of documented traumatic events. *Journal of the American Academy of Child and Adolescent Psychiatry, 27*(1), 96–104.

Thoennes, N., Pearson, J., & Tjaden, P. (1988). *Allegations of sexual abuse in custody and visitation cases: An empirical study of 169 cases from 12 states.* Denver, Col.: Association of Family and Conciliation Courts Research Unit.

7

Assessment of Adolescents Who Have Been Sexually Abused

Luise Greuel and Adelheid Kuehne

Whereas psychological research has been increasingly involved with child credibility, adolescents have been overlooked by researchers. There are specific components that must be taken into account when assessing adolescents (suggestibility, compliance). Assessors have to consider specific developmental tasks of adolescents (self-identity, sex-role orientation) that might affect the process and the result of psychological investigation. Finally, age-specific symptoms and posttraumatic disorders following the sexual abuse of adolescents (i.e., depression, drug use, sexualized behavior) need to be incorporated into the credibility assessment.

While psychological research has been increasingly involved with child credibility in sexual abuse cases, adolescents have been overlooked by researchers. This is quite remarkable, since, according to German criminal statistics, 90.6% of the victims of sexual abuse are children between the ages of six and 14 years (see Mertens, 1994): moreover, over a third of the rape victims are adolescents (Greuel, 1992). We believe that the major reason for the "blind spot" is that youths are not considered "children," and thus in many ways are dealt with as adults.

In this chapter, we first reflect upon general aspects of credibility assessment. We then discuss some specific problems in assessing adolescents in sexual abuse cases: (1) suggestibility, (2) compliance and self-identity, and (3) emotional problems and age-specific posttraumatic disorders. In any investigative assessment of sexual abuse, the assessor has to generate a basic hypothesis ("reality hypothesis"), as well as alternative hypotheses referring to other possible origins of the alleged events. In order adequately to explore the alternative hypotheses, the following considerations are suggested: (1) the adolescent's competence to testify, (2) the credibility of the adolescent's statement, and (3) developmental tasks of adolescents.

GENERAL ASPECTS OF CREDIBILITY ASSESSMENT

Competence to testify includes the cognitive abilities to reproduce a reliable and valid testimony concerning an experienced or perceived event. The question to answer is: Does the statement reflect the original perception/experience in a correct manner, or is it falsified by cognitive mistakes (unconsciously erroneous testimony)? In this context, perception and mnemonic and verbal abilities concerning such factors as reality monitoring need to be assessed by standardized tests or behavioral observation.

In assessing adolescents, basic cognitive functions are usually examined extensively when there are references to cognitive weaknesses or deficits, as in the case of mentally handicapped witnesses. This is in contrast to the investigation of children, where general cognitive competencies are assessed; adolescent witnesses are more often assessed with concerns about specific cognitive competence. Adolescents may also need to be assessed on specific situational factors that might affect their competence to testify. For example, sexual victimization of adolescents often occurs in situations in which alcohol or drugs have been consumed. In such cases, the memory, which might have been affected by intoxication, has to be assessed.

Credibility of the statement involves considering the motivational factors affecting the statement. The question to be answered is: Is the content of the witness's statement based on an experienced event or is it a product of fabrication or coercion (consciously false testimony)? The focus of credibility assessment is the content of the statement. Statement validity analysis (Arntzen, 1993; Steller & Koehnken, 1989) analyzes the extent to which "reality criteria" are included; that is, what features appear in truthful reports about actually experienced events but are missing in untruthful (fabricated) statements?

In addition to the rating of the content criteria (see Steller & Koehnken, 1989), other sources of information (e.g., motivation to testify, characteristics of the investigative interview, psychological characteristics of the witness) are used to evaluate the probability that the witness refers to a real event or to a fabrication.

Statement validity analysis was developed to deal with child sexual abuse complaints (see Undeutsch, 1967). But in forensic practice, the procedure has simply been applied to adolescents and young adults (Greuel, 1993b; Scholz & Greuel, 1992) without first considering the different age-specific characteristics (but see Chapter 9, this volume). From our experience, assessing adolescents is quite different from the assessment of child witnesses. In the following, we discuss some specific problems that arise when assessing adolescents in sexual abuse cases, including suggestibility, compliance and self-identity, and emotional problems and age-specific posttraumatic disorders.

INTERROGATIVE SUGGESTIBILITY

In forensic practice, psychological experts are often asked whether adolescents' testimonies are influenced by suggestibility. The question is: do adolescents have a tendency to answer questions based on information that interviewers (i.e., police interrogators, psychologists) may have suggested?

Interrogative suggestibility is defined as "the extent to which, within a closed social interaction, people come to accept messages communicated during formal questioning, as the result of which their subsequent behavioral response is affected" (Gudjonsson & Clark, 1986, p. 84). Register and Kihlstrom (1988) argue that suggestibility may occur in response to (1) leading questions, (2) negative feedback, and (3) repeated questions.

Whereas a "leading question" implies the answer or assumes facts that are likely in dispute, "negative feedback" may be implicit rather than explicit. For example, negative feedback may occur during interrogation when the interviewer repeats the same question several times and the interviewees begin to believe that the interviewer does not accept their previous answers. Thus the interrogator may shift unwanted but perhaps accurate answers through critical feedback and interrogative pressure.

Research indicates that adolescents in general are no more suggestible than are adults (Gudjonsson & Singh, 1984). They provide as much accurate free-recall information as do adults—unless the interrogation is characterized by negative feedback. When youths are exposed to interrogative pressure such as repeated questions, they become markedly more suggestible than adults (Gudjonsson, 1992). Such pressure may be result if the interviewer criticizes the adolescent's answers or simply repeats the same questions several times. When subjected to pressure, adolescents become particularly vulnerable to giving unreliable information during formal interrogation, and they tend to shift their answers (Gudjonsson & Singh, 1984). Thus it is very important to avoid any kind of critical feedback when interviewing adolescents who allegedly have been sexually abused.

In some cases, it may be useful to measure an individual's interrogative suggestibility; for example, if the previous police interrogation has been suggestive. For forensic applications, the Gudjonsson Suggestibility Scales (GSS; Gudjonsson, 1984) can be used to assess the individual's vulnerability to leading questions and negative feedback. The GSS is a standardized psychological test that can identify people who are particularly susceptible to erroneous testimony during formal questioning; it has also been used to assess confabulations (Gudjonsson, 1992). Further information about suggestibility can be gathered by behavioral observation. If there is suspicion of a suggestible interviewee or the interview style has been suggestive, the demands on the quality of the testimony under consideration have to be increased; that is, the reality criteria in the adolescent's abuse complaint must have a higher score before the testimony can be classified as "credible" (Arntzen, 1993).

COMPLIANCE AND SELF-IDENTITY

According to Zaragoza (1991), it is important to differentiate between suggestibility, as discussed above, and compliance. While suggestibility implies personal acceptance of the proposition offered by the interviewer, the phenomenon of compliance indicates that the individual does not accept the proposition, and that he or she is fully aware that his or her responses are influenced. Compliance has two major components:

1. The person has a need to please or protect his or her self-esteem in a social situation.
2. The person has a need to avoid conflict or confrontation with people, particularly those perceived as being in positions of authority.

The latter component has proved quite important with regard to child witnesses (Goodman & Schwartz-Kenney, 1992). In our experience, adolescents are also vulnerable to giving answers they perceive as being consistent with the anticipated expectations of the interviewer, who is perceived as being an authority. In such cases, response sets such as social desirability and obedience to authority (Milgram, 1974) must be considered. To assess such responses, two assessment methods may be implemented: self-report questionnaires (e.g., Gudjonsson Compliance Scale [GCS]; Gudjonsson, 1989) and behavioral observation. As compliance is primarily situation bound, as opposed to being a predisposing trait (Moston, 1990), we prefer behavioral observation for forensic applications.

Here, a stimulus can be presented to check how the interviewee tends to conform in a given condition, or how the client tries to please or gives in when pressured. However, it is very important to point out that this kind of compliance check should only be applied in a neutral thematic interview context, that is, with themes with no relationship to the alleged abuse. If those conditions are established in the case-related interview, the elicited responses might not be used for statement validity analysis (Arntzen, 1993).

Our experience in assessing adolescents suggests that there is a second, possibly more important source of compliance that has been largely overlooked, namely, the effects of sex-role expectations. More so than young children, adolescents are aware of and operate according to socially established sex-role stereotypes (Fegert, 1993), and have a more differentiated gender-related self-concept than do children. Thus factors related to social identity play an important part in interviewing and assessing adolescents who have been sexually abused. Because sexual abuse implies a violation of personal identity, and because social identity is salient for them (Stevens, 1990), adolescents are particularly susceptible to violations of their gendered self-concept. Thus, for example, if an adolescent experienced pleasure or an adolescent boy became sexually aroused (i.e., had an erection) during the sexual abuse, then it is possible, for the developmental reasons described above, that the adolescent will not report the experience accurately. Such a confabulation might serve to protect self-identity or to meet socially established, victim-related schemata about what a "real victim" feels and does. This tendency to withhold or modify aspects of the abuse in order to preserve self-identity can be observed in both adolescent boys and adolescent girls.

A very specific problem arises with regard to male adolescents who have been sexually abused by a male adult. First, boys are usually socialized into an ethos in which independence, activity, self-reliance, and sexual prowess are highly valued, while helplessness, vulnerability, and homosexuality are devalued. Given that sexual victimization creates strong feelings of shame and deep confusion concerning gender and personal identity, male adolescents can be reluctant to talk about their sexual abuse (Van Outsem, 1993; Watkins & Bentovim, 1992).

For the reasons discussed above, in some cases, it is important to assess sex-role orientations and gender-related attitudes when assessing adolescents who have been sexually abused. For forensic applications, interviews with the adolescent, as well as with his or her parents, can provide valuable information about gender cues and the values, standards, and stereotypes the young person has internalized during socialization. In some cases, self-report questionnaires may be helpful (Brogan & Kutner, 1976). In this context, it is important that sex-role orientation or gendered personal identity be communicated at the end of the assessment, and on no account prior to the forensic interview. This is necessary because thinking and talking about sex-role stereotypes may increase the salience of traditional stereotypes, which may affect the interviewee's responses in an undesired way (Schwarz & Brandt, 1993).

Up until now, we have focused on the problems of assessing adolescents who withhold or modify some aspects of their victimization in order to protect their self-identity. But how does one make sense of adolescents who spontaneously report self-dissonance? In such cases, according to statement validity analysis (Steller & Koehnken, 1989), the presence of self-dissonant statements is a positive indicator of the credibility of the adolescent's statement. Such statements correspond with the reality criteria called "self-deprecation" and "pardoning the perpetrator," which indicate that the statement under consideration is likely to be credible. For example, imagine that an adolescent reports that she enjoyed some caress of the abuser or that she did not resist him. It is unlikely that an adolescent who gives consciously false testimony would report such unprofitable statements, as they are dissonant from socially established schemata about what a "real victim" is doing. On the contrary, in some cases of false accusation, the complainants try to present themselves in a highly positive manner in order to meet the standards of social desirability (Arntzen, 1993). Thus statements that report both the positive and negative aspects of the victim and the abuser reflect the adolescent's objective and neutral attitude, suggesting that there is no motivation for false accusations. The objectivity of the statement indicates the credibility of testimony.

EMOTIONAL PROBLEMS AND POSTTRAUMATIC DISORDERS

When investigating adolescents in sexual abuse cases, the assessor is usually confronted with specific emotional and behavioral problems. These problems may be a response to the investigative procedure itself (e.g., awkwardness, shame), or they may result from an abuse experience (posttraumatic symptoms).

The investigative process may feel awkward for the adolescent who is threatened by publicity and uncontrollability (Roos, 1988) and has to present a part of self that he or she is still uncertain about. It is not uncommon for adolescents to hide behind a front of coolness, provocation, or aggression in order to cope with their shame and anxieties. Assessors may respond to the adolescents' defensive behavior with intense countertransference reactions (Hedlund & Eklund, 1986).

Adolescents are commonly aware of the consequences of their testimony for themselves, as well as for their families, particularly in cases of intrafamiliar sexual abuse. Hence they often suffer from strong conflicts of loyalty, which may lead to false retractions of valid (incest) accusations (Goodwin, Sahd, & Rada, 1982). With regard to the psychosocial implications of sexual abuse, the psychological expert has to focus on the motives for retracting complaints.

Victims of sexual abuse exhibit different posttraumatic symptoms at different age levels. Even if there is no specific syndrome of sexual abuse, empirical findings indicate that depression and suicidal tendencies are symptoms more commonly associated with adolescents than with children (DeYoung, 1982). When a child approaches adolescence, antisocial behaviors such as drug use, promiscuity, and prostitution may be observed (Romney, 1982). Girls may run away from home in order to escape their abuse situation, and it is not uncommon for runaways to turn to prostitution (Gomes-Schwartz, Horowitz, & Sauzier, 1985). Such behavioral problems must be incorporated into the assessment, and the evaluator must assess whether the symptoms, as described above, are a response to former victimization (Scholz & Greuel, 1992). Untrained professionals may misinterpret such symptoms of an alleged victim, which may, in turn, raise doubts concerning the adolescent's credibility. For example, if an adolescent girl is known as a drug user, or as a sexually active person, and claims that she has been abused, the court might conclude that she provoked the abuser or that she is not a credible witness. Ironically, such behavioral problems could be a direct consequence of the sexual abuse, which should serve to support her credibility (Greuel, 1993a). Thus it is one of the expert's tasks to explain various behaviors of the assessed witness.

Undeutsch (1967, 1989) and colleagues suggest that the statement, and not the person, is the focus of credibility assessment. That is, credibility is a feature of a specific statement and it is not a characteristic or trait of the witness's personality. Nevertheless, the witness may provide valuable information supporting the forensic statement validity analysis. Behavioral disorders, which are typically associated with sexually abused adolescents, should be incorporated into the credibility assessment and interpreted as offense-specific details (Steller & Koehnken, 1989). Thus the validity of the statement is supported by the symptoms specific to the sexually abused adolescent. Of course, the assessor needs an extensive knowledge of the criminological and psychological particularities of different types of crime, as well as practical experience in assessing sexual abuse complaints, to identify such offense-specific elements of a statement.

CONCLUSION

A psychological assessment in sexual abuse cases involving adolescents needs to determine whether the witness is credible and competent to testify. Therefore, the psychological expert needs information concerning the psychology of testimony, the developmental tasks and emotional problems of male and female adolescents, adolescent vulnerability to suggestion, compliance behavior, adolescent self-identity, and age-specific posttraumatic disorders.

It is important that the statement be the focus of credibility assessment—not the personality of the adolescent witness.

Recommendations

1. **THAT** assessors have a basic knowledge of the developmental tasks of adolescents.
2. **THAT** assessors avoid any kind of interrogative pressure and critical feedback because of adolescents' vulnerability to suggestion.
3. **THAT** assessors be considerate of adolescents' awe of talking about self-dissonant experiences.
4. **THAT** assessors be aware that adolescents are particularly susceptible to violations of their gendered self-concept.
5. **THAT** assessors consider male adolescents' difficulties with reporting homosexual abuse.
6. **THAT** assessors have a basic knowledge about posttraumatic disorders and their implications for adolescents' complaints.
7. **THAT** assessors consider that the statement, and not the personality of the adolescent witness, should be the focus of credibility assessment.

REFERENCES

Arntzen, F. (1993). *Psychologie der Zeugenaussage.* Munich: Beck.
Bilsky, W., Pfeiffer, C., & Wetzels, P. (1993). *Erste Ergebnisse einer repräsentativen Befragung zu den Themen "Gewalt gegen Kinder," "sexueller Kindesmißbrauch," "Abschaffung des elterlichen Zuechtigungsrechts."* Hannover: Kriminologisches Forschungsinstitut Niedersachen, unpublished manuscript.

Brogan, D., & Kutner, N. G. (1976). Measuring sex-role orientation: A normative approach. *Journal of Marriage and Family, 38,* 31–40.

De Young, M. (1982). *The sexual victimization of children.* Jefferson, N.C.: McFarland.

Fegert, J. M. (1993). *Sexuell mißbrauchte Kinder und das Recht, Band 2.* Cologne: Volksblatt.

Gomes-Schwartz, B., Horowitz, J. M., & Sauzier, M. (1985). Severity of emotional distress among sexually abused preschool, school-age, and adolescent children. *Hospital and Community Psychiatry, 36,* 503–508

Goodman, G. S., & Schwartz-Kenney, B. M. (1992). Why knowing a child's age is not enough: Influences of cognitive, social, and emotional factors on children's testimony. In H. Dent & R. Flin (Eds.), *Children as witnesses* (pp. 15–32). Chichester, England: Wiley.

Goodwin, J., Sahd, D., & Rada, R. T. (1982). False accusations and false denials of incest: Clinical myths and clinical realities. In J. Goodwin (Ed.), *Sexual abuse: Incest victims and their families.* Boston: Wright.

Greuel, L. (1992). *Psychologische Bedingungen polizeilichen Interaktionshandelns in der Vernehmung vergewaltigter Frauen.* Bonn: Dissertation.

Greuel, L. (1993a). *Polizeiliche Vernehmung vergewaltigter Frauen.* Weinheim: Psychologie Verlags Union.

Greuel, L. (1993b). Forensische Psychologie. In A. Schorr (Ed.), *Handwörterbuch der Angewandten Psychologie* (pp. 235–242). Bonn: Deutscher Psychologen Verlag.

Gudjonsson, G. H. (1984). A new scale for interrogative suggestibility. *Personality and Individual Differences, 5,* 303–314.

Gudjonsson, G. H. (1989). Compliance in an interrogation situation: A new scale. *Personality and Individual Differences, 10,* 535–540.

Gudjonsson, G. H. (1992). *The psychology of interrogations, confessions and testimony.* Chichester, England: Wiley.

Gudjonsson, G. H., & Clark, N. K. (1986). Suggestibility in police interrogation: A social psychological model. *Social Behavior, 1,* 83–104.

Gudjonsson, G. H., & Singh, K. K. (1984). Interrogative suggestibility and delinquent boys: An empirical validation study. *Personality and Individual Differences, 5,* 425–430.

Hedlund, E., & Eklund, I. B. (1986). Emotionale Probleme der Beraterinnen bei der Konfrontation mit sexueller Gewalt. In J. Heinrichs (Ed.), *Vergewaltigung* (pp. 62–64). Braunschweig: Holtzmeyer.

Kuehne, A. (1988). *Psychologie im Rechtswesen. Psychologische und psychodiagnostische Fragen bei Gericht.* Weinheim: Deutscher Studienverlag.

Milgram, S. (1974). *Obedience to authority.* London: Tavistock.

Moston, S. (1990). How children interpret and respond to questions: Situation sources of suggestibility in eyewitness interviews. *Social Behavior, 5,* 155–167.

Register, P. A., & Kihlstrom, J. F. (1988). Hypnosis and interrogative suggestibility. *Personality and Individual Differences, 9,* 549–558.

Romney, M. C. (1982). Incest in adolescence. *Pediatric Annals, 11,* 813–817.

Roos, J. (1988). *Die Entwicklung der Zuschreibung komplexer Emotionen am Beispiel der Emotion Peinlichkeit.* Frankfurt: Lang.

Scholz, O. B., & Greuel, L. (1992). Zur Beurteilung der Qualität von Glaubhaftigkeitsgutachten in Vergewaltigungsprozessen. *Monatsschrift für Kriminologie und Strafrechtsreform, 6,* 321–327.

Schwarz, N., & Brandt, J. F. (1993). Effects of salience of rape on sex role attitudes, trust and self-esteem in non-raped women. *European Journal of Social Psychology, 13,* 71–76.

Steller, M., & Koehnken, G. (1989). Criteria-based statement analysis. In D. Raskin (Ed.), *Psychological methods in criminal investigation and evidence* (pp. 217–245). New York: Springer.

Stevens, D. (1990, September). *Social fabrics of rape.* Paper presented at the Second Conference on Law and Psychology, Erlangen-Nuernberg.

Undeutsch, U. (1967). Beurteilung der Glaubhaftigkeit von Aussagen. In U. Undeutsch (Ed.), *Handbuch der Psychologie, Band 11: Forensische psychologie* (pp. 26–184). Goettingen: Hogrefe.

Undeutsch, U. (1989). The development of statement reality analysis. In J. Yuille (Ed.), *Credibility assessment* (pp. 101–119). Dordrecht, Netherlands: Kluwer.

Van Outsem, R. (1993). *Sexueller Mißbrauch an Jungen.* Ruhnmark: Donna Vita.

Watkins, B., & Bentovim, A. (1992). Male children and adolescents as victims: A review of current knowledge. In G. C. Mezey & M. B. King (Eds.), *Male victims of sexual assault* (pp. 17–66). Oxford: Oxford University Press.

Zaragoza, M. S. (1991). Preschool children's susceptibility to memory impairment. In J. Dorris (Ed.), *The suggestibility of children's recollections* (pp. 27–39). Washington, D.C.: American Psychological Association.

PART III

The Interview

8

The Language of the
Child Abuse Interview:
Asking the Questions,
Understanding the Answers

Anne Graffam Walker
and Amye R. Warren

In this chapter, we discuss the assumptions that adults make when speaking to each other, and how those assumptions may be inappropriate, and even harmful, if they are carried over into conversations with children. We recommend that, in any interview of a child, the child's comprehension of word meanings be established, that the complexity of sentences be tailored to the child's level of understanding, that the child's comprehension of questions be monitored, and that a structure be provided for the child's report.

This is a chapter about something so simple that we pay little attention to it, but something simultaneously so complex that we ought to: it is a chapter about *language.* More specifically, it is a chapter about assumptions that adults make about the language children speak, and about how those assumptions can lead interviewers astray when they talk to children.

People make a lot of assumptions when they carry on conversations with each other. They assume that each party intends to make sense, for one thing. And they assume that making sense will be done in a language that each person understands. This does not mean simply that each person agrees to speak a particular language, such as English, or Spanish, or Urdu. It means that whatever the language chosen, both parties assume that the other has an adequate store of words and idioms, a skill comparable to their own in putting those words together to make sentences that others will understand, and a shared cultural knowledge of how to use those words and sentences to get things done.

It is not surprising, then, considering that most of our assumptions about language are below awareness when we speak, that we carry them into our conversations with children. The problem is that we should not do so, because for children, particularly young children, those assumptions do not hold true. We cannot consider here all of the ways in which that is so, but we can make a beginning. We will set out what we see as the basic assumption made by adults everywhere when they have conversations, and then break it down into four parts for discussion. At the end of the chapter, we will make a few practical suggestions and offer some recommendations for future reading, so that those who are interested in pursuing the linguistic complexities of talk with children can do so.

ADULT ASSUMPTIONS ABOUT LANGUAGE

The assumption that acts as a primary source of misunderstanding and misinterpretation when we adults talk to children is that *if someone sounds pretty much the way we do, that person has the same linguistic capacities that we have.* In other words, generally, when we begin our conversations (until or unless we have evidence to the contrary):

1. We assume that if someone uses a word, he or she understands its meaning.
2. We assume that if we can ask a complex question, the hearer can process it.
3. We assume that if the hearer does not understand something we have said, he or she will tell us so–and why, in some cases.
4. We assume that if we ask someone "What happened?" he or she can tell us–if he or she knows.

Let us take a closer look at these assumptions, and how they relate to children.

1. We Assume That If Someone Uses a Word, He or She Understands Its Meaning

The assumption that if someone uses a word appropriately, he or she understands it, is one that adults talking to adults must make, or communication could never be accomplished. It is not one, however, that adults should make when talking to children, yet they often do.

"My stepmother loves us. She's overprotective," a nine-year-old tells a judge, who responds, "Well, that's one thing you don't like about her?" "That's the thing I like about her," the child replies, comfortable with the fact that her stepmother cares for her (adapted from *Baxter v. Baxter*, in Jones, 1984).

In this case, the adult's incorrect assumption about the meaning of a word resulted in no harm. The odd juxtaposition of "loves" and "overprotective" caused the judge to ask a clarifying question, and a potentially significant misunderstanding was cleared up. But if there are no linguistic oddities, no overt clues, the clarifying questions can go unasked. When a five-year-old boy responds appropriately, "Before," to a judge's question, "When did it happen: before Christmas or after Christmas?" it is easy to take for granted that the child's "before" is the same as ours. And if we know that "after" is the correct answer, it is tempting to suspect the child's memory or competence rather than to investigate his stage of language development, since "before" is such an "easy" word. In this case, which hinged on the child's identification of the exact date, the outcome was fortunately different. After several more questions about when the incident happened, the judge discovered the source of confusion when he asked: "Listen carefully now. What number comes *before* the number five?" and the child answered, "Six."

Studies by researchers of evidentiary interviews with children show us that we also take for granted that when children demonstrate for us their command over the easy words we use to count, name colors, recite the days of the week and months of the year, tell time, and talk about "Aunt Mary," their *use* of these words is evidence that they understand them as we do (e.g., Brennan & Brennan, 1988; Saywitz & Snyder, 1993; Walker, 1993). This assumption generates such questions as: "You counted for me, so you know about numbers. So how many times did he do this to you?" And when the children give us answers that sound fantastical ("A hundred"), we can be led to discount their reports rather than to investigate the meaning attached to the words.

Taking words for granted is never a safe step in interviewing children. Preschool children are particularly vulnerable to misunderstandings. Their command of language is far from complete, and their ability to give a reliable interpretation to certain prepositions (e.g., "in front of/behind"), adjectives (e.g., "more/less"), adverbs (e.g., "before/after"; "-ly" forms), pronouns (e.g., "this/that"), verbs (e.g., "ask/tell"; "know/think/guess"), and nouns (distinctions between "lie" and "mistake") is limited. Even older children, up to about the age of 10 or 11, can experience difficulty with many of these words (see Gleason, 1993, for a review).

There is a flip side to the assumption that ties use to understanding—and that is that we adults expect our hearers to understand the words we use. On an intellectual level, of course, we do not really believe that children will understand such words as "perpetrator" or "prior to" or "differentiate," yet we use them nonetheless. And while we might catch ourselves now and then ("Oh: 'testify'; that's not a word a child would understand"), words like "court," "case," and "swear" give us no pause at all. Yet studies of children's knowledge of words like these (e.g., Saywitz, Jaenicke, & Campara, 1990; Warren-Leubecker, Tate, Hinton, & Ozbek, 1989) show us that when we say "court," and mean a place where disputes are settled, a child might well be seeing a place where games are played, such as a basketball court. When we talk about a "case," meaning a particular set of circumstances that we are involved in handling, the child might be thinking of something to carry papers in. And "swear" has a far more earthy meaning in everyday life, even for children, than it does in the law.

Everyday life is, after all, the sole source of our original fund of words. Experience is the source of meaning, and what we need to keep in mind when we talk to children is that mutual experience cannot be assumed. Not with life, and not with words.

2. We Assume That If We Can Ask a Complex Question, the Hearer Can Process It

A five-year-old girl was asked, "What was the name of the street on which you pointed out the house where one of the people lived who hurt Doug?" She answered, "I said 'down the street'." Obviously, the response does not match the question, but that is not surprising. To respond accurately, to give the name of the street, the child had to work her way through three relative clauses (beginning with "which," "where," "who"); remember a past action ("pointed out the house"); tackle an indefinite pronoun in an indefinite phrase ("one of the people"); leapfrog over one verb ("lived") to connect "people" with the verb "hurt"; and recognize "hurt" as the adult's euphemism for "killed." She had to, in effect, collapse five propositions (represented by five verbs) into one thought, and remember from beginning to end that the answer to the question should be a street name. Adults would have little difficulty with this task; for a five-year-old, it was impossible. She could not process it because, as is typical of children her age, she was unable to pay attention to that many ideas at once, and her answer focused on the idea that was the most salient to her: her original action in pointing out the house (Walker, 1993).

This example illustrates, then, two critical factors that create linguistic complexity: the inclusion of more than two central ideas (represented by more than two verbs), and the inclusion within a sentence of other potential sentences (the relative clauses). Some other signs of complexity are the use of the passive voice ("Was he kissed by you?," which a child might interpret as, "Did he kiss you?"); complex negation, as in double negatives ("You were *not un*happy, were you?"); and left-branching sentences, in which one or more clauses come in front of the main subject and verb (*"In the days and weeks that followed your becoming aware that Doug got hurt,* you talked to policemen a lot of different times, didn't you?"). (For a thorough discussion of linguistic complexity, see Davison & Green, 1988.) Utterances that have false starts and changes of directions are also very difficult for children to follow, as are questions that begin "Do you remember" followed by more than one proposition: "And do you remember being asked at about 5 o'clock p.m. by a Detective S____ or others to look at six boys who were standing in what's called a lineup?" The five-year-old's answer to that question—complex in many ways—was "Yes" (Walker, 1993). But we have no real way of knowing to what part of the question the "Yes" referred. Questions without reliable answers are not useful in interviews, and worse yet, responses that are misinterpreted as answers can lead us seriously astray.

The examples just provided are of interviews with a young child, not yet in school. But complexity of syntax continues to present processing problems for children well into their middle and sometimes teen years. Full use and comprehension of passives, for instance, can come as late as age 13 (Romaine, 1984); older children continue to be confused by long, involved questions (Brennan & Brennan, 1988); and problems in processing complex negation continue on into adulthood. If adults want clear, reliable answers to their questions, then they must rid themselves of the assumption that if they can ask a complex question, children can answer it. Simple questions that are couched in the active voice, that are as free of negatives as possible, and that express as few ideas as possible will generate better answers, and, therefore, better information from children.

3. *We Assume That If the Hearer Doesn't Understand Something We've Said, He or She Will Tell Us So (and Why, in Some Cases)*

As the previous examples indicate, children sometimes answer questions that they probably have not understood, and yet they rarely ask us to repeat or rephrase our questions. Young children, especially, give us few explicit cues as to whether they do or do not understand us (Gleason, 1977). Instead, they tend to respond to any adult question or statement with an answer or an action, whether or not the adult intended for the child to respond. For example, if a child is drawing and an adult comments, "My crayon is white," the child may hand the adult his or her own crayon, having interpreted the comment as a request for action (Ervin-Tripp, Strage, Lampert, & Bell, 1987). The tendency to respond first and ask later is especially common when the adult speaker is an authority figure. When an authority figure asks a nonsensical or ambiguous question, such as whether milk is bigger than water, children are more likely simply to answer "Yes" or "No" than to ask for clarification (Hughes & Grieve, 1980). Why don't children tell us when they can't understand us?

First, children have a difficult time in judging the adequacy of someone else's speech. Because children are relatively new to the conversational process, they may not have enough resources to listen, to speak, and to monitor what they are hearing and saying all at the same time (Warren & McCloskey, 1993). In one recent study (Perry, Claycomb, Tam, McAuliff, Dostal, & Flanagan, 1993), children were asked to judge how well they understood questions that were asked in "lawyerese." Kindergarten-age children were wrong about their comprehension of the questions most of the time, saying that they understood the questions, but then answering them incorrectly.

Second, children may not give us feedback about our unclear and inappropriate questions because children sometimes make unwarranted assumptions too: they assume that adults are always right. They assume that adult speakers are following certain conversational principles correctly; that, among other things, adult speakers are being informative, clear, cooperative, and honest (Bonitatibus, Godshall, Kelley, Levering, & Lynch, 1988). Thus children may be reluctant to question what an all-knowing adult authority is saying, regardless of how ambiguous it may be.

Third, children are used to the adults in their everyday lives taking responsibility for their comprehension. In natural conversations between parents and children, parents look for signals of misunderstanding (e.g., failures to respond to requests or to answer questions, incorrect answers to questions, hesitations, and confused facial expressions), and rely on these sometimes subtle signals to keep their speech in line with their children's level of understanding. Children do *not* have to provide explicit verbal cues of noncomprehension (e.g., "What?") during natural conversations in order for adults to tailor their speech to the child's level (a good review of this "fine-tuning" literature may be found in Snow & Ferguson, 1977). So why can't sensitive adult interviewers accomplish this same feat? Perhaps it is due to the fact that an interview rarely resembles a natural conversation. It is a question/answer session, with the adult in total control. Further, interviewers are faced with many demands, and in the course of making sure that they remember to ask all the important evidence-gathering questions, they may forget to make sure that the children have understood the questions.

Because children do not often give us explicit feedback of comprehension or lack of comprehension, and because children are not very good at determining when they do not understand a complex question, it is our responsibility to monitor children's comprehension for them. We should give them "permission" to ask us to repeat and clarify, and to correct our mistakes when they do detect them. We should tell them that we do not know what has happened, and, therefore, may not know the right way to ask questions. We should also closely watch their behavior for subtle signals of misunderstanding. In short, we should not assume that children understand us.

4. We Assume That If We Ask Someone, "What Happened?" He or She Can Tell Us, If He or She Knows

In the course of investigating suspected sex abuse, a detective goes over some details with the five-year-old child involved:

Q: I see. And then you went in the shower?
A: Yes, and then I got out and then after it was all over and then I got a ride to, to Sunnyville.

A seven-year-old victim of sex abuse answers questions during a preliminary hearing:

Q: Can you tell me what he did the other time?
A: He pulled me inside my house and then, and then I fell asleep on my couch.
Q: And what happened?
A: [Silence]
Q: M----, did something happen?
A: No.

Experience tells us, and research verifies (e.g., Todd & Perlmutter, 1980), that even children as young as two and a half or three can give accurate, if incomplete, reports of something that happened to them. As the responses given by the two children above demonstrate, this "accurate but incomplete" characteristic can follow children on into their early school years. In each of those cases, the critical knowledge needed by the adult interviewers—all of the detail in the middle—was missing.

Adults have high standards for "telling what happened," for giving, in other words, a personal narrative of some past event. The model we hold for a satisfactory narrative includes a setting that introduces both place and play-

ers, initiating action, central action, goals of the people involved, and consequences (Labov, 1972; Stein & Glenn, 1979). We expect to be alerted if events
are not related chronologically, and we expect to be given a clear picture
as the events unfold of who is involved in what. In order to produce a satisfactory narrative of a personal past event, then, the teller must have, at a
minimum, a great deal of organizational skill, must be able to give clear descriptions, must provide appropriate pronoun reference, and, critically, must
know what knowledge is important to share with the listener. These are not skills
that children can be relied upon to possess, independently, until, in some
cases, the mid-teens (Labov, 1972; Whitehurst, 1976). Even then, children
who face unfamiliar questioning circumstances, such as evidentiary interviews of any kind, are handicapped in their ability to give a complete narrative, or report, of past events.

Easing the handicap is our job. That means, among other things, that we
must provide an appropriate context for the open-ended questions that we
ask. Rather than expecting the child to provide the setting that helps a story
to make sense, we need to be prepared to provide it for that child. That
means that *we* take the responsibility for naming the topic, as in, "Now let's
talk about _____," and for providing the chronological scaffold that holds
the topics together. In the examples above, that could have been done by
asking: "So you got out of the shower. What happened just before you got
out of the shower?" Or, "Oh. He pulled you inside your house. What was
the very next thing that happened?"

Helping a child to build a coherent story also means that we listen to the
implications of our own questions. Had the attorney in the preliminary hearing above done so, he might have understood the silence that followed his
question, "And what happened?" From the child's perspective, nothing did.
Her story was done ("I fell asleep on the couch"). From the adult perspective, however, the child's response that nothing happened could be, and was,
interpreted as a denial that any abuse had occurred on that occasion. It was
an interpretation that could have been avoided, had the adults not assumed
that the child could tell "what happened" on her own.

CONCLUSION

Just as we need to assume that other drivers know how to operate their
machines and obey the rules of the road, we need to assume that other speakers
operate with the same machinery and rules that we do. Otherwise, we would
never make it out of the house, and never attempt a conversation. But the
assumptions that enable us to work smoothly as adults in everyday life can

work against us when we talk to children. As this chapter has outlined, the essential linguistic assumption that we adults need to discard is that children use and process language in the same way as we do. We need to reexamine our notions that tie the use of a word to the understanding of a concept. We need to rethink children's reception of our complicated utterances. We need to drop our adult belief that children will tell us if they don't understand us; indeed, we need to realize that children often don't even know that they don't understand. And finally, we need to recognize that children do not report events in the framework that we typically expect.

These suggestions are more easily "said" than they are "done" in the demanding context of the child abuse interview. However, we believe that it is critically important for interviewers continually to rethink their expectations and to review their own performance. Only through such practice and feedback can they improve their abilities to relate to children from different backgrounds and with widely varying language abilities.

Recommendations

1. **THAT** the child be given an opportunity to talk about a neutral subject before we approach the subject at hand. If successful, this accomplishes two objectives: it helps the child to relax, and it gives us a sample of the child's language.
2. **THAT** we adapt our language to the child. We can make it a habit to use basic words and clear sentences. We can be alert to simple words that have unusual meanings.
3. **THAT** periodic checks be conducted to see if the child is understanding us and we are understanding the child.
4. **THAT** the child be provided with a framework for reporting what has happened. We can direct the child's attention to the topic under discussion at the moment, and inform her when topics have changed. We can also provide the chronological structure for the child's report.

REFERENCES

Bonitatibus, G., Godshall, S., Kelley, M., Levering, T., & Lynch, E. (1988). The role of social cognition in comprehension monitoring. *First Language, 8,* 287–298.

Brennan, M., & Brennan, R. (1988). *Strange language–child victims under cross-examination* (3rd ed.). Riverina, Australia: Charles Sturt University.

Davison, A., & Green, G. (1988). *Linguistic complexity and text comprehension: Readability issues reconsidered.* Hillsdale, N.J.: Erlbaum.

Ervin-Tripp, S., Strage, A., Lampert, M., & Bell, N. (1987). Understanding requests. *Linguistics, 25,* 107–143.

Gleason, J. Berko. (1977). Talking to children: Some notes on feedback. In C. Snow & C. Ferguson (Eds.), *Talking to children: Language input and acquisition* (pp. 199–205). Cambridge, England: Cambridge University Press.

Gleason, J. B erko. (Ed.). (1993). *The development of language* (3rd ed.). New York: Macmillan.

Hughes, M., & Grieve, R. (1980). On asking children bizarre questions. *First Language, 1,* 149–160.

Jones, C. (1984). Judicial questioning of children in custody and visitation proceedings. *Family Law Quarterly, 18,* 43–91.

Labov, W. (1972). *Language in the inner city.* Philadelphia: University of Pennsylvania Press.

Perry, N., Claycomb, L., Tam, P., McAuliff, B., Dostal, C., & Flanagan, C. (1993, April). When lawyers question children: Is justice served? Paper presented at the biennial meeting of the Society for Research in Child Development, New Orleans, La.

Romaine, S. (1984). *The language of children and adolescents: The acquisition of communicative competence.* London: Basil Blackwell.

Saywitz, K., Jaenicke, C., & Campara, L. (1990). Children's knowledge of legal terminology. *Law and Human Behavior, 14,* 523–535.

Saywitz, K.R., & Snyder, L. (1993). Improving children's testimony with preparation. In G. Goodman & B. Bottoms (Eds.), *Child victims, child witnesses: Understanding and improving testimony* (pp. 117–145). New York: Guilford Press.

Snow, C., & Ferguson, C. (Eds.). (1977). *Talking to children: Language input and acquisition.* Cambridge, England: Cambridge University Press.

Stein, N.L., & Glenn, C.G. (1979). An analysis of story comprehension in elementary school children. In R. Freedle (Ed.), *New directions in discourse processing* (pp. 53–120). Norwood, N.J.: Ablex.

Todd, C., & Perlmutter, M. (1980). Reality recalled by preschool children. In M. Perlmutter (Ed.), *New directions for child development, No. 10: Children's memory* (pp. 69–86). San Francisco: Jossey-Bass.

Walker, A. (1993). Questioning young children in court: A linguistic case study. *Law and Human Behavior, 17,* 59–81.

Warren, A., & McCloskey, L. (1993). Pragmatics: Language in social contexts. In J. Berko Gleason (Ed.), *The development of language* (3rd ed., pp. 195–237). New York: Macmillan.

Warren-Leubecker, A., Tate, C., Hinton, I., & Ozbek, I.N. (1989). What do children know about the legal system and when do they know it? First steps down a less-traveled path in child witness research. In S. Ceci, D. Ross, & M. Toglia (Eds.), *Perspectives on children's testimony* (pp. 158–183). New York: Springer-Verlag.

Whitehurst, G. (1976). The development of communication changes with age and modeling. *Child Development, 47,* 473–482.

9

Assessing the Truth in Children's Statements

Debra A. Bekerian
and John L. Dennett

One of the most difficult problems for investigators of child abuse is deciding whether or not a child's accusations are truthful. General issues of truthfulness, and ways to identify a truthful account, have been the subject of much study by psychologists, in many fields (see Koehnken, 1989). Importantly, psychologists have developed assessment procedures that can be applied to the child's account, and, theoretically, should help to decide whether an account is true. Here, this approach will be referred to as statement assessment (SA).

The SA technique was developed initially by Undeutsch (1967), and thereafter by Trankell (1972), with additional modifications being introduced by, for example, Steller and Koehnken (1989) and Raskin and Steller (1989). Since these developments, SA has been receiving increasing attention, both in terms of theoretical development and in terms of field evaluation, particularly within the context of child abuse. This chapter summarizes the major assumptions behind SA, and reviews the nature of the evidence that has been amassed. It then describes some critical points raised in the discussion of SA in current psycholegal debates.

CRITICAL ASSUMPTIONS IN SA

Definition of Truth

It is first essential to provide some definition of what is meant by a truthful account. The particular definition of truth that is used will depend somewhat on the context in which the child's account is being considered. A good illustration of this point is found by comparing therapeutic and evidential interviews. In the therapeutic setting, it is arguable that the critical factor is whether the child believes himself or herself to be telling the truth. The veracity, or accuracy of details, may take on a lesser value. For example, a child may remember some dialogue with the perpetrator, and then completely omit this information in a later interview. This inconsistency may not necessarily undergo much scrutiny by the therapist.

In contrast, the legal setting requires more than the child intending to tell the truth. The account must also contain accurate information. In the preceding example, inconsistencies in such details as conversations may be grounds for concern, as well as examination in some settings (e.g., legal cross-examination).

It would be incorrect, of course, to suggest that in therapeutic interviews there is no regard for inconsistencies. A child who changes the identity of the perpetrator across repeated interviews would be viewed with concern in both therapeutic and evidential situations. However, the legal setting requires more stringent criteria, that is, both truthful intentions and accuracy. As SA is used extensively in legal settings in some countries, most of its proponents adopt this "legal" definition in their discussions (see Koehnken, 1989; Raskin & Steller, 1989).

Working Assumption

All SA procedures assume that a truthful account differs in consistent and observable ways from an account that is untruthful. This assumption was first put forward by Undeutsch (1967), and represents the working hypothesis of SA procedures. Certainly, many theories of memory have argued that accounts based on real experiences are different from accounts that are based on imagined or prompted experiences (see Johnson, 1988). Related research in the experimental work on memory supports these assumptions (see Schooler, Clark, & Loftus, 1987; Schooler, Gerhard, & Loftus, 1986). Under certain conditions, real experiences are likely to be recounted in more detail, such as perceptual features, and developed in an unstructured, spontaneous manner. For example, the child recounting a real experience may change topics and discuss events that happened earlier, in order to provide background information about the relationship with the perpetrator (e.g., Steller & Boychuk, 1992).

Criteria of Truthfulness

As stated, all SA procedures assume that truthful accounts have a particular quality. That is, certain features of an account are proposed to be good discriminators of experienced events. These features, listed in Table 1, are referred to as *content criteria*. These content criteria are applied to the child's statement. Some SA proponents suggest that the criteria be rated on a scale from "being absent" to "strongly present" (e.g., Raskin & Steller, 1989; Steller & Boychuck, 1992). Overall, evaluation with content criteria is assumed to give an indication of whether the account reveals qualities of an experienced event.

Complementary assessments give important additional information that will help determine whether the account is truthful. Steller and Boychuk (1992) review these additional assessment procedures in terms of a validity

TABLE 1
Content Criteria

General characteristics
  1. Logical structure
  2. Unstructured production
  3. Quantity of details
Specific contents
  4. Contextual embedding
  5. Descriptions of interactions
  6. Reproduction of conversation
  7. Unexpected complications during the incident
Peculiarities of content
  8. Unusual details
  9. Superfluous details
  10. Accurately reported details misunderstood
  11. Related external associations
  12. Accounts of subjective mental state
  13. Attributions of perpetrator's mental state
Motivation-related contents
  14. Spontaneous corrections
  15. Admission to lack of memory
  16. Self-doubts about one's testimony
  17. Self-deprecation
  18. Forgiving/pardoning perpetrator
Offense-specific elements
  19. Details characteristic of the offense

checklist (for earlier references, see Raskin & Steller, 1989; Steller & Koehnken, 1989; Undeutsch, 1982). The validity checklist combines information about the child (e.g., verbal competence, motivation to deceive), the interview environment (e.g., the type of questions, the number of interviews), and the plausibility of the account relative to other factors (e.g., consistency with other evidence). The combined evaluation of content criteria and these additional assessments then form the basis for judging the account's credibility.

It is worth emphasizing that the *absence* of criteria should not be used to conclude that the account is based on an imagined/prompted experience. As discussed in the following, accounts of experienced events do not always have a particular quality, in that some content criteria might not be present. Further, not all criteria seem equally important as discriminators of truthful accounts. Consequently, while the presence of content criteria may be associated more with a memory of an experienced event, their absence does not imply a confabulated one.

SA PROCEDURES

Application of Content Criteria

Identifying the presence of content criteria in an account is a skill that requires considerable training to acquire. The interviewer must understand how the content criteria become translated into real language, as when a criterion has been satisfied in the account. Additionally, the interviewer should be experienced and/or skilled in basic interviewing, as well as informed about the specific skills that are required for interviewing children. It is equally important that the interviewer have some knowledge about the characteristics of the particular event under investigation. With regard to child abuse, the interviewer should have a firm understanding of the dynamics involved in abuse, to the extent that they differ from those in other types of crimes (e.g., familiarity with perpetrators).

Fortunately, there are many opportunities for interviewers to be trained, primarily through formal courses such as those regularly offered by experts in SA in North America, Australia, and Europe. A recent paper by Steller and Boychuk (1992) provides illustrations of the application of content criteria to a written transcript of a child's statement, in a sentence-to-sentence fashion. Examples such as these can serve as preliminary introductions to SA procedures, should formal training be difficult to arrange.

Constraints on SA

As with all procedures, SA is constrained by certain requirements. Some have to do with the child; others pertain to the nature of the alleged abuse. A few of these requirements are discussed here (for more comprehensive discussions see Bekerian & Dennett, 1992; Raskin & Steller, 1989; Steller & Boychuk, 1992; Steller & Koehnken, 1989; and Undeutsch, 1982).

ABILITIES OF THE CHILD. Obviously, SA procedures rely on the child's having some level of verbal competence. This means that the child should be able, in theory, to produce an account that is a narrative, or tells a story. The work of Fivush (e.g., Fivush, 1984; Hamond & Fivush, 1991) and Hudson (e.g., Hudson & Fivush, 1991) convincingly illustrates that a child becomes progressively better at producing narrative, coherent accounts that include such details as time, place, agents, and so on. Younger children (e.g., aged three) seem to require more prompting to produce complete and detailed accounts (e.g., Hamond & Fivush, 1991). In practice, this means that SA procedures will need to be modified to suit the capability of the younger child. In particular, SA is difficult to use with preverbal children or with children who have limited verbal abilities. In order to establish the verbal abilities of the child, most SA proponents advise that the child be asked about an event that is irrelevant to the case (e.g., Steller & Boychuk, 1992). This will enable the interviewer to determine the spontaneous narrative style of the child.

FEATURES OF THE ALLEGED ABUSE. The successful application of SA also is determined by the features of the alleged abuse. For example, the event must be of some sufficient duration. A very short, action-impoverished event is not likely to be remembered in a highly detailed, unstructured manner (see Raskin & Steller, 1989, for an example). Another important feature is the uniqueness of the abusive event. In cases of incest, abusive incidents are likely to be regular and numerous and to span extended time courses (e.g., Furniss, 1991). Under such circumstances, accounts initially may be highly regularized and lack the spontaneity that unstructured accounts have. This is likely to be due to the fact that when events are frequently experienced, it is difficult to remember a specific event (see Bekerian & Dennett, 1992).

INTERVIEW STRATEGIES. The strategies used by the interviewer may also restrict the successful application of SA procedures. Preliminary evidence from Steller and Wellershaus (1992) suggests that instructing the child to use memory-enhancing aids may reduce the discriminative powers of the content criteria. Other authors have also noted the importance of the type and quality of interview when making assessments about the presence of content criteria (e.g., Raskin & Steller, 1989). Therefore, it seems that the interviewer should apply SA procedures only to those interviews that have followed a particular format.

Most proponents of SA advocate that interview strategies follow the same prescribed sequence. For example, Steller and Boychuk (1992), like many others, suggest that the interview begin with a rapport-building phase, where the child is asked about neutral topics, such as hobbies and school activities. This allows some bond to develop between the child and the interviewer. It also enables the interviewer to assess the child's narrative style and verbal abilities. Then the child should be encouraged to give a free narrative account about the alleged sexual incident, followed by the interviewer's asking of specific questions that systematically probe for more detailed information (see Undeutsch, 1982). The interviewer should question in a logical fashion, and try to elicit information that could indicate the presence of content criteria. Prior to closing the interview, the interviewer should answer any questions that the child might have, and attempt to end the interview in a positive fashion.

EVALUATION OF SA

All procedures need evaluating, and SA is no exception. There are two sources of information that provide some preliminary assessment of SA procedures. It should be remembered, however, that the research is ongoing and probably should be regarded as preliminary.

Estimates of True and False Accusations

One source of information is taken from real cases of sexual abuse that have been reported and received attention from authorities (e.g., social services and the police). Researchers have attempted to estimate "baseline" ratios of the proportion of accusations that are regarded as false, at least in the context of the legal setting. Essentially, this information attempts to give the interviewer some idea as to how many children are likely to be making false accusations (see Jones & McGraw, 1987; Wakefield & Underwager, 1988). These estimates should be treated cautiously and must not be generalized to populations other than those sampled. However, there is increasing concern that false allegations, to the extent that they do occur, are more likely in cases of custodial and visitation-access disputes, and other disputes that arise primarily from divorce proceedings (e.g., Furniss, 1991; Steller & Boychuk, 1992; Yuille, 1989; see also Chapter 12, this volume).

Field and Simulated Studies of SA

The other source of information is derived from field and evaluative studies of SA. The reader is advised to consult an important review of empirical support for SA published by Horowitz (1991), which provides extensive discussion of the findings. Here, only a few exemplary studies are discussed.

Field studies analyze transcripts taken from real cases and assess how prevalent the content criteria are in cases where some independent information is available about the validity of the child's accusations (e.g., forensic evidence). For example, Lamers-Winkleman, Buffing, and van der Zanden (1992) analyzed real statements made by 103 children in the Netherlands concerning sexual abuse. The statements were first categorized on the basis of "substantiated abuse," "highly probable abuse," and "unfounded." Substantiated abuse meant that the perpetrator had made a confession or was convicted, or both. The second, "highly probable," required either that the child had given a statement, that other witnesses had given statements or there was other corroborating evidence, and/or that the child had shown behavioral and emotional signs that were consistent with abuse. The third category, "unfounded," referred to cases in which no statement had been given by the child, or the statement had been demonstrated to be either prompted or confabulated. Raters, who were blind to these initial category assignments, then analyzed the statements for the presence of content criteria (specifically, criteria-based content analysis, or CBCA, as discussed by Steller & Koehnken, 1989[*])

The findings suggest that the age of the child is most highly correlated with ratings for content criteria: older children are more likely to have more content criteria present in their accounts. Additionally, some criteria were more strongly represented (e.g., unusual details). Age proved to be the most important factor in determining the presence of content criteria across all three categories of cases. The authors speculate that very young children (e.g., two to three years old) fail to produce highly detailed accounts spontaneously (see Chapter 6, this volume). Other evidence from studies with very young children supports these conclusions (e.g., Hamond & Fivush, 1991).

It must be stressed that these findings are only preliminary. For one, the numbers of children in different age groups across the category assignments were too small for the results to be meaningfully interpreted (e.g., $N = 3$ in some groups). Additionally, serious questions can be raised about the initial categorization of cases into a range from "substantiated" to "unfounded." Perhaps more important, the data suggest that, even when abuse is not suspected, some of the content criteria can still be identified, and are present to the same extent as they are in accounts that are "substantiated." In fact, the content criteria, although correlated with age, did not distinguish among the three categories; the ratings did not relate to the outcome of the case. This

---

[*]Criteria-based content analysis (CBCA) is a set of specific criteria developed by Steller and Koehnken (1989). Although CBCA has unique features, the criteria themselves are not significantly different from other versions of content criteria that have been put forward by other SA proponents.

suggests that analyses with content criteria are not immediately related to the eventual verdict of the courts with regard to the charges of sexual abuse.

Raskin and Esplin (1991) report on preliminary data collected by Esplin, Boychuk, and Raskin from a field study of 40 cases of child sexual abuse. Cases were initially classified into "confirmed" and "unconfirmed." "Confirmed" cases were those in which there had been corroborating evidence for the child's accusations (e.g., confession, physical evidence, polygraph-test results). Unconfirmed cases were those in which the child's accusations had not been corroborated. Transcripts of the interviews of these 40 cases were then given to someone trained in SA, but who did not know the "confirmed/unconfirmed" classification of the case. The data were quite stunning. First, the rater trained in SA accurately differentiated all "confirmed" cases from "unconfirmed." Second, most of the content criteria were found to be good discriminators between the two classes of accounts. Not only did confirmed cases have more of the content criteria, but their presentation was much stronger. In fact, some criteria were never present in the unconfirmed cases, but were found in as many as 95% of those cases considered to be of confirmed sexual abuse (e.g., criterion 8, unusual details).

One must be cautious in placing too strong an interpretation on the data reported by Raskin and Esplin (1991) (see Horowitz, 1991, and Wells & Loftus, 1991, for detailed discussions). For example, there is no obvious reason why the content criteria were successful in discriminating confirmed from unconfirmed accounts in the data of Epslin and colleagues, but failed to do so in the data reported by Lamers-Winkelman, van der Zanden, and Buffing (1992). Nonetheless, information from field studies is promising, and suggests that content criteria, and the SA approach, may have considerable external validity.

It is essential, from a scientific point of view, that the findings from field studies be complemented by data from more controlled studies. In combination, field and experimental work will enable the best possible conclusion to be reached about SA, and when it is best used by practitioners. It is to these more controlled, experimental studies that the discussion now turns.

Simulated, or analog, studies often compare the accounts of children who had experienced an event with accounts of children who were prompted to invent a story about the event, although they had not witnessed it. For example, Joffe and Yuille (1992) compared the performance of two age groups (grades 2 and 4). The children either had experienced the event, were heavily coached about what happened in the event, or were lightly coached. In the heavily coached condition, the child was instructed to include details that would fulfill the content criteria. Interviews were transcribed and then rated for the presence and strength of the content criteria by two trained evaluators (specifically trained in CBCA). The results suggested that, for older children (between nine and 10 years of age), the content criteria were successful in discriminating between real and confabulated accounts, when the coaching was "light." When coaching was "heavy," the content criteria failed to distinguish between real memories and imagined ones. As pointed out by Joffe and Yuille (1992), this finding is disturbing. As the details about content criteria and SA become more available to the general public, there is the increasing danger that coaching might incorporate details that would bias the positive evaluation of the content criteria.

The data for younger children (ages seven to eight) were entirely different. The accounts produced by younger children were not successfully discriminated by the content criteria. Joffe and Yuille argue that such data argue strongly for the limitations of SA procedures with younger children. They suggest that future research will have to determine the age boundaries for the successful application of SA procedures.

A recent paper by Honts, Peters, Devitt, and Amato (1992) also provides evidence regarding the evaluative power of the content criteria. In their study, some children (ages four to 10) were motivated to deceive the interviewer about a serious matter: importantly, the child believed that telling the truth would have very serious consequences, and so it became critical for the child to deceive. The content criteria were then used to determine whether the accounts of the truthful children could be distinguished from those of the children who were motivated to lie. The results did provide support for the validity of the content criteria, in that truthful accounts could be successfully distinguished from deceptive ones on the basis of the evaluation with the content criteria.

Neither the Joffe and Yuille (1992) nor the Honts et al. (1992) study included analyses of the individual content criteria. However, an experimental study discussed by Steller and Boychuk (1992) does include a separate evaluation of the individual content criteria. The data were originally reported by Steller, Wellershaus, and Wolf (1988). In this study, children of two age groups (first and fourth grades) were asked either to remember a real event or to produce an account based on their imagination. Five different scenarios were used, chosen on the basis that they best approximated the emotional, psychological, and physical circumstances of child abuse: giving a blood sample, being physically beaten by another child, being attacked by an animal, undergoing dental work, and undergoing surgery. The children were asked to produce two stories about these experiences, one being on a real event that they had experienced, and the other based on imagination. Thus each child produced two accounts, one "true" and the other "false." Three raters, who were blind to the "truth" of the accounts, evaluated the stories for the content criteria, using a four-point scale (0 = not present, to 3 = strongly present).

The data suggested that nine criteria were significantly absent in fabricated accounts: logical consistency, perceptual details, embedding, complications, unusual details, superfluous details, misunderstood details, associations, and self-deprecation (criteria 1, 3, 4, 7–11, 17 in Table 1).* In contrast, certain criteria failed to distinguish between truthful and false accounts, particularly those that are associated with motivation-related criteria (i.e., criteria 14–16 and 18). This result is perhaps not surprising, given that others have questioned the logic of some of these criteria (see Bekerian & Dennett, 1992). Other interesting features of the data were that some of the criteria were not understood by the raters (e.g., unstructured production). This suggests that interviewers will need more instruction in identifying the presence of some of the criteria. Additionally, some criteria were present so infrequently that no analyses were possible. Taken together, the data argue for the conclusion that although content criteria can be successfully applied, not all of the criteria will be present to the same extent, nor serve as useful discriminators between real and confabulated accounts.

CONCLUSIONS

Statement assessment is one of the most promising sets of techniques that practitioners can use in determining whether a statement about sexual abuse is true. It has been developed systematically, and has received considerable empirical attention. At this time, it is advisable that only certain interview formats be followed if SA procedures are to be used. Interviewers should be most sensitive to the abilities and developmental level of the child, and to the nature of the suspected abuse. Preverbal children, or children with impaired or limited verbal abilities, are not good candidates for SA procedures. However, it should be stressed that age, per se, should not be the only consideration, as the findings are conflicting (e.g., Honts et al., 1992, vs. Joffe & Yuille, 1992). Possible reasons for the conflicting findings concerning the age of the child are suggested by Goodman and Schwartz-Kenney (1992), who argue that many other factors also must be considered, such as the child's emotional state. Equally, characteristics of the abuse itself may make it difficult to evaluate the account with SA procedures; for example, if the event was of short duration, or if the abuse was experienced repeatedly over a long time period. Although content criteria have been shown to be successful discriminators of truthful accounts, not all of the criteria are equally useful. In practice, this means that the absence of content criteria in a child's account does not indicate a false statement. Finally, it is extremely important that

---

*In the Steller and Boychuk (1992) article, there is a discrepancy between the reported significance of criterion 12 (mental states) and its respective *t*-value, as reported in their Table 4.3 (pp. 65–66).

any legal constraints that are imposed on interviews with alleged victims of child abuse be taken into consideration, before evaluating an account with SA procedures. The interviewer must be fully aware of the legal guidelines imposed by his or her own judicial system, in order to be sure that SA procedures do not contravene those guidelines.

Recommendations

1. **THAT** formal training in an SA procedure be undertaken before an attempt is made to use the technique.
2. **THAT** interview techniques be compatible with and complement the SA technique that is used.
3. **THAT** SA techniques only be used for certain events, and not for others.
4. **THAT** SA techniques only be used with children who are fluent verbally.

REFERENCES

Bekerian, D. A., & Dennett, J.L. (1992). The truth in content analyses of a child's testimony. In F. Losel, D. Bender, & T. Bliesner (Eds.), *Psychology and law: International perspectives.* Berlin: Walter de Gruyter.

Fivush, R. (1984). Learning about school: The development of kindergartners' school scripts. *Child Development, 55*(5), 1697–1709.

Furniss, T. (1991). *The multi-professional handbook of child sexual abuse: Integrated management, therapy and legal intervention* (pp. 342–346). London: Routledge.

Goodman, G., & Schwartz-Kenney, B. (1992). Why knowing a child's age is not enough: Influences of cognition, social and emotional factors on children's testimony. In H. Dent. & R. Flin (Eds.), *Children as witnesses* (pp. 15–32). Chichester, England: Wiley.

Hammond, N. R., & Fivush, R. (1991). Memories of Mickey Mouse: Young children recount their trip to Disneyworld. *Cognitive Development, 6*(4), 433–448.

Honts, C. R., Peters, D. P., Devitt, M. K., & Amato, S.L. (1992, May). Detecting children's lies with statement validity assessment: A pilot study of a laboratory paradigm. Paper presented at the NATO Advanced Study Institute, Il Ciocco, Lucca, Italy.

Horowitz, S. W. (1991). Empirical support for statement validity assessment. *Behavioral Assessment, 13*, 293–313.

Hudson, J., & Fivush, R. (1991). As time goes by: Sixth graders remember a kindergarten experience. *Applied Cognitive Psychology, 5*, 347–360.

Joffe, R., & Yuille, J. (1992, May). Criteria-based content analysis: An experimental investigation. Poster presented at the NATO Advanced Study Institute, Il Ciocco, Lucca, Italy.

Johnson, M. (1988). Reality monitoring: An experimental phenomenological approach. *Journal of Experimental Psychology: General, 177*, 390–394.

Jones, D., & McGraw, J. (1987). Reliable and fictitious accounts of sexual abuse to children. *Journal of Interpersonal Violence, 2*(1), 27–45.

Koehnken, G. (1989, June). Psychological approaches to the assessment of the credibility of child witness statements. Paper presented at the International Conference on Children's Evidence in Legal Proceedings, Selwyn College, Cambridge, England.

Lamers-Winkelman, F., Buffing, F., & van der Zanden, A.P. (1992, September). Statement validity analysis in child sexual abuse cases: A field study. Poster presented at the Third Conference of Law and Psychology, Oxford, England.

Lamers-Winkelman, F., van der Zanden, A.P., & Buffing, F. (1992, September). Interviews which did not lead to statements of sexual abuse. Poster presented at the Third Conference of Law and Psychology, Oxford, England.

Raskin, D. C., & Esplin, P. W. (1991). Assessment of children's statements of sexual abuse. In J. Doris (Ed.), *The suggestibility of children's memory (with special reference to the child witness)* (pp. 153–164). Washington, D.C.: American Psychological Association.

Raskin, D. C., & Steller M. (1989). Assessing credibility of allegations of child sexual abuse: Polygraphic examinations and statement analysis. In H. Wegener, F. Losel, & J. Haisch (Eds.), *Criminal behavior and the justice system: Psychological perspectives.* New York: Springer-Verlag.

Schooler, J., Clark, C., & Loftus, E. (1987). Knowing when memory is real. In M. Gruneberg, P. Morris, & R. Sykes (Eds.), *Practical aspects of memory: Current research and issues* (vol. 1). Chicester, England: Wiley.

Schooler, J., Gerhard, D., & Loftus, E. (1986). Qualities of the unreal. *Journal of Experimental Psychology: Learning, Memory and Cognition, 12*, 171–181.

Steller, M., & Boychuck, T. (1992). Children as witnesses in sexual abuse cases: Investigative interview and assessment techniques. In H. Dent & R. Flin (Eds.), *Children as witnesses* (pp. 47–71). New York: Wiley.

Steller, M., & Koehnken, G. (1989). Criteria-based statement analysis. In D. C. Raskin (Ed.), *Psychological methods in criminal investigation and evidence* (pp. 217–245). New York: Springer-Verlag.

Steller, M., & Wellershaus, P. (1992, September). Information enhancement and credibility assessment of child statements: The impact of the cognitive interview technique on criteria-based content analysis. Paper presented at the Third European Conference of Law and Psychology, Oxford, England.

Steller, M., Wellershaus, P., & Wolf, T. (1988). Empirical validation of criteria-based content analysis. Paper presented at the NATO Advanced Study Workshop on Credibility Assessment, Maratea, Italy.

Trankel, A. (Ed). (1972). *Reliability of evidence.* Stockholm: Beckmans.

Undeutsch, U. (1967). Beuteilung der Glaubhaftigkeit von Aussagen. In U. Undeutsch (Ed.), *Handbuch der psychologie, band 11: Forensische psychologie* (pp. 26–181). Gettingen: Hogrefe.

Undeutsch, U. (1982). Statement reality analysis. In A. Trankell (Ed.), *Reconstructing the past* (pp. 27–56). Stockholm: Norstedt & Sons.

Wakefield, H., & Underwager, R. (1988). *Accusations of child sexual abuse.* Springfield, Ill.: Charles C. Thomas.

Wells, G. L., & Loftus, E. F. (1991). Is this child fabricating? Reactions to a new assessment technique. In J. Doris (Ed.), *The suggestibility of children's recollections: Proceedings of the Cornell conference.* Washington, D.C.: American Psychological Association.

Yuille, J. (Ed). (1989). *Credibility assessment.* Dordrecht, Netherlands: Kluwer Academic Publishers.

10

Psychotherapy and the Recovery of Repressed Memories

Elizabeth F. Loftus and Michael D. Yapko

This chapter raises specific questions about the authenticity of repressed memories arising in response to the contaminating influences of therapists' procedures. The major points that memory is malleable and responsive to suggestion are emphasized throughout. Evidence that false memories can be created is presented, and reasons why therapists may unintentionally suggest memories of abuse to suggestible clients are discussed. Specific guidelines for minimizing the likelihood of therapists creating memories of abuse are provided.

As they took turns telling their shocking story, one could look deeply into their eyes, trying to find some sign, some clue, that would help determine the truthfulness of their account. They desperately wanted to be believed, and, if for no other reason, that is what made objectivity seem even more necessary.

John and Rose, both in their early 70s, were obviously distraught. Referred to the junior author (M.Y.) for therapy by the senior author (E.L.), they impressed upon us both the frustration and anguish of their painful circumstances. Their youngest daughter (of four children), Sally, shortly after the birth of her daughter (John and Rose's grandchild), began to recover memories through her dreams of having been sexually abused as a child by her two uncles (Rose's brothers). Sally believes that many of the episodes of abuse involved satanic ritualistic abuse and torture.

Sally "learned" from her brother-in-law that having a baby is often the catalyst for recovering memories of abuse. In her case, the belief that she was abused arose in response to some dreams of babies being hurt that she had soon after her daughter was born. Her dreams were her primary evidence of her abuse. She consulted therapists on the recommendation of her brother-in-law, who is a well-known expert on childhood sexual abuse. He is a strong believer that abuse can be deduced from even very indirect methods, like dreams or vague symptoms. He was the first to suggest directly to her that she must have been abused, in response to some of the dreams she shared with him. When she reported these dreams and her brother-in-law's "expert" interpretations to therapists he recommended that she see, she found that these therapists also believed that her dreams were valid expressions of repressed memory. In fact, they further encouraged her to uncover even more and increasingly bizarre stories of personal abuse through more dreams and guided imagery. As a result, she soon expanded the list of abusers in her past to include John and Rose, who appeared to be genuinely dumbfounded by the allegations. Sally soon refused to have any contact with them at all, and she likewise prohibited them from having any contact with their grandchild.

Sally's siblings, two brothers and a sister, think she has "gone crazy." They are at least as perplexed as John and Rose about Sally's perspective of her childhood. Sally has cut them off contact with them as well, viewing them all as pawns in the conspiracy of silence.

Listening to John and Rose, observing their obvious despair, hearing their confusion, empathizing with their desire to make sense out of apparent madness, what can we conclude? Are they phenomenal liars who actually were participants in horrendous acts of abuse? Are they two innocent and nice old people utterly bewildered by a crazy situation spun out of control?

We don't know.

RECOVERED MEMORIES OF CHILD ABUSE

Long-repressed memories, such as those of Sally, that return after decades, have become highly publicized via popular articles. In 1991, Roseanne Barr Arnold's story was announced on the cover of *People* magazine. This story involved memories of her mother's abusing her from the time she was an infant until she was six or seven years old—memories that returned in therapy. Both parents adamantly deny her charges.

Who is right and who is wrong? Is the adult child misremembering? Or lying? Are the parents misremembering when they deny abuse, or are they deliberately lying? While the rich and famous may use the media to tell their newly found stories, most of the thousands of now adult children who are accusing their parents are doing so in the relative privacy of family reunions or in the absolute privacy of therapy sessions. Sometimes they take their cases to very public county courtrooms.

The case of D.J. is fairly typical. In January 1987, a 32-year-old woman (D.J.) went into therapy, and, soon after, troubling memories—previously re-pressed—were awakened. She began to remember that from the time she was approximately three years old until she was about 12 or 13 (1958–1968), her father had sexually molested her and her mother had failed to protect her. She sued her parents for compensatory and punitive damages, claiming intentional harm, breach of duty to protect, mental and physical distress, and loss of earnings caused by the intentional harm. D.J. claimed that due to the trauma of the experience, she had had no recollection or knowledge of the sexual abuse until her repression was lifted, shortly before she filed suit. The defendant parents moved to dismiss the complaint, claiming that it was barred by the two-year statute of limitations. The motion was denied; the parents would have to stand trial (*Johnson v. Johnson*, 1988).

As a result of recent changes in legislation permitting cases like D.J.'s to be tried, people in general, and juries in particular, are grappling with the ques-tion, "Are these memories authentic?" Even raising the issue of authenticity makes some people cringe because it appears on the surface to imply skepti-cism about sexual abuse in general. Yet, we know that childhood sexual abuse is tragically common (Daro, 1988). Occasionally, the abuse is corroborated, sometimes very cogently, as with pornographic photographs, or, occasion-ally, with open confessions not derived coercively by the alleged offender. Such objective corroboration could show that the memory report has a basis in reality despite its long-delayed return. But the question being asked here is not about children who are abused and come forward to tell, or about adults who have known about abuse all their lives and only recently have devel-oped the courage to disclose it. Their statements are as believable as any other statements that one might make about one's memory. The question asked here is only about one special class of "memories," namely, those that suddenly emerge in adulthood, or that emerge years later while still a child. Are these memories authentic?

Thus, while many of the memories that are reported for the first time in therapy may be authentic, there is reason to believe that at least some of them are not. To begin with, there have been no studies specifically demon-strating the validity of repressed memories of childhood abuse that return in adulthood (Brewin, Andrews, & Gotlib, 1993). Further, in some cases, the memories that return refer to events that occurred well before the offset of childhood amnesia. Most studies of childhood amnesia suggest that one's earliest recollection does not date back to before the age of about three or four (Howe & Courage, 1993; Kihlstrom & Harackiewicz, 1982). When a recovered memory refers to an incident that occurred at the age six months, for example, there may be good reason to believe that the memory is not authentic.

If some of the recovered memories that are surfacing in therapy sessions are not authentic, then where did they come from? Emory University psychiatrist George Ganaway (1989) proposed several hypotheses to explain the more extreme, satanic ritualistic-abuse memories: false memories could be elicited from internal and/or external sources. The internal drive to manufacture an abuse memory may come about as a way to provide a screen for perhaps more prosaic, but, ironically, less tolerable, factual traumatic material of some sort. Creating a fantasy of abuse with its relatively clear-cut distinction between good and evil may provide the needed logical explanation for confusing experiences and feelings. These memories could also arise from illusion or hallucination-mediated screen memories, or be internally derived as a defense mechanism.

Alternatively, the person could have combined a mixture of borrowed ideas, characters, myths, and accounts from exogenous sources with idiosyncratic internal beliefs. Ganaway goes on to argue that, once activated, the manufactured memories are indistinguishable from factual memories. Unauthentic memories could also be externally derived as a result of unintentional implantation of suggestion or expectation by a therapist or other perceived authority figure from whom the client desires a special relationship, interest, or approval. Alternatively, the false memories can be borrowed from the accounts of others who either are personally known or were encountered in literature, movies, and television.

The Creation of False Memories

The hypothesis that false memories can be created invites an inquiry into the important question of what is known about them. Since the mid-1970s at least, investigations have been made into the creation of false memories through exposure to misinformation. Now, some two decades later, we have scores of studies to support a high degree of memory distortion. People have recalled nonexistent broken glass and tape recorders, a clean-shaven man as having a mustache, straight hair as curly, and even something as large and conspicuous as a barn in a bucolic scene that contained no buildings at all (Loftus, 1979, 1991; Loftus & Hoffman, 1989). This growing body of research shows that new, postevent information often becomes incorporated into memory, supplementing and altering a person's recollection. Even details of genuinely experienced traumatic events, like the space shuttle *Challenger* disaster, can be changed over time (Harsch & Neisser, 1989). Moreover, people sometimes remember the experiences of others as happening to themselves (Barclay & Wellman, 1986). Finally, with sufficient suggestion, whole events that never happened can be implanted into one's mind, as in studies where people remembered being awakened in the night by a loud noise when it never actually happened (Laurence & Perry, 1983; Orne, 1979; Weekes, Lynn, Green, & Brentar, 1992).

It has been argued that the new information invades us, like a Trojan horse, precisely because we do not detect its influence (Loftus, 1991). Understanding how we can become tricked by revised data about our past is central to understanding the hypothesis that suggestions from literature, movies, television, and other sources can affect our autobiographical recall. The existence of this body of research makes it imperative that we examine the extent of suggestion that may be going on with clients who report recently returned memories of childhood abuse. Of course, the simple fact that suggestion can create memories, and that some suggestion may precede the development of memories, does not mean that the memories that are produced are false. Still, the discovery that suggestive influences do precede the development of memories makes those memory reports at least open to the hypothesis that they were suggestion induced (Loftus, 1993; Loftus & Ketcham, 1994; Yapko, 1994a, 1994b).

Therapy and Memory

Therapy itself is another potential source of suggestion that could influence a patient's autobiographical memory. In many cases of memory recovery, therapy has clearly played a role. Therapist E. Sue Blume (1990), the creator of the Incest Survivor's Aftereffects Checklist, states this explicitly when she asserts that she has "found that most incest survivors have limited recall about their abuse" (p. 81). She goes on to say, "Indeed, so few incest survivors in my experience have identified themselves as abused in the beginning of therapy that I have concluded that perhaps half of all incest survivors do not remember that the abuse occurred" (p. 81).

Blume's observation that so many individuals enter therapy without memories of abuse, but acquire such memories during therapy, naturally makes us wonder about what might be happening in therapy. According to Ganaway (1989), honestly believed but false memories could come about via unintentional suggestions from therapists. Ganaway notes a growing social trend toward the facile acceptance and expressed validation of uncorroborated trauma memories, perhaps due in part to sensitization from years of accusations that the memories are pure fantasy. Herman (1992, p. 180) makes a similar point: whereas an earlier generation of therapists might have been discounting or minimizing their patients' traumatic experiences, the recent rediscovery of psychological trauma has led to errors of the opposite kind. Some contemporary therapists have been known to tell patients, merely on the basis of a suggestive history or "symptom profile," that they definitely had a traumatic experience. Even if there is no memory, but merely some vague symptoms, certain therapists will inform a patient, after a single session, that the patient very likely had been the victim of a satanic cult. Once "diagnosed," the therapist urges the patient to pursue the recalcitrant memories. While some therapists recommend against persistent, intrusive probing to uncover early traumatic memories (e.g., Bruhn, 1990), others appear, at least anecdotally, to engage enthusiastically in these therapeutic strategies. Evidence for this claim comes in a variety of forms. What follows are a few brief examples straight from the mouths of therapists.

Therapists' Accounts

One therapist, who has treated more than 1,500 incest victims (Forward & Buck, 1988), openly discusses her method of approaching clients. She tells them: "You know, in my experience, a lot of people who are struggling with many of the same problems you are, have often had some kind of really painful things happen to them as kids—maybe they were beaten or molested. And I wonder if anything like that ever happened to you" (p. 161). While some may consider this a mildly suggestive approach, it is not nearly as problematic as some other documented examples. Clinicians claim to know of therapists who say, "Your symptoms sound like you've been abused when you were a child. What can you tell me about that?" (Trott, 1991, p. 18). Or worse, "You sound to me like the sort of person who must have been sexually abused. Tell me what that bastard did to you" (Davis, 1991, p. 82).

Fredrickson (1992), who has worked with many incest survivors, also talks in detail about her methods of getting patients to remember. She recommends that the therapist guide the patient "to expand on or explore images that have broken through to the conscious mind, allowing related images of the abuse to surface. The process lets the survivor complete the picture of what happened, using a current image or flash as a jumping-off point" (p. 97). She also suggests that the therapist help the patient to expand on the images and sensations evoked by dreams "to shed light on or recover our repressed memories" (p. 98). She extols the virtues of hypnosis to "retrieve buried memories" (p. 98). She recommends that patients "jot down suspected memories of abuse you would like to explore. Include your own felt sense of how you think you were abused" (p. 102).

Other published accounts tell us that therapists like to have the client "tell a story" (Olio, 1989); report their dreams, which then are interpreted as abuse (Poston & Lison, 1990); use "trance writing" sessions (Whitley, 1992); use hypnosis or sodium amytal interviewing or age regression.

Ofshe (1992) would argue that these are the very techniques that can readily lead to manufactured beliefs, rather than authentic recollections. Consider hypnosis and age regression, for example. Do these techniques elicit accurate recollections? Unfortunately, the evidence points the other way. There is an extensive literature that seriously questions the reliability of hypnotically enhanced memory in general (Smith, 1983), and hypnotic age regression in particular (Nash, 1987). Not long ago, the *Journal of the American Medical Association* explicitly expressed concern over the finding that recollections obtained during hypnosis can involve confabulations and pseudomemories (Council on Scientific Affairs, American Medical Association, 1985). With hypnotic regression, men and women have been known to recall being abducted by aliens aboard exotic spacecraft, living inside the womb before birth, and past incarnations (Gordon, 1991; Nash, 1992). Therapists are occasionally impressed by the dramatic reliving of a childhood trauma, and have then taken this as evidence of authenticity. But Nash (1992) reminds us that equally dramatic and subjectively compelling portrayals are given by hypnotized subjects who are told to progress to an age of 70 or 80 (Kline & Gaze, 1951).

Therapists also are impressed by the apparent "healing" that takes place after the recovery of repressed memories and the painful reliving that clients experience. However, Nash (1992) has described in detail at least one patient who painfully recovered vivid details of a space alien abduction, complete with details about the spacecraft, the voices, and the peculiar machine that they attached to his penis to obtain samples of sperm. After memory recovery, his symptoms abated. His therapist remarked, "The paradox, of course, is that this utterly believed-in abduction report is not literally true. In this case, at least, getting better had nothing to do with real insight, recovery of real memories, or uncovering of the truth in any historical sense" (p. 13).

What about the evidence of sodium amytal interviewing? Sodium amytal (a central nervous system depressant) has been used to "verify" or to "clarify" memories, but this technique, too, has questionable validity (Loring, Lee, & Meador, 1989).

Especially when clients are at their most suggestive, therapists could unwittingly suggest ideas to them. They might conceivably do so by either the questions they ask or those they refrain from asking (what comments they follow up), or by directly disclosing their initial hypotheses to their clients.

Why Would Therapists Suggest Things to Patients?

During the course of therapy, many psychotherapists will deliberately dig for buried memories. Even those who are less interested in a client's past will consider its influence on the present to some extent. When therapists dig for memories, they usually do so because they believe that their clients, in order to get well, must overcome the protective denial that enabled them to tolerate the abuse during childhood (Sgroi, 1989, p. 112). Memory blocks might be protective in many ways, but they come at a cost; they cut the survivor off from a significant part of his or her past history, and without a good explanation for a negative self-image, low self-esteem, and other mental problems. These memories must be brought into consciousness, not as an end in itself, Sgroi points out, but only insofar as they help the survivor to acknowledge reality and overcome denial processes that are now dysfunctional (p. 115).

Another perspective on a therapist's willingness to elicit, and then believe, patients' accounts of abuse was discussed by Brewin et al. (1993). The argument is that it is essential to gain a fresh point of view regarding the extent of any abuse, and to foster a positive therapeutic relationship.

It is also possible that some therapists may be unwittingly suggesting ideas to their clients because they have fallen prey to a bias that affects all of us, known as the "confirmatory bias." People in general, therapists included, have a tendency to search for evidence that will confirm their hunches rather than for something that will disconfirm them. It is not easy for us to discard our long-held or cherished beliefs, in part because we are eager to verify those beliefs and so are not inclined to seek evidence that might disprove them. One's beliefs can create one's own social reality, a notion that is the essence of the self-fulfilling prophecy (Snyder, 1984).

If therapists sometimes, or even routinely, ask questions that would tend to elicit reports of behaviors and experiences thought to be characteristic of one who has been a victim of childhood trauma, might not they, too, be creating this social reality? If they interpret ambiguous information as abuse, might they not be getting their patients to remember past events as more abusive than they may have actually been? There seems to be ample evidence that at least some therapists develop a hypothesis that a client was sexually abused, and sometimes this happens early in therapy. And they do so even in the face of denials from their clients. As one respected clinician/ researcher (Briere, 1989) has noted, "Most clinicians who specialize in abuse, however, have clients who they are relatively convinced were sexual abuse survivors, despite their clients' claims to the contrary" (p. 118). They tend to adopt the hypothesis of abuse when they see a certain constellation of symptoms (e.g., sexual dysfunction, depression, destructive relationships, eating disorders). With the hypothesis of repressed abuse in mind, might not their questioning techniques be influenced?

Their good intentions not withstanding, the documented examples of suggestive questioning should impel us at least to ask whether therapists might be suggesting illusory memories to their clients, rather than unlocking distant memories that are authentic. Ganaway (1989) worries that once seeded by the therapist, false memories can develop that replace previously unsatisfactory internal explanations for intolerable but more prosaic childhood trauma.

IMPLICATIONS FOR THERAPISTS

Therapists might want to consider whether it is really wise to "suggest" that childhood trauma happened, to probe relentlessly for recalcitrant memories, and then uncritically to accept them as fact. The uncritical acceptance of uncorroborated trauma memories by therapists, social agencies, and law enforcement personnel has fueled public accusations of alleged perpetrators by "survivors." If the memories were fabricated, such accusations will cause irreparable damage to the reputations of potentially innocent people and the destruction of families.

Beyond the problems posed for the innocent families, there are also problems for the patient. Reinforcing the validity of unverifiable memories within the therapeutic setting can send therapy on to diversionary paths leading away from the patient's true problems. If the therapist and patient collaborate in a mutual deception to use a bottomless pit of memories, therapy becomes interminable and financial resources are drained. Worse, the patient's initial wonderings, supported by therapy affirmations, could become fixed beliefs, perhaps precipitating suicidal thoughts and behaviors based on the new belief system. Patients who are reinforced into a new belief system could develop newer, larger problems. If the memories are ultimately shown to be false, therapists can become the targets of complaints of ethics violations and lawsuits. Such lawsuits have already begun.

What should therapists do instead? As a first step, it is worth recognizing that we do not yet have the tools for reliably distinguishing the signal of true repressed memories from the noise of false ones. Until we gain these tools, it seems prudent to exercise caution when some presumed amnestic barrier is probed. Psychotherapists would be wise to be circumspect regarding uncorroborated repressed memories that return. Techniques that are less potentially dangerous would involve clarification, compassion, empathy, and gentle confrontation as patients sort out their personal truths. Continuing consideration of other causes, or even multiple causes, for problems seems not only wise, but essential. Translating this general advice into specific guidelines for clinicians is the next step. We offer some possible guidelines here.

GUIDELINES FOR CLINICIANS

The complex issues raised and the knowledge we have about the malleability of human memory strongly suggest the need to establish some meaningful clinical guidelines in order to minimize the likelihood of therapist contamination. In this section, we discuss the role of a therapist's projections in the face of ambiguity, and then offer specific guidelines for therapists to consider in regulating their interactions with their clients.

It is vitally important to distinguish those cases in which the client now knows, and has known all along, that he or she was abused from those where the person enters treatment plagued by symptoms of an unknown origin. This section deals exclusively with those cases in which an individual seeks treatment, offers no reports of a history of sexual abuse, and even states, when asked, that he or she does not believe that there was any abuse in his or her background.

Ambiguity, Confusion, and the Need for Clarity

The psychological literature is replete with examples of people who blindly obey authority figures whom they perceive as credible, and who conform to others' perceptions of ambiguous events (Aronson, 1992). Suggestibility is an inherent dimension of human personality, and is evident to some degree in virtually every interaction (Yapko, 1990, 1995). The interaction that takes place in the context of psychotherapy is predicated on the inevitable influence on the client by the clinician (Haley, 1973). It is not a question of *whether* such influence ensues, but one of *to what degree* and *with what consequences* (Zeig, 1980).

Someone seeking therapy is already immersed in a perceptual frame that includes the following characteristics: (1) a belief that he or she is personally powerless to effect meaningful change; (2) a feeling of hopefulness that a trained "expert" can, through "objective" perspective and refined techniques, help resolve his or her problems; and (3) the notion that the person must conform to the therapist's perceptions and comply with the therapist's plan if he or she is to improve. The client is in a "one-down" position relative to the therapist, and, therefore, exibits a higher degree of compliance in that special relationship than might exist in any of the person's other relationships (Haley, 1973). In this unique context, conformity and obedience are defined as necessary in order to recover from one's "illness." Thus the perspective of the therapist is critical in determining the focus of treatment.

Most therapists have been trained in the use of projective tests such as the Rorschach and Thematic Apperception tests. The relevant principle is known as the "projective hypothesis," which states that when exposed to an ambiguous stimulus, like an inkblot, one gives meaning to the ambiguous stimulus through the mechanism of projection (Sundberg, Taplin, & Tyler, 1983).

A client's symptoms are, in essence, an experiential Rorschach. The more ambiguous their source or function in a person's life, the greater is the opportunity for the therapist to project his or her personal biases into an interpretation. This can have antitherapeutic results in any case, but these can be even more serious when symptoms are interpreted as "evidence of sexual abuse," although no such abuse was, in fact, reported. On this basis alone, it seems most cautious, and respectful of the client, to avoid drawing an unprovable conclusion that abuse occurred in the absence of a specific report to that effect by the client (Yapko, 1993, 1994a, 1994b).

A main problem in psychotherapy is that causal explanations typically tend to be plausible. For example, if a person were to present with the problem of needing to lose 25 pounds, a physician would likely interpret the problem plausibly as "metabolic." A Freudian analyst would probably interpret that the individual is "fixated at the oral stage of development." A behavior therapist would want to identify the "reward" (i.e., positive reinforcement) for overeating. A gestalt therapist would ask the patient to "identify your polarities and establish a dialogue between your fat and thin selves." The problem here—overweight—is the same in all cases, but the perspectives on how to interpret and then treat it differ markedly. Yet, each of these divergent interpretations is plausible. Can we clearly distinguish between what is plausible and what is actually true? After decades of accumulated research on therapy practices, the answer is hardly an unequivocal response in the affirmative.

Therapists typically want to identify the root cause of a problem. Sometimes they may even succeed in doing so. More often, however, the root cause is inferred, and not known directly. When the inferred cause is not particularly damaging to the person's self-esteem and close relationships, it may provide a reframing that makes the problem easier to solve (Yapko, 1990). However, when the inferred cause is one that is likely to scar someone's self-esteem permanently and inevitably damage his or her closest relationships, the inference provides a perspective that is both damaging and unprovable. The plausible explanation may satisfy the therapist's need to derive clarity from the inkblot of the client's symptoms, but it does so at the client's expense.

Why would a client accept, even reluctantly at first, a therapist's deduction that abuse, though not remembered, must have taken place? There are many possible reasons. Clearly, the need to make sense of seemingly senseless symptomatic behavior is a powerful catalyst (Yapko, 1994b; Zeig, 1980). As past clients have told us, "Believing I was abused explained so many things so quickly. I didn't have to search for reasons anymore." Furthermore, the need for approval, which naturally increases in close relationships, is amplified in the therapy context. Approval is obtained only when one adopts the therapist's perspectives. In short, the dynamics of social influence and the need for explanations that are plausible (if untrue) point to a low tolerance for ambiguity in both therapist and client. Specifically, one must be willing to accept that ambiguity is inherent in some symptomatic pictures, and resist the desire to offer an explanation suggesting abuse merely because it satisfies some need to understand. It is an inference that simply carries too much destructive potential for the client's life.

CONCLUSION

The point from which to analyze one's investigative session for leading statements is when one starts working with a situation that was painful for the client. This is the dangerous phase of the clinical interaction, because this is where the therapist is going to ask such questions as, "How old were you? Where were you? What was going on? Who was around? What was the interaction between you and that person like?" This is the point at which, if one asks leading questions, the client may be most vulnerable to suggestion (Bower, 1981). The reason for this is the uncertainty the client may experience about the meaning or significance of the experience; uncertainty generally increases suggestibility (Yapko, 1990, 1995). If one asks neutral questions (nonleading questions), and a client comes up with a previously unrecalled memory of abuse, then the therapist should consider treating it as authentic, but still be open to the possibility of other sources of influence.

Recommendations

The psychological literature reveals with abundant clarity that people are most likely to conform when there are no clear-cut parameters for interpreting experience. When people are uncertain, they have an increased tendency to adopt the perceptions of others (Aronson, 1992). Abuse is a realm in which people are often unsure, but, in some cases, their therapists seem all too certain that the abuse happened. Can an uncertain client come to adopt the perceptions of a therapist who exudes certainty? The answer is Yes (Laurence, Nadon, Nogrady, & Perry, 1986; Laurence & Perry, 1983; Orne, 1979).

Since there is no reliable way to determine whether a memory is authentic or confabulated, we offer some specific guidelines to help assure that therapists will be the solution, and not the problem. In light of what has been stated here about the role of suggestion in making the "diagnosis" that a client may have been abused when that was not a presenting problem, the following guidelines provide a useful starting place. Thus we suggest:

1. **THAT** clinicians not jump quickly to the conclusion that abuse occurred simply because it is plausible. If one is dealing with a situation in which the client has never raised the word "molest" or has never identified himself or herself as an abuse survivor,

then don't be the one to suggest it. The situation is entirely different, of course, when a person comes in for therapy and says, "I
was molested." At that point, one must treat the allegation as true
because clearly it is real to the client and there is no legitimate
basis for dismissing or refuting it. Whether or not it actually happened might be important for some purposes, but this is not the
point of this chapter. We are specifically addressing the situation
in which the client comes never having a thought about abuse
until the therapist introduced the idea that "you were probably
molested" as a way of explaining the client's symptoms.

2.   **THAT** clinicians not suggest abuse, either directly or indirectly,
outside the therapeutic context simply because it seems plausible.
We are aware of cases in which therapists first "diagnosed" a
molestation survivor over the phone! Recently, a prospective
patient reported, "I spoke to a therapist over the phone whom I
called to set up an appointment. I wanted to see her about my
low self-esteem. She suggested that I was probably molested as a
child. She told me that I should first see you and be hypnotized
to find out." Asked if she had eventually gone to see this therapist, she said, "No." She was diagnosed as an abuse victim over
the phone by someone she had never met! We have both seen
this happen many times, and we think it is a terrible practice.

3.   **THAT** clinicians not refer someone for a quick hypnosis session
in order to try to confirm or disconfirm a suspicion of abuse. Do
not put any clinician in the position of having to provide a
"hypnotic truth serum" or serve as a hypnotic "truth investigator." Hypnosis cannot prevent deception. With regard to
hypnosis, it is essential to recognize the role of suggestion in
interviewing clients. A knowledge of hypnosis allows one to
recognize better the malleability of memory and the power of
suggestion to influence perceptions, including perceptions of
memory. If one does not have a good command of one's suggestions and does not use them deliberately and skillfully, then one
runs a greater risk of introducing information in ways that can
actually be hurtful to the client.

4.   **THAT** clinicians not ask leading questions. Leading questions
imply either a desired or a correct answer. They typically take
such forms as, "When were you abused?" and "How did he or
she molest you?" In the hypnotic framework, such questions
involve what are known as "presuppositions" (Yapko, 1990,
1995). They presuppose that abuse happened, and now it is
purely a matter of trying to determine exactly what happened
and when. Clinicians should be especially careful of their tone of
voice and gestures as a nonverbal basis for leading the client.

5. **THAT** clinicians not assume that repression is in force if the person cannot seem to remember much from his or her childhood. Rather than jump to the conclusion that the person's background must somehow involve trauma, one can consider the equally plausible possibility that it is merely because he or she doesn't really care that much about past experience. For those individuals who tend to be either "here and now" or future oriented, their representations for the past are typically quite impoverished (Yapko, 1988, 1989). Nothing particularly bad happened; they just do not represent the past in much detail because it is not a highly valued dimension of their subjective experience.

6. **THAT** clinicians not rely on their own memories. If you are planning to conduct the kind of session that is aimed at uncovering sensitive information, consider videotaping or audiotaping the session. Then it is possible to go review the tape in order to determine whether any leading or suggestive questions were asked. Was the possibility of abuse inadvertently suggested and so provoked a memory to suddenly arise? Transcribe the questions that were asked: Was anything implied? Were there any presuppositions?

Our key point in this chapter is that memory is suggestible. Therefore, we want to encourage therapists to make sure that, while assessing abuse survivors in treatment, they are not contaminating their clients through their own expectations and biases. We simply want therapists to better recognize that they unwittingly can create the very problems they then must treat.

REFERENCES

Aronson, E. (1992). *The social animal* (6th ed.). San Francisco: Freeman.

Barclay, C. R., & Wellman, H.M. (1986). Accuracies and inaccuracies in autobiographical memory. *Journal of Memory & Language, 25,* 93–103.

Bass, E., & Davis, L. (1988). *The courage to heal: Women healing from sexual abuse.* New York: Harper & Row.

Blume, E. S. (1990). *Secret survivors: Uncovering incest and its aftereffects in women.* New York: Ballantine.

Bower, G. (1981). Mood and memory. *American Psychologist, 36,* 129–148.

Brewin, C. R., Andrews, B., & Gotlib, I. H. (1993). Psychopathology and early experience: A reappraisal of retrospective reports. *Psychological Bulletin, 113,* 82–98.

Briere, J. (1989). *Therapy for adults molested as children: Beyond survival.* New York: Springer.

Bruhn, A. R. (1990). *Earliest childhood memories, Vol. 1: Theory and application to clinical practice.* New York: Praeger.

Council on Scientific Affairs, American Medical Association (AMA). (1985). Scientific status of refreshing recollection by the use of hypnosis. *Journal of the American Medical Association, 253*, 1918–1923.

Daro, D. (1988). *Confronting child abuse.* New York: Free Press.

Davis, L. (1991). Murdered memory. *Health, 5*, 79–84.

Dywan, J., & Bowers, K. (1983). The use of hypnosis to enhance recall. *Science, 222*, 184–185.

Forward, S., & Buck, C. (1988). *Betrayal of innocence: Incest and its devastation.* New York: Penguin Books.

Fredrickson, R. (1992). *Repressed memories: A journey of recovery from sexual abuse.* New York: Simon and Schuster.

Ganaway, G. K. (1989). Historical versus narrative truth: Clarifying the role of exogenous trauma in the etiology of MPD and its variants. *Dissociation, 2*, 205–220.

Gordon, J. S. (1991). The UFO experience. *Atlantic Monthly, 268*, 82–92.

Haley, J. (1973). *Uncommon therapy.* New York: Norton.

Harsch, N., & Neisser, U. (1989, November). *Substantial and irreversible errors in flashbulb memories of the Challenger Explosion.* Poster presented at the Psychonomic Society annual meeting, Atlanta, Ga.

Herman, J. L. (1992). *Trauma and recovery.* New York: Basic Books.

Howe, M. L., & Courage, M. L. (1993). On resolving the enigma of infantile amnesia. *Psychological Bulletin.*

Johnson v. Johnson (1988). 701 F. Supp. 1363 (N.D. III.).

Kihlstrom, J. F., & Harackiewicz. (1982). The earliest recollection: A new survey. *Journal of Personality, 50*, 135–148.

Kline, M. V., & Gaze, H. (1951). The use of projective drawing technique in the investigation of hypnotic age regression and progression. *British Journal of Medical Hypnosis, 3*, 10–21.

Laurence, J-R., Nadon, R., Nogrady, H., & Perry, C. (1986). Duality, dissociation, and memory creation in highly hypnotizable subjects. *International Journal of Clinical and Experimental Hypnosis, 34*(4), 295–310.

Laurence, J-R., & Perry, C. (1983). Hypnotically created memory among highly hypnotizable subjects. *Science, 222*, 523–524.

Loftus, E. F. (1979). *Eyewitness testimony.* Cambridge, Mass.: Harvard University Press.

Loftus, E. F. (1980). *Memory.* Reading, Mass.: Addison-Wesley.

Loftus, E. F. (1991). Made in memory: Distortions of recollection after misleading information. In G. Bower (Ed.), *Psychology of learning and motivation* (vol. 27, pp. 187–215). New York: Academic Press.

Loftus, E. F. (1993). The reality of repressed memories. *American Psychologist, 48*, 518–537.

Loftus, E. F., & Hoffman, H. (1989). Misinformation and memory: The creation of new memories. *Journal of Experimental Psychology: General, 118*, 100–104.

Loftus, E. F., & Ketcham, K. (1991). *Witness for the defense.* New York: St. Martin's Press.

Loftus, E. F., & Ketcham, K. (1994). *The myth of repressed memory.* New York: St. Martin's Press.

Loring, D. W., Lee. G. P., & Meador, K. J. (1989). The intracarotid amobarbital sodium procedure: False-positive errors during recognition memory assessment. *Archives of Neurology, 46*, 285–287.

Nash, M. (1987). What, if anything, is regressed about hypnotic age regression? A review of the empirical literature. *Psychological Bulletin, 102*, 42–52.

Nash, M. (1992). *Retrieval of childhood memories in psychotherapy.* Paper presented at the annual convention of the American Psychological Association, Washington, D.C.

Neisser, U. (1991). A case of misplaced nostalgia. *American Psychologist, 46*(1), 34–36.

Ofshe, R. J. (1992). Inadvertent hypnosis during interrogation: False confession due to dissociative state, misidentified multiple personality, and the Satanic Cult hypothesis. *International Journal of Clinical and Experimental Hypnosis, 40*, 125–156.

Olio, K. A. (1989). Memory retrieval in the treatment of adult survivors of sexual abuse. *Transactional Analysis Journal, 19*, 93–94.

Orne, M. T. (1979). The use and misuse of hypnosis in court. *International Journal of Clinical and Experimental Hypnosis, 27*, 311–341.

Poston, C., & Lison, K. (1990). *Reclaiming our lives: Hope for adult survivors of incest.* New York: Bantam.

Sgroi, S. M. (1989). Stages of recovery for adult survivors of child sex abuse. In S. M. Sgroi (Ed.), *Vulnerable populations: Sexual abuse treatment for children, adult survivors, offenders and persons with mental retardation* (vol. 2). Lexington, Mass.: Lexington Books.

Smith, M. (1983). Hypnotic memory enhancement of witnesses: Does it work? *Psychological Bulletin, 94*, 387–407.

Snyder, M. (1984). When belief creates reality? In L. Berkowitz (Ed.), *Advances in experimental social psychology* (vol. 18, pp. 247–305). Orlando, Fla.: Academic Press.

Sundberg, N., Taplin, J., & Tyler, L. (1983). *Introduction to clinical psychology.* Englewood Cliffs, N.J.: Prentice Hall.

Trott, J. (1991). The grade five syndrome. *Cornerstone, 20*, 16–18.

Weekes, J. R., Lynn, S. L., Green, J. P., & Brentar, J. T. (1992). Pseudomemory in hypnotized and task-motivated subjects. *Journal of Abnormal Psychology, 101*, 356–360.

Whitley, G. (1992, January). Abuse of trust. *D. Magazine*, pp. 36–39, .

Yapko, M. (1988). *When living hurts.* New York: Brunner/Mazel.

Yapko, M. (1989). Disturbance of temporal orientation as a feature of depression. In M. Yapko (Ed.), *Brief therapy approaches to treating anxiety and depression* (pp. 106–118). New York: Brunner/Mazel.

Yapko, M. (1990). *Trancework: An introduction to the practice of clinical hypnosis* (2nd ed.). New York: Brunner/Mazel.

Yapko, M. (1993, September/October). The seductions of memory. *Family Therapy Networker, 17*(5), 30–37.

Yapko, M. (1994a). Suggestibility and repressed memories of abuse: A survey of psychotherapists' beliefs. *American Journal of Clinical Hypnosis, 36*(3), 163–171.

Yapko, M. (1994b). *Suggestions of abuse: True and false memories of childhood sexual trauma.* New York: Simon and Schuster.

Yapko, M. (1995). *Essentials of hypnosis.* New York: Brunner/Mazel.

Zeig, J. (1980). *A teaching seminar with Milton H. Erickson, M.D.* New York: Brunner/Mazel.

11

An Introduction to the Cognitive Interview Technique

Debra A. Bekerian
and John L. Dennett

This chapter examines the Cognitive Interview (CI) technique and considers its potential applications for child witnesses. We review CI and provide a summary of the basic findings. We then consider the most appropriate circumstances under which CI might be used with children, focusing on important factors such as the age of the child, the verbal competence of the child, and the emotional state of the child.

The goals of interviews conducted for alleged child abuse are determined by a number of factors, e.g., the law, the penal system, current police practices, social service mandates, and so on. However, it is probably true to suggest that most interviewers, particularly those conducting evidential interviews, want to determine whether or not the child's accusations are authentic. In arriving at this decision, three features of the child's accusations are crucial. Firstly, the child must be able to remember a *specific* event during which the alleged abuse occurred. In the psychology of memory, this is referred to as episodic remembering, or episodic memory (cf., Tulving, 1973). Secondly, the child should be able to provide details about the episode in question. That is, the account should contain features of the specific context, e.g., what conversations were held. In general, as more contextual details are remembered, the account is rendered more believable. Thirdly, the child should produce details that are accurate. Inaccuracies in the story will undermine the credibility of the account, particularly if they can be challenged with conflicting evidence. In short, the interviewer is more likely to decide that the child's accusations are authentic if the child can remember a specific event, can report contextual details, and is accurate in the details remembered.

Experimental psychologists have devoted much attention to procedures that might improve episodic memory. The research suggests that certain memory techniques can promote more complete and accurate recall. In this chapter we will discuss one technique that has been developed from psychological research, referred to as the Cognitive Interview (CI) technique. Specific attention will be paid to correct application and circumstances in using this technique with children.

CI has been so successfully applied to real interview situations that police authorities have now included CI as a basic part of interview training (Geiselman, 1992; George, 1991). The reader is advised that many books and papers have been written on the topic; a comprehensive review of the literature as a whole is beyond the scope of this chapter. Consequently, the intention is to provide the reader with a useful summary of the issues in using CI with children, and offer further reference sources should the reader be interested in pursuing specific points in greater detail.

INTERVIEWING STRATEGIES IN CI

The Cognitive Interview (CI) technique was originally devised by Edward Geiselman and his colleagues, with Ronald Fisher developing the original concept further (referred to as the revised CI). CI was initially applied to laboratory studies of memory (Geiselman et al., 1984). However, the subsequent application to real interview settings has been very successful (Fisher et al., 1987b; George 1991). CI is distinguishable from other types of interview techniques, such as Conversational Management (Shepard, 1988), in its emphasis on four principal memory strategies.

Principal memory strategies

Reinstate the context. The individual is asked to try and reinstate (or recreate) as much of the surrounding context that was concomitant with the event, including emotional/internal states.

Part of the difficulties people experience when they try to remember an event is initially accessing the information in memory, or isolating information in memory that is relevant to the event in question. For example, suppose a person is asked about what happened on Thursday of last week. The person will somehow have to distinguish information that is relevant to "last Thursday" from information that is relevant to "last Friday." Remembering this type of event information is more difficult, at least initially, than, say, remembering what your name is. Context reinstatement helps the person remember a specific event (engage in episodic remembering) by reinstating, or recreating, original features of the event. It is assumed that the reinstatement of features will help the person to use retrieval cues that will aid memory (Davies & Thomson, 1988; Tulving & Thomson, 1973).

Context reinstatement can be achieved in a variety of different ways. It can involve the internal generation of features through the process of imaging (Malpass & Devine, 1981). Or, context reinstatement can occur through the external reinstatement of features (Bowers & Bekerian, 1984), as might happen when a witness is taken back to the scene of a crime. However, this procedure may be difficult to apply to real investigations of child abuse. Alternatively, the person might be asked to try and remember the sequence of actions, thereby reinstating the original order of events (Eldridge, Barnard, & Bekerian, 1993).

Report everything. *The individual is encouraged to report as much as he or she can remember, irrespective of the level of subjective confidence associated with the information or the perceived importance of the information.*

A common, but erroneous, belief held by many witnesses* is that confidence is a reliable indicator of the accuracy of information (Loftus, 1979; Noon & Hollin, 1987). This means that some witnesses will omit recalling a detail, if they feel uncertain about it. Thus, a witness may feel that a certain piece of information is not relevant or important enough to mention to an interviewer and, consequently, fail to mention that detail (Geiselman, 1992).

However, the empirical work suggests that the relationship between confidence and accuracy is unpredictable (Kassin, Ellsworth, & Smith, 1989; Wells & Lindsay, 1985). Furthermore, it is often the case that the witness may misjudge the relevance of a piece of information (Geiselman, 1992). For these reasons, it is important to try and encourage individuals to disregard the confidence in, or the perceived importance of, a piece of information. Work from the experimental literature strongly suggests that encouraging a person to adopt a lenient attitude in reporting information will result in more complete accounts, e.g., disregarding the confidence associated with the information or the perceived importance of the information (Bekerian & Dennett, 1992).

---

*Throughout the chapter, witness will be referred to, although most points can apply to victims, unless specified explicitly.

Recall events in different order. *The individual is asked to recall the event in more than one sequential order, that is, recall the event from the end to the beginning, or from the middle, etc. This strategy can also be applied to lower-level details, as in the scanning of images.*

As stated above, part of the problem a witness may have is initially accessing relevant event information in memory. Changing the order of recall should help memory by enabling the person to use different retrieval cues. The alternative retrieval cues would be then likely to increase the chances of remembering new information (Geiselman & Callot, 1990; Mingay, Dennett, & Bekerian, 1984).

Change perspectives. *The individual is asked to recall the event as if he or she were viewing it from another person's perspective, e.g., remember the event as if you had been sitting to the left of the perpetrator.*

The rationale for this strategy again is derived from the assumption that different retrieval cues will facilitate retrieving different information from memory. A change in perspective should force the person to consider new retrieval routes, thereby making new information available. Empirical evidence supports this claim (Nigro & Neisser, 1983; Whitten & Leonard, 1981).

However, a potential problem exists with this strategy. If a witness is asked to adopt a perspective that he or she did not actually experience, some information that is reported may be imported from other sources, e.g., general world knowledge. For example, suppose a child is asked to remember what happened when she visited the dentist. The child may not actually remember whether the dentist asked her to sit in the chair on this specific occasion. However, she may "know," from previous occasions, that the dentist sometimes is the person to greet her. A change in perspective, e.g., "Tell me what the dentist would have seen," may encourage her to use this general knowledge, although she does not actually remember it from the specific experience. This imported information is consistent with the event, even though the information was not experienced by the individual (Bartlett, 1932).

Therefore, a change in perspective can lead to the inclusion of information that is confabulated and difficult to distinguish from "authentic" memories. In response to this potential problem, some proponents of the revised CI suggest that changes in perspective should not be used with children (Saywitz, Geiselman, & Bernstein, 1992). Instead, they suggest that the witness should be encouraged to give more than one recall (Fisher et al., 1989; Memon et al., 1992). The assumption is that repeated recall attempts will make the individual more likely to use new and different strategies for remembering, yielding new information. The phenomenon of new information being correctly recalled on successive recall trials has been well documented, and is referred to as hypermnesia in the memory literature (Scrivner & Safer, 1988).

It is important to point out that merely asking the person to recall repeatedly will not guarantee the use of new retrieval strategies. For example, it has been noted that, unless otherwise instructed, people will produce accounts on the basis of what they remember they had said before, rather than attempting to remember from the original event itself (Hammersley, 1981). Additionally, there are certain consequences of repeatedly being interviewed about the same incident. For one, repeated accounts may take on certain qualities that could be used to challenge the authenticity of the child's account, particularly if CI strategies had been used. This point is very important and will be expanded upon later. For these reasons, it is probably important that the witness be explicitly instructed to disregard what was said in earlier accounts, and try to base the account on what is remembered from the event.

Effects of principal memory strategies

Each of the four memory strategies has been demonstrated as being effective in promoting recall. However, they are not equally powerful nor resilient in their effects. For example, context reinstatement has been shown to be the most powerful of the strategies in isolation and also to have the longest lasting effects on recall (Geiselman et al., 1986; George, 1991). Additionally, it is sometimes difficult for the interviewer to identify when a witness is successfully using a strategy (George, 1991; Saywitz et al., 1992). For example, Saywitz et al. (1992) suggest that it is difficult for the interviewer to know when a child is using context reinstatement. This may pose problems, to the extent that the interviewer may wish to confirm that the child can accurately execute the memory aids. Generally, it is recommended that the strategies be used in combination (Geiselman, 1992).

Additional cognitive components

In addition to the principal strategies described above, CI advises the use of other memory aids that are intended to produce more specific detail from a person. These essentially take the form of more guided or specific memory cues that the witness is asked to use (see Appendix A in Saywitz et al., 1992). For example, the witness may be encouraged to try and remember any numbers that were encountered, or any names that might have been mentioned. The use of either of these techniques is helpful if the witness had previously failed to mention such details in his or her narrative account. Additionally, witnesses are questioned about the content of any conversations that may have been overheard, and whether or not the perpetrator(s) in question had any specific speech characteristics, such as distinctive accents.

Communicative skills of the interviewer

CI emphasizes the quality of communication between the interviewer and the witness, e.g., the importance of rapport building. Fisher and Geiselman (1992) also state that it is important for both the interviewer and the witness to share in their expectations of why and how the interview is being conducted. These suggestions appear in most guides to interviewing and, consequently, are not unique to CI (Shepard, 1988).

Fisher et al. (1989) have provided some interesting information concerning problems that seem to arise regularly in interviews, particularly within the American police system.* They note that highly experienced police interviewers seem to suffer from interview practices that might inhibit the witness's account. Three particularly common "problems" are excessive interruptions, excessive use of a question-answer format, and inappropriate sequencing of questions. These problems are pervasive and are likely to occur with any witness, whether an adult or a child. Each will be very briefly considered.

The act of remembering requires some concentration and any interruptions will, by definition, distract the witness. Most experienced interviewers begin an interview by asking for a free narrative account. However, many interviewers interrupt the witness. As noted by Fisher et al. (1989), interviewers, on average, interrupted four times per every response given by the witness (an average of every 7.5 secs.). George (1991) also notes in his field study of English constabularies that officers not trained in CI asked significantly more questions per 10 minutes of interview than officers trained in CI. George's finding supports the notion that interruptions are more common with interviewers untrained in CI.

A second common problem noted by Fisher et al. (1989) is the excessive use of specific question-answer formats. Certainly, all interviews rely on a question-answer format. However, Fisher et al. comment that the format often is one where very specific questions are directed at the witness, e.g., what color was the suspect's shirt. Although there are benefits to short-answer questions, they may inhibit the person from remembering additional information.

The third most common problem reported by Fisher et al. (1989) is the inappropriate sequencing of questions. This takes a number of forms. For example, interviewers sometimes follow a standardized, rather formalized, line of questioning, rather than tailoring the questioning for the specific witness in question. The result is that the line of questioning appears to be

---

*These problems were not noted within the context of child abuse victims, but rather noted with interviews, generally, of witnesses.

motivated by a specified checklist, rather than by the account produced by the witness. This is particularly important in the context of child witnesses, since they represent a group requiring special attention.

Another example of inappropriate sequencing is when interviewers ask questions that are pertinent to information already given by the witness, rather than pertinent to information currently being given by the witness, e.g., returning to a previous point while the witness is trying to answer another question. This interrupts a witness's current train of thought. Finally, interviewers may be very unstructured in their line of questioning. One question may ask about a perceptual feature of a perpetrator, then the following question will ask about an entirely different type of feature, such as the order in which an action took place. This rapid and unstructured shift in topic prevents the witness from concentrating his or her attention on producing an accurate and comprehensive account.

In addition to those mentioned above, there are other guidelines about interviewing that are advised by CI proponents, although they are not considered to be integral to the administration of CI techniques (Fisher & Geiselman, 1992). These include the preference of open-ended questions over closed questions, the care needed in asking questions at a rate that allows the witness to respond, and the need to use language that is compatible with that used by the witness. The last point, namely the use of age-compatible language, is particularly relevant to interviews with younger children (Saywitz et al., 1992). For example, interviewers are advised to use terms that the child witness has used when making reference to genitalia, rather than impose their own, more adult terms (see Chapter 8, this volume).

EXPERIMENTAL AND FIELD STUDIES OF CI

CI has been studied under different methodologies and a wide range of conditions (see Bekerian & Dennett, 1992, for a review). The findings reported on CI are always regarded in comparison to a "standard" interview condition. In experimental settings, a "standard" interview condition might be free recall instructions, where the person is simply asked to remember everything he or she can about the event in question (Geiselman et al. 1984). In field studies, "standard" conditions are those interview strategies that are used by practitioners who are untrained in CI techniques (George, 1991; Saywitz et al., 1992). George (1991) defines "standard" conditions as those interview strategies that are used by experienced police officers, with no formal training in CI techniques. The type of "standard" condition one chooses may determine the types of effects that are observed with CI, particularly in field studies. For example, interviewers who are not formally trained in CI may nevertheless incorporate some of the CI techniques in their interviews, e.g., give the witness time to answer questions, ask the witness to form images of the perpetrator. When compared to these "standard" interviews, CI may not show as great an advantage.

Generally, the pattern of findings is that CI increases the amount of correct information that is recalled, but does not increase the amount of errors produced in the account. Therefore, CI promotes more accurate recall. This seems to be true across a wide range of conditions, subject populations, and event types (Bekerian & Dennett, 1992).

However, important exceptions exist. Sometimes CI does not significantly improve the amount of correct information recalled by children (Memon et al., 1992). Other studies with children have reported that CI increases the number of errors included in an account (Newlands & Macleod, 1992). Further, the beneficial effects of CI do not generalize to all types of information. Recall for some information is increased, while, for others, it remains unaffected (Geiselman et al., 1984; Memon et al., 1992). We will consider these "exceptional" circumstances in greater detail below (see *Conditions for Using CI*).

USING THE TECHNIQUES OF CI

CI is not difficult to implement, either for the interviewer or for the witness. However, it is clear that some type of instruction should be given to interviewers before they attempt to use CI, particularly as there are specific issues that arise within the context of child witnesses. Fisher and Geiselman (1992) have compiled a book on CI that contains, in addition to other useful chapters, details concerning training in the CI techniques. Consequently, discussion of training issues will be brief, with the reader being advised to consult the more comprehensive source.

Fisher and Geiselman (1992, Chapter 11)* suggest that the structure of an interview should follow a prescribed sequence. First, the witness is asked to give a free narrative account. During this free narrative phase, the interviewer should interrupt as little as possible and avoid guiding the witness's account. Following the free narrative, the specific memory techniques of CI are introduced. Again, the interviewer should avoid interruptions. This allows the witness better opportunity to use the memory strategies, e.g., form a perceptual image. Finally, the interviewer should summarize or review

---

*Fisher and Geiselman (1992) do not specifically address developmental issues, and the reader is advised that their text is designed primarily to inform about CI techniques and interview strategies.

what had been said in the interview, prior to closing down the interview. This serves the purpose of reminding the witness about the account, and allows for any corrections or additions.

Interviewers are also likely to require some instruction as to how they might question for more specific details. For example, witnesses who form images should be probed in detail for specifics about these images. This probing requires the interviewer to adopt language and metaphors that are relevant to the specific witness's description. Obviously, the interviewer must be cautious about leading the witness, and this is a particularly important point when one is interviewing younger children (ages four to seven) (Ceci, Ross, & Toglia, 1987).

In short, the interview should combine free narrative and more specific questions. The interviewer should avoid any interruptions during the free narrative phase, and should develop the line of questioning in an open-ended manner. Following this, the interviewer may wish to ask more specific, closed questions, but should be aware of the possibility of restricting, or leading, the child's response. As Fisher et al. (1989) suggest, such "...strategies may be difficult for experienced interviewers to implement, as it is natural to make use of one's professional experience; however, the interviewer should train himself to listen more actively...the interviewer [should] approach each interview as if this were his first source of information about the crime, even if he has prior knowledge" (p. 184).

CONDITIONS FOR USING CI

Although there has been substantial work done on CI, there is very little advice concerning conditions under which it can be applied to optimal advantage. In this section, we consider what requirements, if any, are likely to be important for the successful use of CI, particularly in the context of child witnesses.

The Critical Interview

It is an unfortunate fact that children are interviewed repeatedly in the course of investigations of child abuse. One of the more extreme, and distressing, examples of this was reported in the McMartin case in California, where some children were forced to reconstruct their accounts as many as 15 times. While there is agreement that children should be interviewed as few times as possible, the norm is nonetheless that children will be interviewed on more than one occasion.

The repeated interviewing of a child witness poses certain difficulties for memory techniques like CI. For example, one potential problem that has been noted is the fate of errors that occur under CI techniques (Bekerian & Dennett, 1993). Because CI techniques are so powerful as memory aids, it is possible that any errors in the child's account may become more "real," with a greater likelihood that they will be confused with actual events, or details.

There is relatively little evidence that indicates the point at which CI techniques should be introduced. Because many other factors are involved in decisions about the nature of interviews that are conducted with alleged child victims, this issue is likely to prove difficult to resolve. For example, the emotional state of the child must be considered as one of the critical factors in deciding whether memory enhancing techniques are used (Geiselman, 1992). Additionally, there must be some consideration for other procedures that one might wish to be applied to a child's account. For example, the effectiveness of content-based criteria to determine the credibility of a child's account may be undermined by the use of memory-enhancing techniques like CI (Steller & Wellershaus, 1992).

Characteristics of the Witness

One of the most obvious requirements for using CI is that the witness be "old enough" to understand and use the memory strategies. For example, before a certain age, children do not appear to understand certain memory strategies; and, even when instructed in these memory strategies, they may not spontaneously adopt them in subsequent situations (see Schneider & Pressley, 1989, for a comprehensive review of developmental changes). Saywitz et al. (1992) have provided some guidelines as to how CI can be modified for use with younger children (e.g., ages three to seven). For example, in adult studies, witnesses have been instructed to "imagine" where and when they might have been sitting in a particular location, as part of context reinstatement. With younger children, the use of the word "imagine" may be taken as an indication that the child should fantasize, rather than report what actually happened to him or her. Saywitz et al. suggest that such terms be avoided, particularly with younger witnesses (e.g., four years old).

Another essential requirement is that the witness can produce a narrative account about a specific event (i.e., engage in episodic remembering). Again, the age and/or verbal competence of the child will determine the extent to which this requisite is fulfilled. The ability to "tell a story" develops with age (Fivush & Hudson, 1991). Younger children (e.g., two-year-olds) construct narrative accounts that sometimes omit certain expected features, e.g., temporal coherence. The reader is advised to consult the primary reference sources for further information about developmental changes in narrative competence and style (Schneider & Pressley, 1989). However, some researchers in CI have suggested that CI techniques should be used only with children of, or above the age of seven (Memon, personal communication).

Characteristics of the Event

Another factor that may effect a child's ability to recall a specific event is the frequency or regularity of the incidents (Hudson, 1988). Events that occur frequently may be reported in a very schematic manner, at least initially. The child may initially remember only general features of the events, particularly those that are consistent across different incidents (e.g., actions, times of day). The schematic nature of accounts has been found in cases of prolonged incest, where the abuse was frequent and regular. Data from naturalistic studies with children have similarly reported that repeated experience with a class of events can lead to highly structured accounts, somewhat irrespective of the manner in which the child is questioned (Hudson, 1988; Nelson, 1988).

Should the child experience difficulties in recalling a specific incident, there are certain strategies that one can employ which may help isolate a specific instance or instances. For example, the child might be asked to reconstruct a "time-line," with personally significant events being used as anchor points, e.g., your last birthday, Christmas time, the summer holidays. The child might then be asked whether an incident occurred at any time surrounding these anchor points (Geiselman, 1992).

It also appears that the complexity of an event will determine how successful CI techniques will be. Events can vary in the logical sequence of their actions. For example, events like "eye tests" follow a logical, predictable sequence (Memon et al., 1992). In contrast, an event like "going to the zoo" is not as constrained. Events can also differ in the speed with which actions happen; few things can be happening at any one time, or many things can be occurring simultaneously.

According to Geiselman et al. (1984), events that are logically sequenced and have a slow action pace are "simple." Events that are not sequentially constrained, and where many actions occur simultaneously, are considered "complex." Experimental results have suggested that memory for simple events is not significantly improved with CI, as compared to the improvement noted for complex events (Geiselman et al., 1984; Memon et al., 1992).

There are a number of reasons why CI may not be as effective with simple events. First, if an event is sequential in nature, the occurrence of one action almost predicts another, or at least constrains what might happen next (Ornstein, 1992). Because of this, causally linked events are easier to remember (Bransford & Johnson, 1972). This seems to be the case with even fairly young children (Ornstein, 1992). Second, memory is likely to be better when few actions occur at any one time. There is a greater chance that the person can attend carefully to each action, rather than trying rapidly to switch attention between many actions.

From a practical point of view, CI might not be employed if the event in question is not sufficiently complex. For example, if the child reports having contact with the alleged perpetrator only for a matter of seconds, the child may not benefit from CI techniques. Of course, knowing whether an event is complex or not may pose problems in real cases, given the interviewer is not in the same privileged position as the experimenter. However, even the real interviewer may obtain some indications of the complexity of the event by, for example, carefully reviewing the information that was provided by the child during the free narrative stage.

CONCLUSIONS

CI is successful in helping people remember events that have happened in their lives. At this time, there have been sufficient research and field studies with adult populations to suggest that it can be used, providing certain requisites are fulfilled. Although the research with child populations is not as extensive as that with adults, the preliminary findings suggests that CI can be successfully used with children over the age of seven, provided suitable adjustments are made (Saywitz et al., 1992). For example, CI would appear to be appropriate to use when a child is asked to remember a specific event of a certain complexity and uniqueness. Another point is important to make. In this chapter, much discussion has been given to the importance of using CI techniques on children of a certain age (e.g., seven years and older). Although there is no doubt that the nominal age of the child is one indicator that must be taken into account before using CI, it is inappropriate to judge the individual child's ability on the basis of age alone. A close examination of this has been provided by Goodman and Schwartz-Kenney (1992), where these authors stress that many factors besides chronological age can affect a child's ability to produce an account, such as social, emotional, and situational factors present at the time of the interview. Consequently, the practitioner is advised that the age of the child is only one factor that must be taken into consideration before CI techniques are used.

Generally, it is advisable that interviewers who are interested in CI should be formally trained in the techniques, or at least take advantage of video training that is now available. If used under the correct conditions, CI can provide the interviewer with very powerful interviewing tools. Not surprisingly, this success will depend entirely on characteristics of the child in question, characteristics of the event in question, and the extent to which the interviewer can adopt strategies that will be sensitive to the needs of the child and to the goals of the interview.

Recommendations

1. **THAT** interviewers must receive formal training/experience in using CI techniques.
2. **THAT** CI is probably better suited for children who have reached a certain level of verbal competence (e.g., fluent in constructing a story).
3. **THAT** CI should be used only after other factors have been considered, such as stage in the investigation or emotional state of the child.

REFERENCES

Bartlett, F. (1932). *Remembering: A study in experimental and social psychology.* Cambridge, England: Cambridge University Press.

Bekerian, D. A., & Dennett, J. L. (1992). The cognitive technique: Reviving the issues. *Applied Cognitive Psychology, 7*, 275–297.

Bekerian, D. A., & Dennett, J .L. (1993). The Cognitive Interview: The fate of errors.

Bowers, J. M., & Bekerian, D. A. (1984). When will post-event information distort eyewitness testimony? *International Journal of Applied Psychology, 69*, 466–472.

Bransford, J., & Johnson, M. (1972). Contextual prerequisites for understanding: Some investigations of comprehension and recall. *Journal of Verbal Learning and Verbal Behaviour, 11*, 717–726.

Ceci, S., Ross. D., & Toglia, M. (1987) Age differences in suggestibility: Narrowing the uncertainties. In S. Ceci, M. Toglia, & D. Ross (Eds.), *Children's eyewitness memory* (pp. 79–91). New York: Springer-Verlag.

Davies, G. M., & Thomson, D. M. (Eds.). (1988). Memory in context: Context in memory (pp. 339–344). Chichester, England: John Wiley and Sons.

Eldridge, M., Barnard, P., & Bekerian, D. A. (1993). Schematic influences in autobiographical memory. Manuscript submitted for publication.

Fisher, R., & Geiselman R. E. (1992). *Memory-enhancing techniques for investigative interviewing: The cognitive interview.* Springfield, Ill.: Charles C. Thomas.

Fisher, R., Geiselman, R. E., & Amador, M. (1989). Field tests of the cognitive interview: Enhancing the recollection of actual victims and witnesses of crime. *Journal of Applied Psychology, 74*(5), 722–727.

Fisher, R., Geiselman, R. E., Raymond, D., Jurkevich, L., & Warhaftig, M. (1987). Enhancing enhanced eyewitness memory: Refining the cognitive interview. *Journal of Police Science and Administration, 15*, 291–296.

Fivush, R., & Hudson, J. (1991). *Knowing and remembering in young children.* New York: Cambridge University Press.

Geiselman, E. (1992, May). Cognitive Interviewing Techniques for use with child victim/witnesses. Paper presented at the NATO Advanced Study Institute, Il Ciocco, Lucca, Italy.

Geiselman, R. E., & Callot, R. (1990). Reverse and forward recall of script-based texts. *Applied Cognitive Psychology, 4,* 141–144.

Geiselman, R. E., Fisher, R., Firstenberg, I., Hutton, L., Sullivan, S., Avetissian, I., & Prosk, A. (1984). Enhancement of eyewitness memory: An empirical evaluation of the cognitive interview. *Journal of Police Science and Administration, 12,* 74–80.

Geiselman, R. E., Fisher, R., MacKinnon, D., & Holland, H. (1986). Enhancement of eyewitness memory with the cognitive interview. *American Journal of Psychology, 99,* 385–401.

George, R. (1991). *A field and experimental evaluation of three methods of interviewing witnesses/victims of crime.* Unpublished Master's thesis . University of East London.

Goodman, G., & Schwartz-Kenney, B. (1992). Why knowing a child's age is not enough: Influences of cognitive, social and emotional factors on children's testimony. In H. Dent & R. Flin (Eds.), Children as witnesses (pp. 15–33). Chichester, England: John Wiley and Sons.

Hammersley, R. H. (1981). *Headed records and the multiple representation of information in memory.* Unpublished doctoral dissertation, Cambridge University.

Hudson, J. A. (1988). Children's memory for atypical actions in script-based stories: Evidence for a disruption effect. *Journal of Experimental Child Psychology, 46*(2), 159–173.

Kassin, S., Ellsworth, P., & Smith, V. (1989). The "general acceptance" of psychological research on eyewitness testimony. *American Psychologist, 44,* 1089–1098.

Loftus, E. F. (1979). *Eyewitness testimony.* Cambridge, Mass.: Harvard University Press.

Malpass, R., & Devine, P. (1981). Guided memory in eyewitness identification. *Journal of Applied Psychology, 66,* 343–350.

Memon, A., Cronin, O., Eaves, R., Bull, R., & Küpper, B. (1992, May). The Cognitive Interview and child witnesses. Paper presented at the NATO Advanced Study Instituste, Il Ciocco, Lucca Italy.

Mingay, D., Dennett, J. L., & Bekerian, D.A. (1984). Memory for a staged incident. *Forum, 17,* 58–60.

Nelson, K. (1988). The ontogeny of memory for real events. In U. Neisser and E. Winograd (Eds.), *Remembering reconsidered: Ecological and traditional approaches to the study of memory* (pp. 244–276). Cambridge, England: Cambridge University Press.

Newlands, P., & Macleod, M. (1992, September). Continuing the Cognitive Interview. Poster presented at the Third European Conference of Law and Psychology, Oxford.

Nigro, G., & Neisser, U. (1983). Point of view in personal memories. *Cognitive Psychology, 15,* 467–482.

Noon, E., & Hollin, C. (1987). Lay knowledge of eyewitness behaviour: A British survey. *Applied Cognitive Psychology, 1*, 143–153.

Ornstein, P. (1992, May). Theoretical and applied perspectives of children's memory. Paper presented at the NATO Advanced Study Institute, Il Ciocco, Lucca, Italy.

Saywitz, K. J., Geiselman, R. E., & Bornstein, G. K. (1992). Effects of cognitive interviewing and practice on children's recall performance. *Journal of Applied Psychology, 77*, 1–12

Schneider, W., & Pressley, M. (1989). *Memory development between two and twenty.* New York: Springer-Verlag.

Scrivner, E., & Safer, M. (1988). Eyewitnesses show hypermnesia for details about a violent event. *Journal of Applied Psychology, 73*, 371–377.

Shepard, E. (1988). Developing interview skills. In P. Southgate (Ed.), *New directions in police training.* London: HMSO.F.

Stellar, M., & Wellershaus, P. (1992, September). Information enhancement and credibility assessment of children's statements: The impact of the Cognitive Interview technique on Criteria-Based Content Analysis. Paper presented at the Third European Conference of Law and Psychology, Oxford.

Tulving, E. (1972). Episodic and semantic memory. In E. Tulving & W. Donaldson (Eds.), *Organization of memory.* New York: Academy Press.

Tulving, E., & Thomson, D. (1973). Encoding specificity and retrieval processes in episodic memory. *Psychological Review, 80*, 352–373.

Wells, G. L., & Lindsay, R. C. L. (1985). Methodological notes on the accuracy-confidence relation in eyewitness identifications. *Journal of Applied Psychology, 70*(2), 413–419.

Whitten, W., & Leonard, J. (1981). Directed search through autobiographical memory. *Memory and Cognition, 9*, 566–579.

PART IV

Assessment Issues

12

Evaluating Allegations of Sexual Abuse in the Context of Divorce, Child Custody, and Access Disputes

Marion F. Ehrenberg and
Michael F. Elterman

This chapter focuses on the evaluation of child sexual abuse allegations arising during divorce, custody, and access disputes. Historical and legal issues relevant to this problem are summarized, and research about the extent, nature, and validity of sexual abuse allegations in divorce is reviewed. These research findings taken together suggest that improbable allegations are equally or more likely to occur during custody disputes than in cases where custody is not an issue. In the first half of this chapter, the practitioner is familiarized with a range of divorce-related family dynamics as possible contexts for sexual abuse allegations: abuse leading to divorce, abuse revealed during divorce, abuse precipitated by divorce, and custody/access disputes. A number of issues to be considered by the practitioner involved in

The first author would like to acknowledge support of a Social Science and Humanities Research Council grant while completing this work.

evaluations of child sexual abuse allegations in divorce are reviewed in the second half of the chapter. Knowledge and skills needed to complete such evaluations are summarized, and relevant professional and ethical issues are discussed. A clinical-research approach to evaluation is recommended and described. The practitioner is encouraged to evaluate carefully the specific circumstances of the sexual abuse allegation, including when, how, and by whom the allegation was brought forward. Strategies for differentiating sexual abuse from divorce trauma in children are presented, and characteristics of accused and alleging parents and aspects of their relationships with their children in probable and improbable cases are reviewed. The chapter concludes with 10 specific recommendations relevant to practitioners involved in the evaluation of child sexual abuse allegations in divorce.

OVERVIEW

Many health and mental health professionals are involved in assessing child sexual abuse allegations arising in a wide range of contexts and circumstances. While family dynamics are generally considered when such allegations are evaluated, family disagreements about custody and access visitation decisions can complicate such assessments. The purpose of this chapter is (1) to discuss the extent, type, and validity of sexual abuse allegations in divorce and custody situations; (2) to familiarize the practitioner with a range of divorce-related contexts in which child sexual abuse allegations may occur; (3) to summarize key issues in the evaluation of sexual abuse allegations during divorce, custody, and visitation disputes; and (4) to discuss ethical and professional concerns relevant to clinical practice in this area.

DIVORCE, CHILD CUSTODY, AND
ACCESS DISPUTES AS AN EVALUATIVE CONTEXT

Divorce and Child Custody in Historical Perspective

It is critical for practitioners evaluating sexual abuse allegations in families disputing custody and visitation issues to have a basic understanding of emerging family law, child protection policies, and legal terminology relevant to this area of practice (Deed, 1991). Historically, family laws pertaining to child custody and access decisions were based on a presumption of paternal custody, but were eventually replaced by the "tender years presumption," which favored mothers' claims. Today, custody decisions are guided by the "best interests of the child criterion," which emphasizes the needs of the children over the rights of divorcing parents. Without a legal presumption of maternal or paternal custody, the courts have seen a proliferation of bitter and protracted custody disputes. These disputes typically involve a parent's attempt to discredit the ex-spouse's fitness as a parent and to demonstrate his or her own superiority in meeting the child's needs. In recent years, the courts have looked to mental health professionals to develop recommendations about how the interests of a child involved in such a dispute may be best served (for a review, see Elterman & Ehrenberg, 1991).

In the early 1970s, adultery was the main allegation used to draw attention to a parent's moral fitness, but today evidence of a parent's sexual conduct with other consenting adults will generally not support a denial of custody or access to that parent. In the current climate of increasing social consciousness about the prevalence of child sexual abuse and its traumatic and far-reaching effects on child victims (e.g., Briere, 1988; Browne & Finkelhor, 1986), parents are accusing each other of sexual abuse of their children during custody battles (Benedek & Schetky, 1985; Elterman & Ehrenberg, 1991). If such allegations are substantiated, the perpetrator is often excluded from contact with the children and the plaintiff is usually awarded full custody. Mental health professionals involved in evaluating such cases and making recommendations to the courts tend to lean conservatively, and when necessary, in the direction of least possible risk to the child. This takes the form of increasing the risk of overpredicting the dangerousness of the accused parent (Elterman & Ehrenberg, 1991). Judges are faced with the difficulty of making decisions that strike an appropriate balance between parental rights and child protection. Where there is uncertainty about the validity of an accusation, the choice between two potential errors must be made: an innocent parent and the child may be deprived of a relationship with each other, or a child may be returned to a situation where he or she continues to be sexually abused. If an error is made, a child's physical and psychological health may be jeopardized, or a parent's life and career may be destroyed (Green, 1986). While there is considerable research documenting the effects of sexual abuse on child victims (Briere, 1988; Browne & Finkelhor, 1986), the impact of false allegations of sexual abuse on the children involved has not been researched, but is likely to be harmful (Benedek & Schetky, 1987b).

Extent, Nature, and Validity of Sexual Abuse Allegations

Despite the recent increase in the research on child sexual abuse, the issue of improbable accusations has been largely neglected by behavioral scientists. The available evidence is limited to case reports, anecdotal references, and a few empirical studies. There are several problems that complicate the interpretation of previous findings and continue to compromise research in this area. First, some studies depend on small and possibly biased samples (e.g., reports of a few cases selected, evaluated, and analyzed by the reporting practitioner). Second, important details about the cases may be missing (e.g., whether the allegations were made by the parent or the child, the timing of the allegation), and information about how the allegations were evaluated may be lacking. Even the larger and more extensive archival studies are limited by the type of information recorded in agencies' files. Third, the most serious methodological problem is that it is impossible to validate the truthfulness of an allegation using any absolute, scientifically acceptable criterion measure. At best, after careful investigation, an evaluator or team of evaluators may conclude the extent to which the available assessment findings are consistent or inconsistent with sexual abuse. In addition to detailing a thorough and systematic evaluation process, future research studies may include ultimate court decisions and follow-up data (e.g., details of any allegations and counterallegations following an initial accusation, evidence of sexual abuse revealed after the court hearing, admissions by alleging or accused parents after the court decision) as additional outcome measures. Often the court's decision has been shaped by an expert opinion, and, therefore, the decision and evaluation findings are not independent measures. This problem emphasizes the importance of additional follow-up information to strengthen these studies. While it is important for professionals practicing in this area to remain abreast of the relevant literature, it is equally important that they interpret and weigh ongoing research findings in light of these methodological problems (for a review, see Elterman & Ehrenberg, 1991).

These methodological issues taken into consideration, the current literature suggests that children are accurate in their disclosures of sexual abuse in noncustody cases in 92% to 94% of the cases (Goodwin, Sahd, & Rada, 1978; Jones & McGraw, 1987; Peters, 1979). Although these studies suggest that only 6% to 8% of sexual abuse reports could not be validated, some studies of sexual abuse allegations during custody disputes find that in this context the corresponding figures are significantly higher (Benedek & Schetky, 1985; Green, 1986). These findings indicate that there may be factors present in custody situations that are related to a higher proportion of improbable allegations than in noncustody situations. The discrepancy between the incidence of improbable allegations in custody versus noncustody contexts has since been disputed (Berliner, 1990; Hlady & Gunter, 1990; Jones & Seig, 1988; Thoennes & Tjaden, 1990), although there are insufficient empirical data to speak conclusively to this issue.

Since the mid-1980s, much professional and media attention has been directed at sexual abuse allegations arising during custody and access disputes. Although many of these accounts suggested a dramatic rise in these cases, typically with mothers falsely accusing fathers (e.g., "Child abuse," 1987; "Guilty until," 1987), it now appears that these accounts may have contributed to a limited, if not inaccurate, view of the problem. Thoennes and

Tjaden (1990) conducted a comprehensive study of all families contesting custody and visitation before eight domestic relations courts over a six-month period in jurisdictions across the United States. They found that approximately 2% of these 9,000 cases involved sexual abuse allegations, suggesting only a slightly higher incidence of sexual abuse reports than in the general population. The researchers concluded that even if there had been a recent increase in the number of these cases, it was likely in keeping with the heightened awareness and willingness to report suspected abuse in the general population. Contrary to anecdotal accounts suggesting that these cases almost always involved accusations by mothers against fathers, in only slightly more than half of the 165 cases with sexual abuse allegations did the mothers accuse the fathers (48%) or stepfathers (6%). The remainder of the cases involved fathers accusing mothers or mothers' new partners, and allegations by or against third parties. Typically, the sexual abuse allegation cases referred to a single, female child whose custody was in dispute. Based on an evaluation by a child protection services worker and/or court evaluator, half of the custody dispute cases were believed to involve abuse. In 33% of the alleged cases, no abuse was believed to have transpired, and in the remaining 17% of the cases, no determination could be reached. Furthermore, cases involving allegations made by mothers against fathers were equally likely to be perceived as valid as allegations made by fathers against mothers. In contrast to earlier studies, Thoennes and Tjaden (1990) found that allegations of sexual abuse among families in dispute over custody and visitation are no more likely to be determined as being false than are allegations of child sexual abuse in the general population. It should be noted that Thoennes and Tjaden's study did not include detailed information about who (child, parent, other) disclosed the alleged sexual abuse.

Anthony and Watkeys (1991) studied all referrals of suspected child sexual abuse received by child health units, social services, and the police in one region of South Wales from 1986 through 1989. The evaluations of these possible child sexual abuse cases involved social work/police interviews with the child individually and with family members, a police interview with the alleged offender, a medical evaluation, and integration of assessment information in a multiagency case conference. Of 410 referrals with a possible diagnosis of child sexual abuse, 350 referrals were fully investigated; of these, in 197 cases, the allegations of child sexual abuse were substantiated, typically with the alleged offenders pleading guilty. A majority of substantiated referrals resulted from direct disclosures from children (60%), whereas unsubstantiated cases were less frequently based on children's allegations (22%). Of the unsubstantiated cases, the majority arose because of professional or family concern, but 18% were considered "false" and "malicious" by the investigative team. One third of these "false allegation" cases involved accusations made by a parent against the other parent during a custody or access dispute, where evaluators had noted persistent nondisclosure of abuse by the child, and that the child appeared to have been "tutored" about what to say (Anthony & Watkeys, 1991).

In our view, the practitioner involved in assessing sexual abuse allegations during divorce or custody proceedings has a mandate that extends beyond careful evaluations and recommendations for individual cases. We suggest that practitioners should also provide the courts with information about the extent and validity of these types of allegations, when it is necessary and possible to do so. Currently, considerable misinformation exists and there is much media frenzy about sexual abuse allegations during custody disputes that may unfairly bias how a particular case is handled. While many questions about the extent, nature, and type of sexual abuse allegations arising during custody disputes have not been definitively answered, clearly many reliable allegations of sexual abuse are raised by mothers, fathers, and third parties in this context. The research findings taken together suggest that improbable allegations are equally or somewhat more likely to occur during custody disputes than in cases not involving custody/access matters, but that they should never be dismissed or assumed without careful investigation.

Sexual Abuse Allegations in the Context of Divorce and Custody Dynamics

The practitioner may be asked to evaluate sexual abuse allegations arising in a number of different divorce-related contexts. Routine and thorough assessment of family dynamics and careful questioning about the timing and circumstances of the allegation, as well as familiarity with a range of divorce-related circumstances, may assist the practitioner to evaluate an accusation of child sexual abuse in its proper context. Faller (1991) identified four dynamics resulting in allegations of sexual abuse during or after the dissolution of a marriage in 136 cases referred to a university-based child abuse and neglect agency for diagnosis and/or treatment.

1. Abuse leading to divorce (11 cases).
2. Abuse revealed during divorce (26 cases).
3. Abuse precipitated by divorce (52 cases).
4. Improbable allegations during divorce and custody/access disputes. (Nineteen cases were judged "false" and 12 cases were "inconclusive.")

CHILD SEXUAL ABUSE LEADING TO DIVORCE. This situation involves a parent's initiating a separation, because the parent suspects that the child is or was being abused by the other parent (Faller, 1991). In fact, disclosures of child sexual abuse are followed by parental divorce in approximately half of the cases reported to child-protection authorities (Sirles & Lofberg, 1990). In many families, the alleging parent will have informed child-protection authorities prior to the divorce, and will attempt to prevent visitation by the accused parent after the divorce. However, in some cases, the alleging parent will not have reported the suspected abuse until after the separation or divorce, and this may raise questions about the validity of the allegation. In such cases, it is important that the practitioner not only evaluate by whom, when, and how the alleged sexual abuse was initially disclosed, but also whether there were issues of family violence and fear that prevented a more timely disclosure by the alleging parent (Elterman & Ehrenberg, 1991). As professionals involved in evaluating allegations of this kind will typically also be required to make recommendations to the courts regarding the child's best interests, they will likely need to address the extent to which the parent who delayed reporting child sexual abuse is currently capable of protecting and caring for the child.

CHILD SEXUAL ABUSE REVEALED DURING DIVORCE. There are several reasons why child sexual abuse may be revealed at the time of parental divorce, rather than earlier. First, a child may finally feel safe enough to report long-standing sexual abuse because the perpetrator is no longer living in the home (Faller, 1991). Second, a child may have avoided disclosing the abuse precisely because he or she was told that it would destroy the family. Third, the nonabusing parent may be more prepared to acknowledge the expartner's abuse of the child at a time when conflict between the parents is less threatening and is permitted to come to the surface. The abused child may feel that their disclosure is more likely to be believed and responded to under such circumstances. It is best to avoid assuming that a sexual abuse allegation arising under these circumstances is necessarily valid or invalid. Rather, the practitioner should carefully assess all family members, while also evaluating why, how, and by whom the alleged abuse was disclosed at the time of the divorce.

CHILD SEXUAL ABUSE PRECIPITATED BY DIVORCE. Clinicians and researchers have noted that divorce-related stresses and loss of family structure may bring about behavior that was not previously exhibited (Johnston & Campbell, 1988), and this may include sexual abuse (Faller, 1991). Alleged abusers may appear to be overwhelmed by loneliness, and may be demonstrating regressive behavior in many aspects of their lives. The practitioner who suspects that the alleged abuse may have been precipitated by divorce should evaluate whether there were prior indications of sexual attraction to children that were held in check by the structure of the marriage and supervision by other family members. Faller (1991) reports that an unusual and age-inappropriate amount of touching and caressing of the child, tongue kissing, sleeping with the child, and erections during body contact with the child were noted prior to the divorce in these cases. In some instances, it may be difficult for the practitioner to ascertain whether there is potential for the child to be abused by the accused parent or whether the abuse occurred. Either case should lead to recommendations for protecting the child, and, possibly, for increased supervision and structure for the accused parent.

IMPROBABLE OR FALSE ALLEGATIONS IN DIVORCE. Improbable allegations of sexual abuse appear most commonly in child custody disputes that arise immediately after a separation or divorce has been granted, and center around issues of visitation (Benedek & Schetky, 1985; Green, 1986). An allegation of sexual abuse by the custodial parent is likely to capture the judge's attention and effect an immediate suspension of the noncustodial parent's visitation rights in an otherwise lengthy and bureaucratic legal process, and it may permanently terminate contact between the accused parent and the child. For example, in a study of all children admitted to a children's hospital over a seven-year period with a diagnosis of possible sexual abuse (Jaudes & Morris, 1990), it was discovered that an initial outcry of abuse was reliably associated with a custody change.

A noncustodial parent may allege sexual abuse in an attempt to get the court to change the permanent custody order that was awarded at the time of divorce, but conscious and calculated lies in making allegations or counterallegations are relatively rare (Faller, 1991; Jones & McGraw, 1987). For example, Faller (1991) believed three of the 19 "false allegation" cases (i.e., three of all 136 divorce-related sexual abuse allegation cases) to be calculated untruths. More typically, improbable allegations are based on a "core of reality" (Green, 1986). Emotionally stressed parents may pick up on "marginal symptoms" (Elterman, 1987), jump to unfounded or inappropriate conclusions, and generally assume the worst. Faller (1991) notes that in contrast to intrafamilial abuse dynamics where mothers will find it difficult to believe that their husbands could sexually abuse their children, the opposite problem may arise when parents are divorcing. With the disappointment and disenchantment of marital dissolution, divorcing parents may become convinced that their estranged partners are capable of almost anything, including child sexual abuse. They may overreact rather than underreact to questionable circumstances and events by systematically not giving the benefit of the doubt.

There are several situations in which the noncustodial parent will be particularly vulnerable to accusations by the custodial parent. The child may display regressive symptoms (crying, nightmares, bed-wetting, or clinging), depression, anger, noncompliance, or aggressiveness after a visit with the noncustodial parent. The custodial parent may misinterpret the child's distress about separating from the noncustodial parent—feelings that will be heightened at the end of a visit—as signs of sexual abuse. Similarly, custodial parents may misperceive increases in physical contact—hugging, kissing, holding—between the child and the other parent as sexual. In reality, these physical displays of affection may be triggered by long and unaccustomed absences. The child may exhibit physical symptoms upon return from a visit, such as constipation (change in diet during visits) or redness in the genital area (inexperienced bathing or toileting), and these signs and normal caretaking practices may be misinterpreted (Green, 1991). Postvisit interrogations may ensue— "Did he touch you down there?"—to confirm the custodial parent's suspicions. The child's fears of being abandoned by the custodial parent, an emotional reaction commonly noted in children of divorce (e.g., Garbarino & Vondra, 1987), may strengthen their tendency to assimilate that parent's suggestions as fact. Normal sexual behaviors and sexual exploration in developing children may also be misinterpreted as signs of sexual abuse by a vulnerable parent (Green, 1991), especially by parents who themselves were sexually abused as children.

Once a parent has alleged sexual abuse, a predictable chain of events is set into motion—including involvement of the police, social service workers, lawyers, and mental health professionals—in preparation for a court hearing. Repeated interviewing may shape the child's report of events (Yuille, 1988). Typically, the visitation or custody rights are immediately suspended. Even in cases where there is insufficient evidence to substantiate the sexual abuse accusation or to charge the accused parent, the court may restore only supervised access. Most often under these conditions, the court and the professionals involved will lean systematically toward protecting the child. Although a decision in this direction is ethically and practically unavoidable, the strong possibility remains that innocent parents are being removed from their children's lives. If the accused parent is cleared, the immense stress and the months or years that have elapsed by the completion of the proceedings may have irreparably damaged the relationship with the child. The potential effects on the child may be devastating (Elwell & Ephross, 1987; Pine, 1987).

EVALUATIVE ISSUES AND CONSIDERATIONS

A complete discussion of the procedures and content of child custody/ access evaluations is beyond the scope of this chapter, but is presented elsewhere (e.g., Hodges, 1991; Melton, Petrila, Poythress, & Slobogin, 1987). Instead, this section considers issues relevant specifically to the assessment of sexual abuse allegations in the context of a child custody/access evaluation.

Necessary Knowledge and Skills

Clinicians evaluating sexual abuse allegations in divorce will require knowledge and skills relevant to both sexual abuse and custody/access assessments. Practitioners should be capable in child, adult, and family assessment, including interviewing and the evaluation of intellectual, academic, personality, social, sexual, and emotional development and adjustment. The clinician needs to be knowledgeable about normal and abnormal human development, psychopathology and psychodiagnostics, family theory, and family dynamics. In particular, the practitioner must be familiar with how these major areas of study and practice pertain to child sexual abuse, family violence, separation, divorce, and custody/access issues. Practitioners should be trained in forensic clinical practice and psycholegal assessment, and have specialized information about the specific populations they serve (e.g., mentally/physically challenged, ethnic groups). As it is rare for any one practitioner to meet all of these requirements, teams of evaluators with complementary sets of skills and extensive consultation with other professionals may be recommended.

Professional and Ethical Issues

Extensive reviews of ethical and legal issues relevant to child sexual abuse in Canada and the United States are included in Chapters 19 and 20 of this volume. Because practitioners evaluating allegations of child sexual abuse in divorce and custody cases are faced with the task of integrating information provided by numerous professionals, they need to exercise caution about stepping outside the limits of their professional ethics and standards. For example, nonmedical mental health practitioners may refer to a physician's report documenting physical evidence of child sexual abuse, but they are not in a position to interpret the medical data. Similarly, mental health professionals should be careful not to offer legal advice to clients involved in a sexual abuse/custody evaluation, even if, after years of professional contact with lawyers and judges, they feel well versed in the legal workings of divorce and custody. While the evaluations of experienced practitioners may be consistently requested and trusted by the courts, the role of these health and mental health professionals is to offer information, opinions, and recommendations. The ultimate decision rests with the courts (Melton et al., 1987).

In response to the complexity and likelihood of ethical complaints being brought in the areas of sexual abuse and child custody, some professional organizations have developed specific standards and ethical guidelines to assist members practicing in these areas and to help them avoid the common pitfalls (e.g., College of Psychologists of British Columbia, 1990). A common error is that practitioners may complete a sexual abuse evaluation without realizing that divorce and custody issues are involved. Therefore, it is essential that practitioners evaluating any allegation of child sexual abuse routinely explore family dynamics and ask specifically about marital separations, divorce, and custody and visitation matters. In our experience, it is not unusual for a parent to contact a mental health professional requesting that a child be assessed for possible sexual abuse without mentioning, for example, that he or she is the noncustodial parent visiting with the child. Evaluators should always attempt to include all relevant parties in their assessment—the child who is the focus of the allegation, as well as both the alleging and accused parents or third parties. It may also be necessary to assess the child's siblings, the parents' current partners, and other key family members and authorities (e.g., the child's teacher or day-care supervisor).

Other common pitfalls in evaluating sexual abuse allegations in divorce include (1) a lack of clarity in the final report regarding its purposes, ultimate uses, and distribution; (2) a failure to separate opinions from data; (3) a lack of acknowledgment of the limitations of the report and its recommendations; (4) insufficient attention to relevant individual differences in ethnicity, language, developmental level, and physical or mental disabilities; and (5) lack of clarity about the role of the assessor, confusing assessment and treatment roles, dual relationships, and possible conflicts of interest on the part of the evaluator (College of Psychologists of British Columbia, 1990).

There are few areas of professional practice that evoke greater emotion and involve larger numbers of ethical complaints than do sexual abuse and custody/access evaluations (College of Psychologists, 1990; Schetky, 1991). To ensure objectivity and impartiality in these evaluations, practitioners must be aware of and protect against any personal biases or agenda they bring to this task, such as their age, discipline, theoretical orientation, feelings about the race of the alleged perpetrator, and personal history of child sexual abuse (Jackson & Nuttall, 1993).

The Clinical-Research Approach to Evaluation

Like others practicing in this area (e.g., Brooks & Milchman, 1991), we recommend a clinical-research approach to the complex problem of evaluating sexual abuse allegations in divorce and custody disputes. As clinical researchers, evaluating practitioners or team of practitioners are advised as follows:

1. To approach the evaluation with professional knowledge and skills, which they should attempt to update on an ongoing basis and to document in the final report.
2. To clarify their role as assessor (not as therapist), and to describe the assessment process verbally and in writing to those involved

in the evaluation, including an adequate time frame and the names of those who will receive copies of the final report.

3. To collect as much relevant data through multiple assessment techniques (e.g., interviewing, observation, psychological testing) as feasible from as many sources (all relevant family members, key individuals, previous or concurrent evaluators/investigators/ therapists) as possible, while noting missing or insufficient data and why these data could not be obtained.

4. To develop multiple hypotheses or *possible* explanations for the allegation under evaluation (e.g., the child was abused as was originally alleged; the child was abused but not by the accused parent; the allegation is based on the misinterpretation of normal caretaking practices).

5. To repeat steps 3 and 4 until satisfied that all possible explanations for the allegation have been adequately explored.

6. To document and explain any data that are consistent or inconsistent with any of the hypotheses.

7. To integrate the data in order to conclude whether the child's and parents' and/or third parties' behaviors and psychological functioning are consistent with, inconsistent with, or inconclusive regarding the sexual abuse allegation.

8. Based on the foregoing conclusion, to develop specific recommendations about custody and visitation (and possibly interventions) that, in their opinion, will best serve that child's needs and interests, with first priority given to safety issues.

In summary, the clinical-research approach to these evaluations suggests a dynamic data-gathering and synthesizing process.

Evaluators should also include a statement about what degree of certainty accompanies this conclusion and why. Evaluating practitioners tend to be more confident about conclusions when, for example, allegations involve children over the age of three and where there are reports of multiple recent episodes of sexual abuse (Thoennes & Tjaden, 1990). This does not mean that an allegation of a single such episode involving an infant whose custody is in dispute is unlikely to be true, but that it may be more difficult to reach an acceptable level of certainty about the validity of the allegation than about one involving an older child with multiple episodes of abuse. In cases with greater uncertainty, the evaluator's recommendations may be more conservative regarding the child's safety than in situations where there is greater certainty that the abuse did not occur.

Circumstances of the Sexual Abuse Allegation

The evaluator should investigate the issue of who, how, when, and under what circumstances the allegation of child sexual abuse was originally brought, and its current status. To this end, the evaluator should gather information from all previous or concurrent investigators and assess how these evaluations were conducted and used by the parents (Schuman, 1986). By being familiar with a range of divorce-related family dynamics in which child sexual abuse allegations may occur,* the evaluator can carefully explore the specific timing and family circumstances surrounding an accusation. A time line based on first-hand interviews and corroborating data (e.g., copies of custody orders, court subpoenas) can help the evaluator to understand the time frame in which the allegation occurred. For example, an evaluator may question the validity of an allegation of child sexual abuse brought by one parent against the other parent shortly after he or she was refused a change in the custody.

In general, improbable allegations are more often raised by parents than by the child (Benedek & Schetky, 1985; Jones, 1985). Nonleading and developmentally appropriate techniques for interviewing children who may have been abused, as well as typical patterns of memory, suggestibility, language, and disclosure, are detailed in other chapters in this volume (also see Benedek & Schetky, 1987; Ceci & Bruck, 1993). As repeated interviews and evaluations are not unusual for sexual abuse allegations in divorce cases, the evaluator may wish to review transcripts of previous interviews with the child. (If the evaluator is convinced that previous evaluators have thoroughly investigated an allegation of sexual abuse, in some instances, he or she may refuse to conduct a new evaluation on the ethical grounds that further interviewing of the child is not in the child's best interest and could be harmful.) Although a lack of emotion and immediate outspokenness in disclosing the sexual abuse to the evaluator may suggest an improbable allegation (Haugaard & Reppucci, 1988), some children may begin to recount the experience with muted emotions over successive interviews and contacts with different evaluators (Jones & McGraw, 1987). It is important for the practitioner to assess the nature of a child's distress and conflict during a disclosure to ascertain whether it is related to sexual abuse trauma or to the pressures of not disappointing the alleging parent. It is typical for children in divorcing families to fear abandonment by the custodial parent after the noncustodial parent has moved out, to have greater dependency needs, and to be more susceptible to paren-

---

*See the section on "Sexual Abuse Allegations in the Context of Divorce and Custody Dynamics" for a review of these divorce-related family dynamics.

tal influence (Benedek & Schetky, 1987b; Wallerstein, 1985). Therefore, fears and emotional conflict about not acting in accordance with the alleging parent's wishes may be particularly intense. Similarly, it is important for the evaluator to assess secrecy details carefully, because the child's reactions may stem from pressure to keep genuine sexual abuse a secret or for secrecy about supporting a parent's allegation even when the child is not convinced that it is true. Insistence on an appropriate time frame for the evaluation, including periods of free play and conversation, may permit the practitioner to build a relationship with the child. Not only should a child never be pressured or hurried by the interviewer when discussing sensitive topics, but important details and information are much more likely to emerge in a relaxed relationship with the evaluator.

In cases involving improbable allegations, the child may use adult expressions, sexual terminology, or colloquialisms, and may speak from an adult perspective (Haugaard & Reppucci, 1988; MacFarlane, 1986). In such cases, the evaluator may compare the language used by the alleging and accused parents to learn how the child may have picked up adult terminology (Elterman & Ehrenberg, 1991). Practitioners should also consider that a child may have learned to talk about genuine sexual abuse in adult language through frequent and perhaps inappropriate discussions with the alleging parent. If this is the case and the evaluator decides that the abuse has in fact occurred, he or she may include recommendations to help the alleging parent to be more appropriate and helpful in discussions with the child.

Divorce Versus Sexual Abuse Trauma

Research has demonstrated that children of divorce who are involved in their parents' disputes are likely to suffer emotional trauma and have behavior problems (Amato & Keith, 1991; Hetherington, 1989). The greater the degree of marital conflict, the greater is the extent of parental distress and interparental conflict after separation, and the more likely it is that the children will to be drawn into such conflicts (Tschann, Johnston, Kline, & Wallerstein, 1989). The problem that this poses for the practitioner evaluating sexual abuse allegations in divorce and custody disputes is that it may be difficult to differentiate children's experiences of divorce from sexual abuse trauma. This is particularly true of "nonspecific" psychological and behavioral sequelae that may result from either or both experiences. These sequelae may include depression, fear, anxiety, feelings of betrayal, anger, poor self-esteem, psychosomatic symptoms, and school and peer problems. There are a number of strategies that may help practitioners to differentiate signs of divorce and sexual abuse trauma in children. These strategies assume that

the evaluator is familiar with both the divorce and the sexual abuse litera-
tures.* First, the practitioner should attempt to explore the etiology of a child's
nonspecific symptoms. For example, if the initial assessment of a child suggests he or she is suffering from poor self-esteem, the practitioner might explore, in as much detail as is developmentally possible, how the child sees
himself or herself, and why. Understood in the context of all other evaluation data, the child who feels disgusted by his or her own body and discloses
body-focused inappropriate comments made by the accused parent may have
been sexually abused. On the other hand, the child whose negative self-
esteem stems from feeling unlovable and from perceptions of being abandoned by the noncustodial parent may be suffering from divorce trauma
alone.

A second strategy for differentiating divorce from possible sexual abuse
trauma is for the practitioner to evaluate the presence of any sexually specific
symptoms (e.g., inappropriate sexual knowledge, developmentally inappropriate sexual behavior), which is discussed in detail in other chapters. As
there are several factors known to influence how the child may be affected
by sexual abuse (e.g, duration of the abuse, amount of coercion, use of force;
see Haugaard & Reppucci, 1988), a specific allegation of sexual abuse may
be evaluated in terms of its consistency with this information.

Finally, it is essential that the practitioner learn as much as possible about
the child's emotional and behavioral functioning prior to the alleged abuse
and, if possible, prior to the parents' divorce. As parents' reports of their
children's current and past behavior are often biased in the context of child
custody evaluations (Ash & Guyer, 1991), it is essential that the practitioner
rely on a range of informants' reports, in addition to the child's and parents'
reports and the evaluator's observations. Family physicians, teachers, prin-
cipals, and other individuals likely to be more neutral in their observations of
the child may be valuable sources of information. By learning about the
child's psychological functioning at the time of the evaluation in the context
of his or her earlier development, the practitioner may be in a better position
to assess the extent to which the allegation is consistent or inconsistent with
the picture of the child that emerges.

The Alleging Parent and the Accused Parent

No single profile of the sexual offender has been identified, but there are
certain clinical observations that may raise concern about an individual's

---

*The authors are unaware of any research that directly addresses the issue of differentiating
divorce and sexual abuse trauma. Instead, research about the effects on children of sexual
abuse and of divorce is consulted.

risk for such behavior (Bresee, Stearns, Bess, & Packer, 1986). Ad hoc analyses of the characteristics of known sex offenders suggest that they may show sexual deviations, poor impulse control, difficulties with monitoring or directing emotional reactions, excessive self-centeredness, strong dependency needs, poor self-esteem, developmentally inappropriate expectations and perceptions of their children, generally poor judgment, substance abuse, a tendency to regress under stress, and role reversal and/or other relationship difficulties (Bresee et al., 1986; Famularo, Stone, Barnum, & Wharton, 1986; Sahd, 1980). The practitioner's evaluation of sexual abuse allegations in divorce-related situations should be based on the observation of *patterns* of characteristics in the context of other assessment data because (1) the absence of these characteristics will not necessarily rule out sexually abusive behavior by accused parents, (2) some of these characteristics are also associated with other conditions, and (3) there is little research focusing specifically on accused parents involved in custody disputes (McAnulty & Adams, 1990). It is important for the practitioner to develop an understanding of both the alleging parent's and the accused parent's current and past psychosocial functioning. The possible presence, nature, and outcome of any childhood history of sexual abuse should be explored, because unresolved experiences of child sexual abuse may increase the accused parent's risk for sexually abusive behavior. Similarly, an unresolved childhood history of sexual abuse on the part of the alleging parent may increase the possibility of misinterpreting his or her own child's behavior as suggesting sexual traumatization (Green, 1991).

Observations of children interacting with accused parents are controversial in evaluations of sexual abuse allegations in divorce and custody cases. It is considered standard practice in child custody evaluations to observe the child with each parent (Hodges, 1991). However, sessions including the child and the accused parent in sexual abuse assessments are generally not recommended because of the excessive emotional stress that this may place on the child (e.g., College of Psychologists of British Columbia, 1990). One strategy for resolving this dilemma, is for the practitioner to see the accused parent and child together at the end of the assessment period, but only if the assessor is reasonably confident that the sexual abuse did not occur. Conversely, if other assessment data suggest that the allegation is true, the final joint interview with the child and accused parent can be avoided. Either situation requires ongoing emotional support of the child by the evaluating practitioner.

In cases where the child and the accused parent can be seen together, the practitioner may evaluate the extent to which the parent and child engage in developmentally and role-appropriate interactions, and may attend to any signs of symbolic or overt sexual play. The sexually abused child will often be fearful and withdrawn in the presence of the offender, and may tend to cling to the other parent (Haugaard & Repucci, 1988). This intense fear may generalize to all individuals perceived to be similar to the offender (e.g., men with dark beards) (Faller, 1984; Gardner, 1986). Any unusual reaction to a male or female practitioner should be noted (Faller, 1984). The quality of the interactions between the child and the alleging parent should be compared with the quality of those between the child and the accused parent.

Gardner (1987) has noted that in improbable cases the child may confront the accused parent with the allegation in the presence of the alleging parent, especially when prompted by nonverbal messages from the alleging parent (Green, 1986). Similarly, parents making false allegations may attempt to control the child's responses through eye contact and subtle facial expressions, and the child may respond by checking with the alleging parent before proceeding (Green, 1986, 1991). In such cases, there may be a discrepancy between the child's angry verbal accusations and his or her apparent comfort in the accused parent's presence, when the alleging parent is absent.

In custody disputes involving improbable accusations of child sexual abuse, alleging parents may show no signs of psychopathology, although some may exhibit paranoid, histrionic, or borderline tendencies (Benedek & Schetky, 1985), and, in rare cases, delusional qualities are noted. However, rather than assuming that psychopathology on the part of the alleging parent invalidates the allegation, it is important for the practitioner to recognize that a psychologically disturbed parent still may have discovered genuine evidence of sexual abuse (Bresee et al., 1986). In improbable cases, the alleging parent may appear overzealous about the allegation, but reluctant to have the child interviewed alone. Even after several evaluations with negative outcomes, these parents may appear unwilling to consider the possibility that the child was not abused and immediately reject any other explanations for the child's behavior (Elterman & Ehrenberg, 1991). These alleging parents may appear unaware of or indifferent about the impact of the investigative process on the child, and may not appreciate the psychological trauma and loss suffered by sexually abused children (Gardner, 1987). In cases where children have been sexually abused, alleging parents may feel ashamed or stigmatized, and may blame themselves for not having protected the child. In improbable cases, the alleging parent will be less likely to have this attitude, and may be relatively free in discussing sensitive information concerning the child.

The relationship between the alleging parent and the accused parent should also be explored for any history of family violence (Ayoub, Grace, Paradise, & Newberger, 1991), as these dynamics may add perspective to delayed disclosures in valid cases, and may explain motivations underlying accusations of sexual abuse (e.g., continued attempts to control and intimidate after a violent marriage has ended, retaliation against the violent spouse from the relative safety of a divorce). The practitioner evaluating an allegation of child sexual abuse in such cases must also consider the child's risk of physical abuse by the parents, and, when necessary, take action to protect the child. Although anger between parents disputing the custody of their children is typical of this situation (Johnston & Campbell, 1988), the practitioner should assess the extent to which the anger may be distorting the parents' perceptions. A parent obsessed with hatred and hostility toward an ex-spouse may perceive all aspects of the child's relationship with the other parent in ways that reinforce his or her negative view of that person (Wakefield & Underwager, 1991). Such parents may also do whatever they can to hurt their ex-spouses by influencing the children against them, typically without considering how this may ultimately hurt the children involved (see Gardner, 1987).

Finally, it should be noted that an allegation of sexual abuse made by one parent against the other may prompt the evaluator to focus almost exclusively on the child, the alleging parent and the accused parent. However, there may be cases in which an alleging parent has accurately perceived signs of sexual abuse in the child, but the perpetrator is not the accused parent. In fact, divorce-related changes in the family constellation (e.g., addition of stepparents and stepsiblings), day-care, schools, and neighborhoods, combined with less supervision from an emotionally and economically stressed custodial parent, may place a child with exacerbated dependency needs in a situation in which he or she is more vulnerable to being abused. Careful and routine attention to family dynamics and living circumstances and gathering information relevant to a range of possible explanations for allegations of sexual abuse are most likely to result in thorough and accurate evaluations.

CONCLUSION

The evaluation of sexual abuse allegations arising during divorce, custody, and access disputes is a complex and challenging process with a great deal at stake for the children and families involved. Although there remains much to be learned about this process, the material contained in this chapter may be helpful in introducing the practitioner to research findings, practical considerations, and ethical issues relevant to conducting such evaluations. Practitioners working on sexual abuse and custody matters are encouraged to contribute to the development of this area by sharing their experiences and subjecting their data to empirical analysis.

Recommendations

1. **THAT** practitioners look to research on the extent, nature, and validity of sexual abuse allegations in divorce, custody, and access disputes to contextualize individual cases and to contribute

to an objective view of the problem on the part of health, mental health, and legal professionals.

2. **THAT** practitioners familiarize themselves with a range of divorce-related dynamics and routinely explore family and divorce dynamics in all evaluations of child sexual abuse allegations.

3. **THAT** practitioners assess the extent to which they possess the requisite knowledge and clinical skills relevant to sexual abuse allegations in divorce cases, engage in continuing education, and consider consultative and team approaches to these evaluations.

4. **THAT** practitioners who are making recommendations to the courts clarify their roles as evaluators and detail the evaluative process to all parties involved *prior* to initiating assessments.

5. **THAT** practitioners familiarize themselves with previous investigators' reports and attempt to interview and assess all relevant parties, including *at least* the child, the alleging parent, and the accused parent.

6. **THAT** practitioners adopt a clinical-research approach to evaluations of sexual abuse allegations in divorce by gathering data relevant to a range of explanations for the accusations.

7. **THAT** practitioners carefully evaluate who, how, when, and under what circumstances allegations of child sexual abuse were brought forward.

8. **THAT** practitioners assess the extent to which the child's reports, behavior, and psychological functioning are consistent with divorce and/or sexual abuse trauma.

9. **THAT** practitioners evaluate the past and current psychosocial functioning of both the alleging parent and the accused parent, their past and current relationships with each other, and their relationships with the children involved.

10. **THAT** practitioners state the extent to which the assessment data are consistent, inconsistent, or inconclusive regarding sexual abuse allegations, separate fact from opinion, and indicate how confident they are in their conclusions.

REFERENCES

Amato, P. R., & Keith, B. (1991). Parental divorce and the well-being of children: A meta-analysis. *Psychological Bulletin, 110,* 26–46.

Anthony, G., & Watkeys, J. (1991). False allegations in child sexual abuse: The pattern of referral in an area where reporting is not mandatory. *Children and Society, 5*(2), 111–122.

Ash, P., & Guyer, M. J. (1991). Biased reporting by parents undergoing child custody evaluations. *Journal of the American Academy of Child and Adolescent Psychiatry, 30*(5), 835–838.

Ayoub, C. C., Grace, P. F., Paradise, J. E., & Newberger, E. H. (1991). Alleging psychological impairment of the accuser to defend oneself against a child abuse allegation: A manifestation of wife battering and false accusation. *Child and Youth Services, 15*(2), 191–207.

Benedek, E. P., & Schetky, D. (1985). Allegations of sexual abuse in child custody and visitation disputes. In D. Schetky & E. Benedek (Eds.), *Emerging issues in child psychiatry and law* (pp. 145–158). New York: Brunner/Mazel.

Benedek, E. P., & Schetky, D. H. (1987a). Problems in validating allegations of sexual abuse. Part 1: Factors affecting perception and recall of events. *Journal of the American Academy of Child and Adolescent Psychiatry, 26*(6), 912–915.

Benedek, E. P., & Schetky, D. H. (1987b). Problems in validating allegations of sexual abuse. Part 2: Clinical evaluation. *Journal of the American Academy of Child and Adolescent Psychiatry, 26*(6), 916–921.

Berliner, L. (1990). Protecting or harming? Parents who flee with their children. *Journal of Interpersonal Violence, 5*(1), 119–120.

Bresee, P., Stearns, G. B., Bess, B. H., Packer, L. S. (1986). Allegations of child sexual abuse in child custody disputes: A therapeutic assessment model. *American Journal of Orthopsychiatry, 56*(4), 560–569.

Briere, J. (1988). The long-term clinical correlates of childhood sexual victimization. *Annals of the New York Academy of Sciences, 528*, 327–334.

Brooks, C. M., & Milchman, M. S. (1991). Child sexual abuse allegations during custody litigation: Conflicts between mental health expert witnesses and the law. *Behavioral Sciences and the Law, 9*, 21–32.

Browne, A., & Finkelhor, D. (1986). Impact of child sexual abuse: A review of the research. *Psychological Bulletin, 99*(1), 66–77.

Ceci, S. J., & Bruck, M. (1993). Suggestibility of the child witness: A historical review and synthesis. *Psychological Bulletin, 113*(3), 403–439.

"Child abuse used to win custody feuds." (1987, January). *Toronto Globe and Mail.*

College of Psychologists of British Columbia. (1990). *Guidelines for the conducting of psychological assessments in cases involving sexual abuse: Report of the task force on sexual abuse.* Vancouver, B. C.: Author.

Deed, M. L. (1991). Court-ordered child custody evaluations: Helping or victimizing vulnerable families. *Psychotherapy, 28*(1), 76–84.

Elterman, M. F. (1987, March). *Differentiating true and false allegations of child sexual abuse in custody cases.* Paper presented at the annual conference of Family Court Counsellors, Vancouver, B. C., Canada.

Elterman, M. F., & Ehrenberg, M. F. (1991). Sexual abuse allegations in child custody disputes. *International Journal of Law and Psychiatry, 14*, 269–286.

Elwell, M. E., & Ephross, P. H. (1987). Initial reactions of sexually abused children. *Social Casework, 68*(2), 109–116.

Faller, K. (1984). Is the child victim of sexual abuse telling the truth? *Child Abuse and Neglect, 8*, 473–481.

Faller, K. C. (1991). Possible explanations for child sexual abuse allegations in divorce. *American Journal of Orthopsychiatry, 61*(1), 86–91.

Famularo, R., Stone, K., Barnum, R., & Wharton, R. (1986). Alcoholism and severe child maltreatment. *American Journal of Orthopsychiatry, 56*(3), 481–485.

Garbarino, J., & Vondra, J. (1987). Psychological maltreatment: Issues and perspectives. In M. R. Brassard, R. Germain, & S. N. Hart (Eds.), *Psychological maltreatment of children and youth.* New York: Pergamon.

Gardner, R. A. (1986). *Child custody litigation: A guide for parents and mental health professionals.* Cresskill, N.J.: Creative Therapeutics.

Gardner, R. A. (1987). *The parental alienation syndrome and the differentiation between fabricated and genuine sex-abuse.* Cresskill, N.J.: Creative Therapeutics.

Goodwin, J., Sahd, D., & Rada, R. (1978). Incest hoax: False accusations, false denials. *Bulletin of the American Academy of Psychiatry and the Law, 6,* 269–276.

Green, A. H. (1986). True and false allegations of sexual abuse in child custody disputes. *Journal of the American Academy of Child Psychiatry, 25*(4), 449–456.

Green, A. H. (1991). Factors contributing to false allegations of child sexual abuse in custody disputes. In M. Robins (Ed.), *Assessing child maltreatment reports: The problem of false allegations* (pp. 177–189). New York: Haworth Press.

"Guilty until proven innocent." (1987, June). *New York Times,* p. 11.

Haugaard, J. F., & Reppucci, N. D. (1988). *The sexual abuse of children.* San Francisco: Jossey-Bass.

Hetherington, E. M. (1989). Coping with family transitions: Winners, losers, and survivors. *Child Development, 60,* 1–14.

Hlady, L. J., & Gunter, E. J. (1990). Alleged child abuse in custody and access disputes. *Child Abuse and Neglect, 14,* 591–593.

Hodges, W. F. (1991). *Interventions for children of divorce* (2nd ed.). New York: Wiley.

Jackson, H., & Nuttall, R. (1993). Clinician responses to sexual abuse allegations. *Child Abuse and Neglect, 17,* 127–143.

Jaudes, P. K., & Morris, M. (1990). Child sexual abuse: Who goes home. *Child Abuse and Neglect, 14,* 61–68.

Johnston, J. R., & Campbell, L. E .G. (1988). *Impasses of divorce: The dynamics and resolution of family conflict.* New York: Free Press.

Jones, D. P. H. (1985). Reliable and fictitious accounts of sexual abuse in children. *Journal of Interpersonal Violence, 2*(1), 27–45.

Jones, D. P. H., & McGraw, J. M. (1987). Reliable and fictitious accounts of sexual abuse to children. *Journal of Interpersonal Violence, 2,* 27–85.

Jones, D. P. H., & Seig, A. (1988). Child sexual abuse allegations in custody or visitation cases: A report of 20 cases. In E. G. Nicholson & J. Bulkley (Eds.), *Sexual abuse allegations in custody and visitation cases: A resource book for judges and court personnel* (pp. 22–36). Washington, D.C.: American Bar Association.

MacFarlane, K. (1986). Child sex abuse allegations in divorce proceedings. In K. MacFarlane & J. Waterman (Eds.), *Sexual abuse of young children* (pp. 121–150). New York: Guilford Press.

McAnulty, R. D., & Adams, H. E. (1990). Patterns of sexual arousal of accused child molesters involve in custody disputes. *Archives of Sexual Behavior, 19*(6), 541–556.

Melton, G. B., Petrila, J., Poythress, N. G., & Slobogin, C. (1987). Child custody and divorce. In G. B. Melton et al. (Eds.), *Psychological evaluations for the courts: A handbook for mental health professionals and lawyers* (pp. 329–346). New York: Guilford Press.

Orzek, A. M. (1985). The child's cognitive processing of sexual abuse. *Journal of Child and Adolescent Psychotherapy, 2*(2), 110–114.

Peters, J. (1979). Children who are victims of sexual assault and the psychology of offenders. *American Journal of Psychotherapy, 30*, 398–421.

Pine, B. A. (1987). Forum: When helping hurts–the double jeopardy for sexual abuse victims. *Social Casework: The Journal of Contemporary Social Work, 68*(2), 126–127.

Sahd, D. (1980). Psychological assessment of sexually abusing families and treatment implications. In W. M. Holder (Ed.), *Sexual abuse of children: Implications for treatment* (pp. 71–86). Englewood, Col.: American Humane.

Schetky, D. H. (1991). Ethical issues in forensic child and adolescent psychiatry. *Journal of the American Academy of Child and Adolescent Psychiatry, 31*(3), 403–407.

Schuman, D. C. (1986). False accusations of physical and sexual abuse. *Bulletin of the American Academy of Psychiatry and the Law, 14*(1), 5–21.

Sirles, E. A., & Lofberg, C. E. (1990). Factors associated with divorce in intrafamily child sexual abuse cases. *Child Abuse and Neglect, 14*, 165–170.

Thoennes, N., & Tjaden, P.G. (1990). The extent, nature, and validity of sexual abuse allegations in custody/visitation disputes. *Child Abuse and Neglect, 14*, 151–163.

Tschann, J. M., Johnston, J. R., Kline, M., & Wallerstein, J. S. (1989). Family process and children's functioning during divorce. *Journal of Marriage and the Family, 51*(5), 431–444.

Wakefield, H., & Underwager, R. (1991). Sexual abuse allegations in divorce and custody disputes. *Behavioral Sciences and the Law, 9*, 451–468.

Wallerstein, J. S. (1985). Children of divorce: Emerging trends. *Psychiatric Clinics of North America, 8*(4), 837–856.

Yuille, J. C. (1988). The systematic assessment of children's testimony. *Canadian Psychology, 29*(3), 247–262.

13

The Role of the
Medical Evaluation in
Suspected Child Sexual Abuse

Joyce A. Adams

Medical examination may play an important role in the evaluation of suspected sexual abuse, but it provides conclusive evidence in less than 30% of cases. Examinations may be normal for a variety of reasons, and these need to be understood by the professionals from all the disciplines involved in the assessment of abuse allegations. Research on the delineation of genital and anal findings in nonabused children, and on children with proven abuse, continues to provide additional information to clinicians in this field.

The sexual abuse of children is not a new problem in our society (Oates, 1990), but recognition of this problem by the medical community is a relatively recent phenomenon (Kempe, 1978). In the past 10 years, physicians and other health professionals have been asked to examine children who have given a history of sexual abuse, in an attempt to document any injuries or infections that might have resulted from the abuse (Woodling & Kossoris, 1981). The publication of detailed descriptions of examination methods and techniques for examining the child victim (Emans & Goldstein, 1990; Herman-Giddens & Frothingham, 1987; Paradise, 1990) has provided the medical professional with important guidelines to assist in the evaluation of these children.

The goals of the medical evaluation are:

1. To document the child's description of what has occurred.
2. To identify treatable injuries.
3. To collect forensic specimens.
4. To screen for sexually transmitted diseases and, in girls, pregnancy.
5. To reassure the victim that he or she is "OK" and hasn't been physically injured to a serious degree.
6. To assess the patient's mental and emotional state and refer for treatment.
7. To identify any physical changes that may have been caused by previous injuries.
8. To provide prophylaxis for pregnancy or disease as needed.
9. To provide detailed documentation and court testimony if requested.

This chapter focuses on (1) methods of examining children, (2) new descriptive data on what constitutes "normal" genital findings in children, (3) a description of conditions that have been mistaken for abuse, (4) the determination of which physical and laboratory findings should be considered specific for abuse, and (5) the expectations of what an examination can and cannot tell about the likelihood that abuse has occurred.

EVALUATION

Examination Methods

The medical evaluation of the child with suspected sexual abuse begins in the same way as does the evaluation of any other medical problem: by taking a history. As in all other areas of medicine, the history is the most important part of the evaluation. This fact tends to be overlooked, however, by parents, social service workers, law-enforcement officers, attorneys, judges, and the general public, who expect the physician to be able to "rule out" or "substantiate" whether sexual abuse has taken place by examining the child's genitalia. In the vast majority of cases, this cannot be done.

DeJong and Finkel (1990), in a comprehensive review of child sexual abuse evaluations, state: "Historical indicators are the most important indicators of sexual abuse" (p. 501). The authors provide detailed guidelines on how to interview children and record their statements. The Committee on Child

Abuse and Neglect of the American Academy of Pediatrics (1991), in "Guide-lines for the Evaluation of Sexual Abuse of Children," concludes: "The diag-nosis of child sexual abuse is made on the basis of a child's history. Physical examination alone is infrequently diagnostic in the absence of a history and/ or specific laboratory findings" (p. 256).

In spite of the fact that the importance of the history is well recognized, there is still an overreliance on the medical examination, which is expected to show "evidence" of the abuse. This type of evidence (semen, sperm, fresh sign of injury) is rarely found, especially in cases where there has been a delay in seeking medical treatment.

Medical examination is important, however, especially if it is being con-ducted within 72 hours of the last episode of alleged molestation, when an evidential examination is performed. Detailed guidelines for the medical ex-aminer are available (Emans & Goldstein, 1990; Heger & Emans, 1992; Finkel and DeJong, 1994), and should be consulted by anyone who performs these examinations infrequently. In California, examiners have the advantage of using a detailed protocol for the sexual abuse examination, which is printed on the six-page form used to record the history, examination method, and physical findings. This form is reprinted in the appendix of Emans and Goldstein's text (1990).

In general, the history of how the alleged abuse came to light should be obtained from the caretaker separately from the child, unless the victim is a young infant. Children are often traumatized by the retelling of the circum-stances of the abuse, or by seeing their parents' reactions to the allegations. The child should also be interviewed separately. Simple questions such as, "Do you know why you were brought here today?" or "Can you tell me what happened at Uncle Charlie's house?" will allow the child to tell you, in his or her own words, what he or she has experienced. Younger children may need to be asked more direct questions, such as, "Has someone touched or poked you in your privates?" Taking an accurate history from a child requires sensi-tivity, patience, experience, and a knowledge of child development. The child and parent can be together when the procedure for the medical examination is explained. This explanation can be given by the nurse or by the examiner, showing the positions to be used, the light or magnifying device, and the swabs for obtaining cultures, if these are to be taken.

With the child in a gown, a complete head-to-toe examination is performed. In addition to documenting any signs of injury, this also reassures the child that this is a "checkup" just like other checkups at the doctor's office. Key points to remember when examining children are that the examination should proceed slowly and gently, using a matter-of-fact approach, and should never involve the use of force. A child who cannot be examined without using restraint should be sedated or rescheduled for another time, if that is feasible.

Children with active vaginal or anal bleeding will probably need an examination under anesthesia (Dejong & Finkel, 1990).

Vaginal instrumentation very rarely is needed for the prepubertal child (Herman-Giddens & Frothingham, 1987).The prone knee-chest position, described by Emans and Goldstein (1980), and also by McCann, Voris, Simon, and Wells (1990), is very useful when examining the vagina for foreign bodies and for obtaining specimens for culture or analysis for seminal products. In this position, with good relaxation and distraction, a small premoistened urethral swab can be inserted into the vagina without touching the hymen (DeJong & Finkel, 1990). The child usually experiences no discomfort with this method.

Sedation is also rarely necessary when examining the prepubertal child. By using a support person, letting the child "help" when possible, telling stories or singing songs, or having the child talk about something that is fun, one can entice most children to cooperate fully with the examination. Toddlers who cannot be distracted or reassured, or children who are severely traumatized, may need sedation. Unfortunately, the choices for light sedation in an office setting are limited. Chloral hydrate, administered orally, or a combination of Demerol and Phenergan given as an injection may be effective, although there are disadvantages with both methods. Chloral hydrate has an unpleasant taste, and sometimes does not adequately sedate the child. An injection is painful, and may be perceived by the child as punitive.

Documentation of the medical findings is essential. Photographs and/or detailed drawings of the genital and anal areas are important for clinical as well as medicolegal reasons. A colposcope with a camera or videocamera attachment is a good tool for examining the child's genitalia, because it provides a light source, magnification, a "barrier" between the child's genital area and the examiner, and a photographic record of the examiner's findings. The colposcope is a magnifying instrument that a gynecologist uses to view the cervix of an adult woman. It is utilized in sexual abuse evaluations to view the external genitalia, and is not invasive.

Colposcopic photographs can be reviewed in detail, and can be used in consulting a colleague. They can also be used in court, and for research and teaching (Adams, Phillips, & Ahmad, 1990; McCann, 1990). A colposcope is by no means required, however, to perform an adequate examination. Muram and Elias (1989) found that few, if any, abnormalities are detected using a colposcope that are not noted during an unaided examination by an experienced examiner.

What Is Normal?

Before 1989, there were no published standards for normal genital and anal anatomy in prepubertal children. Genital findings such as erythema, disrupted vascular patterns, "enlarged" hymenal opening, and anal "gaping" were described as being present in sexually abused children and, therefore, suspicious for abuse.

McCann, Voris, Simon, and Wells (1989) described perianal findings in a group of 267 prepubertal children selected for nonabuse. They found perianal erythema in 41%, pigmentation in 30%, venous congestion by the end of the examination (in the prone knee–chest position) in 73%, and anal dilation in 49% of the subjects. Because of their frequency in nonabused children, these findings are now considered nonspecific for abuse. Erythema, venous congestion, and anal dilation also can be seen in abused children, however.

Since that time, other studies have appeared that describe anogenital findings in nonabused children (Berenson, Heger, Hayes, et al., 1992; Gardner, 1992; McCann, Wells, Simon, & Voris, 1990) and newborn infants (Berenson, Heger, & Andrews, 1991; Kellogg & Para, 1991). Because of these studies, it can now be stated with reasonable medical certainty that bumps, mounds, tags, and cysts on the hymen, as well as clefts in the superior half of the hymen, are normal findings.

Findings Mistaken for Sexual Abuse

Symptoms and signs referable to the genital or anal area in children may raise the suspicion of sexual abuse. These symptoms include painful urination, vaginal discharge, vaginal itching, pain with bowel movements, bedwetting, and fecal soiling. The signs (observed by the parent or physician) also include blood on the diapers or underpants, redness in the genital or anal area, "tears" in the genital area, possible scars, and warts.

Both Altcheck (1984) and Emans and Goldstein (1990) present detailed discussions of the evaluation of genital complaints in prepubertal girls. Redness of the genital area, itching, and vaginal discharge are relatively common complaints that usually have a benign etiology. For the most part, the use of sitz baths and the elimination of local irritants such as bubble baths and perfumed soaps will eliminate these problems.

A child who is brought in for an examination because of a finding of blood in the diaper or panties needs, of course, a careful examination. Tears of the labia minora, periurethral area, fossa, and fourchette may be caused by accidental straddle injuries (Muram, 1986). These cases usually present with a clear history. The physician may also discover that the blood is coming from the urethra because of a bladder infection, or from the anus due to an anal fissure. Both of these are common, and are not necessarily related to abuse.

Conditions that had been reported as possible sexual abuse, but were found to have another explanation, include lichen sclerosis, a skin condition (Jenny, Kirby, & Fuquay, 1981); urethral prolapse (Johnson, 1991); a congenital defect called a perineal groove or failure of midline fusion (Adams & Horton, 1989; Stephens & Smith, 1971); an infection of the perianal skin by streptococcus (Bays & Jenny, 1990); and a genital hemangioma (Levin & Selbst, 1988).

Another common condition in infants and young children is the labial adhesion, an agglutination or sticking together of the lower portion of the labia minora. In our experience, this condition has occasionally been interpreted as being a scar, or a laceration, if the adhesion begins to break down and bleed. Condyloma, or genital warts, may cause bleeding as well. Although these warts can be transmitted sexually, the causative virus can also be transmitted to the infant at birth, or possibly by routine familial nonsexual contact (Boyd, 1990).

Physicians and other health professionals who examine children need to remember that while sexual abuse may be in the differential diagnosis for a child with genital or anal complaints, they must consider other possible causes.

Findings Specific for Sexual Abuse

The Committee on Child Abuse and Neglect (1991) of the American Academy of Pediatrics listed the finding of sperm, semen, confirmed positive culture for *Niesseria gonorrhea*, and a positive test for syphilis (acquired) as being conclusive of abuse (see Table 1). Muram and Elias (1989) were more conservative, and only counted the finding of sperm as definitive evidence. Table 2 lists the abnormalities considered to be "specific" for abuse by Muram and Elias (1989), and "consistent with, but not diagnostic of, abuse" by the Committee on Child Abuse and Neglect (1991).

We conducted a written survey of physicians involved in sexual abuse examinations, and found that of 71 physicians who had examined more than

TABLE 1
Sexually Transmitted Diseases in Child Sexual Abuse

Presence Conclusive for Sexual Contact	Presence Suspicious for Sexual Contact	Known Transmission by Other Routes
1. *N. gonorrhea* (confirmed)	1. *Condyloma accuminata* in child over five years of age	1. Condyloma in child under two years of age
2. Syphillis (acquired)	2. Herpes II genital lesions	2. Herpes I (if mouth lesions seen)
3. *Chlamydia trachomitis* from genital source (culture proven) in child over two years of age	3. Trichomonas (nonneonate)	3. Chlamydia in a child under two years of age
	4. Bacterial vaginosis	

Information condensed from DeJong & Finkel (1990).

TABLE 2
Laboratory and Medical Findings Suggestive of Sexual Abuse

Muram & Elias (1989)	Committee on Child Abuse and Neglect (1991)
1. Recent or healed lacerations of the hymen and vaginal mucosa	1. Abrasion or bruising of inner thighs or genitalia
2. Hymenal opening greater than 1 centimeter	2. Scarring, tears, or disruption of the hymen
3. Laceration of the vaginal mucosa extending through the rectovaginal septum to involve the rectal mucosa	3. A decreased amount, or absence, of hymenal tissue
4. Bite marks	4. Scarring of the fossa navicularis
5. Laboratory confirmation of a venereal disease	5. Injury to or scarring of the posterior fourchette
	6. Scarring or tears of the labia minora
	7. Enlargement of the hymenal opening

Journal of Child Sexual Abuse (1992), 1, 91–99. Binghamton, NY: The Haworth Press. Reprinted with permission.

500 children for suspected abuse, there was over 80% agreement on the following findings as being suggestive or conclusive regarding sexual contact: hymenal lacerations, hymenal transections, hymenal remnants, wearing away of the hymen, a laceration of the posterior fourchette, granulation tissue and scarring of the vaginal wall, laceration of perianal tissues, and positive cultures for gonorrhea and chlamydia (Adams, Harper, & Wells, 1993). Bays and Chadwick (1993) add pregnancy and HIV infection, if not acquired by other routes, to the list of findings specific or diagnostic of sexual abuse.

Myths about Medical "Findings"

How often do children with a history of sexual abuse have abnormal findings? The answer depends on the population studied, the definition of "finding," and what terminology is used. These variables make it almost impossible to compare the results of studies of sexually abused children. Paradise (1990) and Finkel and DeJong (1994) have reviewed this topic in detail. Three studies of sexually abused children in cases where the perpetrator pled guilty to sexual abuse showed that even in these children, 77% of the victims will have normal or nonspecific findings on examination (Muram, 1989; DeJong & Rose, 1991; Adams, Harper, Knudson, & Revilla, 1994).

There are several commonly held myths about what a medical examination can tell about the likelihood of sexual abuse (adapted from Adams, 1992).

MYTH NO. 1. *An examination can determine whether or not a child has been molested.* Most cases of child sexual abuse involve touching, fondling, oral–genital contact, or rubbing of the hand or penis against the genital tissues. None of these activities should be expected to leave signs. Also, children are usually unable or unwilling to disclose their abuse immediately, because they believe the abuser's threats of reprisals, so that perishable evidence of semen or sperm is very rarely found.

MYTH NO. 2. *An examination can determine whether or not penetration has occurred.*
There is a common misperception that the hymen is a paper-thin tissue that will always "pop" when an object is inserted. In reality, the hymen is an elastic, stretchable ring of tissue that only partially covers the vaginal opening, and it can and does stretch open to allow partial, or even complete, penetration of objects without tearing.

In girls who have begun puberty, the tissue is so stretchable and tough that it can easily be stretched to allow full intercourse without tearing. We have several cases with photographs of normal pubertal hymens on girls who admitted to repeated intercourse (and even pregnancy!).

The anus is even more expandable, as demonstrated by the ability routinely to pass very large bowel movements without any injury whatsoever. Even if tears to the tissues do occur, they heal so rapidly (10–14 days) that there may be no trace of the previous injury (McCann, Voris, & Simon, 1992).

Another problem arises with the definition of "penetration." To a young child, having an object pushed in between the labia or buttocks seems like something is going "in," even though it may not penetrate beyond the hymen or anal sphincter. Adult investigators need to be careful not to assume that a child who says, "He stuck his finger in my pee-pee," really means that the finger was inserted into the vagina.

MYTH NO. 3. *An examination can tell when and how often a child has been molested.*
Unfortunately, there are not enough data on the follow-up of children with acute genital injuries to be able to date these injuries, except to say that they are "fresh" (probably less than 72 hours) if there is evidence of acute bleeding or bruising, or "old" (probably over two weeks) if there is obvious scar tissue. Studies done by Finkel (1989) and by McCann and associates (McCann et al., 1992; McCann & Voris, 1993) have described the healing of injuries over time in a small number of patients.

More studies are needed, and will probably need to be done as a collaborative research project.

Recommendations

The role of the medical evaluation in suspected sexual abuse is important, but should not be given more weight than it deserves in the overall investigation. Professionals examining children for abuse should acknowledge the following:

1. **THAT** a complete evaluation must incorporate a careful history from the child, a description by the caretaker of any emotional and behavioral changes, and a medical evaluation.
2. **THAT** the child's statement is the most important evidence of molestation.
3. **THAT** the results of the medical examination will usually be normal or nonspecific, because most types of molestation do not leave signs.
4. **THAT** unusual genital or anal findings may or may not be due to abuse.
5. **THAT** further research is needed to determine the psychological effects of medical examinations on children.
6. **THAT** there is a need to establish a consensus on terminology for describing genital findings in children, and their significance with respect to abuse.
7. **THAT** more research is needed, as a collaborative effort, to describe the healing of acute genital and anal injuries in children.
8. **THAT** the field of medical evaluation is expanding rapidly. It is essential for professionals to keep up with the literature and to attend conferences on a regular basis.

A recent textbook and atlas by Heger and Emans (1992) is an excellent resource, both for clinicians who do only a few examinations and for those who examine children regularly. The authors also reiterate that the medical examination will rarely be diagnostic of sexual abuse. Most of the time, the examination will be normal or nonspecific, but still consistent with the history given by the child of molestation, since many types of molestation do not leave signs. As with most conditions evaluated by medical professionals, 90% of the diagnosis comes from the history given by the patient.

REFERENCES

Adams, J. (1992). Significance of medical findings in suspected sexual abuse: Moving towards consensus. *Journal of Child Sexual Abuse*, *1*, 91–99.

Adams, J. A., Harper, K., & Knudson, S. (1992). A proposed system for the classification of anogenital findings in children with suspected sexual abuse. *Adolescent and Pediatric Gynecology*, *5*, 73–75.

Adams, J. A., Harper, K., Knudson, S., & Revilla, J. (1994). Examination findings in legally confirmed child sexual abuse: It's normal to be normal. *Pediatrics*, *94*, 310–317.

Adams, J., Harper, K., & Wells, R. (1993). How do pediatricians interpret genital findings in children? Results of a survey. *Adolescent and Pediatric Gynecology, 6,* 203–208.

Adams, J. A., & Horton, M. (1989). Is it sexual abuse? Confusion caused by a congenital anomaly of the genitalia. *Clinical Pediatrics, 28,* 146–148.

Adams, J. A., Philips, P., & Ahmad, M. (1990). The usefulness of colposcopic photographs in the evaluation of suspected child sexual abuse. *Adolescent and Pediatric Gynecology, 3,* 75–82.

Altcheck, A. (1984). Common problems in pediatric gynecology. *Comprehensive Therapy, 10,* 19–28.

Bays, J., & Chadwick, D. (1993). Medical diagnosis of the sexually abused child. *Child Abuse and Neglect, 17,* 91.

Bays, J., & Jenny, C. (1990). Genital and anal conditions confused with sexual abuse trauma. *American Journal of Diseases of Childhood, 144,* 1319–1322.

Berenson, A., Heger, A., & Andrews, S. (1991). Appearance of the hymen in newborns. *Pediatrics, 87,* 458–465.

Berenson, A. B., Heger, A. H., Hayes, J. M., et al. (1992). Appearance of the hymen in prepubertal girls. *Pediatrics, 89,* 387–394.

Boyd, A. (1990). Condyloma acuminata in the pediatric population. *American Journal of Diseases of Childhood, 144,* 817–824.

Committee on Child Abuse and Neglect, American Academy of Pediatrics. (1991). Guidelines for the evaluation of sexual abuse of children. *Pediatrics, 87,* 254–259.

DeJong, A. R., & Finkel, M. A. (1990). Sexual abuse of children. *Current Problems in Pediatrics, 20,* 495–567.

DeJong, A. R., & Rose, M. (1991). Legal proof of child sexual abuse in the absence of physical findings. *Pediatrics, 88,* 506–511.

Emans, S. J., & Goldstein, D. P. (1980). The gynecologic examination of the prepubertal child with vulvovaginitis: Use of the knee–chest position. *Pediatrics, 79,* 778–785.

Emans, S. J., & Goldstein, D. P. (1990). *Pediatric and adolescent gynecology.* Boston: Little, Brown.

Finkel, M. A. (1989). Anogenital trauma in sexually abused children. *Pediatrics, 84,* 317–322.

Finkel, M. A., & DeJong, A. R. (1994). Medical findings in child sexual abuse. In R. M. Reece (Ed.), *Child abuse: Medical diagnosis and management* (pp. 185–247). Philadelphia: Lea & Febiger.

Gardner, J. J. (1992). Descriptive study of genital variation in healthy, non-abused premenarchal girls. *Journal of Pediatrics, 120,* 251–260.

Heger, A., & Emans, J. (1992). *Evaluation of the sexually abused child.* New York: Oxford University Press.

Herman-Giddens, M. E., & Frothingham, T. C. (1987). Examination for evidence of sexual abuse. *Pediatrics, 80,* 203–208.

Jenny, C., Kirby, P., & Fuquay, D. (1981). Genital lichen sclerosus mistaken for sexual abuse. *Pediatrics, 83,* 597–598.

Johnson, C. (1991). Prolapse of the urethra: Confusion with clinical and anatomic characteristics with sexual abuse. *Pediatrics, 87,* 722–725.

Kellogg, N. D., & Para, J. M. (1991). Linea vestibularis: A previously undescribed normal genital structure in female neonates. *Pediatrics, 87,* 926–929.

Kempe, C. H. (1978). Sexual abuse, another hidden pediatric problem. *Pediatrics, 62,* 382–389.

Levin, A. V., & Selbst, S. M. (1988). Vulvar hemangioma stimulating child abuse. *Clinical Pediatrics, 27,* 213–215.

McCann, J. J. (1990). Use of the colposcope in childhood sexual abuse evaluations. *Pediatric Clinics of North America, 37,* 630–648.

McCann, J., & Voris, J. (1993). Perianal injuries resulting from sexual abuse: A longitudinal study. *Pediatrics, 91,* 390–397.

McCann, J., Voris, J., & Simon, M. (1992). Genital injuries resulting from sexual abuse: A longitudinal study. *Pediatrics, 89,* 307–317.

McCann, J. J., Voris, J., Simon, M., & Wells, R. (1989). Peri-anal findings in prepubertal children selected for non-abuse: A descriptive study. *Child Abuse and Neglect, 13,* 179–193.

McCann, J. J., Voris, J., Simon, M., & Wells, R. (1990). Comparison of genital examination techniques in prepubertal children. *Pediatrics, 85,* 182–187.

McCann, J. J., Wells, R., Simon, M., & Voris, J. (1990). Genital findings in prepubertal females selected for non-abuse: A descriptive study. *Pediatrics, 86,* 428–438.

Muram, D. (1986). Genital tract injuries in the prepubertal child. *Pediatric Annals, 15,* 616–620.

Muram, D. (1989). Child sexual abuse: Relationship between sexual acts and genital findings. *Child Abuse and Neglect, 12,* 211–216.

Muram, D., & Elias, S. (1989). Child sexual abuse—genital tract findings in prepubertal girls—II. Comparison of colposcopic and unaided examinations. *Journal of Obstetrics and Gynecology, 160,* 333–335.

Oates, K. (1990). *Understanding and managing child sexual abuse.* Philadelphia: W. B. Saunders.

Paradise, J. E. (1990). The medical evaluation of sexually abused children. *Pediatric Clinics of North America, 37,* 839–862.

Stephens, F. D., & Smith, E. D. (1971). *Ano-rectal malformations in children.* Chicago: Year Book Medical Publishers.

Woodling, B. A., & Kossoris, P. D. (1981). Sexual misuse: Rape, molestation and incest. *Pediatric Clinics of North America, 28,* 481–499.

14

Assessment of Sexual Preferences in Cases of Alleged Child Sexual Abuse

Howard E. Barbaree and
Edward J. Peacock

Phallometric assessment as an investigative tool in cases of allegations of child sexual assault was examined. Currently, phallometric assessment is being used to assess tendencies toward pedophilic behavior in men accused of child sexual abuse but who deny the allegations. Results of these assessments are taken into consideration in decision making by the courts, by the police, by employers, and by others. While phallometric assessment of the convicted child molester has been found to be valid, and the specificity of the test has been found to be very high (95%), the sensitivity of the test, or its ability to correctly identify known child sexual abusers, was found to be unacceptably low (40%–55%). Ethical issues arising from the use of the test were discussed. The use of the phallometric test in the investigations of allegations of child sexual abuse was discouraged as being an inappropriate use of the test.

The present chapter will examine the use of phallometric assessment as an investigative tool in cases of alleged child sexual abuse. Phallometric assessment involves the direct measurement of erectile responses in the human male in response to sexual stimuli. When the sexual stimuli involve still

242

pictures of human nudes who vary in gender and age, differential responses to the stimuli indicate sexual preferences for gender and age. For example, a heterosexual will show consistently stronger responses to female nudes, while a homosexual will show consistently stronger responses to male nudes. In a similar way, stronger responses to prepubescent children indicate a sexual preference for children and a tendency toward pedophilic behavior. Pedophilia is a diagnostic term indicating a sexual interest in children, often indicating a preference for children over adults as sexual partners.

Phallometric assessments have been used extensively in many jurisdictions in North America as part of the investigative process in response to allegations of child sexual abuse. When a child accuses a man of sexual abuse and when the man claims his innocence, various authorities will suggest that the man submit to the phallometric test as an assessment of his pedophilic tendencies. The results of the phallometric assessment, often incorporated into a more general psychiatric or psychological assessment, are frequently considered by the courts as part of the evidence weighed in making judgements of guilt or innocence, by employers deciding on continuing or terminating employment, by children's protective agencies in justifying actions taken to protect children, and by the police in judging whether or not to proceed with criminal charges. Used in this way, the test assumes a role similar to the lie detector test.

In the spring of 1987, Officer Norman Harrington of the Old Towne Police Force in Bangor, Maine was accused of sexual assault by two children, a 13-year-old boy and a nine-year-old girl. Officer Harrington was suspended from his job while these allegations were investigated. A police investigation was completed, but charges were never laid. However, the police force and the City of Old Towne were unwilling to reinstate Officer Harrington in his job until he had completed a full clinical assessment, satisfying them that he did not have pedophilic tendencies.

The City of Old Towne obtained the services of a psychologist at the University of Maine to conduct a clinical assessment of Mr. Harrington, including a planned phallometric assessment. Once Officer Harrington fully appreciated the nature of the assessment that was being proposed, he refused to proceed with the test. In response, the City of Old Towne fired Officer Harrington. In the summer of 1993, Officer Harrington successfully sued the City of Old Towne claiming that his civil rights had been violated, and he has been awarded nearly $1,000,000 in damages.

The present chapter will argue against the use of the phallometric test for the purpose of investigating allegations. We will not argue against the use of this test generally. The phallometric test has been used effectively with convicted child molesters for various purposes, including: (1) confrontation of patients in therapy who deny deviant interests; (2) pretreatment assessment of deviant sexual arousal as a potential treatment target; (3) assessment of risk for reoffense; and (4) monitoring of treatment progress. These uses of the phallometric assessment are quite appropriate, when conducted by a trained and qualified professional.

The present chapter will question the appropriateness of the use of the phallometric assessment with men who have not been convicted of child sexual assault. With these men, phallometric assessment has been used in two ways: (1) investigation of a man's potential for child sexual abuse after allegations of child sexual abuse have been made, and (2) screening of job candidates when the job involves direct and intensive involvement with children. These two uses of the test are more controversial. The present chapter will address the use of phallometry for screening purposes, but we will focus on its investigative use. We will argue that the investigative use of the test is inappropriate in that its benefits are illusory and its potential harmful effects outweigh any possible benefits.

ASSESSMENT OF SEXUAL PREFERENCES AND PEDOPHILIA

Men who sexually assault children are thought to be motivated by a sexual preference for children, and these men are known as pedophiles (Freund & Blanchard, 1981). The concept of a sexual preference forms the basis of the modern clinical assessment of child molesters (Barbaree, 1990), and some of the most popular classificatory systems are based, at least in part, on the classification of the stimuli that elicit sexual arousal and fantasies in the individual (Knight, Rosenberg, & Schneider, 1985). In the Diagnostic and Statistical Manual (Fourth Edition) of the American Psychiatric Association (American Psychiatric Association, 1994), the paraphilias are characterized by sexual fantasies and arousal in response to sexual objects or behaviors that are not part of normative arousal-activity patterns. In particular, pedophilia is characterized by sexual arousal to children and sexual fantasies involving sexual interactions with children. A sexual preference is thought to be a relatively stable individual trait (Freund, 1981; Freund & Blanchard, 1981).

The laboratory assessment of sexual preferences, or phallometry, follows from this model of child molestation and has become an important part of a complete clinical assessment of child molesters (Abel, 1976; Freund & Blanchard, 1981). The laboratory procedure involves presenting sexual stimuli to men while monitoring their erectile responses (Earls & Marshall, 1983; Laws & Osborn, 1983). In most phallometric laboratories throughout the world, the circumferential method of measurement is used, employing the mercury-in-rubber strain gage (Earls & Marshall, 1983; Laws & Osborn, 1983). The gage is a syslastic rubber tube filled with mercury and it resembles an elastic band. During testing, it is placed around the man's penis midway along the shaft. An electronic device called a plethysmograph passes a small AC current through the mercury column, measuring its ability to conduct electric current (conductance). As the penis increases in circumference during erection, the mercury column is stretched, decreasing its cross-sectional area, thereby decreasing its conductance. The plethysmograph, with the help of a computer, translates conductance into mm change in penile circumference through an equation derived by calibration.

A small minority of phallometric laboratories in the world use the volumetric method (Freund, 1963, 1965). In this method, a glass cylinder closed at one end is placed over the penis, and a donut-shaped pressure cuff is inflated around the base of the penis to seal the penis within the cylinder. With increases in penile volume during erection, the air pressure in the cylinder increases. Air pressure is monitored through a pressure transducer and translated into cc of air displacement by a computer. The volumetric device is preferred by its adherents because of its higher sensitivity to small erectile responses. However, it is not as popular as the circumferential method because the volumetric method is much more expensive, it is much more intrusive, and it requires more technical expertise to use.

Normally, in studies of deviant arousal in child molesters, stimuli have taken the form of still photographs presented as 35-mm slide transparencies projected on a screen in front of the subject. The target persons depicted in the slides were nude or partially clad males and females. In the series of pictures, the age of the targets was systematically varied, with different targets exhibiting different age-related physical attributes, including size, muscular development, maturity of facial features, and secondary sexual characteristics (e.g., the presence or absence of pubic, facial, and body hair, variation in breast size, etc.). Usually, stimuli were presented in durations from 30 sec to 2 min, and the stimuli were presented in a random order. Most often, erectile responses have been quantified as the largest (peak) erectile response during a stimulus presentation. When the man shows significant arousal to children relative to the strength of his arousal to adults, it identifies him to the clinician as a possible pedophile (Freund & Blanchard, 1989).

Critical reviews of the psychometric properties of these assessments have been written (Murphy & Barbaree, 1987; O'Donohue & Letourneau, 1992). Murphy and Barbaree (1987) have evaluated phallometric assessment using the criteria established for psychological tests by the American Psychological Association (American Psychological Association, 1985). These reviews have concluded as follows: (1) phallometric assessment procedures have good criterion-related validity (both concurrent and predictive); (2) criterion groups (offenders and nonoffenders) show different patterns of arousal and the patterns of arousal shown are related to criminal history and reoffense; and (3) individuals who show deviant patterns of arousal are more likely to commit sexual offenses against children in the future. However, the reliability of the procedure has not been adequately tested as yet. The establishment of the validity of these tests depends in part on the results of studies that will be reviewed subsequently in this chapter, but the psychometric issues will not be addressed directly.

Kurt Freund (Freund, 1967a, b) conducted the pioneering work in this area. In some of the studies subsequently reported (Freund, 1981; Freund, McKnight, & Langevin, 1972; Quinsey, Chaplin, & Carrigan, 1979; Quinsey, Steinman, Bergersen, & Holmes, 1975), the target stimuli have been divided into broad categories, such as "children," "adolescents," and "adults," and these studies have compared the strength of sexual arousal to each category. Other studies have divided the stimuli into one- to two-year age groupings and have plotted the strength of sexual arousal over the age-of-target continuum, resulting in what is known as an age-preference profile (Baxter et al., 1984; Marshall, Barbaree, & Butt, 1988; Marshall, Barbaree, & Christophe, 1986; Murphy et al., 1986).

At this point, and before reviewing the findings in this literature, it is important to make a clear distinction between the incest offender, and the nonfamilial child molester. The incest offender is a child molester who has assaulted children who live in his own home, either by assaulting his own biological children, or his stepchildren, or the children of the woman with whom he lives. In contrast, the nonfamilial child molester has assaulted children with whom he has no familial relationship. Once a man has assaulted a child outside his familial relationships, he is considered a nonfamilial child molester, even though he may have also assaulted children with whom he lives.

The studies involving phallometric assessment of age preferences have been quite consistent in their findings. Nonoffenders have shown strong arousal to adult females and a sharp drop in arousal to adolescent and child targets. As a group, men who have molested nonfamilial female children have shown greater arousal to prepubescent girls than did matched nonoffenders, although as a group they have also responded quite strongly to adult women. Men who have molested nonfamilial male children have shown greater arousal to boys than did matched nonoffenders, although again this group has shown at least moderate arousal to adult men and women. Incestuous child molesters, as a group, have not shown strong responses to children, but their responses to adults were also relatively weak compared with the nonoffenders' responses. Some authors have suggested different underlying psychological processes in incest versus nonfamilial child molestation (Williams & Finkelhor, 1990). Whereas, it is thought that preferences for children as sexual partners may play an important role in nonfamilial

child molestation, it is postulated that incest involves more opportunistic behavior, as well as dynamics involving family dysfunction (see Chapter 15,
this volume).

Returning to the studies of phallometric assessment, these studies compared group averages in response strength to each stimulus category. Recognizing that individual men might show idiosyncratic patterns of arousal and
that offender groups might be heterogeneous in the shapes of their individual
age-preference profiles, Barbaree and Marshall (1989) conducted an analysis
of age-preference profiles among 40 nonfamilial child molesters who had
offended against female children, 21 father-daughter incest offenders, and a
group of 22 matched nonoffenders. In this study, a computer program was
written to sort the profiles among five shape categories as follows: (1) an
"adult" profile in which subjects showed strong responses to adult females
aged 20 years and older, moderate responses to 16- and 18-year-old targets,
and minimal or no responses to targets below age 15; (2) a "teen-adult" profile in which subjects showed strong responses to female targets aged 13 and
older, with a decreasing response to younger targets; (3) a "non-discriminat-
ing" profile in which subjects showed moderate arousal to targets of all ages;
(4) a "child-adult" pattern in which subjects showed strong responses both to
targets 18 years and older and to targets 11 years and younger, but showed
only weak responses to targets aged 12–14; and (5) a "child" profile in which
subjects showed strong responses to targets 11 years of age and younger, but
only minimal responses to targets aged 13 and older. The profiles are presented in Figures 1–3.

Almost 70% of nonoffenders showed profiles categorized as "adult" profiles. The remainder of the nonoffenders were approximately evenly distrib-
uted between the teen-adult and nondiscriminating profile categories. Of
incest offenders, 40% showed an adult profile, and an equal number exhibited a nondiscriminating pattern of response. Most of the remaining incest
offenders showed a teen-adult profile, with only one incest offender showing
a child-adult profile. None of the nonoffenders had profile shapes that indicated responses to children, and none of the incest offenders showed responses exclusively to children.

In contrast, the child molesters showed remarkably heterogeneous patterns of response. The largest subgroup (35%) showed a child profile. The
remainder of the child molester group was approximately equally distrib-
uted among the other four profile categories. It is clear from this close examination of individual profile shapes that child molesters do not uniformly
show sexual preferences for children, and they certainly do not show exclusive sexual responses to children. Responders to children (the child and the
child-adult profile groups) were found to have lower than average intelligence and lower socioeconomic status. Further, the men who exhibited the

FIGURE 1
Non-Responders to Children

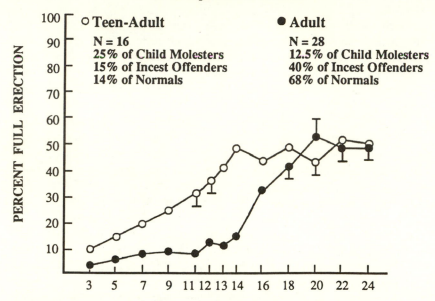

Mean age-preference profiles for the "adult" and the "teen-adult" profile groups. (From H.E. Barbaree & W.L. Marshall, 1989. "Erectile Responses amongst Heterosexual Child Molesters, Father-Daughter Incest Offenders and Matched Non-Offenders: Five Distinct Age Preference Profiles." *Canadian Journal of Behavioural Science, 21,* 70–82.) Copyright 1989, Canadian Psychological Association. Reprinted with permission.

child profile had used more force in the commission of their offenses and reported having offended against a larger number of victims (Barbaree & Marshall, 1989).

SENSITIVITY AND SPECIFICITY OF THE PHALLOMETRIC TEST

The fact that the test can discern different arousal patterns between or among criterion groups does not necessarily mean that the test would serve as an adequate investigative tool in cases of alleged child sexual abuse. The phallometric test used as an investigative tool is akin to using a medical screening instrument to detect the presence or absence of a disease among members of the general public (Abel et al., 1993). Normally, screening tests are

FIGURE 2
Non-Discriminators

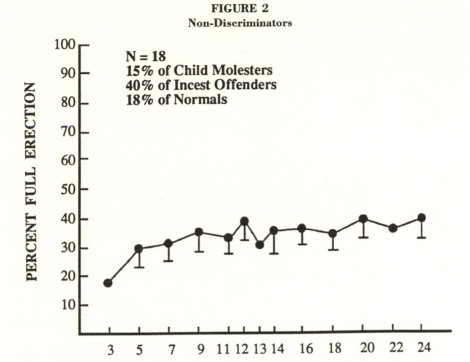

Mean age-preference profiles for the "nondiscriminator" profile group. (From H.E. Barbaree & W.L. Marshall, 1989. "Erectile Responses amongst Heterosexual Child Molesters, Father-Daughter Incest Offenders and Matched Non-Offenders: Five Distinct Age Preference Profiles." *Canadian Journal of Behavioural Science, 21,* 70–82.) Copyright 1989, Canadian Psychological Association. Reprinted with permission.

evaluated as to their usefulness by assessment of their sensitivity and their specificity. In terms of the evaluation of phallometric assessment as a screening device, sensitivity is defined as the percentage of the offenders who are correctly identified as pedophilic, and specificity refers to the percentage of the nonoffenders who are correctly identified as nonpedophilic.

Below, the data from the Barbaree and Marshall (1989) study have been analyzed to provide a determination of the test's sensitivity and specificity. In this analysis, a profile was taken to indicate a nonpedophilic response if the profile was an "adult," a "teen-adult," or a nondiscriminating profile. A profile was taken to indicate a pedophilic response if it was a "child" or a "child-adult" profile. Two separate analyses of sensitivity were done. The first was done on the nonfamilial child molesters and the second was done

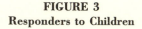

FIGURE 3
Responders to Children

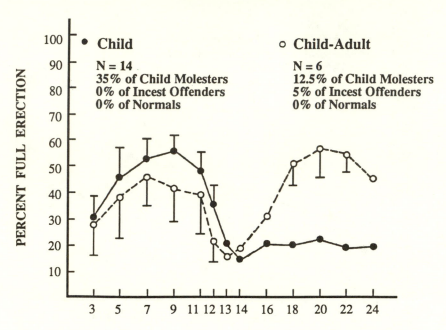

Mean age-preference profiles for the "child" and the "child-adult" profile groups. (From H.E. Barbaree & W.L. Marshall, 1989. "Erectile Responses amongst Heterosexual Child Molesters, Father-Daughter Incest Offenders and Matched Non-Offenders: Five Distinct Age Preference Profiles." *Canadian Journal of Behavioural Science, 21*, 70–82.) Copyright 1989, Canadian Psychological Association. Reprinted with permission.

on the incest offenders. The calculations of the test's specificity were done on the data from the matched nonoffenders. These analyses are presented in Table 1.

As shown in Table 1, 20 of the total 83 subjects were identified as having pedophilic sexual interests, and 63 were found to have nonpedophilic interests. Of the 40 nonfamilial child molesters, 19 were found to have a pedophilic response. Therefore, for the nonfamilial child molester, the sensitivity of the test was 47.5%, indicating that roughly one half of child molesters would be correctly identified by the test as pedophilic. Of the 21 incest offenders, only one was found to have a pedophilic response. Therefore, as applied to the incest offenders, the sensitivity of the test was below 5%, indicating that only a very small proportion of the incest offenders would be correctly identified

TABLE 1.

The Sensitivity and Specificity of Phallometric Assessment as a Screening Instrument for Pedophilia: Nonfamilial Child Molesters and Incest Offenders

			Criterion Groups		
		Nonfam CM's[1]	*Incest[2]*	*Nonoffenders*	
Results of Phallometric Assessment	Pedophile	19	1	0	20
	Nonpedophile	21	20	22	63
Totals		40	21	22	83

Nonfamilial Child Molester Sensitivity = 19/40 x 100 = 47.5%
Incest Offender Sensitivity = 1/21 x 100 = 4.8%
Specificity = 22/22 x 100 = 100.0%

[1] Nonfamilial Child Molesters
[2] Incest Offenders

by the test. It seems that the sensitivity of the phallometric test is quite low. For incest offenders, sensitivity was found to be unacceptably low. For nonfamilial child molesters, more than half of subjects fail to be identified as having pedophilic sexual preferences.

Of the nonoffenders, none were identified as having a pedophilic response. Therefore, with this sample of nonoffenders, the specificity of the test was 100%. This is undoubtedly an overestimate of the test's true specificity, due in this case to sampling error. Obviously, if we were able to sample a large group from the general male population, some pedophiles would be sampled; of these, some (approximately 50%, given the test's sensitivity) would show pedophilic responses. If, for example, 10% of the population were true nonfamilial child molesters, only half of them would show a pedophilic response to the test. Given these estimates of the prevalence of child molestation in the male population, the real specificity of the phallometric test would then be 95%.

Freund and Blanchard (1989) have published a formal study of the sensitivity and specificity of the phallometric test. They estimate that the test's sensitivity is 55%, and that the test's specificity is 95%, figures that are in close agreement with the estimates we have presented based on our analysis of the Barbaree and Marshall (1989) data.

In their study, Freund and Blanchard (1989) divided their offender sample into admitters and nonadmitters, depending on whether or not the offenders denied their offense history. Of course, deniers would be motivated to fake their responses to the phallometric test, trying to show a normal age preference in support of their denial of an offense history. Faking of the age-preference profile can occur in a number of ways. Some offenders are able to suppress erectile responses at will or when instructed to do so (Abel et al., 1975; Freund, 1963; Laws & Rubin, 1969; Wydra et al., 1983), and some nonoffenders are able to produce moderate erectile responses to nonpreferred stimuli (Laws & Rubin, 1969; Quinsey & Bergersen, 1976). Presumably, then, offenders with these abilities may distort their true sexual responses during assessment.

Some offenders have been observed using mechanical methods of control, such as manipulating the strain gage (Laws & Holmen, 1978), and nonerectile responses, like tensing of the pelvic musculature or hyperventilation to influence the strain gage (Quinsey & Bergersen, 1976). These methods of distortion can be easily detected or prevented by the monitoring of the subject during the test with a video camera, movement detectors, or additional psychophysiological measures. Subjects may control stimulus input by averting their gaze from a slide or video presentation (Laws & Rubin, 1969), but this may be prevented by the use of a video monitoring camera focusing on the subject's face and gaze, or by a detection task that requires the subject to report a signal is presented randomly as part of the stimulus display (Laws & Rubin, 1969).

The more difficult faking to detect and prevent is the subject's own cognitive control of the stimulus presentation. For example, when men are required to engage in a complex secondary task, arousal to an erotic stimulus is suppressed (Geer & Fuhr, 1976). Subjects attempting to suppress arousal to deviant stimuli might use self-distraction and, indeed, when subjects have been instructed to fake suppression of response to a preferred erotic stimulus, they reported using such a strategy to minimize arousal (Wydra et al., 1983). At the very least, we have to conclude that some tested pedophiles are able to fake normal sexual preferences in the laboratory.

In the Freund and Blanchard (1989) study of phallometric testing's sensitivity, tests of the nonadmitters were found to have lower sensitivity when compared with tests of admitters. Tests of the admitters yielded a sensitivity of 100%, with each and every one of the admitters showing pedophilic responses during the test. However, in the tests of the nonadmitters, almost half failed to show pedophilic responses, leading these authors to estimate the phallometric test's sensitivity to be approximately 55%. Perhaps, nonadmitters were able to fake nonpedophilic responses, thereby avoiding detection as pedophiles. The Barbaree and Marshall (1989) sample included a number of nonadmitters, including 12 of 40 nonfamilial child molesters and 11 of 21 incest offenders. In samples such as these, those offenders who do not deny their offenses tend to minimize their offensive behavior in some significant way (Barbaree, 1991) and these offenders would be motivated to minimize their pedophilic arousal. Obviously, phallometry would be used as an investigative tool only in cases where the tested subject was a nonadmitter or a partial admitter. Therefore, when the phallometric test is being used as an investigative tool its sensitivity will be lower than when the test is used for other purposes.

In a subsequent study, Freund and Watson (1991) found the sensitivity of the test to be almost 80% for offenders against female children and almost 90% for offenders against male children when the offender had offended against at least two victims. However, the sensitivity of the test was only 45% in offenders who had offended against only a single female child victim. Perhaps, in investigations of alleged child sexual abuse, the sensitivity of the test could be considered to be acceptably high when allegations are being made by more than one victim. However, when only one child is making allegations, the test will not be very good at detecting sexual interest toward children.

One other factor will serve to reduce the test's sensitivity. Both the Freund and Blanchard (1989) and the Barbaree and Marshall (1989) studies eliminated subjects from their samples when they failed to meet a minimum requirement for level of overall arousal. Using the circumferential method of measurement, Barbaree and Marshall (1989) eliminated 20% of the original sample of nonfamilial offenders and 30% of the incest offenders. Using the more sensitive volumetric method of measurement, Freund and Blanchard (1989) eliminated approximately 6% of their sample, and Freund and Watson (1991) eliminated 15% due to low arousal. Subjects who do not meet these minimum level requirements are known as nonresponders, and the results of their test are called a flatline. If the nonresponders were to be added back into the sample, as it seems they should if one were to accurately calculate the sensitivity of the test, these subjects would be added to the denominator in the equation, and the resulting sensitivity would be reduced even further.

Most of the subjects in the studies described here have been convicted, were admitters, or were recruited from the general public. For them, the consequence of the outcome of the test is not as important as it would be for the man under investigation. With a great deal at stake, the man being investigated will be quite a bit more anxious. It is well known that anxiety inhibits or suppresses sexual arousal; thus, men under investigation would be more likely to flatline. With the increased number of nonresponders, the sensitivity of the test will decrease even further. Therefore, for the phallometric test used as an investigative tool, sensitivity should be thought of as being substantially below 50%, possibly as low as 40%.

The consequence of such a low sensitivity will be that not many offenders will be detected as pedophilic and that the test would yield a large proportion of false negatives, men who actually committed a sexual offense against a child, but who do not show a pedophilic response during phallometric testing. If the lack of a pedophilic response is taken to indicate the man's innocence, large numbers of errors in judgement will result.

The problem of the false negative can be seen from another perspective. An accused man may seem to "pass" the test by not showing a pedophilic response. However, if there is widespread recognition of the test's low sensitivity, he will not be seen to have exonerated himself by passing the test, since so many men who have molested children have not shown pedophilic responses during the test. Therefore, an accused man cannot really pass the phallometric test, but he can certainly fail it.

While low sensitivity is characteristic of the phallometric test and may seem to limit its utility, the phallometric assessment is probably the best method for screening for pedophilia. The other methods of clinical investigation include interview and psychological testing. Of course, both of these methods are notoriously flawed when used with a group of men who are motivated to deny their sexual interest in children. While some pedophiles may be able to fake nonpedophilic responses during phallometric testing, almost all are able to fake nonpedophilic responses to questions in interview and while responding to self-report questionnaires. In personality tests, both the questions and answers are not so transparent or obviously related to child sexual abuse, and this seems to address the issue of fakability of the test. Unfortunately, no empirical relationship has yet been established between child molestation and personality traits or types (Hall, 1988; Nadelson & Notman, 1984; Quinsey, 1986; Marshall, 1993). Therefore, personality tests are not a valid method of identifying pedophilia or pedophilic tendencies. Although the sensitivity of the phallometric test may be low, its ability to detect pedophilic tendencies in men is probably superior to any other method of clinical investigation.

The high specificity of the test means that if the phallometric test yields a pedophilic response, then the tested man most likely has a history of sexual interactions with children. One of the fears often expressed concerning the use of the test as an investigative tool is that it would yield a large number of false positives. This would occur if there were a large number of men in the population who experienced pedophilic arousal and had fantasies involving children, but who controlled their behavior and had never molested a child. This would also occur if large numbers of innocent men responded to children during phallometric tests. In these cases, the phallometric test would detect their arousal to children and falsely label them as pedophiles. The apparent high specificity of the test puts this fear to rest, since none of the published studies find significant pedophilic arousal among nonoffender or control subjects. Of course, a pedophilic response during testing does not mean that the individual is guilty of any particular offense against any particular child victim. It does mean, however, that previous sexual interactions with children are likely to have occurred.

In conclusion, while it is true that men who have not been involved in child molestation in the past are not likely to be falsely identified by the phallometric test, it is also true that probably fewer than 50% of actual nonfamilial child molesters will be identified as such by the test. For incest offenders, almost none are correctly identified by the test. Use of the test will lead to numerous false negatives, and this is the most important disadvantage of the test, leading to unfortunate consequences. The dangers of the false negative result are numerous and they include: (1) that the case manager concludes from the test's outcome that the man is safe with children and thereby reduces the level of care and attention to other signs of risk; (2) that the police conclude that following through with criminal charges in the face of the negative result would be inappropriate; (3) that the courts hesitate to find a man guilty given that the test indicates he has no sexual interest in children, even in the case where a victim has given compelling testimony; and (4) that employers will relax in their supervision of a man found to have "passed" the phallometric test, and thus subject children to continuing risk.

ETHICAL CONSIDERATIONS

Of course, use of the phallometric test must comply with ethical principles and the standards of practice of all the relevant professional governing bodies. Probably, the most important principle governing the ethical use of the phallometric test is that of informed consent. By that we mean that the man to be tested is fully informed: before beginning any part of the assessment, regarding the nature of the test, of what different outcomes of the test will mean, of who will be informed of the outcome of the test, and of how different outcomes will likely be interpreted in his individual case. Given our discussion above, the man to be tested should be informed, after the details of the testing procedure itself have been fully described, that failing the test by exhibiting a pedophilic response will be taken to indicate a history of sexual interactions with children or, at least, a propensity for it. Further, the man should be informed that passing the test will not be taken to mean that he has no history of sex with children nor any propensity for it.

Further, it is not just the subject of the test who needs to be fully informed on this issue. The written report of the test outcome, particularly in cases where the outcome does not indicate a pedophilic interest, should clearly indicate that this is not evidence in support of the man's innocence with respect to allegations, nor does it attest to his safety with children.

It is our experience that when men are fully informed of the nature of the test and the meaning of its outcomes, many refuse to be tested. For the man under investigation, this is a "no win" situation. It is a slightly different situation when screening job applicants for jobs involving a high degree of contact with children. After being fully informed, the man to be screened can decide whether or not to go through with the test based on the confidence he has concerning his own sexual interests and the extent of his desire for the job. However, in the case of screening job applicants, the problem of the false negative is just as important as in the investigation of allegations. Men who pass the screening test should not be considered safe on the basis of the test outcome. Negative test results should not lead those in authority to a decision to drop other appropriate precautions or to relax the monitoring of men who work closely with children.

Recommendations

1. **THAT** the phallometric test is the best method we have for detecting pedophilia in men, but even so, it is not very effective at detecting deviant sexual interests in men who have sexually assaulted children.
2. **THAT** negative results should not be taken to mean that the man is innocent or that he is safe with children.
3. **THAT** the consumers of the test results, including the courts, attorneys, police, employers, and child protective case workers need to be fully informed as to the meaning of the test results. In particular, they need to be alerted to the meaning and the dangers of the false negative as a possible outcome of the test.
4. **THAT** the consumers of the test results should be well enough informed so that they do not expect incest offenders to show pedophilic responses, and so that they do not routinely request the test be done with incest offenders.
5. **THAT** men to be tested should be fully informed of all aspects of the testing procedure and clearly informed of the meanings of each of the possible outcomes of the test and what each of these outcomes would mean in his individual case. In particular, the man should be clearly told that if he "passes" the test, it will not exonerate him or "prove" his innocence.
6. **THAT** if the man is hesitant at all about proceeding with the test after he has been fully informed, the test should not be done.
7. **THAT** in most cases of allegations of child sexual abuse, the phallometric test should not be used in the investigation of the allegations.

Although the chapter has argued against the use of the phallometric assessment as a test of sexual preference in the investigation of allegations of child sexual abuse, we feel strongly, as stated earlier in the chapter, that the phallometric assessment has many uses in the assessment and treatment of convicted child molesters. When convicted child molesters deny their offense history, deviant sexual responses in the laboratory can often be used to confront these men with their deviance in therapy. When the convicted child molester shows a deviant sexual interest in children in the laboratory, these responses can often be targeted in therapy, and continuing evaluation of the response in the laboratory will assist in the tracking of progress in therapy (Quinsey & Earls, 1990). Finally, pretreatment assessment of deviant sexual interest in children has been shown to be a predictor of reoffense among child molesters (Barbaree & Marshall, 1988).

REFERENCES

Abel, G. G. (1976). Assessment of sexual deviation in the male. In M. Hersen & A. S. Bellack (Eds.), *Behavioral assessment: A practical handbook.* New York: Pergamon.

Abel, G. G., Barlow, D .H., Blanchard, E. B., & Mavissakalian, M. (1975). Measurement of sexual arousal in male homosexuals: The effects of instruction and stimulus modality. *Archives of Sexual Behavior, 4,* 623–629.

Abel, G. G., Lawry, S. S., Karlstrom, E. M., Osborn, C. A., & Gillespie, C. F. (1993). Screening tests for pedophilia. *Criminal justice and behavior.*

American Psychiatric Association. (1994). *Diagnostic and statistical manual- Fourth Edition.* Washington, D.C.: American Psychiatric Association.

American Psychological Association. (1985). *Standards of educational and psychological testing.* Washington, D.C.: Author.

Barbaree, H. E. (1990). Stimulus control of sexual arousal: Its role in sexual assault. In W. L. Marshall, D. R. Laws, & H. E. Barbaree (Eds.), *Handbook of sexual assault: Issues, theories, and treatment of the offender* (pp. 231–255). New York: Plenum Press.

Barbaree, H. E. (1991). Denial and minimization among sex offenders: Assessment and treatment outcome. *Forum on Corrections Research, 3,* 30–33.

Barbaree, H. E., & Marshall, W. L. (1988). Deviant sexual arousal, demographic and offense history variables as predictors of reoffense among child molesters and incest offenders. *Behavioral Sciences and the Law, 6,* 267–280.

Barbaree, H. E., & Marshall, W. L. (1989). Erectile responses among heterosexual child molesters, father-daughter incest offenders, and matched non-offenders: Five distinct age preference profiles. *Canadian Journal of Behavioural Science, 21,* 70–82.

Baxter, D. J., Marshall, W. L., Barbaree, H. E., Davidson, P. R., & Malcolm, P. B. (1984). Deviant sexual behavior: Differentiating sex offenders by criminal and personal history, psychometric measures, and sexual response. *Criminal Justice and Behavior, 11,* 477–501.

Earls, C. M., & Marshall, W. L. (1983). The current state of technology in the laboratory assessment of sexual arousal patterns. In J. G. Greer & I. R. Stuart (Eds.), *The sexual aggressor: Current perspectives on treatment* (pp. 336–362). New York: Van Nostrand Reinhold.

Freund, K. (1963). A laboratory method of diagnosing predominance of homo- and hetero-erotic interest in the male. *Behaviour Research and Therapy, 1,* 85–93.

Freund, K. (1965). Diagnosing heterosexual pedophilia by means of a test for sexual interest. *Behaviour Research and Therapy, 3,* 229–234.

Freund, K. (1967a). Diagnosing homo- or heterosexuality and erotic age-preference by means of a psychophysiological test. *Behaviour Research and Therapy, 5,* 209–228.

Freund, K. (1967b). Erotic preference in pedophilia. *Behaviour Research and Therapy, 5,* 339–348.

Freund, K. (1981). Assessment of pedophilia. In M. Cook & K. Howells (Eds.), *Adult sexual interest in children* (pp. 139–179). London: Academic Press.

Freund, K., & Blanchard, R. (1981). Assessment of sexual dysfunction and deviation. In M. Hersen & A. S. Bellack (Eds.), *Behavioral assessment: A practical handbook* (pp. 427–455). New York: Pergamon Press.

Freund, K., & Blanchard, R. (1989). Phallometric diagnosis of pedophilia. *Journal of Consulting and Clinical Psychology, 57,* 100–105.

Freund, K., McKnight, C. K., & Langevin, R. (1972). The female child as a surrogate object. *Archives of Sexual Behavior, 2,* 119–133.

Freund, K., & Watson, R. J. (1991). Assessment of the sensitivity and specificity of a phallometric test: An update of phallometric diagnosis of pedophilia. *Psychological Assessment: A Journal of Consulting and Clinical Psychology, 3,* 254–260.

Geer, J. H., & Fuhr, R. (1976). Cognitive factors in sexual arousal: The role of distraction. *Journal of Consulting and Clinical Psychology, 44,* 238–243.

Hall, G. C. N. (1988). Criminal behavior as a function of clinical and actuarial variables in a sexual offender population. *Journal of Consulting and Clinical Psychology, 56,* 773–775.

Knight, R. A., Rosenberg, R., & Schneider, B. A. (1985). Classification of sexual offenders: Perspectives, methods, and validation. In A. W. Burgess (Ed.), *Rape and sexual assault* (pp. 222–293). New York: Garland Publishing.

Laws, D. R., & Holmen, M. L. (1978). Sexual response faking by pedophiles. *Criminal Justice and Behavior, 5,* 343–356.

Laws, D. R., & Osborn, C. A. (1983). How to build and operate a behavioral laboratory to evaluate and treat sexual deviance. In J. G. Greer & I. R. Stuart (Eds.), *The sexual aggressor: Current perspectives on treatment.* New York: Van Nostrand Reinhold.

Laws, D. R., & Rubin, H. B. (1969). Instructional control of an automatic response. *Journal of Applied Behavior Analysis, 2,* 93–99.

Marshall, W. L. (1993). *The use of the MMPI in decisions of guilt or innocence with sex offenders.* Manuscript submitted for publication.

Marshall, W. L., Barbaree, H. E., & Butt, J. (1988). Sexual offenders against male children: Sexual preferences for gender, age of victim, and type of behavior. *Behaviour Research and Therapy, 26,* 383–391.

Marshall, W. L., Barbaree, H. E., & Christophe, D. (1986). Sexual offenders against female children: Sexual preferences for age of victims and type of behavior. *Canadian Journal of Behavioural Science, 18,* 424–439.

Murphy, W., & Barbaree, H. E. (1987). *Assessments of sexual offenders by measures of erectile response: Psychometric properties and decision making.* Rockville, Md.: National Institute of Mental Health.

Murphy, W. D., Haynes, M. R., Stalgaitis, S. J., & Flanagan, B. (1986). Differential sexual responding among four groups of sexual offenders against children. *Journal of Psychopathology and Behavioral Assessment, 8,* 339–353.

Nadelson, C., & Notman, M. (1984). Rape and seasonal variations [letter]. *American Journal of Psychiatry, 141,* 1015–1016.

O'Donohue, W. T., & Letourneau, E. (1992). The psychometric properties of the penile tumescence assessment of child molesters. *Journal of Psychopathology and Behavioral Assessment, 14,* 123–174.

Quinsey, V. L. (1986). Men who have sex with children. In D. N. Weisstub (Ed.), *Law and mental health: International perspectives (*vol. 2; pp. 140–172*).* New York: Pergamon.

Quinsey, V. L., & Bergersen, S. G. (1976). Instructional control of penile circumference in assessments of sexual preference. *Behavior Therapy, 7,* 489–493.

Quinsey, V. L., & Earls, C. M. (1990). The modification of sexual preferences. In W. L. Marshall, D. R. Laws, & H. E. Barbaree (Eds.), *Handbook of sexual assault: Issues, theories, and treatment of the offender.* New York: Plenum.

Quinsey, V. L., Chaplin, T. C., & Carrigan, W. F. (1979). Sexual preferences among incestuous and nonincestuous child molesters. *Behavior Therapy, 10,* 562–565.

Quinsey, V. L., Steinman, C. M., Bergersen, S. G., & Holmes, T. F. (1975). Penile circumference, skin conductance, and ranking responses of child molesters and "normals" to sexual and nonsexual visual stimuli. *Behavior Therapy, 6,* 213–219.

Williams, L. M., & Finkelhor, D. (1990). The characteristics of incestuous fathers: A review. In W. L. Marshall, D. R. Laws, & H. E. Barbaree (Eds.), *Handbook of sexual assault: Issues, theories, and treatment of the offender* (pp. 231–255). New York: Plenum.

Wydra, A., Marshall, W. L., Earls, C. M., & Barbaree, H .E. (1983). Identification of cues and control of sexual arousal by rapists. *Behaviour Research and Therapy, 21,* 469–476.

15

Some Family Considerations in Assessment and Case Management of Intrafamilial Child Sexual Abuse

Brian R. Abbott

It is recognized that specific patterns of maladaptive family relationships are present in incest families. These disturbed family relationships contribute to the occurrence of the sexual abuse. This chapter provides a framework and typology in which to examine and understand these family dynamics. The information is used to explain various case-management and therapeutic decisions that are made with the incest family, including protecting the victim, managing retracted allegations of sexual abuse, dealing with multiproblem families, guiding the family treatment process, and determining the appropriateness of family reunification.

It has been estimated that one in 20 females is sexually abused by a father figure (Finklehor, 1984). It is also recognized that incest perpetrators differ from other types of child molesters, such as preferential pedophiles (Conte, 1990). A major distinction between incestuous offenders and other types of sexual offenders is the nature of the familial relationships, which contributes to the occurrence of the sexually abusive behavior (Conte, 1990; Giarretto, 1982). These dysfunctional family relationships also appear to be associated with the degree of trauma experienced by the victim (Lusk & Waterman, 1986). Such findings demonstrate the importance of determining the nature and extent of the family dysfunction when assessing alleged cases of intrafamilial child sexual abuse—and, more specifically, the degree to which these family dynamics contribute to the etiology of the sexual abuse and the trauma suffered by the victim.

The rationale for including an appraisal of family functioning as part of a comprehensive evaluation is also grounded in principles of best-practice guidelines and current research findings. It is generally accepted that psychological assessments of children include an appraisal of the association between any family or marital difficulties and the child's presenting problem (Wanerman & Cooper, 1977). Contemporary research in developmental psychology emphasizes the role of family-of-origin functioning in the later personality adjustment of clinical and nonclinical populations of children (Berger, 1985; Farber & Egeland, 1987; Swensen, 1985). These conclusions suggest that data concerning family functioning, in alleged or validated cases of intrafamilial child sexual abuse, provide a more ecologically valid context in which to make clinical or case-management decisions regarding child victims of sexual abuse and their families. This chapter provides a brief review of attempts to classify maladaptive patterns of familial relationships associated with incestuous families. A clinical typology is also presented to highlight the function of family dynamics in both the etiology of the sexually offending behavior and the trauma suffered by the victim. This information is a crucial element in the validation process of intrafamilial child sexual abuse allegations and in developing practical, comprehensive plans for the treatment and case management of the incest family.

PATTERNS OF FAMILY DYSFUNCTION: CLINICAL OBSERVATIONS VERSUS EMPIRICAL FINDINGS

Ample clinical observations have discerned common patterns of family dysfunction in intrafamilial child sexual abuse. Role reversal between the child victim and the parents appears to be most prevalent in the incest family. This may become manifest in such phenomena as the child's assuming the responsibilities of a wife in relation to the father, the perpetrator's relating to the child victim as if he or she were an adult lover, and the victim's caring for younger siblings (Giarretto, 1982).

The marital and parental units in the incest family also exhibit characteristic dysfunctions. The offender often maintains an intense emotional dependence on the spouse (Giarretto, 1982; Lusk & Waterman, 1986). This can overwhelm the spouse, who gains distance by establishing emotionally egalitarian relationships outside the family (Giarretto, 1982). As a result, the nonoffending parent may abandon the child victim emotionally or physically (Perlmutter, Engel, & Sager, 1982). Zefran and colleagues (Zefran, Riley, Anderson, Curtis, Jackson, Kelly, McGury, & Suriano, 1982) describe the incest family as having significant marital problems related to a patriarchal power structure. Other clinical observations of incest families have noted a lack of appropriate parent–child boundaries (MacFarlane and Waterman, 1986; Pozanski & Blos, 1975; Zefran et al., 1982), poor communication among family members (Giarretto, 1982; Lusk & Waterman, 1986; Zefran et al., 1982), and isolation of the family from supportive extended family and social relationships (Mrazek, 1981; Vander Mey & Neff, 1982). Little empirical research has been completed that tests the validity of these clinical observations. Similarly, there is a dearth of research that includes comparisons in family functioning between incestuous families and other clinical and nonclinical samples. The studies that have attempted to do so have yielded equivocal results (Abbott, 1990; Maddock, Larson, and Lally, 1991; Peterson, Basta, and Dykstra, 1993).

In an effort to determine differences in family functioning between incestuous pretreatment, incestuous posttreatment, and nonclinical families, Maddock et al. (1991) administered standardized measures of family functioning, communication, sex-role stereotyping, sexual satisfaction of the spouses, distribution of power and control in the marital relationship, and family members' attitudes regarding sex. With the exception of the communication and the power and control measures, there were no significant differences among the groups studied. On the two dimensions that achieved statistical significance, the following results were obtained: (1) wives in the pretreatment incest group perceived having significantly less power and control in their marital relationships than did the women in the posttreatment incest and control samples; and (2) communication between spouses and among parents and children in the pretreatment incest group was significantly poorer than in the posttreatment incest and control groups. These results appear to support the clinical observations that incest families entering treatment differ from nonclinical families in being characterized by a submissive mother figure (Zefran et al., 1982) and in having poor communication among family members (Giarretto, 1982; Waterman & Lusk, 1986; Zefran et al., 1982).

Using matched groups of adolescent sexual offenders, including intrafamilial offenders and delinquent teenagers, Abbott (1990) administered various measures of family functioning and parent–child communication to the parents and adolescents in both groups. It was found that the families of adolescent sexual offenders did not significantly differ from their counterparts in the delinquent group on measures of family cohesion, adaptability, and communication. Dysfunctional family patterns and communication were seen in both samples. There were greater similarities than differences between the two groups in the types of relationship and communication disturbances presented. This suggests that the family dysfunction found with adolescent incest perpetrators does not differ significantly from that of delinquent youths with no history of sexually offending behavior.

In further support of clinical observations, Peterson et al. (1993) report significant findings on the Clinical Analysis Questionnaire (Krug, 1980) when comparing clinical and nonclinical control subjects (mothers whose children were molested by a teacher and a nonclinical sample of mothers) with mothers of incestuously abused children. The incestuous mothers evidenced significantly greater parental emotional maladjustment and ineffectiveness as shown in high levels of preoccupation with bodily functions; low energy; and feelings of worthlessness, blame, suspiciousness, and rejection; as well as unusual impulses, anxiety, and obsessional behavior. The authors reason that these problems among mothers from incestuous families may contribute to the family dysfunction, and thus increase the child's vulnerability to abuse (Peterson et al., 1993).

Keeping in mind that every study has methodological problems that affect the validity and generalizability of the results, it appears that there may be differences in some aspects of family functioning between incestuous families and nonclinical control families; however, there are no apparent differences when incestuous families are compared with other clinical samples of families. This is not surprising as it appears that the family dysfunction characteristic of incestuous families is not qualitatively or quantitatively different from other clinical populations, such as families that present problems of domestic violence or substance abuse, or even some nonclinical populations (Maddock et al., 1991). Based on these assertions, it can be concluded that certain forms of dysfunctional family dynamics can be found in intrafamilial sexual abuse.

Absent other corroborating clinical data, however, the patterns of family dysfunction cannot be used in isolation to predict or confirm sexual abuse in a family. In fact, looking for a direct casual relationship between specific forms of family dysfunction and the occurrence of child sexual abuse not only may be dangerous, but is contrary to the current thinking in this field (Finkelhor, 1986). It is generally accepted that intrafamilial child sexual abuse takes place as a result of a complex interaction among multiple factors. These include, but are not limited to, the psychological disturbance present in each family member, problems with social and family functioning, environmental or situational stresses, and physiological factors.

This view is most succinctly stated in the four-factor model developed by Finkelhor (1984). Within this interactional framework, dysfunctional family dynamics are viewed as an integral part of a combination of factors that play a role in causing intrafamilial child sexual abuse. When examining an incestuous family, the clinician must look for the reciprocal interactions between the intrapsychic functioning of each individual, the family relationships, the intergenerational history of each parent's family, and situational or environmental stresses. It is the combination and interaction of these factors that contribute to the exhibition of sexually abusive behavior in the family. To emphasize one factor over another may lead the clinician to overlook important areas that are in need of intervention.

Keeping in mind the limitations of the association between incestuous abuse and dysfunctional family dynamics, the following clinical typology is presented. This model illustrates the interactions among the intrapsychic, interpersonal (including family relationships), physiological, and situational factors that contribute to the occurrence of the sexual abuse. This information can be utilized by professionals in the validation process and to develop case-management and treatment plans.

A CLINICAL TYPOLOGY OF INCESTUOUS FAMILIES

To assist in the assessment and the therapy and case management of incestuous families, a typology of each of three common family systems (single parent, egocentric patriarch, and the parentless family) is presented. The typology was developed from the author's clinical work with incestuous families, as well as by integrating current clinical and empirical observations of such families. The presupposition is that the offender is a male, as the author has seen too few female incest offenders from which to make generalizations about family patterns. Also, a thorough review of the literature could not uncover information pertaining to the family dynamics involving female incest offenders. This conceptualization examines how various dyads within the family (e.g., victim–offender, victim–nonoffending parent, offender–nonoffending parent), in combination with the intrapsychic and interpersonal problems of each family member, contribute to the fact that sexual abuse takes place. The typology, to be explained in the following, is not exhaustive, as it is not possible to classify all forms of family dysfunction that are seen in incestuous families. Whether or not a family fits into one of the three types of families is not as important as the clinician's or case manager's assessment of how the dysfunction in the various dyads and the family as a whole are involved in the etiology of the sexually offending behavior.

The use of typologies for classifying human behavior must be approached cautiously. The observed symptoms that make up a typology suggest a cause-and-effect relationship. The degree of diagnostic certainty of this relationship varies considerably. In psychology, many typologies or syndromes are considered nondiagnostic because they cannot point to such a relationship with any degree of certainty (Myers, 1993). Although a typology, such as the one described here, cannot establish cause, it does describe the relationship of symptoms to known causes. The following typology provides clinical utility for understanding the influence of family dynamics that are related to incestuous behavior. It can also assist in deciding on points of intervention and in determining progress toward changing dysfunctional patterns.

The Single-Parent Family

The single-parent family derives its label from a common response given by the nonoffending parents in these families: "My husband is just like one of the kids." This family is characterized by an offending parent who is passive and immature and feels inadequate or insecure. Typically, the couple unites because the offender's overly dependent nature is a complement to the nonoffending parent's tendency to fulfill the other's constant need for attention, affection, and recognition. When a child is born in this family, the offender feels rejected or neglected because the partner's full attention has been diverted to the child. This feeling of neglect or abandonment is compounded when subsequent children are born.

The offender finds it difficult to cope with the normal family developmental process because of his sense of isolation from other supportive adult relationships. History may reveal that the offender either has had few close peer relationships or, subsequent to the marriage, divested from supportive peer relationships. Whichever is the case, the offender then becomes overly dependent on the marital relationship to meet adult emotional needs. He places increasing demands on his partner for time and emotional energy, which results in the partner's feeling conflicted over the competing demands of the children and her spouse. In some cases, the offender may feel jealous of the children, and actually compete with them for the attention of the nonoffending parent. It is for this reason that this family system is called "single-parent," as the nonoffending parent perceives that she is having to be a parent to both her children and her husband. The constant neediness of the offender creates a great deal of distress or discord in the marital relationship. As this conflict becomes entrenched, the nonoffending parent begins to withdraw emotionally. This detachment may take various forms, including ignoring the offender, investing more time and emotional energy into the relationship with the children, or spending increasing amounts of time away from home in other pursuits, such as employment or hobbies. This retreat from the intense demands of the offender provides a way for the nonoffending parent to gratify her adult emotional needs. The extent of her withdrawal from the marital relationship can also affect the relationship with the victim.

Typically, there is some estrangement in the relationship between the victim and nonoffending parent. The degree of emotional abandonment felt by the victim can vary considerably, from mild to extreme. The emotional detachment of the nonoffending parent may become manifest in various behaviors, including, but not limited to, ignoring the needs of the child, having a relationship with the child that is characterized by conflict, or unconsciously encouraging the child to develop an overly dependent relationship with the offender, while herself abandoning her relationship with the victim. As a result, the victim reaches out to the offender for emotional support and comfort, perceiving the nonoffending parent as someone who is not protective or cannot be trusted.

When the victim feels chronically abandoned by the nonoffending parent, an interesting phenomenon may arise. The victim will develop an intense emotional attachment to the offender, on whom he or she becomes reliant as the main provider of emotional succor. In essence, the attention and nurturance received from the offender are seen as tantamount to maintaining the victim's sense of self-worth or survival. This intense dependence, coupled with the feelings of guilt, shame, and anxiety associated with the sexual abuse, creates tremendous ambivalence and confusion for the victim. In dealing with these conflicted feelings, the victim maintains a strong love attachment to the offender and projects anger, hurt, and sadness onto the nonoffending parent for the perceived abandonment. In this situation, the victim often presents as being intensely angry with the nonoffending parent, and it appears that negative feelings toward the offender are absent.

As for the offender, he feels helpless to deal with the marital conflict and is unable to meet his emotional needs through this relationship. Thus he turns to one of the children in the family, who later becomes the victim. This child is almost always a female, usually the eldest. Because of his poor social skills, immaturity, or poor self-confidence, the offender cannot turn to other adults, within or outside the family, to fulfill his unmet emotional needs. Instead, a relationship with the child makes the offender feel competent, in control, and loved. Essentially, the offender projects idealized images of an adult relationship onto the victim, projections that are played out in their day-to-day relationship. The hallmark of this projective process is the offender's distortions of the child's behavior and motives. For instance, the victim's seeking of nurturance and attention is misperceived by the offender as the deliberate romantic display of an idealized adult partner. From this behavior, he infers that the child's feelings are romantic or sexual. As the offender becomes increasingly dependent on the victim to meet his emotional needs, he begins to develop sexual fantasies involving the victim. The fantasies develop prior to the onset of the actual sexual abuse, continue during its course, and frequently persist upon termination of the abusive conduct. Typically, the offender fantasizes sexual activity with the victim, to which he believes the victim has the capacity to consent, and imagines that the sexual behavior is a further expression of affection in a romantic relationship. The repetition of these fantasies also serves further to break down the inhibition against incestuous conduct with the child. The offender comes to believe that the fantasy is how the victim actually feels and thinks and this perception provides him with the justification to act upon his sexual thoughts.

The nonabused children or siblings in the family are also affected by the dysfunctional family dynamics. In fact, Kroth (1979) found that when the nonabused siblings are not provided with therapeutic services as part of the treatment plan for the incestuous family, these children, upon conclusion of therapy, may display more symptoms of psychological distress than does the victim. In the single-parent family system, the nonabused siblings appear to suffer the effects of being emotionally neglected both by the nonoffending parent and the offending parent. The nonoffending parent's emotional detachment from the family and the attention the offender showers on the victim leave the nonabused children feeling rejected, as well as angry and intensely jealous of the victim for receiving special attention from the offending parent.

The Egocentric Patriarch

This family system is distinguished by its patriarchal power structure, where the father is king and the wife and children are his subjects. Like the offender in the single-parent family, the egocentric patriarch feels inadequate and insecure, but the manner in which these feelings become manifest is quite different. Both offender types are highly sensitive to rejection, but unlike the passive withdrawal of the offender in the single-parent family, the egocentric patriarch responds with rage and controlling or dominating behavior. He sees the nonoffending parent and the children as objects and perceives a sense of sole ownership of them. The offender is extremely fearful of losing his cherished objects, which leads him to exert absolute control and dominance to maintain possession. As a result, this offender uses intimidation (e.g., critical and demeaning language, threats of physical violence), and, at times, acts out in a physically aggressive manner in an effort to obtain gratification of his emotional needs from family members.

The personality structure of the egocentric patriarch is dominated by strong narcissistic traits, such as a sense of entitlement over family members, egocentric behavior and attitudes, or an overly sensitive reaction to criticism or rejection, even to the extent of being a personality disorder. In more virulent circumstances, the offender may evidence a sociopathic makeup. People outside of the family may describe the egocentric patriarch as passive, shy, or inhibited—a likable sort of fellow who keeps to himself. This offender commonly has few, if any, supportive peer relationships, and it is unusual for him to show the controlling, dominant, or abusive aspects of his personality to outsiders. When an offender exhibits such behavior outside the family, this usually indicates a sociopathic personality.

The nonoffending parent in this family can be described as submissive, helpless, and dependent. These personality traits make it easier for the offending parent to dominate the spouse. Their etiology usually results from the nonoffending parent's having been a victim of chronic physical, sexual, or emotional abuse throughout her life. It is common for her not only to have been abused within her family as a child, but also in other adolescent and adult relationships. In fact, the nonoffending parent may have married the egocentric patriarch in order to leave an abusive family environment.

Other clinicians have seen the nonoffending parent as having some type of nonspecific physical disability that leads to an overly dependent relationship with the offender, and thus makes her more vulnerable to the offender's efforts at control and dominance in their relationship (Stern & Meyer, 1980). Early in the relationship, the offending parent may not show his abusive aspects and his dominating and controlling behaviors are seen by the nonoffending parent as protective and caring. As the relationship progresses, the offender becomes increasingly dependent on the nonoffending parent, and, correspondingly, becomes more fearful of losing her. As the offender perceives instances of rejection, he becomes enraged and lashes out verbally or physically. He becomes more demanding of the nonoffending parent's time and attention and engages in behavior that makes her more dependent on him (e.g., not allowing her to go to work or to leave the home without him). The nonoffending parent responds with helpless and passive behavior that was learned in her childhood.

The offender also perceives his children as chattel and believes that he has the right to treat them as he wishes. The children are extremely fearful of the offender, a fear that usually is based in reality, as they may have been the recipients of physical or emotional abuse and probably have witnessed their mother's being victimized in this manner. The children also take on a passive or submissive response to the egocentric patriarch based on the modeling of such behavior by the nonoffending parent. In addition, the nonoffending parent may encourage the children to act in a pacifying manner toward the egocentric patriarch in an effort to reduce the chances of conflicts that can lead to abusive conduct.

The victim in this family system is usually female, but also may be a male child. It is not uncommon for the egocentric patriarch to sexually abuse more than one victim. The behavior is motivated by the offender's sense of ownership over the child victim, and that he can do what he pleases. The offender's sexually abusive conduct may be acted out impulsively, or, like the offender in the single-parent family, he may develop and act out an "adult love relationship" with the child. Resistance by the victim may be met with intimidation, threats of or actual physical violence, or the withdrawal of affection or nurturance.

Quite often there is a positive bond between the victim and the nonabused children and the nonoffending parent. The nonoffending parent often feels guilty about her spouse's abuse of the children, and so will make extraordinary attempts to give them nurturance and attention. The close emotional ties between the children and the nonoffending parent develop through the common effort to pacify the egocentric patriarch. But in other situations, the children feel intense anger toward the nonoffending parent for not being protected.

When sexual abuse occurs in this family, it is common for the nonoffending parent to be aware of it. In some instances, this knowledge empowers her to report the abuse to the authorities. More frequently, however, the sexual abuse is viewed by the victim and the nonoffending parent as yet another event over which they have no control and so should try to avoid situations that might provoke further abuse. Both the victim and nonoffending parent feel guilty that the sexual abuse occurred. The victim may deduce that he or she acted in a way to incite the offender, and the nonoffending parent may see that she failed to protect the child from the abuse.

The guilt felt by the nonoffending parent may spur her to confront the offender, whose reaction will often be one of rage, resulting in the intimidation or physical abuse of his spouse. This attack will continue until the spouse stops the confrontation or retracts the allegations of sexual abuse. If the abuse has been reported to the authorities, at this time the nonoffending parent, and possibly the victim, will officially retract the allegations. In some instances, the offender may react to the confrontation by the nonoffending parent by forcing her to engage with him in the sexual abuse of the child. In the offender's mind, this action provides insurance that the spouse will not report the sexual abuse because she also will be held legally accountable and will lose the children. In the face of such responses, the nonoffending parent retreats and assumes a stance of passive resignation. As a result, the victim is confronted with the harsh reality that the mother cannot be protective and that he or she should also take an acquiescent position with the offender.

The Parentless Family

This family derives its name from its lack of a parental or executive sub-unit; there is no differentiation between the subsystems of parent and child. This diffusion of boundaries may be evidenced in inconsistent limit setting and discipline by the parents, as well as in their seeking a peer relationship with the children. These are parents who allow their children to drink alcohol or use drugs in the home, who provide few rules for the children to abide by, or who relate to them as peers. When working with these families, professionals are often faced by the question, "Just who are the parents in this family?"

Typically, the husband and wife establish a relationship based on the idea that the other will provide unconditional acceptance and meet every emotional need. Later in the relationship, this fantasy becomes a nightmare, as each realizes that the other does not have the psychological capacity to fulfill every need or to give unconditional approval. Conflicts in the marriage begin to develop at this point, as each partner feels angry, cheated, and empty, and attempts to manipulate the other partner to meet his or her needs. When both conclude that their needs for acceptance and nurturance cannot be met by the other spouse, they seek to attain this through other means.

In order to satisfy his needs for recognition and affection, the offender turns to a child in the family, who subsequently becomes the victim. He develops an overly involved emotional relationship similar to that of the offender in the single-parent family. Essentially, the cognitive, affective, and interpersonal processes that lead both offenders to commit sexual abuse are the same.

To cope with the dysfunctional marriage, the nonoffending parent may turn to one of the children, even possibly the victim, or to another adult outside the family for acceptance and nurturance. In some situations, the nonoffending parent relates to the victim as a peer, and the victim responds by taking on a parental or adult role. In this circumstance, the victim perceives the nonoffending parent as someone who is fragile and needs to be taken care of. As a result, the victim comes to believe that he or she is responsible for the emotional well-being of that parent. In a second instance, the mother may withdraw emotionally or abandon the victim in an effort to find individuals outside the family to meet her emotional needs. It is common, in such cases, for the nonoffending parent to encourage the victim to maintain a close relationship with the offender. As the offender transfers dependence needs onto the victim, this relieves the nonoffending parent of having to respond to the offender's insatiable demands and clinging behavior. In turn, the victim becomes more dependent on the offender to provide nurturance, which reinforces their overly involved emotional relationship. In both circumstances, the victim feels abandoned by the nonoffending parent and does not perceive her as having the ability to be protective or supportive, and so may not inform her about the sexual abuse.

Quite often, the lack of a consistent executive subsystem also affects the nonabused siblings in the parentless family. They experience little limit setting or discipline, and may feel emotionally neglected because of their parents' inability to provide consistent nurturance and attention. As a result, it is common for these children to have behavioral problems, which are most often observed in the school setting. The nonabused siblings may feel anger toward the victim due to his or her favored status with the offender.

As stated earlier, the preceding typology describes common incestuous families seen in clinical settings and is not an exhaustive discussion of family dynamics associated with sexually abusive families. The reader may find families that are a blend of two of the types described or that are quite different. This typology is intended to stress the importance of examining the function that various dyads serve in contributing to the sexually offending behavior. Based on these dynamics, the clinician or case manager can determine appropriate service plans or points of intervention at which to ameliorate the dysfunction in these relationships.

IMPLICATIONS FOR ASSESSMENT AND CASE MANAGEMENT

Caution must be exercised when attempting to use clinical and empirical research results regarding family functioning to make a determination as to the veracity of an allegation of child sexual abuse (see also Chapter 17). This situation is most likely to arise when either the offending or the nonoffending parent denies that the sexual abuse occurred. Often this places the onus on the case manager or clinician to decide whether the allegations are valid. When determining the authenticity of the reported sexual abuse, it is not advisable to use the presence or absence of family dysfunction in a predictive manner, that is, to justify a clinical opinion that sexual abuse did or did not take place. In the absence of other, relevant clinical findings, an objective determination regarding the veracity of the allegation based on the presence or lack of specific symptoms of family dysfunction cannot be supported by current research or clinical thought, although, in practice, such inappropriate assessment strategies may be carried out. When diagnosable family dysfunction exists, in such a situation, the clinician or case manager should provide a description of its nature and extent and make recommendations as to how it should be treated therapeutically and handled through case-management strategies.

Keeping the limitations of the family systems theory in mind (i.e., that family functioning alone cannot distinguish incest families from nonincest families), assessment information regarding family functioning is still crucial to the treatment and case management of the incestuous family. Understanding the nature and extent of dysfunction in certain family dyads or triads can assist in making critical case-management decisions, such as to remove the child or the offending parent or to implement reunification, and in developing appropriate service plans that are geared toward protecting the child victim. Clinicians can also use this information to craft plans for therapeutic intervention with the family as a whole, or family members individually, as well as to utilize baseline family functioning data to measure the outcome of interventions.

Finally, the development and monitoring of treatment goals and service plans for dealing with sexually offensive behavior should reflect an interactional model of etiology. In other words, the treatment and service plans should be individually tailored to ameliorate the unique psychological, interpersonal, and physiological problems of each member of the incest family, as well as to address those family problems and environmental or situational stresses that, in combination, have led to the sexual abuse.

Recommendations

1. **THAT** it be recognized that incestuous families present specific maladaptive patterns of family relationships. These maladaptive patterns are most obvious in the victim–nonoffending parent, the victim–offender, and the marital relationships. The role of the nonabused siblings also must be examined when assessing incest families.

2. **THAT** dysfunctional family relationships found in incest families be viewed as a contributing factor in the etiology of the sexually abusive behavior. It is the maladaptive patterns of family relationships, in combination with other psychological, social, physiological, and situational factors, that lead to the occurrence of sexual abuse.

3. **THAT** incestuous family dynamics be taken into account as part of a comprehensive assessment of the sexually abused child and the family. The disturbed family relationships found in incest cases cannot, in isolation, diagnose or predict the presence of child sexual abuse.

4. **THAT** the role of family dynamics in the etiology of incestuous abuse be recognized as crucial in the development of effective case-management and treatment plans. Case managers and clinicians must take into account the dysfunctional family dynamics, making decisions that include, but are not limited to, validating the sexual abuse allegation, determining appropriateness of reunification, and ascertaining progress in treatment or assessing the risk of additional offenses.

REFERENCES

Abbott, B. R. (1990). *Family dynamics, intergenerational patterns of negative events and traumas, and patterns of offending behavior: A comparison of adolescent sexual offenders and delinquent adolescents and their parents.* Ann Arbor, Mich.: University Microfilms International.

Berger, A. (1985). Characteristics of abusing families. In L. L'Abate (Ed.), *The handbook of family psychology and therapy* (pp. 900–936). Homewood, Ill.: Dorsey Press.

Conte, J. (1990). The incest offender: An overview and introduction. In A. L. Horton, B .L. Johnson, L .M. Roundy, & D. Williams (Eds.), *The incest perpetrator: A family member no one wants to treat* (pp. 19–28). Newbury Park, Calif.: Sage.

Farber, E. A., & Egeland, B. (1987). Invulnerability among abused and neglected children. In E. J. Anthony & B. J. Cohler (Eds.), *The invulnerable child* (pp. 253-288). New York: Guilford Press.

Finkelhor, D. (1984). *Child sexual abuse: New theory and research.* New York: Free Press.

Finkelhor, D. (1986). Sexual abuse: Beyond the family systems approach. *Journal of Psychotherapy and the Family, 2,* 53–65.

Giarretto, H. (1982). *Integrated treatment of child sexual abuse.* Palo Alto, Calif.: Science and Behavior Books.

Kroth, J. A. (1979). *Child sexual abuse: Analysis of a family therapy approach.* Springfield, Ill.: Charles C. Thomas.

Krug, S. E. (1980). *Clinical Analysis Questionnaire manual.* Champaign, Ill.: Institute for Personality and Ability Testing.

Lusk, R., & Waterman, J. (1986). Effects of sexual abuse on children. In K. MacFarlane & J. Waterman (Eds.), *Sexual abuse of young children: Evaluation and treatment* (pp. 101–120). New York: Guilford Press.

MacFarlane, K., & Waterman, J. (1986). *Sexual abuse of young children: Evaluation and treatment.* New York: Guilford Press.

Maddock, J. W., Larson, P. R., & Lally, C. F. (1991). An evaluation protocol for incest family functioning. In M. Q. Patton (Ed.), *Family sexual abuse: Frontline research and evaluation* (pp. 162–177). Newbury Park, Calif.: Sage.

Mrazek, P. B. (1981). The nature of incest: A review of contributing factors. In P. B. Mrazek & C. H. Kempe (Eds.), *Sexually abused children and their families.* New York: Pergamon.

Myers, J. E. B. (1993). Expert testimony describing psychological syndromes. *Pacific Law Journal, 24*(3), 1449–1464.

Perlmutter, L. H., Engel, T., & Sager, C. J. (1982). The incest taboo: Loosened sexual boundaries in remarried families. *Journal of Sex and Marital Therapy, 8*, 46–49.

Peterson, R. F., Basta, S. M., & Dykstra, T. A. (1993). Mothers of molested children: Some comparisons of personality characteristics. *Child Abuse and Neglect.*

Pozanski, E., & Blos, P. (1975, October). Incest. *Medical Aspects of Human Sexuality*, pp. 46–76.

Stern, M. J., & Meyer, L. C. (1980). Family and couple interaction patterns in cases of father–daughter incest. In B. Jones, K. MacFarlane, & L. L. Jenstrom (Eds.), *Sexual abuse of children: Selected readings.* Washington, D. C.: U.S. Department of Health and Human Services.

Swensen, C. H. (1985). Personality development in the family. In L. L'Abate (Ed.), *The handbook of family psychology and therapy* (pp. 73–101). Homewood, Ill.: Dorsey Press.

Vander Mey, B. J., & Neff, R. L. (1982). Adult-child incest: A review of research and treatment. *Adolescence, 17*, 717–735.

Wanerman, L., & Cooper, S. (1977). *Children in treatment.* New York: Brunner/Mazel.

Zefran, J., Riley, H. F., Anderson, W. O., Curtis, J. H., Jackson, L. M., Kelly, P. H., McGury, E. T., & Suriano, M. K. (1982). Management and treatment of child sexual abuse cases in a juvenile court setting. *Journal of Social Work and Human Sexuality, 1*, 155–170.

16

The Assessment of
Children with Disabilities
Who Report Sexual Abuse:
A Special Look at
Those Most Vulnerable

Connie Burrows Horton and
Kimberly A. Kochurka

This chapter examines a number of pervasive myths that interfere with identifying, reporting, and planning interventions in cases of sexual abuse of special-needs children such as those with developmental disabilities. Since children with disabilities are at high risk for sexual abuse, they are entitled to the same sensitivities that are granted other alleged victims. Specific suggestions for accurate, sensitive investigations with this population are discussed.

Clearly, it is a disturbing thought to acknowledge that children, the most vulnerable members of society, are so frequently abused. It may be even more disturbing to accept that children who are extra vulnerable, those with special needs or disabilities, are also frequently victims of sexual abuse. Unfortunately, this, too, is a reality that society, and especially mental health professionals, must begin to address. Since current estimates suggest that children with disabilities are sexually abused at a rate four to 10 times higher than that of the general population (Baladerian, 1991), this travesty no longer can be ignored. These child victims need, and deserve, appropriate therapeutic interventions; their offenders must be dealt with. However, before such actions can take place, accurate investigations must be conducted.

The public and professional preoccupation with determining the accuracy of children's sexual abuse allegations has been suggested as having its origin "in the difficulty many people experience in believing that adults can choose to be sexual with children" (Faller, 1988, p. 389). Likewise, some concerns about determining the accuracy of allegations made by children with disabilities may begin with a difficulty in believing that adults could choose to be sexual with these children.

Once professionals accept the possibility that the special-needs children with whom they work may be victimized, they are in a position to equip themselves to assess—sensitively, effectively, and accurately—sexual abuse allegations made by these children. All special populations must be considered at risk for abuse, and professionals working with them must be trained in specific techniques to handle their allegations appropriately. This chapter focuses on one such special population as an example: children with developmental disabilities. (Note: While in some regions and settings, "mentally retarded" is still used, the term developmentally disabled is preferred by many, and will be used throughout this chapter to refer to children with impaired intellectual and adaptive behavior capabilities.)

Professionals who do not believe that children with disabilities could ever be victims of sexual abuse may overlook obvious signs of abuse and ignore even direct reports. When this occurs, child victims are not provided adequate protection or intervention services. Those not trained in the techniques and procedures appropriate to handle such allegations may arrive at invalid conclusions that potentially could harm the child victims, their families, and their caregivers. Thus a balance must be obtained in which professionals not only accept the possibility that a child with developmental disabilities may have been abused, but also are careful to use sensitive and accurate investigation techniques before coming to definitive conclusions.

THE VULNERABILITY ISSUE: MYTHS AND REALITY

While there is an increasing recognition that children with developmental disabilities are more vulnerable to sexual abuse than other children (Ammerman, 1990; Hewitt, 1987; Krents, Schulman, & Brenner, 1987), there are still a number of prevalent myths that interfere with preventing, identifying, and reporting the abuse and intervening in these cases.

Myth 1: Children with developmental disabilities are at low risk for sexual abuse because people feel sorry for them and would not take advantage of their disability.

In reality, the very nature of their disability may make these children easy targets for perpetrators. Cognitive limitations, as well as communication difficulties, lead to an increased vulnerability. Offenders generally choose victims who not only are unlikely to resist, but also are unlikely to report their assaults (Crossmaker, 1991). Since children with developmental disabilities may be unable to explain what happened, perpetrators may view them as "safe risks."

Additionally, as overwhelming as the disclosure and investigation stages are for any child, this process is likely to be even more confusing for a child with developmental disabilities. Questions that cross any sexually abused child's mind, such as "Who should I tell?" "Why are they asking me the same questions over and over again?" "Am I in trouble?" "Who will help me?" are likely to be extremely confusing for these children.

In addition to the communication difficulties, children with disabilities are vulnerable because of their often lifelong dependency on their caregivers (O'Day, 1983). Compared with their peers, these children are less likely to grow out of their dependent stage. Thus the vulnerability for abuse may be increased when they are taught to follow unquestioningly the directions of "nurturing" adults (Varley, 1984).

Furthermore, because of the nature of their disabilities, these children often have a large number of caretakers and/or service providers in their lives who have intense contact and direct access. In fact, it is likely that some of these caregivers and/or service providers may actually seek out a work setting that allows them sexual contact with a vulnerable population (Froemming & Fuestel, 1991; Sobsey & Doe, 1991).

Myth 2: Restricting the activities of the child with developmental disabilities and eliminating contact with strangers will help eliminate the chances of sexual abuse.

Unfortunately, when parents learn about the alarming rates of abuse, with the best of intentions, they will often restrict their child's activities (Krents et al., 1987). However, as is true with the majority of child victims, the assailants of children with developmental disabilities are most likely to be family members, or people known to and trusted by the victim, such as teachers, residential care providers, and aides (Baladerian, 1991; Heighwey, Webster, & Shaw, 1990; Varley, 1984). In fact, it has been reported that as many as 99% of perpetrators were well known to and trusted by their victims with developmental disabilities (Baladerian, 1991).

Therefore, restricting the contacts of these special children, and allowing them to develop only a few close relationships with caregivers and family members, is not likely to decrease the risk of sexual abuse. In fact, this parental or institutional decision actually has the potential to increase the risk of abuse by creating lifelong dependence and a paucity of safe people in whom to confide in the event of abuse.

If family and friends can victimize children with developmental disabilities sexually, the question arises: Does institutionalization offer increased protection? Unfortunately, the very institutions designed to protect these children may facilitate abuse. Institutions that reinforce children for compliant behavior, rather than independent judgment, further increase the risk for abuse. Also, as mentioned before, some offenders may deliberately seek out such work environments, where an opportunity for abuse exists.

In addition, there is a tendency for institutions to try to handle disclosures of sexual abuse "in house" (Sullivan, Vernon, & Scanlan, 1987). Too often in institutional settings, alleged offenders are harassed or threatened, or forced to resign, but no formal legal action is taken. Thus the offender will leave that institution, and if background checks are not conducted on staff, will be able to find employment in another institution, where the abuse can be repeated (Sobsey & Doe, 1991). As a result, rather than protecting children, some institutions are perpetuating the problem of sexual abuse.

Myth 3: Since a child with an intellectual disability does not know what is happening, the sexual abuse will have no negative impact.

While many abusers, and sometimes caretakers, may use such distorted logic to rationalize their actions, there is no evidence to suggest that children with developmental disabilities are less affected than are other victims.

Developmentally disabled children often do not understand what is happening to them when they are being sexually abused, but this is true for most children. Further, if a lack of understanding were related to less severe effects of abuse, one would expect that children abused at an early age would be less affected than those abused when older. However, research has not consistently found such a pattern. In fact, there is a trend in research findings to suggest that children abused at younger ages appear to be more affected by the abuse (Browne & Finkelhor, 1986).

Another important predictor of how severely a child will be affected by abuse is related to prior emotional functioning and the degree of resiliency the child possesses (Anthony, 1987). Since epidemiological studies have repeatedly found a greater prevalence of psychiatric disorders among the developmentally disabled population as compared with the general population (Lewis & MacLean, 1982), many children with developmental disabilities may have a predisposition toward emotional problems and an impaired sense of resiliency even before their abuse.

Therefore, while the research literature examining the effects of sexual abuse among developmentally disabled children is limited, there is reason to believe that their reactions may be qualitatively different (Varley, 1984) and more severe (Tharinger, Horton, & Millea, 1990) than in the nonhandicapped population.

Myth 4: If they were really being abused, children with developmental disabilities could just say "No"!

The naive belief that any child can simply say "No" to sexual abuse fails to recognize the coercive dynamics and the power differential that exists when an adult has sexual contact with a child. Although saying "No" is tremendously difficult for any child victim of sexual abuse, it may be even more difficult for a child with developmental disabilities.

Children with developmental disabilities, in some cases, have been deprived of the affection, nurturing, and caring they need. This can happen when they are removed from their families at early ages to be placed in an institutional setting, or when social interaction with friends and neighbors is limited (Krents et al., 1987). Any "affectionate" attention from an offender, even in the form of sexual advances and exploitation, thus may be difficult to refuse (Brantlinger, 1988; Froemming & Fuestel, 1991; Kempe & Kempe, 1984; Muccigrosso, 1991).

Additionally, these children tend to lack assertiveness skills. Some children with disabilities have been reinforced by caretakers for being compliant, for obeying authority, and for following directions. Since they have not been reinforced for saying "No," it is difficult for them to do so, even when the situation calls for it (Froemming & Fuestel, 1991; Muccigrosso, 1991).

The lack of experience with evaluative thinking and decision making contributes to this population's difficulty in declining sexual advances (Brantlinger, 1988; Muccigrosso, 1991). Some children with disabilities are deprived of opportunities to develop sound judgment (Muccigrosso, 1991). For example, many caregivers find it easier to do for their child with disabilities than to teach them. In institutions, chemical and physical restraints are often used to control the behavior of these children, eliminating the opportunity for them to use their own judgment. All of these actions render them more powerless, further destroying their ability to say "No" (Crossmaker, 1991).

The odds that a child with a developmental disability will say "No," or will try to disclose, are further decreased by the child's lack of information about sexuality and sexual abuse. Due to misconceptions held by parents and staff alike, children with developmental disabilities are rarely included in quality sex education or sexual abuse prevention programs that could give them some sense of normal sexual behavior (Brantlinger, 1988; Foxx, McMorrow, Storey, & Rogers, 1984; Fuestel, 1991; Gordon, 1971; Heighwey et al., 1990; Mitchell, Doctor, & Butler, 1978). Therefore, exploitive sexual practices may be perceived by these children as acceptable since there is no source of information or basis for comparison (Froemming & Fuestel, 1991).

Finally, saying "No" is extremely difficult for those children who want desperately to fit in with "normal" children (Tharinger et al., 1990). Much like any child, children with developmental disabilities need to feel valued and accepted (Matson & Sevin, 1988). Since these children and adolescents experience multiple obstacles to acceptance, such as being viewed by their peers as "different" or "weird," they may be willing to do almost anything to fulfill that need including submitting to sexual exploitation, especially if they are told that this will make them "like everybody else."

Partially because of biases and myths such as these, the sexual abuse of children with developmental disabilities continues to be minimized, ignored, disbelieved, or undiscovered (Crossmaker, 1991). Specifically, behavioral and emotional signs may be ignored and direct disclosures discounted. Accurate investigations are often not instigated.

ACCURATE ASSESSMENT

Indicators of Abuse

While there is not a unique list of signs and symptoms of the sexual abuse of children with developmental disabilities, behavioral and emotional signs could be expected to be much the same as in the general population (Tharinger et al., 1990; Vevier & Tharinger, 1986). Too often, however, symptoms that normally would cause a professional to wonder about abuse are ignored. For example, a young girl with developmental disabilities who wears multiple layers of clothing may be thought of as dressing inappropriately due to a lack of understanding of social norms or weather conditions, rather than because of a desire to protect her body from further abuse. Thus front-line workers should be aware of typical indicators of sexual abuse and encouraged not to ignore them because of a child's disability (Tharinger et al., 1990; Vevier & Tharinger, 1986).

Direct Disclosures

Children with developmental disabilities are not likely to discuss sexual abuse freely unless they are specifically asked about it (Sullivan et al., 1987). Thus, given all of the obstacles to disclosure discussed above (e.g., fear of losing affection, caretaking, or friends), any disclosure should be taken seriously and investigated carefully.

In sum, when professionals are willing to replace myths about the sexual abuse of children with developmental disabilities with sobering facts, they are in a position to watch for signs and symptoms of abuse, take disclosures seriously, and begin accurate investigations.

Sensitive Investigation

In many ways, appropriate, sensitive investigation techniques used with this population may not differ significantly from those used with other children. However, certain aspects of the process should be highlighted, as practitioners are reminded that children with disabilities are entitled to the same sensitivities that are available to other alleged victims of child sexual abuse. Aspects of the assessment procedures need to be adapted to accommodate the cognitive and communication levels of these children. Finally, it should be noted that while there are some important issues to consider, as discussed in what follows, the ability to conduct a sensitive and accurate assessment may depend largely on adopting an individualized approach that is responsive to the child's needs and abilities.

SETTING. In choosing the setting for an interview with a child or adolescent with developmental disabilities, the professional should consider issues of privacy, neutrality, and dignity (Sgroi, 1989). While these issues should be considered in choosing the setting for working with any alleged child victim, their importance should not be minimized when working with children with developmental disabilities.

Privacy, for example, may be a very important, yet rarely experienced, concept for a child with disabilities. Given the needs for additional assistance in self-care and the plethora of caretakers and professionals who may be involved in their lives, such children may feel that they have no place to themselves and that "their business is everybody's business." Thus in talking to children with disabilities about such a personal matter as sexual victimization, their rights to privacy should be respected. A hallway or a corner of the special education classroom, for example, are choices that do not reflect a respect for privacy rights.

Neutrality may also be a particularly important consideration for children with developmental disabilities. As discussed above, there tends to be a naive belief, even among some professionals, that no one, and especially no one the child has known and trusted, would victimize that child. However, children with disabilities *are* abused, and they tend to be abused by those closest to them. Therefore, the professional should not choose a setting for an interview that implies an a priori assumption of the alleged offender's innocence. For example, it is generally not appropriate to conduct an interview in the child's home, especially if a family member is an alleged offender. Again, while such precautions are a given in most child sexual abuse interviews, professionals should not change their procedures because of a naive belief that when working with a child with disabilities, "it just couldn't be true." The importance of making choices based on a concern for the dignity of such a child cannot be overstated. While the location of the interview may not appear to be a critical issue in this regard, if an appropriate site is selected, a message is conveyed that "You matter. I have time for you. You are safe. I want to hear your story."

Since many of these children have communication difficulties, it is not surprising that they may have enormous difficulty expressing themselves when they are especially upset and anxious, as in the case of talking about a sexual assault. Every effort, therefore, should be made to help the child feel comfortable and safe, and an important part of that is the selection of an appropriate setting.

THE INTERVIEWER. A critical aspect of the investigation is the interviewer. The expertise of the professional and his or her comfort with this special population are critical in determining the appropriateness of an individual to conduct the interview. While consideration of gender may seem a sensitive point, such an issue is complex, and depends on the individual situation. Whether to match the gender of the investigator with the gender of the child depends on such factors as the gender of the alleged offender, the gender of the caretakers with whom the child has felt safest, the age of the child, and the child's comfort/embarrassment in speaking about sexual issues with a person of the opposite sex. Matching the gender of the interviewer to the interviewee, however, should be considered secondary to choosing the person who is most supportive, accepting, and nonjudgmental in nature (Sgroi, 1989).

Ideally, someone who is trained in both child protection and disability concerns will be able to conduct the assessment. When this is not possible, someone skilled in sexual abuse investigations with very young children may best understand the appropriate developmental level of questions (Patterson, 1991). Those without specific training with developmentally disabled children may feel "deskilled" (Wescott, 1992), and may need reminders that many of the same skills that apply to young children apply in these cases (e.g., determining appropriate levels of communication, choosing responses, and determining how much the child has understood).

When the professional conducting the actual investigation does not have expertise in dealing with children with developmental disabilities, it may be helpful to have a human service worker who is familiar with the child's disability and communication style help the investigator "craft" questions or approaches in communication (Wisconsin Council on Developmental Disabilities, 1991). For example, the investigator may need help in choosing an appropriate vocabulary level, keeping questions simple and straightforward, and rewarding effort in the interview. Such consultation may take place before the interview with the child. At the very least, the interviewer should be familiar with abuse investigation basics. If the investigator is not an expert in developmental disabilities, there must be a willingness to be flexible and open to suggestions made by those familiar with the child's abilities.

Additionally, in some situations, it may seem appropriate to involve an interpreter in the interview itself. Such a decision should be carefully considered. If it is determined that an interpreter is needed, the person should be carefully chosen so as not to embarrass or cause further trauma. For example, one child may be embarrassed to have a teacher from school, who will hear the intimate details of one's traumatic experience, serve as an interpreter. On the other hand, another child victim may find the presence of such a person empowering or comforting (Wescott, 1992). The relationship of the interpreter with the alleged offender should be carefully considered to avoid a sense of divided loyalty and subtle pressure for the alleged victim to recant. For example, it is inappropriate to have one parent serve as an interpreter when the other parent is the alleged perpetrator.

In conclusion, multiple factors must be balanced. While the emotional needs and communication disabilities of the child should be considered (Wescott, 1992), these concerns must not outweigh the need for a private, objective interview in which the child is allowed to speak the truth. Sgroi (1989) suggests a blended approach in which a supportive person is included in the initial stages of the meeting when introductions are made and the purpose of the interview is discussed, and later excused so that the interviewer can meet with the child privately. Again, an individual decision must be made depending on the child's abilities and needs and the circumstances of the alleged abuse.

INTERVIEWING TECHNIQUES. While the issues mentioned are critical, communication is perhaps the most fundamental concern in the assessment of allegations. It is most important that the investigation be conducted at the child's functional level (Wescott, 1992). When working with these children, the interview approach must be very clear and concrete. Initial stages that are important in all interviews should be handled deliberately with developmentally disabled children.

Aspects of the early stages of interviewing, such as establishing the purposes of the interview and teaching the child to answer questions (Hoorwitz, 1992), may be particularly important. Again, each should be discussed specifically and concretely. Since children with developmental disabilities have a "lifetime of experiences of failing or being found deficient when their cognitive capacities are tested" (Sgroi, 1989, p. 259), it is especially important that they understand that this is not a test, and that the interviewer just wants to understand what happened. Further, children with developmental disabilities must be explicitly told that they do not need to know all of the answers, and that it is okay to say, "I don't know" or "I forgot." It is also important that they know not to "fake it" or to make up an answer if they do not know or cannot remember.

Choosing appropriate interview formats is a critical, but sophisticated, skill. Some have argued that the nonleading questions, generally recommended for use with alleged victims of sexual abuse, are even more significant in working with those with developmental disabilities (Sgroi, 1989). These children must be encouraged to use their own words rather than agree with an option the interviewer has proposed because it is what they thought they were supposed to do. When using nonleading questions, only simple interrogatives such as "Yes, what happened next?" are used.

While most would agree that the use of open-ended questions is generally the ideal way to proceed, this may not always be possible. Open-ended questions have been demonstrated to be largely inadequate with this population since many are unable to answer them (Sigelman, Budd, Winer, Shoenrock, & Martin, 1982). "Tell me what happened" may be met with a blank look or an "I don't know" or "I forgot." The inclusion of an example of possible responses should be avoided, as this seems only to confuse the issue.

Yes/no question and answer formats may be even more problematic because of the tendency for persons with developmental disabilities to acquiesce, or say "Yes" to questions, even if this is contradiction of their response to previous questions (Sigelman, Budd, Spanhel, & Shoenrock, 1981a). For example, the question "Did he pull down your pants?" is likely to be met with a "Yes" even though the previous question "Did he leave your clothes on?" was also answered "Yes."

Either/or question formats represent a slight improvement over yes/no formats; however, there is some bias toward choosing the latter option (Sigelman, Budd, Spanhel, & Shoenrock, 1981b). For example, the developmentally disabled child who is asked "Was he alone or did he have friends with him?" is more likely to say that the alleged perpetrator had friends with him. For this reason, open-ended questions are the preferred format, even with this population.

Part of the interview with, for example, a young girl with developmental disabilities, might go something like this.

INTERVIEWER: Can you tell me what happened?
CHILD: Uncle Charlie touched me...
INTERVIEWER: Tell me more about that.
CHILD: He touched me on my privates. (Gestures toward her crotch)
INTERVIEWER: And then what?

In this example, the child is doing well with open-ended questions with simple interrogatives to prompt further elaboration. The responses in this type of interview are more likely to be valid since the child is using her own words to tell her own story rather than acquiescing to something the interviewer has suggested that she believes she is supposed to confirm.

Other children with developmental disabilities may not be able to respond to open-ended questions, so interviewers may try yes/no, either/or, or multiple-choice formats as in the following example.

INTERVIEWER: Can you tell me what happened?
CHILD: I don't know...
INTERVIEWER: Saturday night. What happened?
CHILD: When?
INTERVIEWER: Did someone touch you?
CHILD: Yes.
INTERVIEWER: Tell me more about that.
CHILD: What?
INTERVIEWER: Who touched you?
CHILD: When?
INTERVIEWER: Who touched you? Your dad? Uncle Charlie?
CHILD: Uncle Charlie.
INTERVIEWER: Where did he touch you?
CHILD: I don't know.
INTERVIEWER: On your arm? On your feet? Or on your privates?
CHILD: My privates.

In this case, the child's responses are highly questionable for a number of reasons. The child never "told her own story" to open-ended questions; she always acquiesced by answering yes to yes/no questions, and she consistently chose the latter option on either/or or multiple-choice formats. Additionally, the interviewer's questions were leading (e.g., Did he touch you? Your privates?). If the interview questions were nonleading and the child's patterns were not so consistent (e.g., if she sometimes answered "No" and chose options that were in different positions in the multiple-choice sequence), she would have been more credible.

When it is unclear as to whether a child is answering accurately, it may be helpful to test the child's ability with the question format. This can be accomplished by asking a series of questions in which "Yes" cannot always be the accurate answer. For example, the interviewer might ask, "Do you live in a house?" and "Do you live in an apartment?" or "Do you have brothers or sisters?" and "Are you the only child in your family?" If the child acquiesces by answering "Yes" to both questions in the pair, demonstrating an inability to handle this question format, this style of questioning should be avoided in the investigation. Similar tests can be used with multiple-choice and either/or formats.

If a child does answer the open-ended questions, the answer should be taken seriously, even if the responses to more closed-ended formats (yes/no; either/or; multiple choice) appear inconsistent and unreliable. According to Sgroi (1989):

> There is no more reason to believe that a person with mental retardation will misinform or give an inaccurate response to an open-ended question than would be likely for a person with normal cognitive functioning. By contrast, the combination of cognitive impairment coupled with lifelong training toward compliance with authority figures probably increases the likelihood that persons with mental retardation will give an inaccurate response to a leading question. (p. 265)

For example, consider the following interview.

INTERVIEWER: Can you tell me what happened?
CHILD: Yes, my mother went to the store and I was home alone with Dad. He told me to take off my clothes. He took off his clothes and told me to suck his hot dog.
INTERVIEWER: Then what happened?.
CHILD: I did it, and it squirted white stuff.
INTERVIEWER: Was anyone else there?
CHILD: Yes.
INTERVIEWER: Was it just you and your Dad at home?
CHILD: Yes.
INTERVIEWER: Have you ever done this with anyone else?
CHILD: Yes.
INTERVIEWER: With Uncle Charlie?
CHILD: Yes.
INTERVIEWER: With your brother?
CHILD: Yes.

In this case, the child clearly has an acquiescent response style, so any responses to leading questions are highly suspect. Thus the interviewer does not know whether anyone else was home, and certainly should not assume that there was sexual contact with Uncle Charlie or the child's brother. At the same time, the response to the open-ended question regarding her father should not be dismissed. During that portion of the interview, the child appears to be telling her story, rather than acquiescing. She is no more likely to be misinforming than would be a child with normal cognitive functioning.

Interviewers may find it especially helpful to use visual aids when working with children with developmental disabilities. Anatomically correct drawings, anatomically correct dolls, props, and free drawing have been suggested as useful adjuncts to verbal interviews (Sgroi, 1989). It is still equally important not to "lead" the interviewee, but to use the tools in open-ended ways: "You say he touched you. Can you show me where?" "Can you draw what happened?" "Use these dolls to show me what happened last night."

Finally, as is appropriate in working with anyone reporting sexual abuse, the interviewer should monitor his or her own response to avoid communicating shock, disgust, or anger. Children with developmental disabilities who are in this overwhelming, confusing situation may be especially sensitive to these nonverbal messages and fear that the adult is disgusted or angry with them.

CONCLUSION

In sum, it is vital that professionals remember that children with disabilities are sexually abused, and thus are entitled to the same sensitivities that are granted other alleged victims of child sexual abuse. Additionally, aspects of the assessment procedures must be adapted to match the developmental level of a child. As the field learns more about investigations with children with developmental disabilities, additional specific recommendations can be made.

Recommendations

1. **THAT** professionals in this field remain aware of the pervasive myths that interfere with accurate detection, sensitive investigation, and the provision of appropriate services to children with developmental disabilities who are sexually abused.
2. **THAT** practitioners use investigation techniques that balance sensitivity and accuracy and are based on available information regarding best practice adapted to meet the needs of the individual child.
3. **THAT** research continue to inform the field regarding effective investigation and intervention techniques with this special population.

REFERENCES

Ammerman, R. T. (1990). Predisposing child factors. In R. T. Ammerman & M. Hersen (Eds.), *Children at risk: An evaluation of factors contributing to child abuse and neglect.* New York: Plenum.

Anthony, E. J. (1987). Risk, vulnerability, and resilience: An overview. In E. J. Anthony & B. J. Cohler (Eds.), *The invulnerable child.* New York: Guilford Press.

Baladerian, N. (1991). Sexual abuse of people with disabilities. *Sexuality and Disability, 9,* 323–335.

Brantlinger, E. (1988). Teachers' perceptions of the sexuality of their secondary students with mild mental retardation. *Education and Training in Mental Retardation, 3,* 24–37.

Browne, A., & Finkelhor, D. (1986). Impact of child sexual abuse: A review of the research. *Psychological Bulletin, 99,* 66–77.

Crossmaker, M. (1991). Behind locked doors–institutional sexual abuse. *Sexuality and Disability, 9,* 201–219.

Faller, K. C. (1988). Criteria for judging the credibility of children's statements about their sexual abuse. *Child Welfare, 37*(5), 389–401.

Foxx, R. M., McMorrow, M. J., Storey, K., & Rogers, B. M. (1984). Teaching social/sexual skills to mentally retarded adults. *American Journal of Mental Deficiency, 89,* 9–15.

Froemming, R., & Fuestel, J. (1991). *At greater risk: Legal issues in sexual abuse of adults with developmental disabilities.* Madison, Wis.: Wisconsin Council on Developmental Disabilities.

Gordon, S. (1971). Missing in special education: Sex. *Journal of Special Education, 5,* 351–354.

Heighwey, S., Webster, S. K., Shaw, M. (1990). *STARS: Skills training for assertiveness, relationship-building and sexual awareness.* Madison, Wis.: Wisconsin Council on Developmental Disabilities.

Hewitt, S. (1987). The abuse of deinstitutionalised persons with mental handicaps. *Disability, Handicap and Society, 2,* 127–135.

Hoorwitz, A. N. (1992). *The clinical detective: Techniques in the evaluation of sexual abuse.* New York: Norton.

Kempe, R. S., & Kempe, C. H. (1984). *The common secret: Sexual abuse of children and adolescents.* New York: Freeman.

Krents, E., Schulman, V., & Brenner, S. (1987). Child abuse and the disabled child: A parent's perspective. *Volta Review, 89,* 78–95.

Lewis, M., & MacLean, W. (1982). Issues in treating emotional disorders. In J. L. Matson & R. P. Barrett (Eds.), *Psychopathology in the mentally retarded* (pp. 1–36). New York: Grune and Stratton.

Matson, J. L., & Sevin, J. A. (1988). *Psychopathology in persons with mental retardation.* Oxford, Miss.: Behavior Intervention Specialists.

Mitchell, L., Doctor, R. M., & Butler, D. C. (1978). Attitudes of caretakers toward the sexual behavior of mentally retarded persons. *American Journal of Mental Deficiency, 83,* 289–296.

Muccigrosso, L. (1991). Sexual abuse prevention strategies and programs for persons with developmental disabilities. *Sexuality and Disability, 9,* 261–271.

O'Day, B. (1983). *Preventing sexual abuse of persons with disabilities: A curriculum for hearing impaired, physically disabled, blind, and mentally retarded students.* Santa Cruz, Calif.: Network Publications.

Patterson, P. M. (1991). *Doubly silenced: Sexuality, sexual abuse and people with developmental disabilities.* Madison, Wis.: Wisconsin Council on Developmental Disabilities.

Sgroi, S. M.(1989). Evaluation and treatment of sexual offense behavior in persons with mental retardation. In S. Sgroi (Ed.), *Vulnerable populations* (vol. 2, pp. 245–283). Lexington, Mass.: Lexington Books.

Sigelman, C. K., Budd, E. C., Spanhel, C. L., & Schoenrock, C. J. (1981a). When in doubt, say yes: Acquiescence in interviews with mentally retarded persons. *Mental Retardation, 19,* 53–58.

Sigelman, C. K., Budd, E. C., Spanhel, C. L., & Schoenrock, C. J. (1981b). Asking questions of retarded persons: A comparison of yes-no and either–or formats. *Applied Research in Mental Retardation, 2,* 347–357.

Sigelman, C. K., Budd, E. C., Winer, J. L., Schoenrock, C. J., & Martin, P. W. (1982). Evaluating alternative techniques of questioning mentally retarded persons. *American Journal of Mental Deficiency, 86,* 511–518.

Sobsey, D., & Doe, T. (1991). Patterns of sexual abuse and assault. *Sexuality and Disability, 9,* 243–259.

Sullivan, P. M., Vernon, M., & Scanlan, J. M. (1987). Sexual abuse of deaf youth. *American Annals of the Deaf, 10,* 256–261.

Tharinger, D., Horton, C.B., & Millea, S. (1990). Sexual abuse and exploitation of children and adults with mental retardation and other handicaps. *Child Abuse and Neglect, 14,* 301–312.

Varley, C. K. (1984). Schizophreniform psychoses in mentally retarded adolescent girls following sexual assault. *American Journal of Psychiatry, 141,* 593–595.

Vevier, E., & Tharinger, D. (1986). Child sexual abuse: A review and intervention framework for the school psychologist. *Journal of School Psychology, 24,* 293–311.

Wescott, H. L. (1992, May). *The disabled child witness.* Paper presented to the NATO Advanced Study Institute, "The Child Witness in Context: Cognitive, Social, and Legal Perspectives," Il Ciocco, Lucca, Italy.

Wisconsin Council on Developmental Disabilities. (1991). *Sexual abuse of adults with developmental disabilities: Legal issues and proposals for change.* Madison, Wis.: Author.

17

Assessment of Children Who May Have Been Abused: The Real World Context

Jon R. Conte

There has been increasing concern over the assessment of children for possible sexual abuse. This concern has been especially great in the case of certain children. This chapter discusses the nature of "difficult cases" that present for an assessment of possible sexual abuse, reviews selected research on key aspects of the assessment of these cases (e.g., the difference between "true" vs. "false" cases and children as witnesses), and identifies some of the real world issues and experiences that make assessment of some cases more difficult than others. Suggestions are made for research and practice in this area.

Among the many aspects of practice in child sexual abuse, the one area receiving perhaps the most attention from professionals in law, mental health,

---

Note: The term "validation" has come to be synonymous with the assessment of young children who may have been sexually abused. It is not a term I am altogether comfortable with as it implies that some official action or approval is necessary before a child and family deserve mental health intervention. Nonetheless, since it is in common usage, I will from time to time use it as a short form for "the assessment of children who may have been sexually abused."

social service, and (to a lesser extent) medicine is that of the assessment of children who may have been sexually abused. The outcome of an assessment of whether or not a child was sexually abused has important implications. For example, the outcome may determine whether or not service is provided: children who are labeled as not-abused frequently do not receive service, and yet, require service.

Additionally, errors in professional judgment may result in an abused child being diagnosed as not having been abused, or in a child who was not abused being diagnosed as abused. Either alternative places the child at risk. Similarly, such assessments may result in an adult accurately or inaccurately being identified as a sexual abuser. This may result in prosecution, stigmatization, inappropriate treatment, or other consequences. Nor is practice in this area without risks for the mental health and social service professional. Professional judgments are often under tight scrutiny from other professionals and may result in court appearances (sometimes of a frequent and intense nature) that are often hotly contested by other mental health, social service, and allied professionals.

What is known or not known from research about various aspects of assessment is often misrepresented in court. Research bearing on this work is ever increasing, (as indicated by this volume) and keeping current requires considerable energy for practitioners engaged in "real-world" work with these cases. The purpose of this chapter is to discuss the presentation of "difficult cases" where sexual abuse may have taken place and to suggest research topics that might clarify our understanding of these cases. Such an exploration is an opportunity to raise questions, concerns, and ideas for both researchers and front-line workers.

WHAT CASES ARE WE CONCERNED ABOUT?

It is helpful to place current concerns about the assessment of children who may have been abused in the context of all sexual abuse cases. Although public and professional interest has been directed toward difficult cases, it is not completely clear what constitutes a "difficult case." Practice experience suggests that such cases usually involve young children, although the same concerns are raised about older persons (and the problem of "false memory" in adult survivors of abuse). "Difficult cases" often arise in divorce or custody actions, although the same concerns raised in these cases (e.g., children make reports to confirm parental statements or beliefs) are also raised in cases in which the alleged offender and child victim(s) are not related. "Difficult cases" sometimes refer to cases in which the judgment about whether the cases are "true or false" appears particularly difficult. The case characteristics (e.g., age of child, marital status of child's parents) that make a case difficult seem to vary greatly depending on who is doing the defining, whether a defense attorney, child protection investigator, or mental health professional.

Characteristics of cases where there is little professional doubt that an allegation is true need to be understood. Although there is likely to be some cross-discipline variation in agreement, our ability to understand the characteristics that serve to verify an allegation may be helpful in understanding how cases come to be defined as "clear-cut" versus one of the "difficult cases" (that is contested, unclear, or difficult to assess).

Some of the professional literature that proposes ideas or procedures to use in validating allegations of sexual abuse is based on analysis of small samples in specialized forensic medical practices, where cases are classified anecdotally without the aid of any kind of measurement (Green, 1986). There is at least one published criticism (Corwin et al., 1987) suggesting that one of the authors in one of these reports (Green, 1986) classified as false a case that in fact should have been classified as true.

Consequently, there is little reason to believe that small samples from highly specialized clinics or practices in single locations or even large samples from single sources are representative of cases from other settings or locations. It is a well-known research maxim that samples may vary in how well they represent the population from which they are supposedly drawn. Additionally, sample characteristics should be described to determine how representative that sample is of the population of interest.

From a research point of view, our understanding of the phenomena of "contested cases" would be aided by a clearer understanding of what makes cases "difficult" so that samples could be better described along the variables of real interest. For example, if the parents' marital status and child's age and IQ make the assessment of sexual abuse "difficult," then samples should be described in terms of these factors. Research should also explore the role of these factors in assessment.

To date, much of the research data on sexual abuse focuses on the age of the victim, duration and frequency of abuse, relationship between victim and offender (alleged in the case of contested cases), and the type of sexual behavior. Such data from a large number of sites using common definitions, are helpful in increasing our understanding of sexual abuse of children and assessment of sexual abuse. Ultimately, however, some attention has to be paid to other variables (such as psychological functioning of all parties in a "difficult" case) that may be important in understanding "difficult cases." Indeed, it is likely that such cases are not a unitary phenomenon and may actually consist of subtypes defined by specific characteristics.

It would also be helpful to understand how various professional groups come to define some cases as "difficult"; to look at the extent to which the factors within disciplines correlate with the mission of that discipline (e.g., do nonmedical professionals rate medical aspects of cases as more important in defining difficult cases than do medical personnel, or do defense attorneys define a difficult case based more on a current case than on stable characteristics across cases?), or whether the factors which are important in defining "difficult cases" have some research bases.

"True" vs. "False" Cases

There has been a great deal of interest in the difference between "true" and "false" cases. For example, Benedek and Schetky (1987a, b) describe 10 false cases out of 18 and indicate that false reports are more likely to be brought forward by parents. They suggest these reports are based on parental distortions of reality, not ulterior motives. In the only study on "false" reports using reliable measurement procedures (e.g., a measure of child behavior), Horowitz, Gomes-Schwartz, and Cardarelli (1990) report on 181 cases, of which 16 were judged to be false (seven of these initiated by the child). No differences between "true" and "false" cases were found in sex or age of child. The "lying children" were more likely to come from families with higher socioeconomic status, and more likely to be Protestant. Those who made false allegations usually did so against a family member, reported intercourse more often, appeared more intelligent, and showed more delinquent behavior.

In another study, Faller (1988) reports on 103 cases in which she compared aspects of the child's statements (e.g., emotional reaction of victim consistent with abuse) to three levels of offender confession—full, partial, and indirect. The characteristics clinically attributed to a true allegation by a child include: information about the context of sexual abuse (how and where it happened) the description or demonstration of sexual victimization and emotion consistent with being victimized.

While it now appears that "false reports" are rare and, when they do occur, more likely to be initiated by adults, there are a number of problems with this literature. For example, with the exception of Horowitz et al. (1990) and Faller (1988), there has been little effort, even when criteria for discriminating between false and true cases are provided, to identify the specific criteria that discriminate between true and false cases. No study provides us with an estimate of the reliability of classification into true and false groups. We are asked to accept on faith that the investigators are accurate in their classification.

Most critically, there appears to be no external standard for what is a true and what is a false case. Although Faller (1988) provides an innovative approach to the external criterion by making comparisons within the sample, there are no data supporting the proposition that there are reliable differences in the characteristics of true and false statements about sexual abuse made by a child. Indeed, Faller (1988) reports that statements made by children in 6.5% of cases where there was a full confession by the offender (N=4) lacked any of the characteristics that are thought to make a statement true, such as sexual knowledge in a child's statements or behavior that is inappropriate for a child's developmental age.

The inability to verify whether a report of sexual abuse is true or false has profound implications for both researchers and practitioners. Yet, "true" or "false" may not be the best way to think about the difficult cases. There may be cases where it is never clear what did or did not happen, or what is "true" or "false."

Emphasizing "true" or "false" cases creates further problems. In cases with legal involvement, the determination of truth, at least truth as it is defined in the court, lies with the trier of fact (Melton & Limber, 1989). However, there are cases where allegations have been made, but legal evidence and psychosocial information supporting the allegations vary. Although a clear, definite determination will not be possible, the child and adults in the case still need service. A simple dichotomous diagnosis (true or false, substantiated or unsubstantiated) serves to prevent such cases from getting service. If nothing else, a three part determination—substantiated, not-substantiated-but-needing-service, and unsubstantiated—would increase the possibility that service will be provided as needed.

More central to our discussion here, it would be extremely helpful if some effort could be given to developing an empirically generated topology to describe difficult cases. Such a topology might include: (1) case characteristic information, such as age, developmental level, and psychological profile of alleged victim and adult parties to the case; (2) a classification of the service needs of the child and family—e.g., needs supportive counseling to explore abuse allegations further, or parent needs therapy to deal with own issues, or child and mother need concrete resources away from alleged offender; and (3) a description of additional relevant factors, including nature of alleged abuse, course of disclosure, relationship between alleged offender and alleged victim, etc.

PRESENTATION OF CASES TO PROFESSIONALS

Cases in which a child may have been sexually abused present to the mental health and social service professional with considerable variation in characteristics that may or may not influence the assessment process. Professional understanding of the validation process would be aided by greater understanding of how these characteristics influence both the child as witness and the validation/assessment process.

Child Victim

Probably that area of assessment that has received the most attention in courts and in the scientific literature is that of the child as witness. This research builds on a long line of eyewitness research. However, as Goodman, Aman, and Hirschman (1987) have pointed out, much of the eyewitness literature is not directly applicable to the situation of a child who may have been abused (see also Ceci & Bruck, 1993). For example, much of the research is based on exposing subjects in an artificial situation, such as a university laboratory, to a novel stimulus (e.g., a white dog walking across a playing field), conditions that lack any personal significance to the subject. Moreover, since much abuse (as much as 70%) takes place more than one time, abused children are not passive witnesses but have direct involvement in the activity, and the event to be remembered is real abuse, not artificial (remembering details of a story).

Nonetheless, recent research has tried to more closely duplicate the situation of the abused child by involving stimulus material with some degree of trauma, such as inoculations (Saywitz, Goodman, Nicholas, & Moan, 1991). Goodman et al. (1987) summarize the research: 1) children are more suggestible than adults, especially young children (three years old and younger); 2) adults recall more information, but they recall both correct and incorrect information; 3) young children are quite accurate in free recall, but don't recall as much information as adults; 4) children are more likely to elaborate on correct responses than on incorrect responses; 5) stress does not appear to interfere with memory; 6) younger children do have less ability to answer objective and suggestive questions accurately and their ability deteriorates over time; 7) free recall is more accurate than cued recall, but free recall does not elicit as much information; 8) if cued recall is necessary, questions that allow for multiple-choice answers are better than yes/no or short answers; and 9) there is no evidence that children make up false stories.

Recent research by Ceci and colleagues (Ceci & Bruck, 1993) recognizes the methodological problems in conducting research on children as witnesses, and while this research approximates the real-world experience of children who may have been abused by increasing the salience of the experienced events, methodological problems still exist. For example, in one study, a stranger, "Sam Stone," made a two-minute visit to young children (ages three to six) in a day-care center. Children were interviewed four times over a 10-week period. One month following the fourth interview, a new interviewer using "forensic procedures" asked the children about two "non-events," which involved the stranger doing things to a teddy bear and book. (Stranger Sam had done nothing to the bear or book). A second group of children were given a "stereotype" about Sam before his visit. The author suggests, "We did this to mimic the sort of stereotypes that some child witnesses have acquired about actual defendants" (p. 14). The "stereotyping" had an effect.

Forty-two percent claimed, in response to suggestive questioning, that Stranger Sam had ripped the book or soiled the bear. Of the youngest children, 19% claimed to have seen Stranger Sam do the misdeeds.

While this research and other work in the same tradition are helpful in cautioning interviewers about "stereotyping," suggestive questioning, and the like, the "experienced" events are still quite dissimilar to sexual-abuse experiences. In the Stranger Sam study, destruction and soiling of property are likely to be nearly universal experiences of childhood. The effects of poor interviewing techniques on children's reports of common (destroying property) vs. uncommon (vaginal rape) childhood experiences may be different.

Mostly critically, the real forensic question is how an interviewer (or other adults) can distinguish between a child's report of a real event and one of an unreal experience (that may have been constructed by suggestive questioning). No amount of research demonstrating that human beings can be led, manipulated, or tricked into saying that something happened when it did not happen assists us in knowing if what a child describes is accurate.

To date, age of the child has been the primary variable examined in research on children's capacities as witnesses. This has had a real-world foundation since state laws have tended to specify an age after which children were presumed to be competent to testify, and because children are often attacked as incapable of saying what happened to them because of age alone. However, it may not be age alone that accounts for variation in children's abilities to report events. Within the same age, children's abilities may vary by IQ or developmental capabilities. For example, perhaps children who have started to read have already begun the process of learning how to store and retrieve information from memory. Preexisting psychological conditions within the child, such as depression, anxiety, conduct disorders, or dissociation may interfere with or heighten a child's capacity to recall events.

In addition, a child's social standing and pattern of relationships in a family or peer group may influence what the child reports about family members or peers. Especially in cases where some children in a group report abuse and some children in the same group do not, an analysis of peer-group membership may be helpful. Such an analysis may assist in understanding if children within a peer group were alone or together at a time that they may have been abused, or if the children's reports represent a shared story or misrepresentation by the group based on the statements of one significant peer leader in the group (Goodman & Schwartz-Kenney, 1992).

There is much that child victims who are not the subjects of contested cases can tell us about how children perceive abuse, what they can remember, why they tell, when they tell, and how they choose to disclose. Clinically, it is recognized that children often make more or less conscious decisions about telling. For example, a child may not tell about abuse to protect a parent or sibling, or a child may tell because she sees the offender grooming a sibling for abuse. There has been little systematic effort to learn what abused children can tell us about the disclosure process.

Investigations examining aspects of the abused child that may influence the ability of a child to recall, report, or elaborate must carefully frame the findings, since there may well be psychological conditions, such as dissociation, depression, or withdrawal from friends and activities, that negatively impact on ability to recall real events. These conditions, however, may result from abuse and not from preexisting factors. Research examining such factors may well begin with children who have not been abused and, in time, move on to the study of these factors in abused children who are not the subject of legal proceedings at the time of study. In this way, research will move beyond efforts to discredit children (e.g., by studying suggestibility) toward a comprehensive understanding of when, how, and under what conditions children fail to disclose abuse, disclose abuse, and are led by adults to make "false" disclosures.

Child's Family

The influence of a family on a child's report requires more extensive investigation. In part because of the failure of early "family" views on incest (Conte, 1986) to accurately portray the nature of sexual abuse of children and partly because of the difficulty of accurately assessing predisclosure family functioning, insufficient attention has been paid to what virtually every mental health professional recognizes as an important aspect of young children—their family (see Chapter 15, this volume).

The disclosure of sexual abuse is a crisis for most families. Denial, repression, and avoidance are well-known mechanisms used by adults to protect themselves from anxiety-producing events. For parents, abuse of a child is a significant traumatic event that may elicit feelings of anger, failure, depression, and the like. For other parents, abuse of a child may trigger feelings of their own child abuse. When the offender is a family member, a range of additional emotions may be experienced, including conflicted loyalties and betrayal. The assessment of families at the time of disclosure may not adequately assess predisclosure functioning, although research on the assessment of families at various points in time (pre-, during, and posttrauma) would be useful in understanding this issue. Nonetheless, aspects of the family may be associated with a number of factors that may influence a child's ability to remember, report, and explain events. These factors may well have complex relationships with children's reports; they may inhibit the report of abuse, or confuse or distort the report.

One might speculate that in cases where a family member is the offender, family dynamics may be more powerfully associated with the child's ability to report. There are a number of factors that deserve to be investigated to determine if they have some relationship with children's reports of abuse. These include: (1) the relationship between the child's family of origin and extended family; (2) the quality of intrafamily relationships; (3) the resources available to the family (e.g., Can Mom support the children and herself without the alleged offender in the home?); (4) the psychological history of the individual family members; and (5) the history and quality of the marital relationship (especially when one partner is the alleged offender). Such factors might be associated with what children report, how willing they are to report abuse, or what they say about abuse.

In a significant effort to shed light on mothers as "accomplices" in child sexual abuse cases, Gomes-Schwartz, Horowitz, and Cardarelli (1990) report that 80% of mothers in their clinic sample took some action to protect their child when abuse was disclosed. Mothers were the least protective and most angry and punitive toward the child when the abuser was not a biological father. Mothers exhibited no single personality pattern (in fact only 18% had a prior psychiatric history), although significant proportions had major symptoms of submission (21%), emotional lability (25%), social withdrawal (19%), reality distortion (13%), and negativism (15%). Further, a mother's history of relationships had some impact on her ability to protect her child. Thus, mothers with a history of abuse with their own fathers were less capable of taking protective action.

The focus here is how psychological factors may influence the child's report of abuse. This type of research may have considerable payoff toward understanding assessment of children who may have been abused. Children, even quite young children, are capable of knowing what parents want and what they can handle. A few days before this paragraph was written, a mother in a parent group told me that her child told her that the child's father could not handle her disclosure of what he had done to her. Protecting her father's fragile emotional makeup was more important than telling other people what he had actually done to her. This child's sense of her father as a weak, dependent adult needing to be taken care of was consistent with how his ex-wife saw him. Research may well identify a host of psychological factors in various family members that are associated with children's abilities or willingness to report.

Clearly, there are many intra- and interpersonal factors that may influence children's reports of events. It may be instructive to explore what children indicate their parent(s) (and other professionals) wanted them to say, whether this is consistent with what, in fact, the child said, and what the child thought the consequence to the parent and others would be if the child had revealed what did or did not happen. In short, exploring other aspects of the child's perception of a parent's and family's emotional and psychological life will render useful information.

Service Provider's History

Cases come to the attention of professionals after a variety of previous professional contacts. In the survey of 212 professionals reported by Conte, Fogarty, and Collins (1991), 24% of children had been interviewed by one other professional before contact with the professional completing the survey. Contacts with professionals prior to the assessment, as well as interactions with significant adults in the environment, may influence children's reports. There is little understanding of how contact with professionals may influence what a child reports to another professional. Such influence, likely in some cases, may suppress willingness to report or may result in "false" reports. Insensitive interviewing, promises made to a child that are not kept (e.g., tell me what happened and you will be protected), and unintentionally induced versions of events may influence what children recall or are willing to report. Most useful would be research investigating children's resistance to suggestion, the incorporation of experimenter versions of events, and the ability of children to sort out what was real and what was induced by the experimenter, and how these change over time with various types of children.

Professional belief and behavior have been looked upon as benign sources of influence, except when defense attorneys have tried to raise questions about the processes used to support disclosure. Although I am aware of only preliminary data supporting such claims that children can be led by professionals to make false reports, it seems naive to assume that professional effects do not exist. Everson and Boat (unpublished manuscript) have reported that Child Protective Service (CPS) workers who had recently seen cases of false reports were more likely to question children's veracity than CPS workers who had not recently seen false cases. Conte et al. (1991) report that some professional knowledge is at considerable variance from what research evidence suggests, especially in terms of knowledge about sexual offenders (see Chapter 14, this volume). A better understanding of how children react to adult versions of events, of how children understand aspects of the disclosure and intervention process (for example, no contact orders), and of the ways that professional knowledge and bias appear in these cases will help the field begin to understand the potential influences of professional intervention.

Indeed, investigation of professional behavior, its absence, and its impact on children may be quite helpful. There has been little research on professional relationships and their influence on case outcome. Nor has there been investigation of the influence of prior reports from selected professionals on other professionals' behavior. Within communities, certain agencies and individuals develop reputations for competent or less than competent work. If a professional evaluates a case and relies, in part, on a report from a prior agency with a good reputation, is greater weight placed on this prior report than on one from an agency with a less competent reputation? Indeed, how is reputation established and how accurate is it? How accurate are prior reports and how do they influence subsequent professional activities?

I have read any number of reports that seem to paint a conclusive picture that a child was abused, only to learn that the reports omitted significant details about the child's situation or the assessment process. A CPS investigator once told me that she was going to substantiate a report against a father because she knew "he is guilty, he reminds me of my ex-husband." What impact will a substantiated child abuse report have on subsequent assessments of this case, especially given that the reader of subsequent reports will not have the workers' verbal statements for the basis of the substantiation? A professional who has evaluated hundreds of children and has an excellent local reputation, testified in court that she knew a child had been abused because the child used red ink in drawings. I am aware of no data supporting such a statement. What effect will the conclusion of this professional have on the court or on other professionals?

While these "horror" stories may or may not be rare examples of professional practice, they illustrate the profound power that professionals exercise in these cases. The following characteristics of professional behavior need to be investigated: 1) professional decision making, 2) factors that predict various judgments; 3) the level of knowledge in various professionals and how this is related to case recommendations; 4) levels of agreement among different disciplines working in the same case; and 5) how individual worker personality and other psychological variables are associated with case outcome. Answers to such questions will provide greater understanding about the factors that influence the assessment of children who may have been abused.

CONCLUSION

If one of the first tasks of science is description, the science that supports the assessment of children who may have been sexually abused has much to accomplish. Large N, multisite studies using common definitions and measurement procedures directed toward describing the cases that present for an assessment of possible sexual abuse should be encouraged. It would be extremely helpful if such studies assessed cases along a number of dimensions to determine how these dimensions interact and how they are associated with various outcomes of assessment. In this chapter, a number of possible dimensions have been suggested. These include: 1) aspects of the target child, including IQ, specific developmental capabilities, psychological functioning, etc.; 2) aspects of the child's family, such as marital relationships, relationships between parents and extended family, amount of resources available, and quality of intrafamily relationships; and 3) aspects of the service history of the case, including number and nature of prior professional contacts, level of training of previous professionals, and previous outcomes of assessment.

Although there are many variables subsumed within these domains, it is not beyond the capability of our science to sort and group these into meaningful subcategories. Such an effort might result in a classification of cases within a multidimensional system describing case characteristics, child and family characteristics, and previous professional contact. Such a classification at intake might ultimately lead to an assessment process designed to assess each of the dimensions of relevance in a case.

Recommendations

1. **THAT** each professional who seeks to know if a child has been sexually abused should carefully analyze what characteristics of a case make such an assessment particularly "difficult" for the professional. These characteristics should be held up against the existing body of research to determine what is known about the relationship between those characteristics and sexual abuse.
2. **THAT** it is very unlikely that any assessment procedure or "validation model" will ever be 100% accurate in classifying a case as either abused or not abused. Professionals should be cautious in not overvaluing untested models.
3. **THAT** in many cases the absence of a clear indication that a child was abused should not keep the child from receiving other indicated social and mental health services.
4. **THAT** no existing research on the abilities of children to report events directly deals with the critical forensic assessment issue of knowing whether or not a child's statement is an accurate description of events. The implications of research on children as witnesses should not be misapplied to this critical assessment question.

REFERENCES

Benedek, E. P., & Schetky, D. H. (1987a). Problems validating allegations of sexual abuse: I. Factors affecting perception and recall of events. *Journal of the American Academy of Child and Adolescent Psychiatry, 26*(6), 912–915.

Benedek, E. P., & Schetky, D. H. (1987b). Problems validating allegations of sexual abuse: II. Clinical evaluation. *Journal of the American Academy of Child and Adolescent Psychiatry, 26*(6), 916–921.

Ceci, S. J., & Bruck, M. E. (1993). Child witnesses: Translating research into policy. *Social Policy Report, 20*(10), 34–38.

Conte, J. R. (1986). Child sexual abuse and the family: A critical analysis. *Journal of Psychotherapy and the Family, 2*(2), 113–126.

Conte, J. R., & Berliner, L. (1981). Sexual abuse of children: Implications for practice. *Social Casework, 67*(10), 601–606.

Conte, J. R., Fogarty, L., & Collins, M. (1991). National survey of professional practice in child sexual abuse. *Journal of Family Violence, 6*(2), 149–166.

Conte, J. R., Wolf, S., & Smith, T. (1989). What sexual offenders tell us about prevention. *Child Abuse and Neglect, 13*(2), 293-302.

Corwin, D. L., Berliner, L., Goodman, G., et al. (1987). Child sexual abuse and custody disputes: No easy answers. *Journal of Interpersonal Violence, 2*(1), 91–105.

Everson & Boat (Unpublished manuscript)

Faller, K. (1988). Criteria for judging the credibility of children's statements about their sexual abuse. *Child Welfare, 67*(5), 389–401.

Goodman, G., Aman, C., & Hirschman, J. (1987) Child sexual and physical abuse: Children's testimony. In S. J. Ceci, M. P. Toglia, & D. F. Ross (Eds.), *Children's eyewitness memory* (pp. 1–23). New York: Springer-Verlag.

Goodman, G. S., & Schwartz-Kenney, B. (1992). Why knowing a child's age is not enough. In H. Dent & R. Flynn (Eds.), *Children as witnesses* (pp. 15–32). New York: Wiley.

Gomes-Schwartz, B., Horowitz, J. M., & Cardarelli, A.P. (1990). *Child sexual abuse: The initial effects.* Newbury Park, Calif.: Sage.

Green, A. (1986). True and false allegations of sexual abuse in child custody disputes. *Journal of the American Academy of Child Psychiatry, 25*, 449–456.

Melton, G. B., & Limber, S. (1989). Psychologists' involvement in cases of child maltreatment: Limits of role and expertise. *American Psychologist, 44*, 1225–1233.

Saywitz, K., Goodman, G. S., Nicholas, E., & Moan, S. (1991). Children's memories of physical examination involving genital touch: Implications for reports of child sexual abuse. *Journal of Consulting and Clinical Psychology, 59*, 682–691.

18

The Assessment and Investigation of Ritual Abuse

Grant Charles

A divisive debate has arisen in the professional community regarding the existence of ritual abuse. There has been a split between those who believe the accounts of the victims and survivors and those who maintain that the reports are delusional or factious. The current controversy has created confusion among clinicians, child-protection workers, and criminal justice personnel. This chapter provides an overview of the issue and makes recommendations regarding assessment and investigation directions.

During the past few years, there have been numerous reports by child victims and adult survivors of what has been, at various times, labeled ritual, ritualistic, cultic, or satanic abuse (Cook, 1991; Hudson, 1990; Kelley, 1989, 1990; Smith & Pazder, 1980). These people have given horrific accounts of sexual, physical, psychological, and spiritual maltreatment. Clinicians, child-protection authorities, and criminal justice personnel have had to deal increasingly with such allegations. However, their ability to respond effectively has been handicapped by often contradictory information regarding the problem. This chapter provides a review of the current knowledge of ritual abuse, along with an overview of some of the complex and controversial concerns involved in the issue.

THE EXISTENCE OF RITUAL ABUSE

There is a great deal of discussion in the helping and criminal justice professions on whether ritual abuse actually occurs. For the most part, the debate is not so much about whether some children at various times have been abused in extreme ways; most professionals would agree that there are people who are quite capable of inflicting terrible abuse on children. Rather, the disagreement tends to focus upon whether the alleged abuse is as widespread, organized, and severe as some have stated. Unfortunately, many of the professionals have taken polarized positions that leave no middle ground: ritual abuse is rampant, or ritual abuse does not exist.

The consequence of this polarization is that clinicians must rely on information from the "experts" at either extreme of the issue. For therapists first becoming involved with individuals who claim they have been ritually abused, these polarized views complicate a situation that is already difficult. There is a need to go beyond such positions as, "Everything that is alleged must be a delusion, a confabulation, or a lie" or, "Everything that is alleged must be completely believed."

Those who maintain that ritual abuse does not exist point out that it was not until the publication of *Michelle Remembers* by Smith and Pazder in 1980 that any mention of this form of abuse began to surface (Hicks, 1991). However, Kent (1993) has uncovered a 1959 account in a Canadian newspaper that mentions human sacrifice. There also appear to be historical accounts of similar types of activity dating back to ancient and medieval times (Driscoll & Wright, 1990; Kent, 1993; Layton, 1987). It is extremely difficult to make valid comparisons or connections between past reports and current allegations because of our inability to verify the previous accounts. Many of the older accounts, while they may or may not be true, are clouded by the religious and cultural contexts in which they were written. Indeed, the debate as to whether ritual abuse is a recent phenomenon or a historical, but recently uncovered, one is irrelevant in terms of determining the validity of the current allegations.

It is possible that these polarized debates arise because of the extreme nature of the allegations, which are often unsettling, and at times unbelievable. Some of the material being reported, including the practice of cutting people up and then reassembling them (Lanning, 1991), is remarkable; however, much of what is alleged, such as various bizarre sexual and religious practices, has been documented in both ancient and modern times (Daraul, 1990; Eskapa, 1987; Homes, 1991; Kent, 1993). The unbelievable nature of the allegations does not necessarily detract from the validity of an individual's account, just as the believability of an allegation does not necessarily make it true.

DEFINITION

Perhaps not surprisingly, there is no consensus on the definition of ritual abuse. In a general sense, it has been defined as the "sexual molestation of children, usually by multiple perpetrators, in conjunction with rituals that ceremonially evoke magical or supernatural powers" (Nurcombe & Unutzer, 1991, p. 272). But this definition is somewhat limiting in that it precludes other forms of abuse as being components. Kelley (1989) addresses this concern by suggesting that ritual abuse is the "repetitive and systematic sexual, physical and psychological abuse of children by adults as part of cult or satanic worship" (p. 502). While more precise than the previous definition, it emphasizes a religious motivation for the activities. This is problematic in that, while the motivations of the perpetrators may be religious in nature, they may just as easily be financial or sexual. Some of the perpetrators may be involved in the worship of a deity, whereas others may be using the religious trappings of the abuse as a means of controlling the victims in order to ensure their cooperation for financial or sexual gain.

Lanning (1989, 1991) suggests that ritual abuse should not be seen as a separate classification. He argues that from a criminal justice point of view, there is no need for specific statutes dealing with ritual abuse, as the perpetrators' actions are illegal under existing child sexual and physical abuse laws. There is some benefit to this idea in terms of removing the religious aspect from the argument, since its inclusion can evoke a strong emotional reaction that can complicate the investigation of the allegations. It also implies that the worship of a particular god is illegal or that nonmainstream religions may be, by association, abusive.

The most widely accepted definition includes the term ritualistic abuse. Finkelhor and Williams (1988) use this term to refer to any abuse that "occurs in a context linked to some symbols or group activity that have a religious, magical, or supernatural connotation, and where the invocation of these symbols or activities, repeated over time, is used to frighten and intimidate the children" (p. 59). This definition recognizes the religious context of the abuse without suggesting that the motivation of the perpetrator is necessarily based on a religious belief. More work is needed in developing a definition that ensures that professionals working in the area are operating from the same reference point in order to assist in the detection, assessment, and study of the problem.

PREVALENCE

There are those who believe that ritual abuse is a pervasive, epidemic problem that is symptomatic of a wider, satanic conspiracy to take control of society (Core & Harrison, 1991; Raschke, 1990). There are also those, on the other extreme, who suggest that apart from victim and survivor accounts, there is little or no evidence to suggest that ritual abuse exists, and that, if it does exist, it is rare (Hicks, 1991; Lanning, 1991).

In actual fact, the prevalence of ritual abuse is difficult to determine owing to a number of factors. First, there is no central tracking system for reports of ritual abuse so that allegations are not necessarily recorded anywhere other than in clinical notes. This is likely to be the case with many adult disclosures. Child disclosures are often tracked under general abuse categories, and as such are not officially recorded as ritual abuse. Second, it is possible that practitioners are mistaking indicators of ritual abuse for indicators of other forms of abuse (Kelley, 1989; Snow & Sorenson, 1990). Also, some professionals mistake such disclosures, because of their horrible details, as signs of delusional or severe pathological conditions (Cozolino, 1989). It is critical that investigators and clinicians working in this area have an appropriate level of training that will enable them to distinguish between delusional and nondelusional thinking.

DYNAMICS

Ritual abuse is a complex combination of abuses ranging from sexual, physical, and psychological mistreatment, to religious oppression. The abuse usually involves multiple perpetrators and victims and generally takes place within the context of a religious or pseudoreligious ceremony (Nurcombe & Unutzer, 1991). It tends to be highly intrusive and pervasive, and often appears to be quite sophisticated and terrifying (Cozolino, 1989; Kelley, 1989). The abuse also seems to meet more than one need of the perpetrators, such as sexual or sadistic gratification, the furthering of a religious belief, or as a way controlling and silencing the victims (Cozolino, 1989, 1990; Finkelhor & Williams, 1988; Kelley, 1989).

The ritual abuse strategies take many forms. Generally speaking, the psychological and physical abuses seem to be intended to terrorize the victims, thus ensuring compliance and silence. Victims and survivors have reported being buried alive or placed in confined spaces such as coffins, open graves, or cages, often with animals, insects or reptiles, or what appear to be human or animal remains (Cook, 1991; Driscoll & Wright, 1990; Hudson, 1991). There have also been reports of systematic torture using electric shock; puncturing with needles for the purpose of withdrawing blood, inflicting pain, or injecting drugs; or inserting wooden or metal objects into body cavities (Cook, 1991; Hudson, 1991).

Further reports describe children as being forced to ingest excrement, urine, semen, and blood (Finkelhor & Williams, 1988; Fraser, 1990; Hudson, 1990;

Kelley, 1989; Snow & Sorenson, 1990), or made to eat what they believe to be human flesh (Cook, 1991; Cozolino, 1990; Driscoll & Wright, 1990). There are descriptions of children being defecated, urinated, or ejaculated upon or having blood ritualistically poured on them. Victims have also told of taking part in ceremonies involving animal or human sacrifice (Cook, 1991; Cozolino, 1989; Hudson, 1990, 1991; Jonker & Jonker-Bakker, 1991; Snow & Sorenson, 1990). Many female survivors maintain that they were used as "breeders" whose function it was to provide fetuses and infants for sacrificial purposes (Cook, 1991; Driscoll & Wright, 1990).

Victims and survivors frequently report that they were threatened with mutilation, supernatural harm, or the death of themselves or of significant people in their lives, such as parents or siblings (Cook, 1991; Cozolino, 1989; Kelley, 1989). Many of the threats seem to serve to heighten normal childhood fears (Finkelhor & Williams, 1988). As with physical abuse, these threats are meant to ensure compliance and silence.

The sexual abuse of the children ranges from fondling, oral–genital sex, and vaginal and anal intercourse (Finkelhor & Williams, 1988) to bestiality and necrophilia (Driscoll & Wright, 1990). There have also been reports of children being filmed for pornographic purposes (Nurcombe & Ununtzer, 1991). The abuse often involves multiple perpetrators and victims of both sexes, and frequently includes forced sexual activity between the children (Cook, 1991; Driscoll & Wright, 1990; Finkelhor & Williams, 1988; Hudson, 1991; Jonker & Jonker-Baker, 1991; Kelley, 1989).

The abuses often take place within the context of religious ceremonies in which Christian practices are reversed and defiled (Driscoll & Wright, 1990; Fraser, 1990). Indeed, Kent (1993) has suggested that the rituals may be inspired by deviant interpretations of Judeo-Christian religious texts. Many include the use of so-called occult-related materials, such as animal horns, animal and human body parts, candles, and pentagrams, as well as chants and prayers to various deities (Finkelhor & Williams, 1988; Fraser, 1990). Although this has resulted in the labeling of the rituals as satanic, which may be true of many of them, there are also reports of abuses in seemingly Christian-oriented cults (Cook, 1991). It is important as well to note that the use of such materials by certain religious groups does not necessarily mean that their members are ritual-abuse perpetrators.

Adults have been described as wearing masks and robes (Driscoll & Wright, 1990) and as dressing as authority figures such as police officers (Cook, 1991) or as cartoon characters (Finkelhor & Williams, 1988). The purpose of these actions may be to intimidate and confuse the children or to decrease their credibility in the event of a disclosure. In any case, the costumes serve to disguise the perpetrators, thus making identification difficult.

While there is no doubt that many of the abuses are carried out to meet the sexual and/or religious needs of the perpetrators, there may be alterna-

tive explanations for the more extreme behaviors. Cozolino (1989) has speculated that the abuses may be a means to bind the child to the group by sever-
ing his or her ties with mainstream belief systems. Nurcombe and Unutzer
(1991) have suggested that many of the extreme and persistent abuses are
purposeful attempts to induce dissociative reactions in the children, thus ensuring victim silence and cooperation. Pervasive and severe abuse seems to
trigger in some people a psychological fragmentation whereby they lose conscious awareness of the abuse (Burgess, Hartman, Wolbert, & Grant, 1987). It
also may be true that the forced mutual abuse of the children by one another
further ensures victim silence by turning victims into perpetrators. Whatever
the reasons for the abuses, submission to the power of the group appears to
be the only option for the children. The oppressive techniques employed
render the child powerless.

INDICATORS

As with other forms of abuse, there is a need to develop a set of indicators
in order to facilitate the detection, assessment, and treatment of people who
have been ritually abused. Accurate diagnosis allows for more effective intervention. Gould (1992) has developed a set of symptoms and signs of ritual
abuse that appear to be the most widely referenced indicators. They are divided into 12 broad categories, and include problems and/or fears associated with the following.

1. Sexual behavior and beliefs
2. Toileting and the bathroom
3. The supernatural, rituals, occult symbols, and religion
4. Small spaces and being tied up
5. Death
6. The doctor's office
7. Certain colors
8. Eating
9. Emotional problems
10. Family relationships
11. Play and peer relationships
12. Miscellaneous fears, which often take the form of strange beliefs

Within each of Gould's categories are numerous indicators that will not be
duplicated here. However, it is important to note that many of the behaviors
would be considered indicators of "mainstream" abuse, and as such are no
different than would be found in a sexually abused but not ritually abused

child. It should be noted the Gould's sample size was relatively small and as she notes "hardly represents a controlled study of ritual abuse survivors" (p. 201). It is, therefore, unknown whether these indicators are generalizable to other people who have been ritually abused.

Many of the other indicators mentioned in the literature are problematic. Behaviors such as age-inappropriate sexual knowledge or behaviors, night terrors, somatic complaints, soiling, regression, and anxiety (Finkelhor & Williams, 1988; Nurcombe & Unutzer, 1991; Snow & Sorenson, 1990) are identical to the behaviors one could find in any traumatized child. There are also indicators, such as eating problems, dissociative disorders, self-destructive behaviors, which could be connected with severe, nonritualistic, abusive experiences. The indicators that deal with occult activity appear to be the only ones that are exclusively associated with ritual abuse.

The issue of indicators is made even more complex by the suggestion that some victims may present as asymptomatic (Snow & Sorenson, 1990). It may be that these individuals have dissociated their experiences to such an extent that they are able to maintain a resemblance of normality on a daily basis. For an inexperienced caseworker, this could mean that children who are dissociating their experiences may be difficult to diagnosis. Similarly, an emotional numbing may become manifest as a shock reaction to the traumatic events, which means that the child may appear to be symptom-free. Thus it would appear that an understanding of dissociation and posttraumatic stress reactions is critical in order to be able to assess accurately the possibility of severe abuse (Terr, 1990). Both require further research.

Any discussion of indicators needs to conclude with a reminder that they are often misused and misunderstood. They are not diagnostic tools, but rather, at best, guideposts that may indicate that some kind of abuse has occurred. As mentioned, many of the behaviors considered indicators of ritual abuse can be found in other mainstream and clinical populations. Checklists of symptoms put forth without consideration of such factors as a child's age and developmental level can contribute to suggestions of abuse, where, in fact, there is none.

ASSESSMENT AND INVESTIGATION

It is critical to make a distinction between the role of a clinical assessor and that of a child-protection or criminal justice investigator. A clinician, whose function is treatment, is able to accept the statement of a victim based on internal measures of validity, such as a congruency in the person's affect, symptoms, or allegations (Greaves, 1992). Are the clinicians observations consistent with what is being alleged? Child-protection workers and criminal justice personnel, owing to the nature of their work, are usually required to use external measures of proof, such as medical indicators of abuse or the confession of an abuser. The question here is, "Will the gathered evidence be accepted in a court of law?" Too often, the necessity for the two types of validation is misunderstood.

No specific diagnostic tool is available by which clinicians can determine whether a young person has been ritualistically abused. Mangen (1992) reports some success in assessing adult survivors using the Wechsler Adult Intelligence Scale–Revised, the Rorshcach Inkblot Test, and the Thematic Apperception Test, combined with other projective tests. However, there is no agreed-upon profile of a ritual abuse victim—which is as one would expect. The impact of trauma depends on a variety of variables, such as a child's age at the onset of the abuse, the pervasiveness and regularity of the abuse, internal strengths and external supports, and other related environmental factors.

The key to diagnosis for the clinician may be to look for indications of dissociative experiences on the part of the young person. While these experiences are not exclusively limited to ritual abuse victims, there is growing evidence that many survivors have responded to their abuse by psychologically removing themselves from the threatening situation (Mangen, 1992). Questioning of the individual regarding dissociative experiences such as consistent lapses in memory may prove helpful as a beginning point of diagnosis.

Another important related diagnostic strategy relates to the manifestation of severe trauma-related symptoms. Many adult ritual abuse survivors show strong posttrauma reactions that may be diagnosed as dissociative identity disorder or posttraumatic stress disorder. Any sign of extreme, unusual behavior in children may be a useful guide for diagnosing the possibility of ritualistic abuse. However, clinicians should note that these behaviors may be, but are not necessarily, related to ritual abuse, and that there may be other reasons for the behaviors.

It has also been suggested that ritual abuse should be considered in any situation involving multiple perpetrators and multiple victims (Snow & Sorenson, 1990). These authors recommend, as well, that the possibility of ritual abuse be considered if, in intrafamilial abuse situations, a parent has abused his or her children collectively, or the children have been forced to abuse each other.

Despite these diagnostic guidelines, a confident diagnosis of ritual abuse can only be made if the victim or survivor discloses that such abuse actually took place, or if the perpetrators confess. No matter how strongly a clinician may suspect ritual abuse, he or she cannot be sure of it without confirmation by the young person. However, disclosures of abuse and extreme abuse involving threats are not often made spontaneously or concurrently. This creates a problem for the assessor in that he or she may be convinced that an abuse has occurred, yet has not been able to elicit a disclosure from the individual. It is critical that the disclosure be offered freely and not be the result of intrusive or aggressive questioning on the part of the clinician. It is also important that the young person feel in control of the situation.

Confirmation of abuse through a disclosure is very difficult to accomplish. Kelley (1989) has reported that a purposeful and spontaneous disclosure is rare. This is attributable to a variety of factors, such as the rise of threats by the perpetrators to intimidate the victims, the fear of not being believed because of the bizarre nature of the abuse, and anxiety that the victims themselves will get into trouble because of the mutual abuse in which they participated (Cook, 1991; Snow & Sorenson, 1990). For these reasons, it is imperative that clinicians provide an environment that facilitates disclosure—one that ensures that the young person will not be rushed into making statements in order to meet the assessor's need to confirm or disconfirm the allegations. Such sensitivity can make assessment a time-consuming process.

The objectives of child-protection workers and criminal justice personnel are somewhat different from those of clinicians. While the clinician uses assessment to develop a course of treatment, child-protection agencies and criminal justice personnel focus on whether certain activities are in violation of the law. Lanning (1989) has recommended that investigators deal only with the aspects of the alleged activities that fall under the criminal law. As such, he suggests that it is important to minimize the religious or pseudoreligious aspects and concentrate on the legal aspects of the case. He reminds investigators that it is also essential that they keep their investigative role separate from their personal religious beliefs. For example, some investigators may harbor a literal belief in Satan and feel that they have a spiritual responsibility to combat evil that supersedes their corporeal responsibilities. But regardless of a person's personal perspective, the investigation must focus on the child-protection and criminal justice frame of reference.

The clinician and the investigator share some common concerns. Both need to refrain from using coercive information-gathering techniques. The offer of rewards for providing "correct" answers, repetitive questioning, demands for the truth, threats, and the refusal to accept a given answer should all be avoided (Robin, 1991).

Clinicians and investigators also need to be aware of the possibility of contagion, malingering, or coaching (Lanning, 1992; Robin, 1991). Contagion or the contamination of information can occur during assessments or investigations if the clinicians or investigators ask leading questions or provide information to the victims rather than allowing free recall. Malingering is noted when the individual making the allegation has alternative goals, such as profit or the exaggeration of symptoms or circumstances as a means of soliciting attention. While profit is unlikely to be a motive for younger children, this author has met older adolescents who appear to be "showboating" their "symptoms" and alleged occult activity for personal gain.

Coaching serves as a means by which an adult can achieve a personal goal through the manipulation of a child. Kinscherff and Barnum (1992) describe two cases in which the children may have developed symptoms in response to the desires of the parents rather than from an actual abusive situation. These cases parallel the dynamics evident in the Munchausen syndrome by proxy. It is also possible that clinicians, investigators, and other helpers may solicit certain responses or symptoms from children as a result of poor interviewing skills or due to their own personal agendas.

It is essential that clinicians and investigators use appropriate interviewing techniques in order to gather accurate information (Kinscherff & Barnum, 1992). Providing the opportunity for free recall, whereby younger people can tell their stories in their own way and at their own pace, is the ideal manner in which to conduct an interview (Robin, 1991). It decreases the likelihood of any suggestion that a child has been coached or influenced by the interviewer. Allegations of interviewer contagion or coaching can have a major influence on the results of a trial. The interviews also need to be based on the frame of reference of the child rather than that of the interviewer. This means that the child's developmental level and language skills must be taken into account (see Chapters 3–8, this volume).

While it is perhaps impossible to avoid leading questions completely, their use should be restricted. It is important that the questions do not suggest to the child that there is a right or a wrong response. This holds true for both clinicians and investigators. Indeed, clinicians need to be aware that it may be their interviewing style and not the evidence collected by the investigators that contributes the most to the outcome of a trial. This, of course, can create a conflict for clinicians who have to deal with young people who rarely want to talk spontaneously about their abuse.

CONCLUSION

The allegations of ritual abuse by child victims and adult survivors detail combinations of sexual, physical, psychological, and spiritual oppression in the context of religious or pseudoreligious ceremonies. The response to these allegations by the professional community has been mixed, with some members unconditionally accepting everything that is said, while others have searched for alternative explanations. There needs to be a midpoint between these two positions. Some allegations very well may be psychotic manifestations or stories told for ulterior motives, but it also must be recognized that other allegations may be based on true experiences. Definitive statements regarding many of the aspects of ritual abuse may be premature because of a lack of empirical investigation of the dynamics, characteristics, and prevalence of the problem. Speculative suggestions guised as empirical proof add nothing to the credibility of the professional community, and, more important, may impede the development of effective responses to the situation.

Recommendations

1. **THAT** clinical assessment and child-protection/criminal- justice investigations be kept separate. Each plays an important yet distinct role.
2. **THAT** all information gathered from the assessment or investigation be clearly documented. These cases are almost always quite complex and require an appropriate recording system.
3. **THAT** one's personal and/or religious view be separated from the assessment/investigation. Objectivity ultimately will serve the client best.
4. **THAT** it be recognized that there is a critical difference between the validity or verification requirements of clinicians as opposed to those of investigators.
5. **THAT** the clinician develop a clear definition of validity regardless of his or her role. How does one determine whether someone is believable? Does one use the same criteria in every case?
6. **THAT** since the investigation of ritual abuse is in its infancy, and much that appears to be presented as fact is speculation, further research be carried out. Much more work is needed before we fully understand this phenomenon.
7. **THAT** clinicians and investigators undergo special training in order to deal with complex and extreme abuses of this nature.

REFERENCES

Burgess, A. W., Hartman, C. R., Wolbert, W. A., & Grant, C. A. (1987). Child molestation: Assessing impact in multiple victims. *Archives of Psychiatric Nursing,* *1*(1), 33–39.

Cook, C. (1991). *Understanding ritual abuse through a study of thirty-three ritual abuse survivors from thirteen different states.* Sacramento, Calif.: Ritual Abuse Project.

Core, D., & Harrison, F. (1991). *Chasing satan.* London: Gunter Books.

Cozolino, L. J. (1989). The ritual abuse of children: Implications for clinical practice and research. *Journal of Sex Research, 26*(1), 131–138.

Cozolino, L. J. (1990). Ritualistic child abuse, psychopathology, and evil. *Journal of Psychology and Theology, 18*(3), 218-227.

Daraul, A. (1990). *A history of secret societies.* New York: Citadel Press.

Driscoll, L. N., & Wright, C. (1990). *Survivors of childhood ritual abuse: Multi-generational satanic cult involvement.* Unpublished manuscript, University of Utah, Department of Family and Consumer Studies, Salt Lake City.

Eskapa, R. (1987). *Bizarre sex.* London: Grafton Books.

Finkelhor, D., & Williams, M. L. (1988). *Nursery crimes: Sexual abuse in daycare centers.* Newbury Park, Calif.: Sage.

Fraser, G. A. (1990). Satanic ritual abuse: A cause of multiple personality disorder. *Journal of Child and Youth Care, Special Edition,* pp. 55–60.

Gould, C. (1992). Diagnosis and treatment of ritually abused children. In D. K. Sakheim & S. E. Devine (Eds.), *Out of darkness: Exploring satanism and ritual abuse* (pp. 207–248). New York: Lexington Books.

Greaves, G. B. (1992). Alternative hypotheses regarding claims of satanic activity: A critical analysis. In D. K. Sakheim & S. E. Devine (Eds.), *Out of darkness: Exploring satanism and ritual abuse* (pp. 45–72). New York: Lexington Books.

Hicks, R. D. (1991). *In pursuit of Satan: The police and the occult.* New York: Prometheus Books.

Homes, R. M. (1991). *Sex crimes.* London: Sage.

Hudson, P. S. (1990). Ritual child abuse: A survey of symptoms and allegations. *Journal of Child and Youth Care, Special Edition,* pp. 27–54.

Hudson, P. S. (1991). *Ritual child abuse: Discovery, diagnosis and treatment.* Saratoga, Calif.: R &E Publications.

Jonker, F., & Jonker-Bakker, P. (1991). Experiences with ritualistic child sexual abuse: A case study from the Netherlands. *Child Abuse and Neglect, 15,* 191–196.

Kelley, S. J. (1989). Stress responses of children to sexual abuse and ritualistic abuse in day care centres. *Journal of Interpersonal Violence, 5*(4), 502–513.

Kelley, S. J. (1990). Parental stress response to sexual abuse and ritual abuse of children in day-care centers. *American Journal of Nursing, 39*(1), 25–29.

Kent, S. A. (1993). Deviant scripturalism and ritual satanic abuse. Pt. 1: Possible Judeo-Christian influences. *Religion, 23,* 229–241.

Kinscherff, R., & Barnum, R. (1992). Child forensic evaluation and claims of ritual abuse or satanic activity: A critical analysis. In D. K. Sakheim & S. E. Devine (Eds.), *Out of darkness: Exploring satanism and ritual abuse.* New York: Lexington Books.

Lanning, K. V. (1989, October). Satanic, occult, ritualistic crime: A law enforcement perspective. *Police Chief,* pp. 62–82.

Lanning, K. V. (1991). Ritual abuse: A law enforcement view or perspective. *Child Abuse and Neglect, 15,* 171–173.

Lanning, K. V. (1992). A law enforcement perspective on allegations of ritual abuse. In D. K. Sakheim & S. E. Devine (Eds.), *Out of darkness: Exploring satanism and ritual abuse* (pp. 109–146). New York: Lexington Books.

Layton, B. (1987). *The Gnostic scriptures.* Garden City, N.Y.: Doubleday.

Mangen, R. (1992). Psychological testing and ritual abuse. In D. K. Sakheim & S. E. Devine (Eds.), *Out of darkness: Exploring satanism and ritual abuse* (pp. 147–174). New York: Lexington Books.

Nurcombe, B., & Unutzer, J. (1991). The ritual abuse of children: Clinical features and diagnostic reasoning. *Journal of the American Academy of Child and Adolescent Psychiatry, 30*(2), 272–276.

Raschke, C. A. (1990). *Painted black.* New York: Harper and Row.

Robin, M. (1991). The social construction of child abuse and "false allegations." *Child and Youth Studies, 15*(2), 1–34.

Smith, M., & Pazder, A. L. (1980). *Michelle remembers.* New York: Pocket Books.

Snow, B., & Sorenson, T. (1990). Ritualistic child abuse in a neighborhood setting. *Journal of Interpersonal Violence, 5*(4), 474–487.

Terr, L. (1990). *Too scared to cry.* New York: Basic Books.

PART V

Legal and Ethical Issues

19

The Child Witness in Sexual Abuse Cases: Professional and Ethical Considerations

Lorne D. Bertrand, Joseph P. Hornick, and Floyd H. Bolitho

Legislation recently enacted in Canada dealing with the prosecution of alleged child sexual abuse cases attempted to reduce the possibility of revictimization of child victims/witnesses during the process of testifying in court. This chapter presents an overview of the concept of revictimization, as well as a discussion of a research project designed to evaluate the effectiveness of the new legislation. Based on this discussion, several specific recommendations to professionals dealing with these cases are presented.

Although few professionals dispute the fact that child sexual abuse is a societal problem that has existed for many years, since the mid-1970s public awareness of and concern over this issue have increased rapidly (Finkelhor, 1986). As a result, there has been a substantial growth in the number of child sexual abuse cases alleged, and ultimately dealt with by the criminal justice system, as well as a substantial increase in the number of professionals who come into contact with these cases. A number of ethical issues relevant to the professionals dealing with such cases arise as they pass through the judicial system. One of the most sensitive areas that must be considered is whether the child victim of sexual abuse should testify against the accused in criminal proceedings.

As noted by Pogge and Stone (1990), reported cases of child sexual abuse frequently pass through three distinct professional systems: (1) the social service system, (2) the legal system, and (3) the mental health system. While these systems do overlap to a certain extent in their responsibilities as related to these cases, each has distinct responsibilities and duties to perform. The primary function of the social service system is the protection of child victims and the determination of their best interests. The legal system, in comparison, strives to ensure that justice is carried out and that the legal rights of both the accused and the child victim are preserved. The mental health system in child sexual abuse cases frequently serves the function of assessment and treatment, which may focus on both the accused and the victim. Although the mandates of these three systems and the professionals who work within them are not necessarily at odds with one another, the possibility exists that instituting legal proceedings against an accused offender can result in further trauma for the child victim, which raises the issue of whether these proceedings are in the child's best interests. Consequently, the responsibility of the legal system to ensure that justice is served and the responsibility of the social service system to protect the child may result in a situation characterized by conflict.

The potential for this conflict is perhaps greatest in situations where children are required to give evidence and testify in court against the accused. In fact, it has been argued that these children may be revictimized by the judicial process. Many advocates for children suggest that the child victim who is compelled to give evidence, and thus is required to relate the events surrounding the abusive incident in a courtroom setting, is likely to experience a "reliving" of the abuse, and thereby is placed in a situation where he or she is being victimized by the events of the abuse a second time. However, the principle of due process, which drives the justice system, requires that an accused individual have the opportunity to face his or her accuser; in most cases of sexual abuse, the child is the only witness to the abuse, and there may be no choice but to have the child provide testimony in cases that proceed to trial. In addition to the potential for causing the child emotional and psychological distress, the trauma experienced by some children who are compelled to testify may adversely affect their ability to accurately recount the circumstances surrounding the abuse. Clearly, in an allegation of child sexual abuse, it is crucial that the accuracy of the testimony of the child witness be maximized. Given this reality, the problem in many cases becomes one of attempting to reduce the stress and trauma associated with testifying to as great an extent as possible, both to protect the child and to allow for the most accurate testimony possible, while at the same time ensuring that the rights of the accused are not compromised.

This chapter focuses on a case study of how one jurisdiction–Canada–has attempted to deal with the issue of having child sexual abuse victims testify. Following a discussion of the concept of "revictimization," the chapter outlines child sexual abuse legislation recently enacted in Canada that was designed to reduce the negative consequences of testifying for child victims of sexual abuse. Finally, the effectiveness of the legislation is discussed briefly, and some specific recommendations for professionals dealing with child sexual abuse are proposed.

THE CONCEPT OF REVICTIMIZATION

There is no doubt but that being a victim of sexual abuse is a traumatic experience for a child. However, in addition to the initial trauma suffered by these child victims, several authors have argued that requiring children who have been sexually abused to participate in the prosecution of their abusers and to provide testimony in court against them can also be a traumatic experience, resulting in the child's being revictimized by the judicial system (e.g., Bull, 1988; Claman, Harris, Bernstein, & Lovitt, 1986; Flin, 1990; Flin, Davies, & Tarrant, 1988; Glaser & Spencer, 1990; Libai, 1969). Unfortunately, because the child victim is usually the only witness to the sexual abuse, the prosecution of the accused can proceed only if the child gives testimony.

As noted by Bala (1991), historically the legal system has failed to recognize that child victims of sexual abuse may require special consideration when they are called as witnesses. The criminal justice system has been structured to deal primarily with adults, both as witnesses and accused persons, a situation that creates an inherent bias against children who become involved with the system. In many cases, expecting children to perform well as witnesses in court without special considerations is unreasonable owing to the developmental, emotional, and intellectual differences between children and adults. Further, where children do receive special consideration or are treated differently than are adults, this often has a negative tone. For example, Bala (1991) pointed out that "children are victims of a discriminatory justice system which developed rules premised on the notion that children are inherently unreliable witnesses whose testimony must be specially scrutinized" (p. 3). Thus, in court settings, child witnesses are frequently placed in situations where prior expectations exist that they will be unable to perform adequately.

Several aspects of the legal process surrounding the prosecution of child sexual abuse cases can be traumatic for the children. Flin (1990) has argued that causes of stress for children in these cases can be found in the pretrial period, as well as during the actual trial. With regard to the pretrial period, the often lengthy delay between the abuse and the trial can be a source of stress for the child victim due to the uncertainty of the outcome of the legal process. In addition, therapy is often withheld from children who require it in the interval between the disclosure of abuse and the trial to avoid a charge by the defense that the testimony has been contaminated by the therapist. Many young children may also have a sense of powerlessness because they do not understand the nature of the legal proceedings or the evidence-gathering stage, and what their role is during these proceedings. For example, Saywitz (1989) found that children frequently do not understand the meaning of certain words, such as "court," "hearing," and "charges," in a legal context. Further, Yates (1987) found that some child witnesses are apprehensive of the court process because they fear that they will be sent to prison. Also during the pretrial phase, child victims frequently are required to go through repeated interviews by different professionals, such as police officers, lawyers, and social service workers, during which the details of the abuse must be recounted. Young children frequently do not understand the roles and responsibilities of the different professionals involved, and thus do not understand why they must continue to repeat their disclosure of the abuse. This necessity to recount the circumstances of a traumatic event several times can be stressful for the child, and may contribute to a feeling of reliving the abuse.

In addition to the stressors encountered by many child victims during the pretrial period, the trial itself is another potentially traumatic event. As noted by several authors, one of the most frightening aspects of the trial for child witnesses is facing the accused in the courtroom, as well as a fear that this confrontation will lead to retribution by the accused (Flin, 1990; Libai, 1969; Yates, 1987). Also contributing to the stress engendered by the trial is the fact that many children do not have knowledge of courtroom procedures, and may find the formality frightening. Similarly, the physical attributes of the courtroom may be intimidating for a child—for example, the size of the witness chair, the fact that microphones may be pointed at the child, and having the judge's chair raised higher than the witness stand. In addition, child witnesses frequently do not understand the roles of the various people in court, and, in many cases, they do not understand their own role in the courtroom proceedings (Flin, 1990). For example, Flin, Stevenson, and Davies (1989) found that children who were asked how they would feel if they had to go to court reported that they would feel frightened or worried because they might be sent to prison if their testimony was not believed.

Another major source of stress for the child witness during the trial is the process of testifying during the direct examination, followed by the cross-examination. During the examination, the witness has to recount the circumstances of the abuse in detail in a courtroom that typically contains several people who are strangers to the child, a procedure that holds the potential for further traumatization for the victim (Berliner & Barbieri, 1984). The cross-examination presents an even greater possibility for revictimizing the child, since its purpose is to discredit the child's testimony, which, in many cases, means accusing the child of telling lies (Glaser & Spencer, 1990). The final major source of stress relates to the ultimate disposition of the case. Whether the accused is convicted or acquitted, the verdict can be traumatic for the victim. If the accused is convicted and sent to prison, the child may feel extreme guilt at having caused this outcome, especially if the accused is a family member or a close acquaintance of the child (Glaser & Spencer, 1990). Conversely, if the accused is acquitted, the child may assume that this outcome is an indication that he or she was not believed (Berliner & Barbieri, 1984).

It should be noted that, while the sources of stress discussed above have the potential to revictimize the child, some authors have suggested that the process of testifying may not be particularly traumatic for some children, and, in fact, may even exert beneficial or therapeutic effects. For example, Tedesco and Schnell (1987) state that "the experience could be cathartic, provide a feeling of control, provide vindication, and symbolically put an end to an unpleasant experience" (p. 268). While it may be true that some child victims do derive some benefit from participating in the prosecution of the accused, most authors agree that, in the majority of cases, the potential for inducing further trauma to these children outweighs the probable benefits. Given this fact, the ethical burden placed on professionals who deal with such cases is to attempt to find methods whereby the potential for revictimization is minimized as much as possible. One strategy that can be taken to achieve this goal is to adopt legislative changes in the procedure that governs how these cases are processed in the judicial system. The difficulty is preserving the legal rights of the accused, while, at the same time, minimizing the trauma for the child victims. The next section discusses recent legislation in Canada that was enacted in an attempt to attain this goal.

CANADIAN LEGISLATION RELATED TO CHILD SEXUAL ABUSE

In Canada, both the child welfare system and the criminal justice system have a responsibility for dealing with allegations of child sexual abuse. The determination of whether one or both systems become involved in a case depends on the particular circumstances. The criminal justice system, which has a national mandate, is responsible for investigating all reported sexual abuse cases regardless of the relationship of the accused to the victim. The child welfare systems, which are under provincial mandate, become involved primarily in cases where either a child is believed to be at risk of being sexually abused by a guardian, or the guardian cannot or is unwilling to protect the child from abuse, although there is considerable variation in practice by province.

Recently, legislators at the federal level have attempted to respond to the problem of child sexual abuse, largely as a result of the findings of the 1984 *Sexual offences against children: Report of the committee on sexual offences against children and youths* (the Badgley Report). This report, commissioned by the federal government, presented factual information on the incidence and prevalence of sexual offenses against children, and contained recommendations for dealing with the problems it identified. In all, the report made 52 recommendations directed at all levels of government, as well as the private sector.

Far-reaching changes grew out of the Badgley Report. On January 1, 1988, Bill C-15, An Act to Amend the Criminal Code and the Canada Evidence Act, was proclaimed. This act contained a number of major revisions to both substantive and procedural laws governing the sexual abuse of children. The substantive changes to the Criminal Code were designed to eliminate a number of limitations of the previous legislation. For example, previous legislation covered a limited range of activity, prohibiting only vaginal sexual intercourse and not the range of behaviors that would constitute child sexual abuse. Previous legislation was also gender biased since in many instances it did not protect male victims. Further, prior legislation provided a time limitation of one year for reporting certain sexual offenses, and issues of age and consent were also a problem. In an attempt to deal with these substantive issues, Bill C-15 created three new offenses: sexual interference, invitation to sexual touching, and sexual exploitation.

Most relevant to the present discussion are those changes that affect the evidentiary procedures employed when children testify in court. The changes were designed to improve the experience of child victims who are compelled to give testimony at the trial of the accused abuser, while at the same time protecting the rights of the accused. Implicit in these changes was the recognition that making the process of testifying less traumatic for children could enhance the value and accuracy of the testimony, in addition to decreasing the level of revictimization experienced by the child, without contravening the rights of the accused.

In terms of evidentiary procedures, a number of specific changes were made to protect children giving testimony and to improve their experiences as witnesses. For example, Bill C-15 made allowances for a child witness to testify outside the courtroom via closed-circuit television or behind a screen in the courtroom. This provision was intended to facilitate testimony from children who experience excessive anxiety at facing the accused or appearing in the courtroom. In addition to alleviating some of the stress associated with testifying, it was hoped that these techniques would allow a child who otherwise would be too anxious to perform as a witness to provide valid testimony.

Second, the new legislation allowed for the use in the courtroom of video-taped interviews in which the child described the abuse. This provision was intended to avoid, as much as possible, repetitious interviews with the child. It also permits the use of the videotape to refresh the child's memory prior to testifying. Third, the new legislation ruled that corroboration of the child's testimony was no longer required. Fourth, it stated that judges could issue orders restricting publication of any information that could be used to reveal the identity of the victim or any of the witnesses. This provision was intended to provide protection to the child victim by preventing broad public knowledge of the child's identity and the circumstances of the case. In addition, an existing section of the criminal code that is relevant to the present discussion provides for the exclusion of the public from the courtroom during the child's testimony if the presence of strangers makes it difficult for the child to testify.

Finally, amendments to the Canada Evidence Act allow both victims and witnesses under 14 years of age to give sworn evidence, if they understand the nature of the oath and are able to communicate the evidence. The amendment also makes it possible for a child under 14, who does not understand the nature of the oath, to give unsworn evidence if he or she is able to communicate and "promises to tell the truth."

The changes to legislation described above were made in an attempt to improve the experience of the child witness in court, based on the premise that doing so would reduce the potential for revictimization of the child by the judicial system. An additional clause in Bill C-15 required that it be reviewed after four years to determine whether this goal had been achieved. In 1989 and 1990, three research projects funded by Justice Canada were initiated at selected sites across Canada that were designed to evaluate the effectiveness of the bill in realizing its goals. A synthesis of the results of these projects is presented by Hornick and Bolitho (1992). The following section discusses the results of this synthesis as they relate to the issue of revictimization when children are required to give testimony in court proceedings.

EFFECTIVENESS OF CHANGES TO EVIDENTIARY PROCEDURES RESULTING FROM BILL C-15

Research projects designed to assess the effectiveness of Bill C-15 were conducted at several sites across Canada, including Hamilton, Ontario; Regina and Saskatoon, Saskatchewan; and Edmonton and Calgary, Alberta. A central purpose of the studies was to examine the nature of the child witness experience in the judicial system since the proclamation of Bill C-15. This included determining the extent to which the changes to evidentiary procedures allowed in the legislation had been implemented, as well as the extent to which these changes, if implemented, had improved the experience of the child witness.

A posttest/longitudinal tracking design was utilized in all studies. Data were gathered from several different sources and were aggregated into three separate data sets. These included:

1. Court observations that were conducted to collect information on the nature and quality of the child's testimony, as well as the overall effect of the experience on the child.
2. Interviews that were conducted with a small number of child witnesses following their appearance in court to determine their perceptions of the experience, in terms both of how they felt that they had been treated during the trial, and of their overall feelings about the court process.
3. A mail survey that was utilized to obtain perceptions and information related to Bill C-15 from key informants, including child welfare workers, police officers, defense lawyers, prosecutors, and judges.

The data collected reflect on three key questions that address the issue of whether child witnesses tend to be revictimized under the new legislation: (1) What were the observable effects on the child giving testimony? (2) How did children feel about being involved with the criminal justice system? (3) How did the professionals involved with the criminal justice system feel about the procedural changes resulting from Bill C-15? The findings relevant to these questions are discussed in the following section (summarized from Hornick & Bolitho, 1992).

Observable Effects on the Child

In the Calgary study, which observed 15 male and 58 female victims/ witnesses ages six to 18 years, children giving testimony who had experienced physical injury during the abuse incidents demonstrated significantly higher anxiety (82%) than did those children who had not been physically injured (48%). Further, children involved in cases where the incident was reported immediately were rated as much more able to communicate than were children in cases where the abuse was reported more than one year after the incident.

In the Edmonton study, seven male and 37 female victims/witnesses were observed. These children ranged in age from seven years to 18 years, but were generally older than the children observed in Calgary. In these cases, children who had a high number of court experiences were significantly more anxious and withdrawn. Those who experienced two or more court appearances were highly anxious as compared with those who were in court for the first time, or who had had only one previous court experience. One explanation for this finding is that "having to tell the story repeatedly," and being challenged about it, results in stress.

The number of court appearances was also the most significant predictor of crying and being sad in the Edmonton study. Obviously, children who had to retell their story found it difficult. The Edmonton study also found that clearing the courtroom during testimony significantly reduced the probability of their crying and being sad, and female witnesses scored higher on the cry/sad scale than did male witnesses. Finally, the number of people in the courtroom was found to be significantly related to the children's ability to communicate. When there were fewer than 10 people in the courtroom, 79% of the child witnesses demonstrated a high ability to communicate, as compared with 53% for situations in which more than 10 people were present.

Court observation data in the Regina and Saskatoon studies showed that, overall, child witnesses ($n = 21$) did not exhibit an excessively negative response to the experience of testifying in court, suggesting that they were coping reasonably well under very difficult circumstances. Child witnesses' ability to communicate was lowest during the oath/communication stage, highest during the direct examination, and intermediate during the cross-examination (Stevens, Fischer, & Berg, 1992). From the court-observation material of the Hamilton study, it was concluded that the children ($n = 12$) were, in fact, very competent witnesses (Campbell Research Associates and Social Data Research Ltd., 1992).

Perceptions of Child Victims/Witnesses

In Calgary and Edmonton, seven children were interviewed after court proceedings were completed. All seven had been to court, and six of these children actually testified.

(*Note:* Data were not available from the Hamilton and Saskatchewan studies.)

COURT PREPARATION. Two of the children stated that they had attended scheduled precourt visits, one conducted by the prosecutor and a police officer together, and the other by the prosecutor and a therapist. The other five children reported no precourt visit. The two children who attended precourt visits thought that the visit helped them to understand where they were going and what the court looked like.

The children who described what the prosecutor did ($n = 4$) all stated that the prosecutor was on their side; one said that the prosecutor protects the innocent, and one that the prosecutor "protects me." Six of the seven children reported that the prosecutor explained what would happen in court. Four of these children remembered the prosecutor's explaining that they should tell the truth, and three remembered being told to give definite answers. Most of the children ($n = 5$) thought this helped them. These responses show an alliance with the prosecutor and the importance of precourt meetings with the prosecutor in order to help the children feel prepared and supported.

Six of the seven children had at least one support adult in addition to the prosecutor—either a parent or a guardian (in three cases), a social worker (in three cases), or a therapist or other family member. One way in which supportive adults helped was by telling the children that it was normal to feel frightened. Five of the children mentioned this, suggesting the importance of including supportive adults in the process and of validating and normalizing the children's feelings of fear.

When the children were asked how they would help to prepare another child for court, the most common response was that they would advise the child to tell the truth. Other responses included general encouragement, such as: "Be confident," "Be brave," "Don't be afraid," "Believe in yourself," and "It will be fine." Other advice included: "It's not your fault," "Ask questions if you don't understand," "It will take a long time," "The person may not be punished," "It gets frustrating, but go ahead," "Don't let them force words in your mouth," "Even if you lose, he will get caught eventually," and "It will be scary, but you should tell so that it doesn't happen to someone else."

TESTIMONY EXPERIENCE. The general consensus of the child victims/witnesses was that the judge was there to listen to testimonies and to make decisions about the guilt or innocence of the accused. One child stated, "The judge is there to protect you." Only one child felt that the judge did not understand her. The children thought judges could improve their questions by using "normal language," by not being so aggressive, and by listening to the children's stories more closely.

Most of the children also felt understood by the prosecutor. However, three children thought the questions were confusing or not specific enough. Generally, the children were more negative about the cross-examination. Most of the children who were cross-examined felt that the defense lawyer did not understand them.

Four children said that having family members in the courtroom made it easier for them to testify. One child even pretended she was talking to them while testifying. Another child felt more secure with the judge and the police in the courtroom so that the accused could not hurt her. Three children said they felt that having other people (except family members) in the courtroom made it harder to testify. Generally, having family members in the court-room gave the children a lot of support during the testimony. There is some indication that the presence of authority figures offered the children security, but that the presence of strangers seemed to increase stress.

Two children brought items (i.e., one wore her favorite pants and one carried a rosary) that they felt were helpful to have with them. Three of the children thought having a favorite object in court might have been helpful. No screens were used in these cases, but three children agreed that it might have made the testimony easier. None of the children sat in chairs while testifying; all stood. One eight-year-old boy said he got very tired standing and would have liked to sit down.

When asked about the general court process, the children described a range of feelings; some were happy and some were sad. It appears that these overall feelings about the court process were strongly influenced by the out-come, because the two children who felt very sad were witnesses in cases in which either the accused was acquitted or the charges were dismissed. Both of these children described intense feelings of anger and a perception that no one believed them. Other children made general comments to the effect that the process took much too long, that they had to tell their story too many times, and that they did not understand what an acquittal is. One child thought it was good for her to be able to tell her father (the accused) what she thought of him in court.

PROFESSIONAL PERCEPTIONS OF THE IMPACT OF TESTIFYING. Key informants (including child welfare workers, police officers, lawyers, prosecutors, and judges) were asked to respond to the open-ended question: "In your experience, what is the overall impact of the justice system on children who were required to testify in sexual assault cases?" In response to this question, most Alberta and Saskatchewan respondents, regardless of their professional affiliations, felt that giving testimony in court was a traumatic experience for children. The majority of social workers, police officers, and prosecutors expressed similar levels of concern on this issue, whereas defense lawyers and judges, although reporting concern, were not as strong in their beliefs that testifying was "worse than the sexual abuse." In contrast to these findings, the next most often cited impact of testifying on the child was the feeling that it could have a positive effect. Some prosecutors, defense lawyers, and judges in Saskatchewan, and a defense lawyer and judges in Hamilton, reported that they felt that the act of testifying had little effect on children. Defense lawyers and judges in Saskatchewan tended to report that they did not know what the effects of testimony were on children.

Prosecutors, lawyers, and judges in Alberta were also asked about their experiences with the use of new procedures introduced as part of the evidentiary changes to Bill C-15. Results indicated that while not all of the new provisions allowed by the bill were frequently requested, those that were requested were usually allowed by the judge. For example, banning publication, allowing supporting adults in court, and clearing the public and other witnesses from the courtroom were frequently requested by prosecutors and were usually permitted by the judge. Procedures that were less frequently requested, but were usually allowed following a request, included the use of a videotape, allowing the child to sit on the knee of a support adult while giving testimony, and allowing the child to testify behind a screen.

CONCLUSIONS

This chapter has presented a brief review of the literature related to the issue of revictimization, as well as the results of a research project established to assess the effectiveness of Canadian legislation designed to reduce the stress that may be associated with children's court experiences. In conclusion, based on the literature review, as well as on the results of the evaluation studies discussed here, it is evident that, for many children who have been sexually abused, testifying in court is a traumatic and anxiety-provoking experience. Legislation enacted in Canada attempting to alleviate these negative effects by allowing for changes to courtroom procedures appears to be effective in reducing the levels of stress experienced by these children. Results of the studies indicate that professionals need to be made aware of the procedural changes allowed by Bill C-15, and that their requests to implement these changes will generally be regarded favorably by members of the judiciary. The use of such procedures may greatly improve the legal outcome of an allegation of child sexual abuse.

Recommendations

Based on this discussion, several specific recommendations to professionals involved in such cases may be made. Thus it is observed and recommended:

1. **THAT** since children who have been physically injured during the abuse may experience greater anxiety in the process of testifying than do those who were not physically injured, professionals be made aware of this possibility and recognize that these children may require special treatment and counseling in the pre- and posttrial periods.

2. **THAT** since children who are required to undergo several court appearances may experience higher levels of stress than those who testify only once or twice in court, the courtroom be cleared of the public and other witnesses in an effort to reduce this stress.

3. **THAT** since the child's ability to communicate during the court appearance appears to be related to the number of people in the courtroom, with communication levels decreasing with increasing numbers of spectators, the provisions of Bill C-15 allowing for the courtroom to be cleared be invoked to enhance the child's level of communication.

4. **THAT** since children who visited the courtroom prior to the trial reported experiencing less anxiety than children who did not have this opportunity, such visits be arranged, as well as pretrial meetings with the prosecutor, at which he or she can explain the proceedings, which may serve to reduce the amount of stress experienced by the child.

5. **THAT** since some children reported feeling intimidated by the judge, and indicated that they would have felt less anxious if he or she had used language that the child could understand, professionals involved in the trial process attempt to ensure that the proceedings are comprehensible to the child witness, and that, to whatever extent possible, the formality of the courtroom is played down.

6. **THAT** since children who had supportive adults present in the courtroom, whether parents/guardians or social service workers, were less anxious than those who did not have supportive adults with them, children who are experiencing stress should have the option of being accompanied to court by someone they trust and in whom they have confidence.

7. **THAT** since child witnesses may be more likely to experience negative posttrial emotions when either the accused is acquitted or the charges are withdrawn, professionals be made aware that these children may have special needs, and may require additional counseling following the conclusion of the trial.

8. **THAT** although some professionals recognize that testifying can be a traumatic experience for children, others believe that it has little or no negative impact, and thus professionals who are involved be made aware of the possibility of revictimization and of the provisions that are available to reduce this possibility.

9. **THAT** since judges receiving requests to implement changes to evidentiary procedures allowed for in Bill C-15 in a particular

case are quite likely to agree to the request, prosecutors be made aware of the changes allowed by Bill C-15, and of the fact that judges are, for the most part, open to implementing these changes once they have been requested.

10. **THAT** although data were not available in the present study concerning the effects of the use of screens or closed-circuit television, it be recognized, as suggested by the literature, that these provisions may be beneficial in cases where the child witness expresses fear of facing the accused.

REFERENCES

Bala, N. (1991). Double victims: Child sexual abuse and the Canadian criminal justice system. *Queen's Law Journal, 16*, 3–32.

Berliner, L., & Barbieri, M. K. (1984). The testimony of the child victim of sexual assault. *Journal of Social Issues, 40*, 125–137.

Bull, R. (1988). Children as witnesses. *Policing, 4*, 130.

Campbell Research Associates and Social Data Research Ltd. (1992). *Review and monitoring of child sexual abuse cases in Hamilton-Wentworth, Ontario.* Ottawa: Research and Development Directorate, Department of Justice Canada.

Claman, L., Harris, J. C., Bernstein, B. E., & Lovitt, R. (1986). The adolescent as a witness in a case of incest: Assessment and outcome. *Journal of the American Academy of Child Psychiatry, 25*, 457–461.

Committee on Sexual Offences Against Children and Youths. (1984). *Sexual offences against children: Report of the committee on sexual offences against children and youths* (vol. 1). Ottawa: Minister of Supply and Services Canada.

Finkelhor, D. (1986). *A sourcebook on child sexual abuse.* Beverly Hills, Calif.: Sage.

Flin, R. (1990). Child witnesses in criminal courts. *Children and Society, 4*, 264–283.

Flin, R., Davies, G., & Tarrant, A. (1988). *The child witness.* Final report to the Scottish Home and Health Department, Grant 85/9290.

Flin, R., Stevenson, Y., & Davies, G. M. (1989). Children's knowledge of court proceedings. *British Journal of Psychology, 80*, 285–297.

Glaser, D., & Spencer, J. R. (1990). Sentencing, children's evidence and children's trauma. *Criminal Law Review*, 371–382.

Hornick, J. P., & Bolitho, F. (1992). *A review of the implementation of the child sexual abuse legislation in selected sites.* Ottawa: Communications and Consultation Branch, Department of Justice Canada.

Libai, D. (1969). The protection of the child victim of a sexual offense in the criminal justice system. *Wayne Law Review, 15*, 977–1032.

Pogge, D. L., & Stone, K. (1990). Conflicts and issues in the treatment of child sexual abuse. *Professional Psychology: Research and Practice, 21*, 354–361.

Saywitz, K. J. (1989). Children's conceptions of the legal system: "Court is a place to play basketball." In S. J. Ceci, D. F. Ross, & M. P. Toglia (Eds.), *Perspectives on children's testimony.* New York: Springer-Verlag.

Stevens, G., Fischer, D. G., and Berg, L. (1992). *Review and monitoring of child sexual abuse cases in selected sites in Saskatchewan.* Ottawa: Research and Development Directorate, Department of Justice Canada.

Tedesco, J. F., & Schnell, S. V. (1987). Children's reactions to sex abuse investigation and litigation. *Child Abuse and Neglect, 11,* 267–272.

Yates, A. (1987). Should young children testify in cases of sexual abuse? *American Journal of Psychiatry, 144,* 476–480.

20

Ethical and Legal Issues in Cases of Child Sexual Abuse in the United States

Susan P. Limber

The legal and ethical issues faced by mental health professionals in cases of child sexual abuse in the United States are both complex and controversial. This chapter focuses on two of the most highly disputed areas of professionals' involvement in such cases: reporting instances of suspected maltreatment and providing expert testimony at case adjudication. It suggests that many mental health professionals remain underinvolved in reporting cases of suspected maltreatment, yet frequently are overinvolved in providing expert opinions in courts.

During the past two decades, there has been a dramatic increase in the number of reports of sexually abused children. Indeed, by the 1980s, Freud's conclusion that it was "hardly credible that perverted acts against children were so general" (Freud, 1954, cited in McCord, 1986, p. 2) had given way to the recognition that child sexual abuse was a societal problem of staggering

This chapter was partially prepared with the support of a grant from the National Institute of Mental Health.

proportions (McCord, 1986). With the increase in the reporting of child sexual abuse, the involvement of mental health professionals (primarily psychologists, psychiatrists, and social workers) in such cases has changed both quantitatively and qualitatively. Historically, the extent of such involvement included treating a victim or perpetrator of sexual abuse, occasionally reporting a case of suspected sexual abuse, or advising the court about dispositional aspects of the case (e.g., predictions of likely outcomes for the child and family). Today, mental health professionals perform these functions with increasing frequency. In addition, however, they also participate regularly in the adjudicatory stage of child sexual abuse proceedings–the stage of the proceedings at which the occurrence of sexual abuse is determined (Lloyd, 1986; Melton & Limber, 1989; Melton, Petrila, Poythress, & Slobogin, 1987; Quinn, 1992). Here, mental health professionals may be asked to assess allegedly abused children to determine if harm has occurred; to document the chronology, context, or consistency of the abuse complaints; and to offer expert testimony regarding their findings (Melton et al., 1987; Quinn, 1992).

Currently, perhaps the most widely debated roles that mental health professionals fulfill are as reporters of suspected cases of child sexual abuse (see, e.g., Kalichman, Craig, & Follingstad, 1990) and as expert witnesses in court (see, e.g., Melton & Limber, 1989, 1991; Melton et al., 1987; Myers, 1991). The legal and ethical issues raised by the involvement of mental health professionals in these positions are both complex and controversial, and are examined in this chapter in detail.

THE ROLE OF THE MENTAL HEALTH PROFESSIONAL IN INITIATING AN INVESTIGATION OF CHILD SEXUAL ABUSE

The initial involvement of many mental health professionals in cases of child sexual abuse is in reporting suspected maltreatment to authorities. Unfortunately, professionals are frequently perplexed by confusing or ambiguous legal requirements and seemingly conflicting ethical duties.

Reporting Requirements

Modern legislation in the United States regarding the mandated reporting of child abuse and neglect was stimulated by the seminal article by Kempe and colleagues (Kempe, Silverman, Steele, Droegemueller, & Silver, 1962) describing the "battered child syndrome." So great was the influence of this article on legislators that between 1963 and 1967, all 50 states and the District of Columbia passed laws requiring certain classes of individuals to report suspected cases of child abuse and neglect.

WHO MUST REPORT? Initially, under state laws, only physicians were mandated to report suspected instances of child abuse or neglect (Bulkley, 1988; Otto & Melton, 1990). Gradually, however, states have expanded the requirement to include many other individuals who may have regular contact with families and children. The specific identities of these mandated reporters differ from state to state, but include such professionals as teachers, dentists, social workers, psychologists, nurses, religious leaders and counselors, child-care personnel, child-protective service (CPS) workers, and, in a few states, attorneys. In addition to these specified individuals, approximately half of the states require that "any person" report a suspected case of abuse or neglect. As a general rule, mental health professionals are mandated to report, either by being named specifically in a state statute, or by being subsumed under the "any person" requirement (Swoboda, Elwork, Sales, & Levine, 1978).

WHAT MUST BE REPORTED? Generally, mandated reporters must report a "reasonable suspicion" of child abuse or neglect by a parent or parent figure to authorities who are designated in the state statute (child protective services or the police). What acts constitute "child abuse" or "neglect" and what level of certainty constitutes "reasonable suspicion" generally are not clearly defined. The Child Abuse Prevention and Treatment Act of 1974 defines child abuse and neglect as "the physical or mental injury, *sexual abuse* or exploitation, negligent treatment or maltreatment of a child by a person who is responsible for the child's welfare under circumstances which indicate that the child's health or welfare is harmed or threatened" (1988, emphasis added), but it does not define sexual abuse. State laws frequently are no more specific. All include sexual abuse as a triggering incident for a report (either explicitly or implicitly), but few provide guidelines as to its identification.

INCENTIVES TO REPORT. As an incentive for mandated professionals to report suspected cases of child abuse and neglect, most state statutes provide specific criminal penalties for failing to report (MacMurray & Carson, 1991). Generally, these statutes require a showing that the mandated reporter knowingly failed to report a suspected case of child abuse or neglect. If convicted, professionals may be found guilty of a misdemeanor and face penalties of a jail term of up to six months and/or a fine of $100 to $1000. In addition to criminal penalties, some states have specific statutory provisions that establish civil liability for professionals who fail to fulfill their mandated reporting duties. Furthermore, on the basis of a landmark case in California (*Landeros v. Flood*, 1976), failure to report may leave the mandated reporter civilly liable for harm to the child if there are repeated incidents of abuse soon after the unreported incident. As a positive incentive to report suspected child abuse or neglect, all states provide the reporter with statutory immunity from criminal penalties and from civil liability for making a report in good faith. Further, most state statutes explicitly abolish the therapist–client and doctor–patient privileges in such cases. Finally, many states have statutes that shield the reporter from having his or her identification revealed (Davidson, 1988).

To What Extent Is the Law Followed?

Although compliance with mandatory reporting laws has likely improved since the 1960s and 1970s (Garbarino, 1991), it is far from universal. Numerous studies have investigated the reporting behaviors of a wide range of professionals, including psychologists, social workers, nurses, law-enforcement personnel, teachers, and Head Start volunteers (see Kalichman, 1993). Professionals' rates of compliance with reporting laws vary significantly according to the design of the study and the professionals interviewed, as well as a number of case variables. Compiling results from existing studies, Brosig and Kalichman (1992) reported that an average of 40% of the nearly 3,000 mental health professionals surveyed indicated that they had failed to report a case of suspected abuse at some time during their professional careers. Summarizing results from studies that employ hypothetical scenarios to examine reporting rates of mental health professionals, they concluded that approximately 42% of respondents noted hypothetical instances when they would not report suspected maltreatment.

Factors That Influence Professionals' Decisions to Report

Professionals' propensities to report suspected maltreatment have been found to be influenced by legal considerations (e.g., their knowledge of a legal duty to report, the specificity of language in reporting statutes, and their interpretation of the laws' requirements [Abrahams, Casey, & Daro, 1992; Hibbard & Zollinger, 1990; Kalichman & Brosig, 1993; Miller & Weinstock, 1987; Swoboda et al., 1978; Wurtele & Schmitt, 1992; Zellman, 1990a]); characteristics of the case (e.g., the nature and severity of the abuse, characteristics of the child victim, characteristics of the perpetrator, and the amount of evidence [Attias & Goodwin, 1985; Kalichman & Brosig, 1992; Kalichman & Craig, 1991; Kalichman, Craig, & Follingstad, 1988, 1989, 1990; Zellman, 1990a, 1990b, 1992]); and characteristics of the reporter (e.g., professionals' occupations, professionals' fears of personal and professional consequences [Attias & Goodwin, 1985; Newberger, 1991; Pollak & Levy, 1989; Zellman, 1990a; Zellman & Antler, 1990]).

However, the most widely cited rationale for professionals' failures to report cases of suspected child maltreatment is their concern that the report will cause harm to the child and/or the child's family (see, e.g., Kalichman et al., 1989; Miller & Weinstock, 1987; Zellman & Antler, 1990). Indeed, in the study by Kalichman and colleagues (Kalichman et al., 1989), only 14% of psychologist respondents felt that reporting would have a positive effect on the family, while 37% believed that reporting would have a clearly negative effect.

According to many mental health professionals, reporting a suspected case of child abuse or neglect may cause harm in several different ways. First, in cases where abuse is revealed during the course of therapy, harm may arise from the therapist's breaching the client's confidentiality by reporting the maltreatment (see, e.g., Muehleman & Kimmons, 1981; Zebrowski, 1984). Confidentiality is an ethic that protects the client from unauthorized disclosure of information about the client by the treating professional (Jagim, Wittman, & Noll, 1978). Providing a client with an assurance of privacy and a feeling of trust is generally seen as a condition necessary for effective therapy (Guyer, 1982). If confidentiality is breached in order to report suspected cases of child maltreatment, many mental health professionals fear that treatment will be disrupted or terminated (Kalichman & Craig, 1991; Kalichman et al., 1989; Miller & Weinstock, 1987; Zellman 1990a). For example, 42% of psychologists in Kalichman's (Kalichman et al., 1989) survey believed that reporting would have a negative effect on family therapy. Further, a policy of breaching confidentiality to report suspected child maltreatment may cause harm by discouraging clients from disclosing incidents of abuse in therapy (where, presumably, the abuse could be addressed) or by dissuading them from seeking therapy in the first place (see, e.g., Miller & Weinstock, 1987).

Second, harm may arise from a report of maltreatment because the report sets in motion a series of responses by CPS that the mental health professional views as injurious to the child and his or her family (see, e.g., Newberger, 1991; Zellman, 1990a). Professionals are aware of the inadequate investigatory resources of CPS (Otto & Melton, 1990), and many have had bad experiences with CPS investigations (Newberger, 1991; Zellman & Antler, 1990). Mental health professionals appear particularly likely (as compared with physicians) to consider the poor quality of CPS services in deciding whether to report a case of child maltreatment (Zellman, 1990a).

Ethical Dilemmas

Concern over the harm that it may cause children and families has prompted a heated debate among professionals regarding the ethics of reporting suspected child maltreatment. A small minority believe that client–therapist confidentiality should not be breached under any circumstances because it would cause significant, irreparable harm to the client–therapist relationship. Others who are concerned about the negative effects of reporting on the child and family advocate discretionary reporting (e.g., Ansell & Ross, 1990; Miller & Weinstock, 1987), permitting the professional to use his or her discretion in making a report in those instances where suspected perpetrators and victims are in therapy and where the child is not deemed to be in danger of future abuse. Still other professionals support existing reporting laws, but advocate improving the responses of the reporters and CPS (e.g., Butz, 1985; Davidson, 1988; Leong, Silva, & Weinstock, 1988; Racusin & Felsman, 1986).

Professional codes of ethics provide guidance to mental health professionals facing the dilemma of breaching client confidentiality to report suspected maltreatment. Ethics codes state that mental health professionals have a clear duty to comply with the law (e.g., American Psychological Association, 1992, principle F). They also mandate that professionals "respect the confidentiality rights of those with whom they work or consult" (APA, 1992). Recognizing that there may be situations where these two principles conflict (as where reasonable suspicions of child sexual abuse are aroused by a mental health professional's interactions with a client), codes assert that professionals may violate clients' confidentiality when mandated by law or where there is clear physical or psychological danger to an individual (e.g., APA, 1992, Standard 5.05a). In such cases, the ethical principle of nonmaleficence toward the child (refraining from harming) takes precedence over that of fidelity to the client's wishes of confidentiality (Thompson, 1990).

Some argue, however, that nonmaleficence is best achieved by permitting mental health professionals to use their discretion to report maltreatment only in those situations that they deem to be dangerous for the child (see, e.g., Ansell & Ross, 1990). They contend that, in some instances, the harm to the child and family caused by breaching confidentiality and reporting the suspected maltreatment is greater than the harm that might befall the child by not making a report. Thus these professionals believe that they are upholding a higher standard of ethical conduct by not reporting suspected abuse (Kalichman, 1993; Wells, 1988). Indeed, professional codes assert that when laws and ethical standards conflict, mental health professionals are obligated to meet the higher standard (APA, 1992, Introduction).

However, clinical predictions of dangerousness are notoriously difficult to make (Butz, 1985), and mental health professionals have no special expertise in making them (Melton et al., 1987). Moreover, although more research on the effects of CPS involvement on children and families is urgently needed, recent studies on the effects of reporting indicate that CPS involvement in cases of suspected maltreatment may not be as negative as many professionals have presumed (Brosig & Kalichman, 1992; Finkelhor, 1992; Fryer, Bross, Krugman, Denson, & Baird, 1990; Petretic-Jackson & Koziol, 1992). Harper and Irvin (1985) concluded from their survey of 107 cases of child neglect that reports that were made in the context of ongoing treatment rarely severed the clinician–client relationship. In the vast majority of cases (71%), these reports appeared to have positive effects on the parents' willingness to continue to work on the child's behalf. Similarly, Watson and Levine (1989) examined therapy outcomes of 65 cases in which a report of child maltreatment either was made or was considered (and made known to the client). In 25% of these cases, clients withdrew from therapy as a result of the report, but in the remaining 75%, the therapeutic relationship either remained unchanged or improved. Finally, in a survey of 176 Iowa families that had been reported to CPS because of suspected child maltreatment, Fryer and associates (1990) reported that nearly three quarters of the respondents rated the quality of child welfare services as good or excellent, while only 11% rated the services as poor. Moreover, 72% indicated that CPS intervention resulted in a better life for the family. As Finkelhor (1992) concludes, to date "[t]here is simply no evidence to back the assertion that child protective investigations are 'unavoidably traumatic'" (p. 4). In the absence of such evidence, I maintain that it is ethically imperative for mental health professionals to comply with reporting laws (see also Petretic-Jackson & Koziol, 1992). If future research should contradict these findings to indicate that reporting proves harmful to a substantial percentage of children (or to an identifiable subpopulation), then mental health professionals must seek to resolve the conflict between the higher principle of nonmaleficence and legal mandates through proactive changes in legislation, and not merely through private acts of noncompliance (Kalichman, 1993).

Responsible Reporting

Not only do mental health professionals have an ethical duty to report suspected sexual abuse, but they also have an ethical duty to make reports in a responsible manner. Before therapy begins with a client, principles of professional ethical codes require that the mental health professional fully inform the client of the extent of confidentiality (e.g., APA, 1992, Standard 5.01; National Association of Social Workers, 1990). They must be advised that any information they volunteer about abuse (past or present) may trigger a report to authorities. Further, periodic verbal reminders of the limits of confidentiality may be necessary. If child sexual abuse is suspected, mental health professionals are ethically bound to inform the client of their suspicions and intentions to report, unless doing so would put the child victim at risk (Racusin & Felsman, 1986). Unfortunately, surveys of mental health professionals indicate that informing clients about the limits of confidentiality is far from universal practice (see, e.g., Baird & Rupert, 1987, where only half of the practicing psychologists who were surveyed informed their clients of such limits). If mental health professionals are unsure of whether sufficient evidence exists to support a "reasonable suspicion" of child sexual abuse, they should be encouraged to consult colleagues. However, they should be discouraged from delaying a report in order to gather evidence, as this is clearly beyond their professional role and legal duty (Kalichman, 1993).

Improving the CPS Response

Although available research fails to show that reporting has the universally harmful effects that professionals had presumed, nevertheless, it is clear that there is room for improvement in the CPS response to reports. Toward this end, mental health professionals should work to build a cooperative relationship with child welfare services and with individual caseworkers surrounding case management issues (Petretic-Jackson & Koziol, 1992). At a minimum, mental health professionals should be kept abreast of actions taken (or not taken) by CPS in response to the professionals' reports (Davidson, 1988). Ideally, the CPS caseworker should work with and through the therapist to determine the best course of action for the child and family involved (Butz, 1985). Mental health professionals must be vigilant and cooperative in encouraging such a working relationship.

THE MENTAL HEALTH PROFESSIONAL AS AN EXPERT AT ADJUDICATION

Clearly, the role of the mental health professional in reporting cases of suspected child sexual abuse has been, and continues to be, legally and ethically controversial. An equally controversial role of mental health professionals is as an expert at adjudication. During the past 10 years, the admissibility of expert testimony in child sexual abuse cases has been addressed by a number of legal scholars and social scientists (see, e.g., Bulkley, 1992; Lloyd, 1986; Melton & Limber, 1989; Myers, Bays, Becker, Berliner, Corwin, & Saywitz, 1989), as well as numerous state appellate courts (for review, see Bulkley, 1992; Myers et al., 1989).

Expert testimony increasingly is relied upon in cases of child sexual abuse in order to assist the fact finder (the judge or the jury) in determining whether or not sexual abuse has occurred (Melton & Limber, 1989). Often, a child victim is the sole witness to the abuse and his or her testimony is the only direct evidence available. In such circumstances, expert testimony frequently is employed either to buttress or to attack the child victim's assertions of abuse.

General Rules of Admissibility of Expert Testimony

In the United States, the admissibility of evidence at trial generally is determined by the U.S. Federal Rules of Evidence. The majority of states have adopted the Federal Rules (Bulkley, 1992; Michaels, 1987), and those that have not adopted them frequently use them as a model for admissibility of evidence (Michaels, 1987). Under Rule 701 of the Federal Rules, an ordinary witness is not permitted to give opinion testimony. However, an expert witness is allowed to do so under specified circumstances. First, as with all testimony, expert testimony must be deemed relevant to the case in order to be admissible (Federal Rule of Evidence 401). If the expert testimony is considered by the judge to be relevant, it further must be shown that the witness is "qualified as an expert by knowledge, skill, experience, training, or education" and that the expert's opinion is based on "scientific, technical, or other specialized knowledge [that] will assist the trier of fact to understand the evidence or to determine a fact at issue" (Federal Rule of Evidence 702). In states that have not adopted this rule, expert testimony typically is admissible only if the substance of the testimony is beyond the ken of the average layperson (Bulkley, 1992). A further requirement of expert testimony is that its probative value outweigh its prejudicial value (Federal Rule of Evidence 403).

In addition to or in place of the Federal Rules of Evidence, a court may impose its own standard of admissibility of expert advice. Traditionally, most jurisdictions have followed the test enunciated in *Frye v. United States* (1923), which requires that the scientific support for the opinion "be sufficiently established to have gained general acceptance in the particular field in which it belongs" (p. 1014). However, the U.S. Supreme Court recently found that the *Frye* standard was excessively restrictive and superseded by the Federal Rules of Evidence (*Daubert v. Merrell Dow Pharmaceuticals, Inc.*, 1993). Although the Supreme Court's finding is binding upon federal courts, it is not yet clear the extent to which state courts will follow the ruling in *Daubert.*

Admissibility of Expert Testimony: Legal Conclusions

In the adjudicatory phase of child sexual abuse cases, several different types of expert testimony may be sought by the prosecution and defense. The legal admissibility of each type is discussed, as are ethical issues arising from offering each.

TESTIMONY ABOUT ABUSER CHARACTERISTICS. There is little debate on the admissibility of expert testimony about typical characteristics of child sex abusers. Although the prosecution may attempt to introduce such evidence to prove that the defendant has characteristics similar to those of abusers, such testimony is universally excluded by courts (Bulkley, 1988; 1992, Melton et al., 1987; Melton & Limber 1989; see, e.g., *State v. Loebach*, 1981) because it is character evidence (which is inadmissible under Federal Rule of Evidence

404). Further, admission of such evidence violates Rule 702 because mental health professionals have no "specialized knowledge" about characteristics that distinguish child abusers from nonabusers. There is no unique personality type among abusers; rather, there is a wide scope of behaviors that may contribute to the development of molestation behavior (Bulkley, 1988; Melton et al., 1987; Walker, 1990). Moreover, the description of the general behavior patterns of child sexual abusers is not directly relevant to whether a particular defendant abused a particular child (Melton et al., 1987). Thus such testimony is legally inadmissible and ethically unjustified.

TESTIMONY ABOUT CHARACTERISTICS OF SEXUALLY ABUSED CHILDREN. A second type of expert testimony that may be offered in cases of child sexual abuse is testimony about common characteristics of sexually abused children. The least objectionable testimony of this type describes aspects of the victim's behavior that otherwise might be confusing to the fact finder (Melton & Limber, 1989). Frequently, such testimony is referred to as "rehabilitative testimony" (see, e.g., Bulkley, 1992), because it is offered by the prosecution to rehabilitate the credibility of the child by explaining behaviors the jury may incorrectly believe to be inconsistent with having been sexually abused. Typically, rehabilitative testimony is offered to explain a child's clouded, conflicting, or vague accounts; affection for the offender; or retraction of initial accusations (Bulkley, 1992; Lloyd, 1986; Melton & Limber, 1989).

Such testimony generally is ruled admissible in court (Bulkley, 1992; see, e.g., *Bostic v. State*, 1989; *People v. Sanchez*, 1989; *People v. Stark*, 1989). Courts assume that average jurors are unaware of typical behaviors of sexually abused children, and that they may misinterpret their actions during or after the abuse (e.g., failing to resist the abuse, failing to report the incident). Whether such evidence *should* be admitted depends on the knowledge of the average juror. If jurors are not knowledgeable about sexually abused children or if they have misperceptions about how these children should react to sexual abuse, then expert testimony should be encouraged because it will assist them in making an informed decision about the evidence in the case. If, on the other hand, jurors are already aware of common reactions of sexually abused children, then the evidence may be an unnecessary intrusion on the trial process (Melton & Limber, 1989). Currently, little is known about the lay public's knowledge about sexually abused children. However, a survey of parents in metropolitan Boston (Finkelhor, 1984) indicates that the public may be conscious of a child's tendency to delay reporting an incident of sexual abuse. Future research will help to inform judges and policy makers regarding the admissibility of rehabilitative testimony.

In part due to the courts' receptivity to rehabilitative expert testimony in sexual abuse cases, prosecutors soon began to offer expert testimony about typical behaviors, common reactions, and syndromes (see, e.g., Summit, 1983) of sexually abused children (Bulkley, 1992). Such behaviors and emotions include anxiety, secrecy, fear of men, nightmares and other sleep disorders, and unusual sexual knowledge or behaviors (Melton & Limber, 1989; Summit, 1983; see, e.g. *State v. Kim*, 1982; *State v. Myers*, 1984). Many appellate courts have admitted expert testimony that describes these "typical" reactions of sexually abused children, although a significant minority do not (Bulkley, 1992). Courts have been somewhat less likely to admit testimony about whether the behavior of a particular victim/witness is consistent with the behavior of sexually abused children (Bulkley, 1988; 1992; Gothard, 1987; see, e.g., *U.S. v. Azure*, 1986; *Ward v. State*, 1988; but see *State v. Lawrence*, 1988; *State v. Jensen*, 1987).

Should courts admit testimony concerning a child sexual abuse syndrome? Currently, the scientific basis for this syndrome is weak. It was devised for therapeutic treatment purposes, not for determining the truth or accuracy of an abuse allegation (Lloyd, 1986). Many victims of sexual abuse exhibit no obvious signs of maltreatment (Browne & Finkelhor, 1986). Furthermore, numerous children who have not been abused exhibit "symptoms" of child sexual abuse (Emans, 1988; Melton & Limber, 1989; Risin & McNamara, 1989). Thus the syndrome is far from a litmus test for abuse. Indeed, if a child exhibits characteristics of sexual abuse, such as bed-wetting or anxiety, the probability is that he or she has *not* been abused.

Furthermore, presenting evidence to suggest that a child has been sexually abused does not speak to the issue of the specific allegation. Just because a child exhibits signs of having been abused does not mean that the child was abused at the time in question by the defendant on trial (Melton & Limber, 1989). For example, a child who exhibits such signs may have been abused by someone other than the defendant. Thus syndrome testimony about typical characteristics of sexually abused children probably will not be helpful to jurors, and may unduly prejudice them (see, e.g., *People v. Knupp*, 1992). For these reasons, it should not be admitted in cases of child sexual abuse.

ULTIMATE ISSUE TESTIMONY. A third type of testimony that may be offered by mental health professionals in cases of child sexual abuse is testimony about whether or not they believe that a particular child was sexually abused. Such opinion testimony is offered to address the ultimate legal question faced by a court of law. It has not been allowed by a majority of courts (Bulkley, 1988, 1992; Melton & Limber, 1989; Myers et al., 1989). Many courts and commentators have recognized that such opinions clearly exceed any expertise of mental health professionals, and, therefore, are unethical (see, e.g., Bulkley, 1992; Melton & Limber, 1989). Further, these opinions usurp the fact finder's function of determining the veracity of the charges and the guilt of the defendant (Bulkley, 1988, 1992; Lloyd, 1986; Melton & Limber, 1989).

Recommendations for Professionals

If courts permit experts to testify about "typical" characteristics of sexually abused children, or even, on occasion, on the ultimate issue of whether a particular child was abused, *should* mental health professionals agree to provide this evidence?

TESTIMONY ABOUT CHARACTERISTICS OF SEXUALLY ABUSED CHILDREN. Mental health professionals can, with good conscience, inform the court about typical characteristics of sexually abused children, provided that they clearly explain the limits of their knowledge and expertise and take steps to ensure that the court and the jury are aware of these limits (Melton & Limber, 1989). However, to testify that a child's behavior is consistent with sexual abuse implies a degree of certainty that mental health professionals do not currently possess, and, as a result, it may mislead the jury by improperly bolstering the credibility of the child victim.

ULTIMATE ISSUE TESTIMONY. Similar arguments may be used against the admissibility of expert opinion as to whether or not the child victim was sexually abused. As noted above, such determinations by mental health professionals clearly exceed their expertise and usurp the duties of the judge and jury. Unfortunately, a large number of mental health professionals believe that they do have the expertise to determine whether a child has been so abused. In a recent survey of mental health and medical professionals (Oberlander, 1992), over 60% of forensically certified professionals and over 80% of nonforensically certified professionals said they believed that an evaluation could establish whether the child had been sexually abused.

Testimony About the Child's Use of Anatomically Detailed Dolls

The use of anatomically detailed dolls (AD dolls) as assessment tools in cases of child sexual abuse has become particularly controversial, and underscores the need for mental health professionals to be careful not to exceed their expertise when testifying as experts in such cases. Mental health professionals' use of these tools is worth examining in some detail to illustrate this point.

USE OF AD DOLLS BY MENTAL HEALTH PROFESSIONALS. The AD dolls were first developed and used by a handful of professionals in the mid-1970s. Today, these dolls are used extensively by a wide variety of mental health and law enforcement professionals as tools to assess children for signs of sexual abuse, and as therapeutic aids to help them deal with these experiences. A recent study of Boston-area professionals (Kendall-Tackett & Watson, 1992) indicates that their use among mental health professionals is widespread. A clear majority (70%) of their respondents who worked with sexually abused children reported that they utilized AD dolls. The use of the dolls was particularly common in evaluating young children between three and six years of age. A survey by Oberlander (1992) suggests that most medical and mental health professionals find the dolls of help in assessing children for psychological signs of sexual abuse. Professionals in this survey who were not forensically certified were particularly apt to find AD dolls of value in such assessments (86%, as opposed to 59% of forensically certified respondents).

AD DOLLS AS A BASIS FOR EXPERT DETERMINATIONS OF ABUSE. Not only do many mental health professionals find AD dolls useful in assessing allegedly sexually abused children, but some have relied upon findings from AD doll interviews to offer expert testimony about typical behaviors of such children or about whether a particular child was sexually abused (see, e.g., *In re Amber B. and Teela B.*, 1987). But despite their widespread use as assessment tools, conclusive evidence as to their reliability and validity currently is lacking. Although several suggested protocols for using AD dolls have been published (see, e.g., Boat & Everson, 1988; White, Strom, Santilli, & Halpin, 1986), neither the dolls themselves nor their use in assessment interviews has been standardized (APA, 1991). Social scientists (e.g., Cohn, 1991; Glaser & Collins, 1989; Melton & Limber, 1989; Skinner & Berry, 1993; Terr in Yates & Terr, 1988), as well as a number of courts (e.g., *In re Amber B. and Teela B.*, 1987; *In re Christine C. and Michael C.*, 1987), have emphasized that the dolls do not constitute a behavioral "test" of child sexual abuse. As the American Psychological Association (1991) concluded, "Neither the dolls, nor their use, are standardized or accompanied by normative data."

RESEARCH FINDINGS. Although recent studies have begun to answer many of the research questions related to the use of AD dolls, researchers currently do not have clear answers to many of the questions surrounding children's interactions with the dolls. Primary among these questions are: (1) Do AD dolls assist children's recall of an event and/or response to specific questions about an event? (2) What are the normative responses of children at different ages to AD dolls?

To date, few investigations have examined the extent to which the use of AD dolls in an interview enhances children's accurate memories of an event. Goodman and Aman (1990) investigated three- and five-year-olds' memories of interactions (i.e., playing games) with a confederate. In interviewing the children one week after the event, the researchers observed that the use of both AD dolls and nonanatomically detailed dolls enhanced five-year-olds' abilities to recall information correctly or to answer specific questions correctly about an event. The memories of the younger children in this study were aided by nonanatomically detailed dolls, but not by AD dolls. In a study of five- and seven-year-olds, Saywitz and colleagues (Saywitz, Goodman, Nicholas, & Moan, 1991) observed that children who were encouraged to use AD dolls and other props to describe their experiences at a recent medical examination provided twice as much accurate information as did children who were not permitted to use AD dolls and props.

Most investigations of AD dolls have focused on whether the dolls improperly elicit sexualized responses from nonabused children. The majority of these studies have determined that they do not have highly suggestive effects upon most children (Boat, Everson, & Holland, 1990; Cohn, 1991; Dawson, Vaughan, & Wagner, 1992; Everson & Boat, 1990; Glaser & Collins, 1989; Goodman & Aman, 1987, 1990; Sivan, Schor, Koeppl, & Noble, 1988; White et al., 1986). These studies show that although it is not uncommon for them to explore the body parts of the dolls, it is unlikely for nonabused children to act out specific sexual behaviors with the dolls. Two studies (Everson & Boat, 1990; Jampole & Weber, 1987), however, have reported somewhat higher rates of sexualized behaviors among children. Twenty percent (two of 10) of the nonabused children studied by Jampole and Weber (1987) demonstrated sexualized play with AD dolls. Further, Everson and Boat (1990) observed somewhat higher rates of sexualized play among a specific subpopulation of the children in their study. Although only 6% of all children in their study exhibited sexualized play with AD dolls, over 20% of older, male, low-socioeconomic-status, African-American preschoolers displayed such behaviors.

To date, research is inconclusive in determining the extent to which sexually abused children differ from nonabused children in their interactions with AD dolls. Some researchers have observed clear differences in the reactions of abused (or referred, and presumably abused) children versus control children. Jampole and Weber (1987) saw significantly more sexualized behaviors in the AD-doll play of young (ages three to eight) sexually abused children than among nonabused children. Indeed, whereas 90% of the sexually abused children demonstrated explicit sexual behaviors in such play (e.g., demonstrated intercourse between dolls or between the doll and the child), only 20% of the nonabused children in this study did so. White and colleagues (1986) used a structured interview to rate the reactions of children (ages two to six) toward AD dolls. They found that those children who were referred for sexual abuse evaluations received higher ratings of suspected abuse (determined solely by their interactions with the AD dolls) than did nonreferred children.

Other researchers, however, have failed to distinguish such differences. Cohn (1991) observed no significant differences in the reactions of referred versus nonreferred preschoolers toward AD dolls. Both groups of children exhibited similar levels of comfort, aggressive behavior, curiosity, humor, and sexually explicit or acting out behaviors in their interactions with the dolls. Similarly, Kenyon-Jump, Burnette, and Robertson (1991) found no significant differences in the explicit sexual behaviors of the abused versus nonabused preschoolers in such interactions. Given the discrepant findings of these preliminary studies, further research clearly is needed to determine the normative reactions of children of different ages, genders, races, and socioeconomic statuses to AD dolls under different interviewing conditions.

SUMMARY. Because of the questionable validity of AD dolls as an assessment tool and the nontrivial potential of the dolls to mislead professionals and/or jurors about sexual abuse allegations, they should be used with the utmost care in child sexual abuse investigations. Use of the dolls is appropriate to inquire about children's terminology of sexual parts or to assist the child to tell a story of abuse. However, it is inappropriate for mental health professionals who testify in sexual abuse cases to conclude, based upon a child's interactions with AD dolls, that the child was or was not sexually abused. Such testimony would exceed the extent of professional expertise (and, as previously argued, would usurp the role of the judge or jury). Moreover, until further studies provide a more complete picture of children's behaviors with AD dolls, it is premature for mental health professionals to testify about "typical" AD-doll behaviors of abused versus nonabused children.

CONCLUSIONS

Mental health professionals play key roles in the battle against child sexual abuse. However, their participation in such cases is rarely clear cut. Two of their most controversial roles are as reporters of suspected abuse and as expert witnesses at the adjudication of a case. In these roles, mental health professionals may experience significant tensions between perceived ethical duties and legal requirements. This chapter has suggested that while mental health professionals remain underinvolved in the reporting of child abuse and neglect, they may be frequently overinvolved in the adjudication of the case. Mental health professionals must, through education, training, and dialogue, encourage appropriate participation by their colleagues in child sexual abuse cases. It is hoped that the current controversy surrounding the legal and ethical involvement of mental health professionals in cases of child sexual abuse will continue to impel a healthy discussion of their proper roles in these cases. Research that will (1) help us to understand and improve reporting practices, (2) provide a better understanding of the effects of reporting on children and families, and (3) help to determine the validity and usefulness of expert testimony will play a crucial pay in informing participants in this discussion and advising future policies.

Recommendations

1. **THAT** mental health professionals recognize their ethical and legal duty to report all suspected cases of child sexual abuse.
2. **THAT** mental health professionals fully inform clients of the limits of confidentiality in a therapy relationship before therapy begins, and that they provide periodic reminders of these limits during the course of therapy.
3. **THAT** mental health professionals work cooperatively with CPS caseworkers once a report of child maltreatment has been made, following the actions taken in the case and consulting with the caseworker to help determine the best course of action for the child and family.
4. **THAT** mental health professionals who testify in court refrain from providing scientifically unfounded opinions about whether a child (a) fits a "profile" of sexual abuse, (b) likely has been sexually abused, or (c) is telling the truth.
5. **THAT** mental health professionals recognize the questionable validity of AD dolls as assessment tools and their nontrivial potential to mislead professionals and courts about sexual abuse allegations.
6. **THAT** mental health professionals consequently refrain from providing ultimate issue testimony based on children's interactions with AD dolls and from testifying about "typical" play behaviors of children with the dolls, until further research can consistently delineate such behaviors.

REFERENCES

Abrahams, N., Casey, K., & Daro, D. (1992). Teachers' knowledge, attitudes, and beliefs about child abuse and its prevention. *Child Abuse and Neglect, 16,* 229–238.

American Psychological Association. (1991). *Statement on the use of anatomically detailed dolls in forensic evaluations.* Washington, D.C.: Author.

American Psychological Association. (1992). Ethical principles of psychologists and code of conduct. *American Psychologist, 47,* 1597–1611.

Ansell, C., & Ross, H. L. (1990). Reply to Pope and Bajt. *American Psychologist, 45,* 399.

Attias, R., & Goodwin, J. (1985). Knowledge and management strategies in incest cases: A survey of physicians, psychologists and family counselors. *Child Abuse and Neglect, 9,* 527–533.

Baird, K. A., & Rupert, P. A. (1987). Clinical management of confidentiality: A survey of psychologists in seven states. *Professional Psychology: Research and Practice, 18,* 347–352.

Boat, B. W., & Everson, M. D. (1988). Use of anatomical dolls among professionals in sexual abuse evaluations. *Child Abuse and Neglect, 12,* 171–179.

Boat, B. W., Everson, M. D., & Holland, J. (1990). Maternal perceptions of nonabused young children's behaviors after the children's exposure to anatomical dolls. *Child Welfare, 69,* 389–400.

Bostic v. State, 772 P.2d 1089 (Alaska Ct. App. 1989).

Brosig, C. L., & Kalichman, S. C. (1992). Clinicians' reporting of suspected child abuse: A review of the empirical literature. *Clinical Psychology Review, 12,* 155–168.

Browne, A., & Finkelhor, D. (1986). Initial and long-term effects: A review of the research. In D. Finkelhor (Ed.), *A sourcebook on child sexual abuse* (pp. 143–179). Beverly Hills, Calif.: Sage.

Bulkley, J. (1988). Legal proceedings, reforms, and emerging issues in child sexual abuse cases. *Behavioral Sciences and the Law, 6,* 153–180.

Bulkley, J. A. (1992). The prosecution's use of social science expert testimony in child sexual abuse cases: National trends and recommendations. *Journal of Child Sexual Abuse, 1,* 75–95.

Butz, R. A. (1985). Reporting child abuse and confidentiality in counseling. *Social Casework, 66,* 83–90.

Child Abuse Prevention and Treatment Act of 1974, 24 U.S.C.S. §5105-5115 (1979, Cum. Supp. 1988).

Cohn, D. S. (1991). Anatomical doll play of preschoolers referred for sexual abuse and those not referred. *Child Abuse and Neglect, 15,* 455–466.

Daubert v. Merrell Dow Pharmaceuticals, Inc. 113 S. Ct. 2786 (1993).

Davidson, H. (1988). Failure to report child abuse: Legal penalties and emerging issues. In A. Maney & S. Wells (Eds.), *Professional responsibilities in protecting children: A public health approach to child sexual abuse* (pp. 93–101). New York: Praeger.

Dawson, B., Vaughan, A. R., & Wagner, W. G. (1992). Normal responses to sexually anatomically detailed dolls. *Journal of Family Violence, 7,* 135–152.

Emans, R. L. (1988). Psychology's responsibility in false accusations of child abuse. *Journal of Clinical Psychology, 44,* 1000–1004.

Everson, M. D., & Boat, B. W. (1990). Sexualized doll play among young children: Implications for the use of anatomical dolls in sexual abuse evaluations. *Journal of the American Academy of Child and Adolescent Psychiatry, 29,* 736–742.

Federal Rule of Evidence 401.

Federal Rule of Evidence 403.

Federal Rule of Evidence 404.

Federal Rule of Evidence 701.

Federal Rule of Evidence 702.

Finkelhor, D. (1984). *Child sexual abuse: New theory and research.* New York: Free Press.

Finkelhor, D. (1992). New myths about the child welfare system. *Child, Youth, and Family Services Quarterly, 15,* 3–5.

Frye v. United States 2993 F.1013 (D. C. Cir. 1923).

Fryer, G. E., Bross, D. C., Krugman, R. D., Denson, D. B., & Baird, D. (1990, Winter). Good news for CPS workers. *Public Welfare,* pp. 38–41.

Garbarino, J. (1991). The incidence and prevalence of child maltreatment. In D. D. Knudsen and J. L. Miller (Eds.), *Abused and battered: Social and legal responses to family violence* (pp. 219–261). New York: Walter deGruyter.

Glaser, D., & Collins, C. (1989). The response of young, non-sexually abused children to anatomically correct dolls. *Journal of Child Psychology and Psychiatry, 30,* 547–560.

Goodman, G. S., & Aman, C. (1987, April). Children's use of anatomically correct dolls to report an event. Paper presented at the meeting of the Society for Research in Child Development, Baltimore, Md.

Goodman, G. S., & Aman, C. (1990). Children's use of anatomically detailed dolls to recount an event. *Child Development, 61,* 1859–1871.

Gothard, S. (1987). The admissibility of evidence in child sexual abuse cases. *Child Welfare, 66,* 13–24.

Guyer, M. J. (1982). Child abuse and neglect statutes: Legal and clinical implications. *American Journal of Orthopsychiatry, 52,* 73–81.

Harper, G., & Irvin, E. (1985). Alliance formation with parents: Limit setting and the effect of mandated reporting. *American Journal of Orthopsychiatry, 55,* 550–559.

Hibbard, R. A., & Zollinger, T. W. (1990). Patterns of child sexual abuse knowledge among professionals. *Child Abuse and Neglect, 14,* 347–355.

In re Amber B. and Teela B., 191 Cal.App. 3rd 682 (1987).

In re Christine C. and Michael C., 191 Cal. App. 3rd 676 (1987).

Jagim, R. D., Wittman, W. D., & Noll, J. O. (1978). Mental health professionals' attitudes toward confidentiality, privilege, and third-party disclosure. *Professional Psychology, 9,* 458–466.

Jampole, L., & Weber, M. K. (1987). An assessment of the behavior of sexually abused and nonsexually abused children with anatomically correct dolls. *Child Abuse and Neglect, 11,* 187–192.

Kalichman, S. C. (1993). *Mandated reporting of suspected child abuse: Ethics, law and policy.* Washington, D.C.: American Psychological Association.

Kalichman, S. C., & Brosig, C. L. (1992). The effects of statutory requirements on child maltreatment reporting: A comparison of two state laws. *American Journal of Orthopsychiatry, 62,* 284–296.

Kalichman, S. C., & Brosig, C. L. (1993). Practicing psychologists' interpretations of compliance with child abuse reporting laws. *Law and Human Behavior, 17,* 83–93.

Kalichman, S. C., & Craig, M. E. (1991). Professional psychologists' decisions to report suspected child abuse: Clinician and situation influences. *Professional Psychology: Research and Practice, 22,* 84–89.

Kalichman, S. C., Craig, M. E., & Follingstad, D. R. (1988). Mental health professionals and suspected cases of child abuse: An investigation of factors influencing reporting. *Community Mental Health Journal, 24*, 43–51.

Kalichman, S. C., Craig, M. E., & Follingstad, D. R. (1989). Factors influencing the reporting of father–child sexual abuse: Study of licensed practicing psychologists. *Professional Psychology: Research and Practice, 20*, 84–89.

Kalichman, S. C., Craig, M. E., & Follingstad, D. R. (1990). Professionals' adherence to mandatory child abuse reporting laws: Effects of responsibility attribution, confidence ratings, and situational factors. *Child Abuse and Neglect, 14*, 69–77.

Kempe, C. H., Silverman, F. N., Steele, B. F., Droegemueller, W., & Silver, H. K. (1962). The battered child syndrome. *Journal of the American Medical Association, 181*, 17–24.

Kendall-Tackett, K. A., & Watson, M. W. (1992). Use of anatomical dolls by Boston-area professionals. *Child Abuse and Neglect, 16*, 423–428.

Kenyon-Jump, R., Burnette, M. M., & Robertson, M. (1991). Comparison of behaviors of suspected sexually abused and non-sexually abused preschool children using anatomical dolls. *Journal of Psychopathology and Behavioral Assessment, 13*, 225–240.

Landeros v. Flood, P.2d 389 (1976).

Leong, G. B., Silva, J. A., & Weinstock, R. (1988). Ethical considerations of clinical use of Miranda-like warnings. *Psychiatric Quarterly, 59*, 293–305.

Lloyd, D. W. (1986, August). Legal issues for psychologists. Paper presented at the annual meeting of the American Psychological Association, Washington, D. C.

MacMurray, B. K., & Carson, B. A. (1991). Legal issues in violence toward children. In R. T. Ammerman & M. Hersen (Eds.), *Case studies in family violence* (pp. 57–71). New York: Plenum.

McCord, D. (1986). Expert psychological testimony about child complainants in sexual abuse prosecutions: A foray into the admissibility of novel psychological evidence. *Journal of Criminal Law and Criminology, 77*, 1–68.

Melton, G. B., & Limber, S. (1989). Psychologists' involvement in cases of child maltreatment. *American Psychologist, 44*, 1225–1233.

Melton, G. B., & Limber, S. (1991). Caution in child maltreatment cases. *American Psychologist, 46*, 82–84.

Melton, G. B., Petrila, J., Poythress, N. G., & Slobogin, C. (1987). *Psychological evaluations for the courts: A handbook for mental health professionals and lawyers.* New York: Guilford Press.

Michaels, L. F. (1987). Evidentiary issues in cases involving children. In D. C. Bross & L. F. Michaels (Eds.), *Foundations of child advocacy* (pp. 101–116). Longmont, Col.: Bookmakers Guild.

Miller, R. D., & Weinstock, R. (1987). Conflict of interest between therapist–patient confidentiality and the duty to report sexual abuse of children. *Behavioral Sciences and the Law, 5*, 161–174.

Muehleman, T., & Kimmons, C. (1981). Psychologists' views on child abuse reporting, confidentiality, life, and the law: An exploratory study. *Professional Psychology, 12*, 631–638.

Myers, J. E. B. (1991). Comment on Melton and Limber. *American Psychologist, 46,* 81–82.

Myers, J. E. B., Bays, J., Becker, J., Berliner, L., Corwin, D. L., & Saywitz, K. (1989). Expert testimony in child sexual abuse litigation. *Nebraska Law Review, 68,* 1–145.

National Association of Social Workers (1990). *Code of ethics.* Washington D.C.: Author.

Newberger, E. H. (1991). The obligation to protect. *Ethics and Behavior, 1,* 148–149.

Oberlander, L. B. (1992, August). Recommendations for standards of practice in child sexual abuse evaluations. Paper presented at the meeting of the American Psychological Association, Washington, D.C.

Otto, R. K., & Melton, G. B. (1990). Trends in legislation and case law on child abuse and neglect. In R. T. Ammerman & M. Hersen (Eds.), *Children at risk: An evaluation of factors contributing to child abuse and neglect* (pp. 55–83). New York: Plenum.

People v. Knupp, 579 N.Y.S.2d 801 (1992).

People v. Sanchez, 256 Cal. Rptr. 446 (Cal. Ct. App. 1989).

People v. Stark, 261 Cal. Rptr. 479 (Cal. Ct. App. 1989).

Petretic-Jackson, P., & Koziol, R. (1992). Mandatory child abuse reporting: The child and family perspective. *Child, Youth, and Family Services Quarterly, 15,* 7–10.

Pollak, J., & Levy, S. (1989). Countertransference and failure to report child abuse and neglect. *Child Abuse and Neglect, 13,* 515–522.

Quinn, K. M. (1992). Child sexual abuse. In M. G. Kaloerakis (Ed.), *Handbook of psychiatric practice in the juvenile court* (pp. 97–104). Washington, D.C.: American Psychological Association.

Racusin, R. J., & Felsman, J. K. (1986). Reporting child abuse: The ethical obligation to inform parents. *Journal of the American Academy of Child Psychiatry, 25,* 485–489.

Risin, L. I., & McNamara, J. R. (1989). Validation of child sexual abuse: The psychologist's role. *Journal of Clinical Psychology, 45,* 175–184.

Saywitz, K. J., Goodman, G. S., Nicholas, E., & Moan, S. F. (1991). Children's memories of a physical examination involving genital touch: Implications for reports of child sexual abuse. *Journal of Consulting and Clinical Psychology, 59,* 682–691.

Sivan, A. B., Schor, D. P., Koeppl, G. K., & Noble, L. D. (1988). Interaction of normal children with anatomical dolls. *Child Abuse and Neglect, 12,* 295–304.

Skinner, L. J., & Berry, K. K. (1993). Anatomically detailed dolls and the evaluation of child sexual abuse allegations: Psychometric considerations. *Law and Human Behavior, 17,* 399–422.

State v. Jensen, 415 N.W.2d 519 (Wis. Ct. App. 1987).

State v. Kim, 645 P.2d 1330 (Hawaii 1982).

State v. Lawrence, 541 A.2d 1291 (Me. 1988).

State v. Loebach, 310 N.W. 2d 58 (Minn. 1981).

State v. Myers, 359 N.W. 2d 604 (Minn. 1984).

Summit, R. (1983). The child sexual abuse accommodation syndrome. *Child Abuse and Neglect, 7,* 177–193.

Swoboda, J. S., Elwork, A., Sales, B. D., & Levine, D. (1978). Knowledge of and compliance with privileged communication and child-abuse-reporting laws. *Professional Psychology, 19,* 448–457.

Thompson, A. (1990). *Guide to ethical practice in psychotherapy.* New York: Wiley.

U.S. v. Azure, 801 F.2d 336 (8th Cir. 1986).

Walker, L. E. A. (1990). Psychological assessment of sexually abused children for legal evaluation and expert witness testimony. *Professional Psychology: Research and Practice, 21,* 344–353.

Ward v. State, 519 So. 2d 1082 (Fla. Dist. Ct. App. 1988).

Watson, H., & Levine, J. D. (1989). Psychotherapy and mandated reporting of child abuse. *American Journal of Orthopsychiatry, 59,* 246–256.

Wells, S. (1988). On the decision to report suspected abuse or neglect. In A. Maney & S. Wells (Eds.), *Professional responsibilities in protecting children* (pp. 191–202). New York: Praeger.

White, S., Strom, G. A., Santilli, G., & Halpin, B. M. (1986). Interviewing young sexual abuse victims with anatomically correct dolls. *Child Abuse and Neglect, 10,* 519–529.

Wurtele, S. K., & Schmitt, A. (1992). Child care workers' knowledge about reporting suspected child sexual abuse. *Child Abuse and Neglect, 16,* 385–90.

Yates, A., & Terr, L. (1988). Anatomically correct dolls: Should they be used as the basis for expert testimony? *Journal of the American Academy of Child and Adolescent Research, 27,* 254–257.

Zebrowski, S. (1984). Influences on psychologists' perceptions of physical child abuse and their stated willingness to report suspected cases. *Dissertation Abstracts, 45,* 1300.

Zellman, G. L. (1990a). Child abuse reporting and failure to report among mandated reporters: Prevalence, incidence, reasons. *Journal of Interpersonal Violence, 5,* 3–22.

Zellman, G. L. (1990b). Report decision-making patterns among mandated child abuse reporters. *Child Abuse and Neglect, 14,* 325–336.

Zellman, G. L. (1992). The impact of case characteristics on child abuse reporting decisions. *Child Abuse and Neglect, 16,* 57–74.

Zellman, G. L., & Antler, S. (1990). Mandated reporters and CPS: A study in frustration. *Public Welfare, 48,* 30–37.

Name Index

Milchman, M. S., 92–93, 219
Milea, S., 279, 280
Milgram, S., 143
Miller, R. D., 337, 338
Mingay, D., 195
Mitchell, L., 279
Moan, S., 90–91, 110, 112, 114, 295, 347
Moran, T., 50–51
Morris, M., 216
Moser, J. T., 25, 50–51
Mosk, M. D., 51
Mossler, D. G., 90
Moston, S., 144
Mrazek, P. B., 262
Mucigrosso, L., 279
Muehleman, T., 338
Mumme, D. L., 78–80
Muram, D., 234, 235, 237
Murphy, W., 245–46
Murphy, W. D., 246
Myers, J. E. B., 83–85, 90, 93, 265, 335, 341, 344
Myles-Worsley, M., 105, 107

Nadelson, C., 254
Nader, K., 87–88
Nadon, R., 187
Nash, M. R., 51, 182
Nathanson, R., 111, 112–13, 114
Nauful, T., 75–76
Naus, M. J., 101
Neff, R. L., 262
Neilsen, D., 86–87
Neisser, U., 180, 195
Nelson, K., 105, 202
Newberger, E. H., 225–26, 337, 338
Newlands, P., 199
Ney, Tara, xii, 3

Nicholas, E., 110, 112, 114, 295, 347
Nida, R. E., 107–8, 112, 113
Nigro, G., 195
Noble, L. D., 52, 347
Nogrady, H., 187
Noll, J. O., 338
Notman, M., 254
Nurcombe, B., 305, 306, 307, 308, 309
Nuttall, R., 8, 10, 219

Oates, K., 231–32
Oberlander, L. B., 345, 346
O'Day, B., 277
O'Donohue, W. T., 245–46
Ofshe, R. J., 182
Ogilvie, D., xvi
Olio, K. A., 181
Orne, M. T., 180, 187
Ornstein, Peter A., xii, 99, 100, 103, 104, 105–6, 107–8, 110–11, 112–13, 114, 202–3
Osborn, C. A., 244–45, 248–49
Otto, R. K., 336, 338
Ozbek, I. N., 156

Packer, L. S., 224, 225
Palmer, J. C., 108
Palmer, S., 6
Para, J. M., 235
Paradise, J. E., 225–26, 231–32, 237–38
Parker, J., 93
Pazder, A. L., 303, 304
Peacock, Edward J., xii, 242
Pearson, J., 126
Pepin, L., xvi
Perlman, N. B., 23

Perlmutter, L. H., 262
Perlmutter, M., 159
Perner, J., 75, 78–80
Perry, C., 180, 187
Perry, Nancy Walker, xii, 73, 78, 84–85, 90–91, 158
Peters, D. P., 7, 91, 103, 114, 171, 172
Peters, S., xviii
Peterson, C. C.,75
Peterson, J. L., 75
Peterson, R. F., 262, 263
Petretic-Jackson, P., 339, 340, 341
Petrila, J., 335, 339, 343
Pettit, R., 8, 9, 115
Phillips, P., 234
Phipps-Yonas, S., 127
Pine, B. A., 217
Pipe, M. E., 90–91
Pogge, D. L., 320
Pollak, J., 337
Poole, D. A., 107
Porter, F. S., 24
Porter, S., 23
Poston, C., 181
Poythress, N. G., 335, 339, 343
Pozanski, E., 262
Pressley, M., 201–2
Prosk, A., 198–99, 202
Proudfoot, P., xvi
Putnam, F. W., 51
Putnick, M., 7
Pynoos, R. S., 82–83, 87–88

Quinn, K. M., 6, 32
Quinsey, V. L., 246, 254, 257

Rabinowitz, D., 25, 34
Racusini, R. J., 339, 340
Rada, R. T., 26, 146, 212

Subject Index